Butler County
Alabama
it the
Nineteenth Century

Compiled by:
Marilyn Davis Hahn

Southern Historical Press
Greenville, South Carolina

This volume was reproduced
from a personal copy located in
the Publishers private library

Please direct all correspondence and book orders to:
SOUTHERN HISTORICAL PRESS, Inc.
1071 Park West Blvd.
Greenville, SC   29611

Originally printed Birmingham, AL 1978
ISBN #978-1-63914-328-3
Printed in the United States of America

Dedicated to my mother
GLADYS SCOTT SIMS DAVIS
who was born in Butler County

Inscription on the Confederate Monument

on

Capitol Hill in Montgomery, Alabama

"When this historic shaft shall crumbling be,
In ages hence, in woman's heart will be,
A folded flag, a thrilling page unrolled
A deathless song of Southern chivalry."

by

Mrs. I. M. P. Ockenden

of

Greenville & Montgomery

TABLE OF CONTENTS

Chapter 1.   1.
     Butler County Reminiscenses
     The Massacres
     Captain William Butler
     Eli Stroud
     Fort Dale

Chapter 2.   15.
     Register of Civil & Military Appointments
     Early Postmasters and Postal Routes
     First Election in Butler County
     The Greenville Whig, 11 July 1835.

Chapter 3.   27.
     Butler County Men in the Revolutionary War
     Pensioners of the War of 1812
     The Creek War of 1836-1837
     The War Between the States
     The Greenville Observer, 22 Apr. 1865,
     Confederate Veterans Reunion, 12 August 1897.
     Decoration Day, 9 May 1872.
     Military Companies
     Father Ryan Chapter, U. D. C.

Chapter 4.   39.
     Cemetery Records
     Joseph R. Abrams' Patent for Grave-Mounds.

Chapter 5.   86.
     Income Tax List for 1865-1866.
     1886 Gazeteer of Alabama Businesses.

Chapter 6.   103.
     Land Office Removal
     Probate Records
     Henry West Estate
     Early County Marriages
     Probate Notices
     Reminiscense of Over 40 Year Age

Chapter 7.   117.
     Butler Springs
     Kolb City
     Chapman
     McKenzie
     Greenville
     Forest Home

Chapter 8.   131.
     Election of May 1859
     Letters in Post Office 1860 and 1875
     Seventh Annual Distribution of the Advocate
     Butler County Hotels
     Butler County Newspapers
     Hipp & Kelley

Chapter 9.   149.
     Family Sketches

Chapter 10.   166.
     Real Estate Taxes for 1856
     Jury Lists and Lodge Officers
     Pictures.

PREFACE

This book has been written as the result of a program presented to the Butler County Historical Society in October, 1977, the program being for the most part on the early days in Butler County. Many requests for copies of the material gathered for the program have led me to this publication.

Everyone who has done research in this county soon learns that when the Court House in Greenville burned April 12, 1853 all Probate records were destroyed with the exception of the Land Track records. My goal has been in trying to supplement or replace some of the information lost in the fire. This book admittedly falls short of my expectations, but at least it is a start in the right direction. Hopefully, in the years to come another book can be printed when additional information becomes available.

It will be readily noticed that family names have been spelled in a variety of ways. If this is your first journey into early records you will need to understand that people apparently didn't place much importance on the correct spelling of names. No effort has been made on my part to correct the spelling, but, instead I have tried to group surnames together in the Index with the first name listed the most commonly spelled form.

Inasmuch as a comprehensive history of the county was printed by Professor John Buckner Little in 1885 and because of material published by the Butler County Historical Society this publication does not contain many events and subjects which might otherwise have been included.

It is to be hoped that this book will appeal to historians and genealogists as well as to those of us whose lineage can be traced to the pioneers whose names appear between these covers.

M. D. H.

ACKNOWLEDGEMENTS

There have been many sources from which material has come for this book, with the foremost one being the Greenville Advocate. Since its beginning in 1865 this has been an outstanding weekly paper and the articles found therein have been invaluable in revealing to us today life as it was in Butler County in the 113 years since its beginning. It is with permission of Mr. Gene Hardin, the present Editor of the Advocate, that this material is being reproduced.

My gratitude is extended to all those many members of the Butler County Historical Society who worked on the cemetery census, because their efforts have made possible the recording and preservation of this valuable information in book form. This was a major undertaking of the Society and one of which we can all be proud.

My special thanks to Judge Calvin Steindorf and his staff in the Butler County Court House for their assistance, understanding and trust; to Dr. Marvin Whiting, Archivist in the Birmingham Public Library and to his aide-de-camp, Rachael Farmer; to W. Warner Floyd, Executive Director of the Alabama Historical Commission in Montgomery; to the staff in the Southern Room (Tutwiler Collection) of the Birmingham Library; to the Dept. of Archives & History in Montgomery, and to Joseph Caver in particular for all of his assistance; to the Dept. of Archives and History in Atlanta; to Mrs. Dorothy Speir Parrish, not only for her encouragement, but for room and board as well; and to the following people for articles and pictures: Mrs. William Blackwell, Tom Braxton, T. A. Brook, Mr. & Mrs. Lewis Crenshaw, Mrs. Ramona Garrett, Mrs. Guy Hartley, Mrs. Maxena Gandy Lewis, Mrs. Henry Porter Martin, Earl M. McGowin, Allen Pendergraft, Mrs. Joe N. Poole, Sr., Miss Mary Lou Price of the AHC, Herbert Russ, Mrs. Florence Vaughn, Miss Frances Sims, Miss Myra Williams, Mrs. Bennie Ann Washuleski, and Mrs. Aubrey Cheatham.

I like to think of this book, not as just mine, but ours, because it would have been impossible without the cooperation of each of you and many others. Thank you, not only for myself, but for all those people in the years to come who will one day open the covers of this book and delight in reading the information that you had to share.

                       M. D. H.

Butler County proudly recognizes one of its most illustrous citizens of the nineteenth century, the Honorable Hilary Abner Herbert, who served our nation as Secretary of the Navy during the administration of Pres. Grover Cleveland. He received this distinction as a result of his outstanding success while in Congress in building up the American Navy to fighting strength during the Spanish-American War.

INTRODUCTION

Madge Hahn's book on Butler County is an extraordinary work written by an unforgettable Alabamian. Using the cemetery and church as her cornerstones, Madge Hahn portrays Butler County's people and places with objectivity, accuracy and warmth.

Butler County abounds with significant Alabama landmarks. While the area was the setting for Creek Indian battles, the county came into its own with the settling of Greenville, McKenzie, Georgiana, the winding Crenshaw's Ridge, and the sprawling W. T. Smith Lumber Company lands.

Madge has covered Capt. William Butler, the Pooles, Milners, Stallings and Bensons of Butler County, but she has not neglected the substantial middle class, the common folk who contributed to the county's achievements.

Madge has traveled the highways and backroads to gather her on-site data. She has devoured courthouse records and the documents available from other depositories relating to Butler County. Numerous church and family records have been uncovered which flavor this work.

She has made numerous important discoveries during her research on heritage-rich Butler County. She pursues Alabama Heritage with intelligence, talent and calm fervor. She is a historian, genealogist, amateur archaeologist, and skilled communicator and has combined this expertise in this worthy work.

W. Warner Floyd
Executive Director
Alabama Historical Commission

CHAPTER 1

BUTLER COUNTY REMINISCENCES

Greenville Advocate, June 18, 1874					by J. C. Wade

"Thinking that a sketch of the incidents connected with the early settlement of Butler County might not be uninteresting to the many readers of your valuable paper; and believing that there is now no one living who has a more distinct recollection of them than I--I will, by your indulgence, proceed to sketch a few of them.

To begin. On the 25th of December, 1818, my father with his family, left his old home near Macon, Ga., and on the evening of the 13th of January, 1819, reached his place of destination, two and a half miles south of Fort Dale, four northwest of Greenville, on a bold-running little stream which flows south and empties into Persimmon Creek.

At the time of our arrival; the country looked fresh as if just from the hands of its Creator; there were few bushes to obstruct the view, the grass when it came forth in the spring about two feet high, whilst the creeks, branches, marshes, etc., were covered with reed from four to fifteen feet high. The Indians had vacated the country, leaving no trace behind, save here and there a few camps constructed of pine bark. The forests were alive with wild beasts, consisting of bears, panthers, wolves, wild cats, catamounts and deer, the latter in point of numbers greatly preponderating; indeed it was not an unusual sight to see as high as sixty in a drove. Fine sport was given to the lovers of the chase. The enlivering sound of the huntsman's horn, the commingled notes of Fido and Blucher, and Ringwood and Trackwell, and the oft repeated peals from old Betsy, Long Tom, and Never Fail, rang loud and long over the hills and valleys, to the great delight and excitement of those engaged in hot pursuit. Conspicuous among the Nimrods of the day were John Tinsley, John Williams, Phil Cook, Tom Herbert, Jim Wade, and old Bill Dulany; at the crack of whose rifles, the music of the pack would generally cease, they being regarded as dead shots.

The old Fort was still standing, William Martin had a store there, the first and only one in the limits of the county. In the village lived William McDaniel, a Mr. Livingston, Richard Ringold, Matthew Wood and Andrew T. Perry. The latter afterwards rose to the rank of Colonel of the Militia, Sheriff, Representative, and Receiver in the Land Office at Sparta. In 1828 he emigrated to Mississippi, settled near Jackson, where after a residence of a few years he died. One half mile above Fort Dale lived old Mr. McDaniel, and his son, Ennis; south of Fort Dale and on the west side of the stream first mentioned, lived a Mr. Hill, Micajah Wade, John Herbert, Parr Hutchinson and John Arnold. On the east side lived John Cook, Frederick Jolly, Ward Taylor, John Tinsley, Ben and William Dulaney, Isaac Cook, Webster Gilbert and Casswell Vines. On Persimmon Creek, commencing at its source and going south, lived the Talley's, Harrisons, Paynes, William Collins, William Lee, the Rowdons, Gaffords, Dr. H. Herbert, Henry Vincent, Ephraim Parmer, Calvin Leonard, William and John Williams, John Bolling, James and William Dunklin. Commencing at Fort Dale and going west lived Charles Davenport, the Garys,

Mrs. Gordon, Mr. Dickson, whose family was murdered by the Indians in 1817, and Simon Easterwood. On the Ridge lived the Womacks, the Lewis', Carters, Elijah Manning, Judge Crenshaw and the Earnests. I have been thus particular, so that the present inhabitants may know who were the first settlers in the localities mentioned.

The first work was to build camps, in which the settlers lived the first year. Then clearing lands, all of which was planted in corn. The spring opening, the cattle got very fat and gave for the settlers vast quantities of the richest milk. There being no mills, the meal, such as it was, was ground on steel and hand mills. Every man had his fire pan. The toil of the day over and supper eaten, the gun was loaded, the pan lighted up, the wallet filled with lightwood for the occasion, the hunters would set out, following blazes which had been made for the purpose, and often at a late hour would return with a deer swung on a pole. The skins, the only chance for shoes, were carefully stretched and nailed to the walls of the camps, whilst the horns were placed in some conspicuous place as an exhibition of the hunter's exploits. Fort Claiborne being the only market, and pork being thirty-five dollars per barrel, and corn from three to five dollars per bushel, little was purchased, and some of the inhabitants were hard pressed.

The crop pretty well off hand, the 4th of July approaching, and every man surcharged with patriotism; a meeting was held at Fort Dale preparatory to a celebration. The place selected was on the road leading from Fort Dale to Greenville, one and a half miles from the former place, and near the residence of Ward Taylor, who was elected orator of the day. The day being propitious, the citizens turned out in mass. The affair went off joyously, and the effort of Taylor, though by no means a literary man, was considered very fine. Mr. Taylor afterwards rose to the rank of Major, was elected to the Legislature in 1822, was a merchant in Greenville, figured extensively in the stage business between Montgomery and Blakely, was a member to the anti-tariff convention in Philadelphia, in 1831, moved to Texas many years ago, where not long since he died an octogenarian.

Early in 1822, his brother, Elias Taylor, moved out from Georgia, lived there a number of years, moved to Holmes County, Mississippi, where a few years ago he died. He was a man of sterling integrity, always commanded the respect of his fellow citizens; and on the Mississippi Central Railroad runs a magnificent engine bearing his honored name.

In July, 1819, the first school ever taught in the county, commenced, Samuel Farrar, teacher; the school house was on the old Federal road, one and a half miles west of Fort Dale, and near a celebrated limestone spring. The second school was in 1820, one mile south of Fort Dale, James Lane teacher. Mr. Lane was a teacher by profession, and as an educator of the rising generation for several years, came to Mississippi some thirty years ago, where, after a short residence, he died. He was a man of generous and noble impulses, and although in some things a little eccentric, was emphatically a good man.

The first, a Methodist church, was built in 1820, half a mile west of Fort Dale on the old Federal road, and the first camp meeting was in the fall of that year, half mile west of Fort Dale, and half a mile north of the main road. The meeting was conducted by Thomas Nixon, Thomas Clinton, and Benjamin Dulany. Mr. Clinton is still living. The first Baptist church was three miles east of Fort Dale, near the residence of Col. William Lee.

In 1819 the Convention met in Huntsville to frame a constitution for the State Government. John Herbert and William Lee were our accredited delegates. In a few weeks it was announced that the work was completed. The constitution ratified, organization commenced. John Herbert the first Representative; James Lane first Judge of the County Court; Jesse Womack first Sheriff; Edward Herbert first Circuit Clerk, and James Dickson first clerk of the County Court.

As I shall not have occasion to again mention the names of John Herbert and William Lee, I will make a slight digression for the purpose of giving a sketch of each of them. Mr. Herbert was once a citizen of Georgia, in the legislature of which State he served with great distinction for many years, and at one time came within one vote of being elected her Governor. He came to Butler in 1818; was, as above stated, a member of the convention, first representative, and at the time of his death, Receiver in the Land Office at Sparta. In person he was tall, very straight and slender, well educated, clear intellect, immaculate character, unbending integrity, and was considered, and I doubt not justly, the ablest man in the county. He died in 1826, and sleeps four miles northwest of Greenville.

Col. Lee was a Georgian, commanded a company in the war between the United States and the Creek Indians; came to Butler in 1818; was 1st Captain, 1st Major and 1st Colonel of the militia, and, as stated a member of the convention that framed the State Constitution. He was a magnificent looking man, and in principle and deportment the beau ideal of a gentleman. He died in 1824; was buried near his residence, three and a half miles east of Fort Dale, and over his grave was the first Masonic demonstration ever made in Butler County.

County Commissioners were also elected, on whom devolved the duty of looking out and purchasing a location for the county town. My father, Micajah Wade, being one of the Commissioners, I well remember the night he came home and told the family of the place selected. Soon arrangements were made for a survey of the town. My brother, Capt. James W. Wade, was employed to do the work. The day was set, the Commissioners with my brother, met, and as his apparatus was minus a "Jacob Staff" he cut a small sassafras out of which he made one that answered the purpose. He was consequently the first man that ever struck a lick toward the erection of the town of Greenville. He was at the time only 18 years of age. He afterwards held several important positions in the militia; was elected to the legislature from Butler; was a merchant in Greenville; director of one of the banks in Montgomery; came to Mississippi in 1841; was elected to the legislature in 1843; held the position for many years; was during the time Speaker of the House, and afterwards superintendent of the penitentiary.

When the war broke out, he, although fifty years of age, raised a company, led them to the arena of battle, and fought gallantly in defense of his native land. He was six feet high, of symmetrical proportions, ponderous intellect, great dignity and urbanity of manner, and always commanded the respect, admiration and confidence of his fellow citizens. He died December 30, 1869.

The town laid out and lots sold, building begun. First, and at the same time, the Parmer House on the left, and the I. C. Caldwell House on the right, going east from the Court House, were built- the former by Mr. Ephraim Parmer, and the latter by Messrs. Caulfield and Bell of Claiborne, who furnished it with a small stock of goods, and placed Henry Yancy there as clerk.

In 1822 William Blackshire came over from Pike, and improved the lot on the northwest corner of the square; building both a hotel and a store house, in which he sold goods for several years. About this time the first court was held, Judge Crenshaw on the bench. Lawyers: Jack Herbert and Nathan Cook from Butler; Gen. Greening, Samuel W. Oliver and Judge Hunter from Conecuh; Henry Goldthwaite and Ben Fitzpatrick, from Montgomery; Horatio G. Perry and ____ Walker from Dallas, and Gen. Parsons from Monroe.

In the spring of 1821, whilst the town was being built, a Mr. Vincent, who lived half a mile north of the place, was at work in the forest opening a little field; breakfast ready, his good wife blew the horn, when his two little sons, aged four and two, ran to meet him, but missing their way, they were soon lost in the wilderness. The parents immediately commenced a search, which proving ineffectual, the mother in great distress ran over to town and implored the citizens to go and aid in the search. All, with one exception, responded to the call. He, a carpenter from Claiborne, seized the occasion to insult her. This coming to the ears of the citizens, he was tied to a tree, his shirt taken off, and he received at their hands a sound, constitutional drubbing. The news of the lost children spread over the county in a few hours; every man and boy able to aid in the search, rallied to the spot. Two days and nights passed, and no tidings. On the morning of the third day some signs were discovered; the party was collected and placed in a line some fifty yards apart; it was agreed that the finder should fire a signal gun. The search again commenced, and in a short time the signal announced that "the lost was found". At the same instant, and as if all were guided by the same brain, they turned to the spot. The sound of horses' feet was heard in every direction. They reached the place, and there sat the poor little fellows, both unable to walk. Then it was that strong men, for the moment, became as little children, and tears fell like rain from every eye. They were placed in charge of a committee, who bore them in triumph to their parents at the Hotel in Greenville. They were then placed in charge of Dr. Hillary Herbert, who kindly watched over them till the danger was over.

On the 1st day of January, 1826, an academy was opened in the southwestern part of Greenville, James G. Tigner, of Autauga, as teacher; under whose management it flourished for several years, and much good was accomplished. His health failing he was forced to discontinue, and the institution went down. Afterwards he was elected Clerk of the Circuit Court, which position he held for several years. About the year 1840, he died of consumption, and sleeps in the lonely cemetery near the Methodist church. He was one of nature's noblemen!

Butler county was called after Capt. William Butler, a citizen of distinction, (State Senator) whose residence was in Clinton, Georgia. In 1817 he, with a Mr. Gardner, from the same place, visited Alabama in the purpose of looking at the country, and in that portion of Butler called "The Ridge" were killed by the Indians. Hence the title. After his death his family moved to Alabama, settled in Autauga, and remained there a short time, when they removed to this (Copiah) county, Mississippi. When the war broke out between the United States and Mexico, Col. James Butler, eldest son of Capt. B., volunteered, and whilst en route for the scene of conflict, died on board the ship, and found a watery grave in the Gulf of Mexico. Mrs. B. and the other children died in this county. Some of their descendants remain.

Greenville was at first called Buttsville, after Samuel Butts, who fell at the head of his company, in the war with the Creek Indians. The name was changed by the legislature in 1822.

The writer of the foregoing sketches went to Butler at eight and left at twenty-one years of age. Although the country to which he came is a good one; and although all reasonable expectations have been met, he, after an absence of forty-two years, is free to say; that he regrets ever having left. May the star of Butler ever be in the ascendant!

One thought more and I will close. The scenes about which I have been writing, with those who participated in them, have passed away. One by one they have retired from the world's great stage. Some sleep in Alabama, some in Mississippi, some in Louisiana, and some in Texas. Their voices are now forever hushed; their manly forms and cheerful faces will never again be seen in the streets of Greenville; and in a few years more it will not be known that such men had an existence".

Hazlehurst, Miss., June 1874

THE MASSACRES

Many articles have already been written about the massacres which took place in the early days of Butler County, however, some facts were brought out by Peter A. Brannon in an articles in the Montgomery Advertiser dated January 31, 1943, that I felt should be included in this new history of the county.

"There is a section of Western Butler County which was referred to quite early as "the flats". As you travel today from Greenville, out West to the fork of the road at Awin, you pass a small post which bears the name "Fort Bibb." It is east of the plantation of Mr. Poole on that ridge road known as the Greenville to Monroeville highway. Fort Bibb was erected in the late Winter of 1818 as a stockade--to enclose the home of Captain James Saffold. Records of the county say he had moved from the "Ridge" to that place in the flats. The Militia Ridge in that case designated the route of the old Federal Road which ran generally southwest from a point east of Montgomery, along the line of Monroe and Conecuh Counties, to Claiborne. The erection of Fort Bibb was for the protection of the few settlers who had even that early come into that region after the treaty of Fort Jackson signed in August 1814.

Captain Saffold, whose house was inclosed by the stockade to form Fort Bibb, was a veteran of the battle of Calabee fought in our present Macon County some five or six miles east of Pole Cat Springs, in January, 1814. He commanded a company of artillery under Maj. McIntosh. Subsequent to the fight at Calabee, Gen. John Floyd and his Georgia Militia, fell back to Fort Mitchell, but records indicate that some of these Georgia commands were later at Fort Decatur which had been established opposite the Indian town of Tuckabatchi on the south (or east) bank of the Tallapoosa by the 7th North Carolina Regiment in January, 1814, and Capt. Saffold was in that command. Other settlers living in this western part of the county were William P. Garner, Daniel Shaw, James D. Garrett, and that section of the wooded country not far from what is now Manningham and west of Fort Dale site, lived John Dickerson and William Ogle, (or "ley" or by some spelled "Oglesby"). The people who lived near the northeastern corner of what is now Butler erected a stockade, or a blockhouse, at the home of one Thomas Gary and near this privately fortified place was later erected Fort Dale where all the settlers could come for protection. The site of Fort Dale is between Montgomery and Greenville, some six miles north of the court house at Greenville, while Fort Bibb site is some 12 miles west.

Fort Bibb was named for Gov. William Wyatt Bibb, late of Georgia, who had just recently assumed office as governor of the Alabama Territory. The capital was then in Saint Stephens and Gov. Bibb rode back and forth from his home at our present Coosada, some 12 miles north of Montgomery, to Saint Stephens going by Fort Claiborne and crossing the Tombigbee at McGrew's Shoals.

Capt. William Butler for whom Butler County was named, was born in Virginia, but had resided in Georgia prior to the campaign against the Indians in 1813-14, and had already served as a member of the Legislature in that State. He commanded a company of militia under Gen. John Floyd, at the Battle of Calabee and moved to Alabama in 1817, settling in the region later to be referred to as the "Dogwood Flats." (Also referred to as Pine Flat).

When Butler County was created on Dec. 13, 1819, the original bill as reported out designated the thirty townships embraced in the original survey as Fairfield County. Friends of the recently martyred Captain changed the name of the County to read "Butler" in his honor. The death of Capt. Butler occurred about a week after the Ogly Massacre which took place March 13, 1818. This attack on the Oglys and the Strouds occurred at the Ogly home, on the Federal Road, some four miles west of Fort Dale. Mr. Ogly attended a military muster on the 13th of March, 1818, and on his way home that evening met an old acquaintance, Eli Stroud, who with his wife and children was passing through the country, & he persuaded them to accompany him to his home. That same night the house was attacked by Indians who robbed the settlers and murdered Mr. Ogly and four children. Mrs. Stroud was wounded as well as were two or three of the children. One of these, a girl who had been scalped, recovered and lived for many years at the home of Dr. John Watkins of Burnt Corn.

Mrs. Stroud died on the way to Claiborne where she was being carried for medical attention. Five or six days after the massacre, Capt. Butler, Capt. Saffold, William Gardner, Daniel Shaw, and John Hinson left Fort Bibb to proceed in the direction of Fort Dale. Near Pine Barron Creek, some four miles from Fort Bibb, they were set on by a band of Indians under Savannah Jack. Mr. Gardner and Mr. Shaw were killed and Butler and Hinson were wounded, but Mr. Hinson succeeded in getting away on his horse, whereas Capt. Butler who was trying to escape back to Fort Bibb, was captured and immediately murdered by the Indians. (The remains of Capt. Butler, Mr. Gardner and Mr. Shaw were moved at a later date to the town of Greenville and were buried in the Old Cemetery).

Col. Sam Dale at Claiborne, by order of Gov. Bibb, brought a detachment of Alabama Militia, some men of the 7th U. S. Infantry, as well as some from the 3rd Infantry Regiment, and scoured the swamps of the Conecuh and Escambia rivers, as well as Pine Barren Creek and other large streams in Butler County, and finally rid the county of the marauders.

Local records say that Col. Dale's Militia was at Poplar Springs erecting the Stockade destined to be called Fort Dale when Captain Butler was attacked. He sent aid to the frightened people at Fort Bibb who were but once more molested, this when they stole some horses from Dave Reddock, Thomas Carter and Josiah Hill, and killed some of Mr. Thomas Hill's fine cattle. Only one casualty resulted in this attack. Mr. William Cogburn, who lived at the home of Mr. James K. Benson, (the first white settler in Butler County), was killed when he exposed himself--having too much curiosity--by getting on top of a log, into view of the enemy.

Thomas Gary, a Royalist[1] in the American Revolution, to whose home the early settlers first went for protection even though he charged them a fee, is buried in the old Fort Dale Cemetery. You may see his tombstone today. Col. H. T. Perry, James Garrett, Andrew Jones, John Murphy, and several other Georgians and Carolinians had settled about this time at Butler Springs. Thomas Hill and his two sons, Warren Thompson, Capt. John H. Watts and two or three others had settled in the forest of the "Pine Flats", but they were fortunate enough not to be molested by these Indians. Thomas Hill Watts, some forty-five years later Governor of the State, is a descendant of these families who reached Butler County in the Fall of 1816.

While Butler County claims more settlers from Georgia than from any other Eastern State, many of her early ones came from the upper portion, or rather the northwest corner of South Carolina, in the Fairfield District, and this would explain the origin of the determination on the part of the Legislators to call the County "Fairfield". When Capt. Butler was killed on March 20th, this brought him to the attention of these early settlers in such a pertinent way that they sought to honor him.

Savannah Jack who led the Indians in their attacks on the white settlers, recently come into the new country, was born at what Montgomerians know as old Augusta Town site. Some Georgians came into Montgomery County in 1816 and settled at the old Sauwonoga site (which was in late years Bachtel's Lumber Mill), and founded there the first Post stop in the county. There was a tavern and two blacksmith shops at this place, a road fork, one going Southwest and the other West to old Fort Toulouse, (Fort Jackson). By this place went the first regular mail route through the territory, the one provided to carry the mail from Fort Mitchell, by Augusta, by Fort Jackson, to Claiborne and Saint Stephens. Savannah Jack, born at the old Shawnee Town site of Sauwonoga, was the half-breed son of an Irishman from Detroit who had an Indian woman for a wife and who lived at this one-time Shawnee settlement on the Tallapoosa River. At this place today you may see the remains of one Indian Mound and one large flat top Mound on which there is a residence erected, as well as the family burial place of some of the Lucas family, some of the Ross family, and several other early Montgomerians. Savannah Jack was one of the most ruthless of the early half breeds reared in this section of the State. He bitterly opposed William Weatherford's Treaty with Andrew Jackson at old Fort Toulouse on August 9, 1814, and he led the Indians in their attacks on the white settlers. He subsequently went to Florida and joined the Indians there. Josiah Francis and several other Indians from this region were among those who went with the Seminoles. Savannah Jack spent his last days in that State. Col. Pickett says that he boasted that he had killed so many men and women on the Cumberland and Georgia frontiers that he could swim in their blood if it was collected in one Pool. That was probably an exaggeration, but he, no doubt, was a bad man.

The country South of the North line of Montgomery County, which was created in 1816 extending to the Falls of the Coosa River at Wetumpka, was included in the Land Session of August, 1814, and the settlers from the Eastern States who came into Montgomery, Butler, Conecuh and those counties as far Southwest as Monroe, took possession of this recently ceded land, but even though there were only a limited number of Indians

---

[1]. From DAR lineage books, Thomas Gary served as a Private in the State Militia in S. C. in 1780 and provided provisions for the Continentals and Militia from 1781 to 1785. His grave is the only one in the county of a Patriot with a DAR marker.

living in this region, most of them were quite reluctant to move out. Some moved into the reservation, that section East and North of Line Creek and bordered by the Chattahoochee River on the East and the Cherokee Country on the North, and some went to Florida."

CAPTAIN WILLIAM BUTLER

One of the main objectives in writing this book has been to learn more about Capt. Butler for whom the county was named. To a great degree he remains a man of mystery, as the information available on him has been difficult to find and repetitious at best. However, with assistance from the Archives in Atlanta and Montgomery and several helpful correspondents a picture of this patriot began to take shape.

Butler was born in the State of Virginia around 1775, the son of Edmund and Mary Butler, and the grandson of Edmond Butler and Frances Cooke of Goochland County, Virginia, emigrants from England. The Will of Edmond Butler was probated on September 15, 1747 in Goochland Co. Two of his sons, John and William, of Orange Co., N. C. served in the Revolutionary War. Edmund and Mary Butler moved to Greene Co., Ga. prior to April 9, 1788 when he was listed as a Witness to a deed for 200 acres from Milly and Benjamin Gilbert, Jr. to James Garrett of Charlotte Co., Va. for 100 pounds.[1] Milly was one of the daughters of James Garrett. The arrival of the Garrett family to Georgia was of utmost importance to young William as it was one of the daughters, Charity, with whom he later fell in love and married in 1796.[2] By this time Greene County had been divided with part of the land being used to form Hancock County in December 17, 1793.

Edmond died in Hancock County and his Will was probated January 11, 1804,[3] mentioning along with his wife, Mary, his sons, Edward, John, William and Harry, son-in-law, Benjamin Gilbert and granddaughters, Fanny, Polly and and Patsey Gilbert. Family tradition is that one of the sons was killed in an Indian massacre.

Charity Garrett was born in 1778, the daughter of James and Mourning Garrett.[4] James' Will was probated April 13, 1795 in Greene County naming his wife and children, Hannah Woodham, Fanny Butler, Elizabeth Barksdale, Ann Ford, Susanna Butler, Mary Garrett, William Garrett, Charity Garrett, Edmond Garrett and James O. Kelly Garrett.

Additional information came to light on Butler from the application made by Charity on June 7, 1851 for bounty land as follows: "State of Mississippi, County of Copiah. On the 7th day of June in the year of our Lord one thousand eight hundred and fifty one, personally appeared before me, Elisha Douglass, a Justice of the Peace within and for said County, Charity Butlar, aged 72 years, resident of Copiah County in the State of Mississippi, who being duly sworn according to law declares that she is the widow of Captain William Butlar, deceased, who was a Captain of a Company of drafted Militia in the Regiment of

---

1. "Some Georgia Records" Vol. 2. Rev. Silas E. Lucas, Jr. pp 174.
2. Charity Butler's application for Bounty Land filed in Copiah Co., Miss. June 7, 1851.
3. "Hancock Co., Ga. Early Records". Comp. Alden Assoc. pp 108.
4. "Some Georgia Records" Vol. 2. Rev. Silas E. Lucas, Jr. pp 324-325.

Georgia Militia commanded by General John Floyd in the Creek Indian Wars of 1813-14 and that said husband entered the service in Jones County, Georgia on or about the 15th day of October A. D. 1813 for the term of 6 months, and continued in actual service in said war for the term of six months, and was honorably discharged at Fort Hawkins, Georgia, on or about the 15th day of April A. D. 1814 as will appear by the muster rolls of said company, she having in her possession no written certificate of discharge.

She further states that to the best of her recollection and belief she was married to the said William Butlar in Hancock County, State of Georgia, sometimes in the A. D. 1796 by a minister of the Gospel named Courtney and that her name before her marriage was Charity Garrett, and that her said husband was killed by the Indians in what is now Butlar County, Alabama in the A. D. 1818, and that she is still a widow.

She makes this declaration for the purpose of obtaining the Bounty Land to which she may be entitled under the Act passed September 28, 1850. Sworn to and subscribed before me the day and year above written. E. Douglass, J. P. (Seal) Signed Charity (Her X Mark) Butlar."

Butler and his family had moved to Clinton, Jones County, Georgia by 1807 where he was appointed a Justice of the Peace on March 24, 1808 and on July 21, 1812 was appointed a Justice of the Inferior Court. He served two terms in the State Senate from Jones County in 1810 and again in 1814.[1] One of the last mentions found in Jones Co. about the Butlers was on February 5, 1818 when the sale of some of his property was recorded in the Court Records with the right of dower being given by Charity Butler, wife of William Butler. This date was just over a month before the death of Butler on March 18, 1818. From his headstone and from an article written by Peter Brannon, Alabama Archivist, we learn that Butler was a pioneer settler of the County. Although no land was entered in his name we do find his brother-in-law, James O. Kelly Garrett along with other Butlers and Gilberts who were possibly related to him, among the early settlers in this part of the country. It would appear he was in the process of locating a place to settle in Alabama while his wife was perhaps still in Georgia settling their affairs in that state. After his death Charity moved with her children to Autauga County, Ala. where she remained for some years. One of their sons, James G., married in that county to a Miss Alsy Dickson Holloway, daughter of Judith Holloway.[2] He later enlisted to fight in the Mexican War; became ill on board ship; died and was buried at sea. By 1840 Charity had moved to Copiah Co., Mississippi where she remained for the rest of her life. Other children born to this marriage were Susan, Leander, Polly, Frances and John T. S. Butler. Susan and John apparently were the only children to survive their mother who died in 1854 or 5. John died soon after in the latter half of 1855. Leander was married first to a Hill and second to a Bissell. Her children were Julia Hammell (Harvill), George W. Hill, Green Hill, Amelia Womack (Mrs. Stephen) and Mary Pitts (Mrs. Peyton). Polly was married to a Smoot and had a son, William. Frances married a Bailes and had a daughter, Eliza Flowers (Mrs. James).[3]

1. Information provided by the Georgia Department of Archives and History, Manuscripts Section.
2. "Alabama Records" Vol. 206. Compiled by Kathleen Paul Jones and Pauline Paul Gandrud. pp 76.
3. Copiah County, Mississippi Estate Settlement Records. Dated 24th January, 1856.

There are no records on file in Washington on William Butler for service after 1813-14. On the day of his death he was on volunteer service making the dangerous journey from Fort Bibb to Fort Dale a distance of about 15 miles to carry the message of the Indian uprising. Being the civic minded patriot that he was when the need arose for a job to be done he answered the call and gave his life for the safety of others. Such was the spirit of the early settlers of our frontier lands in the Alabama Territory.

In 1858 his remains along with his companions were moved from the woods where he fell to Pioneer Cemetery. Four of the oldest citizens of Greenville served as pallbearers, Joseph Dunklin, Samuel J. Bolling, Ezekiel Pickens and Joseph Parmer with young Hilary A. Herbert delivering the address that honored the fallen hero.[1] This cemetery has been placed on the Alabama Register of Landmarks & Heritage.

ELI STROUD[2]

Eli Stroud was born June 4, 1789 in Hancock Co., Ga., the son of Mark Stroud and Martha Strother Thompson. Other children identified in Mark's Will were William Levi, Mary, Sarah Allen, Orion and Tallatha. Eli married Elizabeth, the daughter of Luke Derbin, in April 1808, and moved to the Mississippi Territory in what is now part of Conecuh Co. near the Butler Co. line. Their marriage was blessed with 4 children born between 1809 and 1818; Tinsey, Mark, Martha and Thomas, the latter being the child killed in the Indian attack. After Elizabeth's death Eli took the three children back to his old home where in 1820 he married Elizabeth, the daughter of Joseph East of the Mars Hill Community. The family once more moved to Butler Co. and to this second wife four children were born. Elizabeth East Stroud died in 1829 and was buried by the side of his first wife on the side of the Federal Road. Eli eventually became dissatisfied with his place due to illness and other troubles and in 1833 moved to Russell Co., Ala. where he remained the rest of his life. He married there his third wife, Eliza Perry, and to this marriage were born two more children.

CAPTAIN WILLIAM BUTLER   ELIZABETH DERBIN STROUD

1. Paper written by Ella Herbert Stuart 15 June 1934 on file in the Dept. of Archives & History in Montgomery, Ala.
2. "The Strouds" by Ab Stroud, 1919, pp 116-128.

FORT DALE

THE PALINGS

The following is a letter written to Governor William Wyatt Bibb from Burnt Corn Spring. The letter was dated only Friday evening.

"Sir:
On last Tuesday morning I left Manac and on that evening I met Dale's detachment with Gays (Garys[1]) family at Jones' where the Col. has established his headquarters. On Wednesday Lt. Riddle with 17 men and 9 Choctaws got up. Yesterday morning Dale ordered a general fatigue for the purpose of completing a little stockade with two blockhouses at diagonal angles which might be done_____night. This morning he intended to move the effectives with 7 or 8 days provisions and go in pursuit of the Indians and to leave such (the sick) lame and lazy to feed the horses and take care of the stores.

1. "Territorial Papers of the U. S. Vol. XVIII. Alabama Territory 1817-19". pp 290-291. An examination of the original letter on file in the Archives in Montgomery led to the discovery of several errors in the book which have been marked by brackets. The James referred to in the letter is probably the William James, postmaster, whose name appears on the outside of the letter. The lines in the above indicate where portions of the letter have disintegrated.

It is probable that twenty or more of Manacs Indians came down last evening and will this day pursue the hostiles-a premium of near 1000($) being offered them for capturing or destroying "Savana Jacks Lor" and his party. The path from Manacs to Brakens, a few miles north of this, is deserted except at Dale Camp and James Hales (James states) that half his neighbors have fled westward for safety.

That 17 Indians should desolate the broad side of an extensive and keep possession of it is astonishing- and unless they are captured by Manacs hunters or Riley's party they will do so. Dales men cannot operate on horse back and with the exception of himself and a few more they cannot walk. However he will see what they are made of and what they can do.

Would it not be well enough to let Dale meet the Regulars and Choctaws on the road___with his volunteers___They are___and useless except for escorts and they will do as well to accompany wagons___. Indeed I wish you could let Dale off for his business requires his attention. I know he wishes it but he will not tell you so.

Most respectfully I am Yr. Obt. Servant.   Gilbert C. Russell"

On the outside of the letter is written ___(Postage ?) Free, William James, P. M., Gov. Bibb, Pleasant Level. This letter is in very poor condition with numerous holes worn in the paper. However the writing is still legible and has been laminated and preserved from further deteriation. The Gary family referred to in this letter was no doubt the family of Thomas Gary whose home had been fortified and called Fort Gary. He died on April 23, 1818 just one month after the murders of Capt. Butler and his associates, William P. Gardner and Daniel Shaw. His widow, the daughter of Charles Jones, very likely would have been living with some of her family for comfort at this time of sorrow and for protection from the Indians. It comes as no surprise to learn that Col. Dale was staying with her family at the time the Fort was being constructed.

Another letter was written to Gov. Bibb from Fort Dale on September 14, 1818 which gives additional insight into this period in Butler's history.[1] The original of this letter was not located in the Archives.

"Sir:
In obedience to your request and the Order of Major General Gaines I herewith recount to you the issue of my march from Fort Claiborne to this station. On Saturday the 5th Inst. I took up the line of march with detachment of infantry commanded by Capt. Matley, and promised to scout the Country in the most sequestered parts near the river-also the creeks and swamps which have the least suspicion of an Indian harbour-which I persued as far as the mouth of Pine Barron Creek. In many places I found the camps of Indians and other signs tho none later than three or four weeks ago.

Magerts and Bayls Company neither have yet arrived at the post nor have made any report of their proceeding to me agreeably to the order of Maj. Gen. Gaines.

[1]. "Through the Years", a column written by Peter Brannun on file in the Dept. of Archives & History. Titled "Around About Buttsville". Not dated.

Lieut. Riddle with a detachment of Regulars also a detachment of Capt. Curtis' company with those which I brought are with me. I shall proceed today to scour the country lying between this and the Mouth of Cedar Creek--after which I shall endeavor to oust a party of Indians which I understand have lodged on the west side of the Alabama near the waters of the Cahawba. On the return from the waters of Cedar Creek I will give you the event of my march.

> With much Respect
> Believe me
> Your humble Servt.
> Sam Dale
> Col. Comdg."

James Stuart, a Scotsman passing through Butler County in 1830 arrived at Fort Dale to find Matthew Wood as the tavern keeper. When he reached there in March of that year the Colonel and the stage driver (who was to carry the coach on southwest), were out hunting, and at length appeared with a fine buck. Dinner at the Tavern was indifferent, the entre was dried venison which was not very agreeable. They did serve one excellent article of food, according to Mr. Stuart, beer brewed from molasses.[1] Matthew Wood was elected Colonel of the 29th Infantry Regiment on December 20, 1823 and was commissioned June 8, 1824. His certificate of election was signed by James Craig, Isaac Cook and Nathan Cook.

Adam Hodgson, a British traveler in the early part of 1820 paid a visit to Fort Dale and recorded the following description of his stop there. "We arrived in the evening at a few palings, which have dignified the place with the appelation of Fort Dale, where travellers are accomodated tolerably, on a flourishing plantation. Our landlord was an intelligent man; and among his books I saw the Bible, the Koran, a hymn book, Nicholson's Encyclopedia, Stern, Burns, Cowper, Coelebs, Camilla, and the Acts of the Alabama Legislature, of which he was a member. The next morning we breakfasted at a retired house, 20 miles distant, kept by one of three families who came out of Georgia two years since to settle and to protect each other. The husband of one of the party had since been shot by the Indians in the woods. He died in three hours after he was found. The wife of another of the party was murdered by the Indians a few days afterwards when on a visit to some friends 15 miles distant, where five women and four children were butchered and scalped; and the house of the narrator was soon afterwards burnt to the ground by the same enemy, provoked probably by some injury or insult offered by travellers through their nation, which they would retaliate on the whites whenever they had an opportunity. We passed in the afternoon by Indian Path; and about twilight arrived at Murder Creek, a deep glen, where we took up our abode for the night."

According to Peter Brannon, Mr. Hodgson had reference to Nathan Cook, an early settler of Fort Dale. Mr. Cook was the Clerk of the County Court, commissioned March 2, 1820, and he served more then two years in that office. He was a native of Hancock County, Georgia, the son of a South Carolinean who came from Brunswick County, Virginia and of a family of English ancestry. He was a member of the Alabama Legislature in 1824. He served as the first postmaster in Fort Dale earning in 1822 $55.52. The last postmaster was John Dickson in 1830 and his income for that year was $13.18. Fort Dale ceased to exist as a town when the post office closed. From Pickett's History and the few remaining documents in our Archives we learn that the Fort served as a Military Post during the early days of the County. Major Ward Taylor

1. "Through the Years" by Peter Brannon. "Around About Buttsville"

operated a stage coach line which made stops at the Fort, in Greenville and in the adjoining territories. Major Taylor also ran a blacksmith shop in Greenville as well as a hotel. The hotel in Greenville was not the most desirable one. The rooms were too small and he did not furnish bedding, though he did furnish matresses into which the feathers had been thrown loosely and not half so many as they should have contained.

The Palings had at one time been a lovely plantation home of huge proportions. The stairway to the second floor was on the left hand end of the front porch. On the inside there was another stairway which led to the third floor--a half story with several large rooms. The original kitchen was a separate structure connected to the main building by a breezeway as was the custom in the early days. One of the early owners of this historic edifice was Joseph Hartley and his wife, Mary.

THOMAS GARY
DAR marker in the background

Letter postmarked from Greenville, Alabama   May 26, 1837

Mr. E. M. Thompson, Hayneville, Lowndes Co., Alabama

Dear Sir:
   I rec'd your letter on this instance stating that I had in my possession one yoke of oxen belonging to the Estate of Standwood Watson, Dec'd, and also 40 lbs. of corn & 2 sacks of salt belonging to Standwood Watson & so forth. Someone informed you wrong when he gave it to you and furthermore if you think I have you can assertain & assure the facts by coming to see, and also I have no note against the Estate of Watson.

                                        Yours with respect & so forth,
                                              Benjamin Rhodes[1]

1. Letter in Scruggs Collection, Dept. Archives & Mss., B'ham. Public Library.

CHAPTER 2

REGISTER OF CIVIL & MILITARY APPOINTMENTS [1]
CONECUH, SEPTEMBER 1817

Butler County was still a part of Conecuh County in September 1817. State Senator from Conecuh was John Herbert. State Representatives were William Lee and Thomas Watts.

TERRITORY OF ALABAMA
1818-1819

Hillery Herbert	Clerk Circuit Court	2 Mch. 1820
Nathan Cook	Clerk County Court	2 Mch. 1820
Jesse Womack	Sheriff (failed to give bond)	2 Mch. 1820
Jesse Womack	Sheriff	2 Apr. 1820
Absalom Carter	Treasurer	2 Apr. 1820
Isaiah Hill	Collector	2 Apr. 1820
John S. Livingston	Surveyor	2 Apr. 1820
Henry Powell	Coroner	22 Aug. 1820
Jesse Womack)	Auctioneers	22 Aug. 1820
Samuel Farrior)		
Micajah Wade	Justice of Peace	26 June 1820
James Wallace	Justice of Peace	26 June 1820
Charles Devanport	Justice of Peace	8 July 1820
John Womack	Justice of Peace	8 July 1820
John Graydon	Justice of Peace	24 July 1820
Marcellus Black	Justice of Peace	24 July 1820
James K. Benson	Justice of Peace	24 July 1820
Thomas Elliotte	Justice of Peace	24 July 1820
James W. Ernest	Constable	20 Apr. 1820
Isaac Smith	Constable	2 June 1820
Elisha Wade	Constable	8 June 1820
Peter Martin	Constable	24 July 1820
Nathan Branceford	Constable	24 July 1820

BUTLER COUNTY
1820-1842

James Lane	Judge City Court	25 Feb. 1825
James H. Dixon	Clerk City Court	4 Aug. 1823
William Lee	Judge County Court	14 June 1821
Nathan Cook	Judge County Court	4 Jan. 1823
Daniel Gafford	Judge County Court	14 Jan. 1834
Herndon L. Henderson	Judge County Court	31 Jan. 1837
John F. Johnson	Judge County Court	3 Aug. 1842

CLERK CIRCUIT COURT

Edward H. Herbert	4 Aug. 1823	James G. Tignor	13 Aug. 1831
Samuel L. Caldwell	5 Sept 1827	William T. Streety	13 Aug. 1840

1. On file in the Alabama Department of Archives and History

CLERK COUNTY COURT

Rubin Read	17 Feb. 1825	William T. Streety	20 Aug. 1835
Vice, J.H. Dickson	8 Aug. 1825	Vice, J.G. Feagin, dec'd	
Robert Reid	19 Sept 1829		29 Aug. 1836
Benjamin Newton	15 Aug. 1833	Samuel J. Bolling	31 Aug. 1837

JUSTICE OF PEACE

Micajah Ward	26 June 1820	Solomon Beesley	4 May 1828
James Wallace	26 June 1820	Ephraim Bowan	4 May 1828
Charles Davenport	8 July 1820	Benjamin Manning	11 June 1828
John Womack	8 July 1820	James Burnsides	11 June 1828
John Graydon	8 July 1820	Vice, Elisha Ward	
Marcellus Black	8 July 1820	Raleigh Jones	4 Sept. 1828
James K. Benson	8 July 1820	Vice, Benjamin Tarver	
Thomas Elliott	8 July 1820	Joseph Ainsworth	25 Sept. 1828
George Norwood	20 July 1822	Vice, Solomon Beesley	
James W. Earnest	3 Mch. 1823	Patterson Rogers	7 Sept. 1829
George Norwood	3 Mch. 1823	Vice, Thomas Skaines	
James K. Benson	3 Mch. 1823	Etheldred Bozeman	7 Sept. 1829
Elhanan Gibbs	15 Apr. 1824	Vice, E. Burk	
Frederick Jolly	30 Aug. 1824	G. W. Wilson	7 Sept. 1829
(Died in office)		Vice, R. Jones	
Jeremiah Gafford	30 Aug. 1824	David Roach	7 Sept. 1829
John Graydon	30 Aug. 1824	Sherard Sprig	7 Sept. 1829
Mercellus Black	30 Aug. 1824	Joseph Rhodes	10 July 1832
William Graydon	1 Jan. 1824	Ambrose Smith	20 May 1832
Jesse Womack	15 Apr. 1824	Joseph Downing	20 May 1832
Matthew Patton, Sr.	7 June 1824	Etheldred Bozeman	20 May 1832
Vice, G. W. Earnest		Thomas Briggs	20 May 1832
Arthur Gary	7 June 1824	G. W. Spear	20 May 1832
Vice, George Norwood		John B. Coker	7 Sept. 1829
Etheldred Bozeman	10 June 1824	David Bird	7 Sept. 1829
Thomas Skanes	10 June 1824	Jeremiah Watts	2 May 1829
William Taylor	4 Aug. 1824	Vice, Thomas Elliott	
John Dickson	30 Aug. 1824	George Opy	2 May 1829
Vice, E. Bozeman		Vice, Ephraim Brown	
Nathan Bozeman	5 Feb. 1825	Jacob L. Womack	2 May 1829
Ephram Bowen	22 July 1825	Vice, James Burnside	
Solomon Beavely	22 July 1825	Robert Black	19 Mch. 1830
Abijah D. Pinson	26 Nov. 1825	Vice, William Graydon	
Vice, N. Bozeman		James W. Williams	19 Mch 1830
Daniel Payne	11 Jan. 1826	James Lowry	12 May 1830
Vice, A. D. Pinson		Vice, David Roache	
Elzathan Burk	30 Mch. 1826	A. Pate	12 May 1830
Vice, William Taylor		Vice, Sherard Sprig	
Burrell B. Hutchinson		F. Smith	4 June 1830
	12 July 1826	Francis Sheppard	4 June 1830
William Graydon	22 Feb. 1827	Ennis McDaniel	13 Sept. 1830
for Greenville		Isaac Smith	29 Oct. 1830
John C. Caldwell	22 Feb. 1827	David Rogers	29 Oct. 1830
Jesse Womack	26 July 1827	Vice, John Dickson	
Richard Pruit	10 Aug. 1827	John Matthews	28 Jan. 1831
Isaac Smith	10 Aug. 1827	Vice, Patterson Rogers	
Thomas Shines	10 Aug. 1827	John Brewer	28 Jan. 1831
John Dickson	27 Oct. 1827	Vice, G. W. Wilson	
James K. Benson	26 Jan. 1828	Joseph Ainsworth	15 May 1831
Joseph Taylor	1 Mch. 1828	Peter Parker	15 May 1831

William McCurry	28 Jan. 1831	John Matthews	6 Aug. 1832	
Vice, J. N. Taylor		Jeremiah Watts	6 Aug. 1832	
John M. Talley	15 May 1831	Malcom McPherson	6 Aug. 1832	
Vice, A. Pate (?)		Raleigh Jones	6 Aug. 1832	
Luke J. Hester	2 July 1831	Micajah Wade	4 Mch. 1833	
Vice, Jackson Brewer		Francis A.B. Wheeler	15 Apr. 1833	
John C. Ley	22 Oct. 1831	Francis Sheppard	12 May 1833	
Henry S. Staggers	22 Oct. 1831	Luke J. Hester	12 May 1833	
James Staggers	20 May 1832	T. C. Phillips	12 May 1833	
George Opy	20 May 1832	Vice, Henry Stagger		
Daniel McIntire	20 May 1832	Thomas H. Briggs	11 May 1835	
John L. Womack	26 Sept. 1832	Joshua Barnett	11 May 1835	
Henry T. Jones	26 Sept. 1832	Joseph Rhodes	21 May 1837	
James A. Benson	6 Aug. 1832	Vice, G. W. Speir		

CONSTABLES

Jackson Sims	10 July 1832	William R. Fuller	13 Apr. 1842
James Wren	11 Nov. 1832	Albert G. Gaffe	13 Apr. 1842
John McCoy	11 Nov. 1832	Richard Bedgood	23 May 1842
George W. Solomon	13 Apr. 1842	James McCan	23 May 1842
William Perry	13 Apr. 1842	James Hodges	26 Oct. 1842
Frederick Adams	13 Apr. 1842	Larry Wilson	6 Mch. 1842
William McKain	13 Apr. 1842	Thomas Smith	7 Apr. 1842
John J. Vickory	13 Apr. 1842	John Colquhoan	10 June 1842
John McCoy, Sr.	13 Apr. 1842		

SHERIFFS

Andrew T. Perry	4 Aug. 1823	Herndon L. Henderson	20 Sept. 1835
William Payne	4 Sept. 1826	Thomas B. Windham	20 Sept. 1836
Vice, A. T. Perry		and	31 Aug. 1837
James Taylor	19 Sept. 1829	Vice, David Rogers	
Sam'l Wright	29 Sept. 1832	Phillip B. Waters	13 Aug. 1840
David Rogers	11 Aug. 1835	John T. Henderson	13 Aug. 1843
Thomas B. Windham	20 Sept. 1835		

EARLY POSTMASTERS

The following list of early postmasters and postal routes in Alabama are from two booklets compiled by J. H. Scruggs, Jr. which can be found in the Birmingham Public Library. These booklets are "Alabama Postal Roads with Maps, 1818-1819" and "Alabama Postal History".

P. O. 1825
Ernest's Store
Greenville

Postmaster
Asa Arrington
Samuel L. Caldwell

P. O. Box 1830
Ernest's Store
Greenville
Hemphill
Manningham
Middletown

	Miles	to Wash.	to Tusc.
Matthias Jones		920	125
S. L. Caldwell		903	143
Wm. Hemphill		924	164
Benjamin Manning		912	152
George W. Wilson		925	165

P. O. Box 1835
Barge's
Greenville
Manningham
Ridgeville

	$	¢
John Barge	14	44
J. M. Parmer	152	17
Robert S. Ware	8	41
(G. W. Coleman	35	60
(Daniel W. Coleman	10	83

P. O. Box 1839	Postmaster	$	¢
Barge's	John Barge	30	28
Fort Dale	Isaac Jones	17	44
Greenville	F. J. Edmonson	135	12
Kirkville	Zeno Pickens	21	28
Manningham	R. S. Ware	21	00
Ridgeville	D. W. Coleman	24	00
Starlington	S. Parker	3	88

P. O. July 1, 1844-June 30, 1845		Comp.	Net Prcds.
Barge's	John Barge	22.08	43.09
Greenville	James L. Dunklin	254.35	283.30
Manningham	(Rbt. S. Ware 12/31	11.35	21.69
	(Joseph McGhee	12.20	23.39
Ridgeville	John B. Lewis	13.86	26.53
Starlington	Albert Butler	9.43	16.60

P. O. Box July 1, 1850-June 30, 1851			
Barge's	J. K. Benson	33.71	44.55
Butler Spring	---------	no ret'n	
Butlersville	H. S. Staggers	.67	.92
Greenville	(Jos. L. Dunklin 9/17	57.97	84.26
	(J. N. Dennis 12/21	74.17	76.64
	(W. C. Caldwell	145.93	158.31
Kirkville	James Kirkpatrick	69.14	85.85
Manningham	D. J. Ray	39.56	53.58
Millville	James L. Thagard	41.14	54.82
Monterey	J. M. Yeldell	38.63	48.51
Ridgeville	(L.M. Watters, 1 qr.	5.61	7.62
	(P. B. Waters	10.85	14.57
Salsoda	---------	no retn.	
So. Butler	(S. H. Slocomb 5/7	15.55	20.70
	(L. M. Wright	83.61	84.96

P. O. 1855			
Big Patsaliga	J. F. Nixon, 1 qr.	.19	.14
Butler Spring	James Reynolds	47.27	18.29
Butlerville (discon. 1/11/55)	J. P. Cook, 3 qr.	4.10	2.50
Dead Falls est. 11/15/1854	(James Daniel 2 qr.	13.45	8.37
	(William Hightower	13.98	9.47
Greenville	Alex McKellar	252.00	350.14
Kirkville	James Kirkpatrick	32.98	16.51
Manningham	Darius J. Ferguson	39.15	12.65
Millville	J. L. Thagard	19.68	10.70
Monterey	Y. M. Yeldell	53.61	23.35
Oaky Streak	N. L. Weaver	12.95	6.83
Rainesville	---------		
Sal Soda	Stephen Bishop	17.95	9.53
So. Butler	J. T. Henderson	24.30	17.59
Starlington	Young Lee		
Three Runs	Joseph Steiner	19.86	22.04

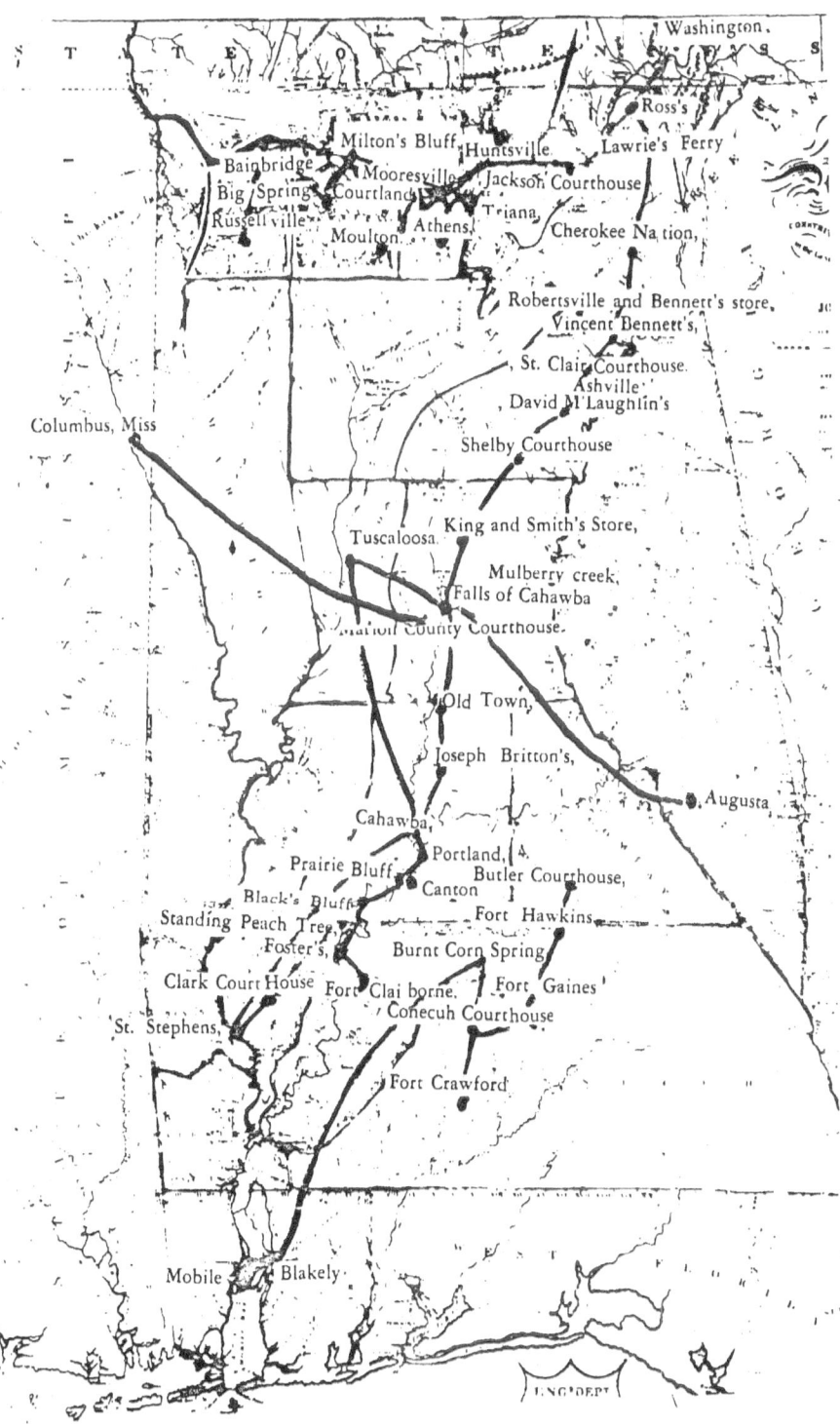

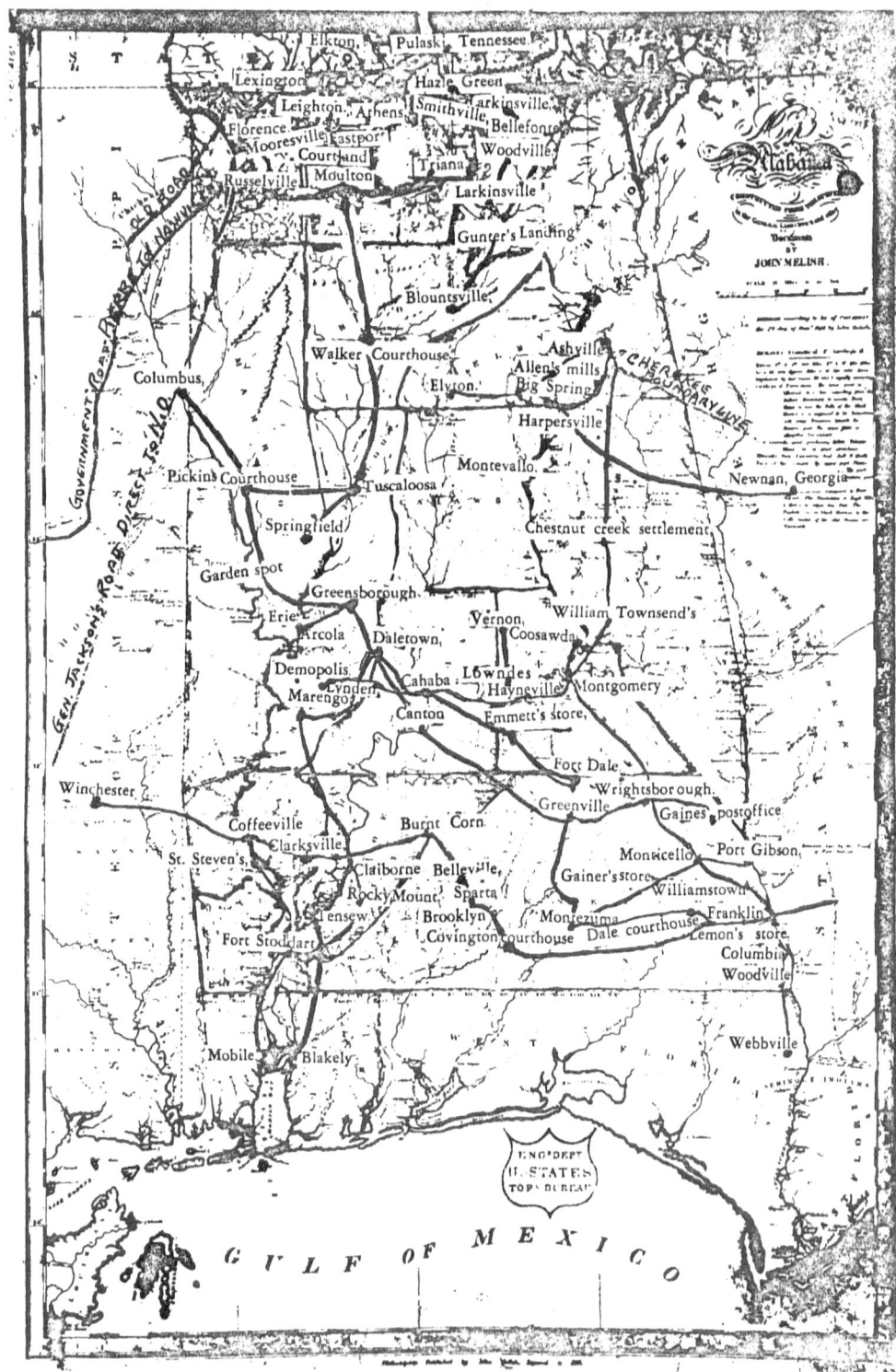

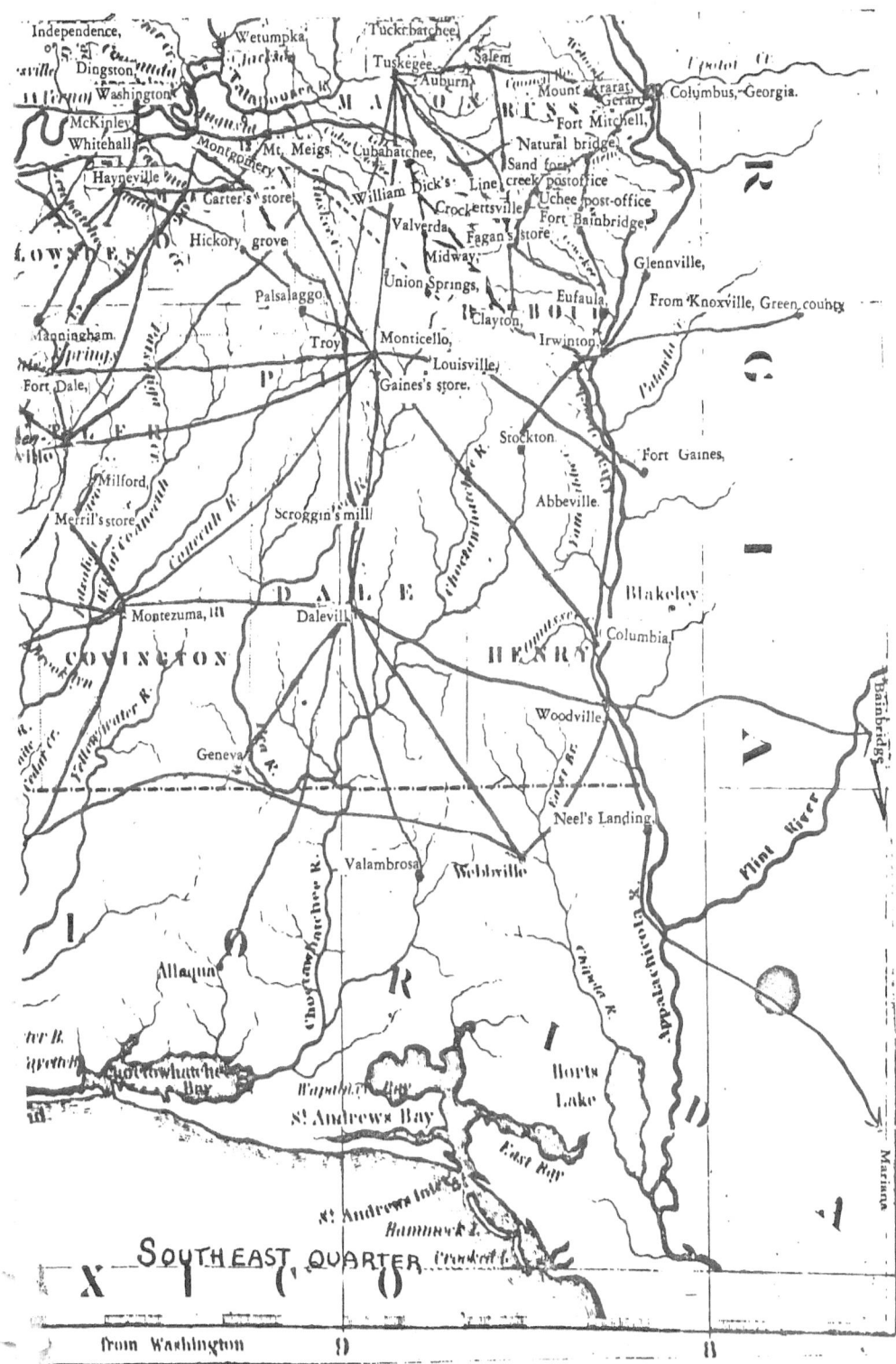

FIRST ELECTION IN BUTLER COUNTY[1]

A list of voters at an election held at Fort Dale on the first Monday in August in the year 1820, for Sheriff for the county of Butler. Original on file with Election Returns of Butler County 1820, in the Department of Archives and History.

William Banks
Robert Black
John Bolling
William Collins
Charles Cook
Henry Cook
Isaac Cook
Nathan Cook
James Craig
Charles Davenport
James Davis
Heram Davison
Archilaus Dickinson
Benjamin Dulaney
James Dunklin
Simeon Easterwood
James O. I. Garrett
Webster Gilbert
John Graydon
William Graydon
George Harrison
King Harrison
Levi Harrison
John Heaton
Hillary Herbert
William Herbert
Par Hutchinson
Frederick Jolly
Johnathan Harrison

John A. C. Jones
William Lee
Calvin Leonard
Taliferro Livingston
Elijah Mannis
Ervine McDaniel
Daniel Paine
John Paine
Samuel Paine
Ephraim Palmer
Andrew J. Perry
John Pierce
Abraham Pivy
Richard Rengold
William Reid
William Rotten
Daniel Safford
Grant Safford
Reuben Tally
Ward Taylor
John Tensley
George Thigpen
George Tillman
Micajah Wade
James Wallace
Elisha Ward
Daniel Williams
John Williams
Samuel Williams

A statement of the polls of an election held at Fort Dale on the first Monday in August in the year 1820, for Sheriff of Butler County.

State of Alabama) We the undersigned managers do hereby certify
Butler County) the within to be a true list of voters and the above a true statement of the polls taken at an election held on the first Monday in August in the year 1820, at Fort Dale for Sheriff of said county and that the accompanying certificate was made of an election held at the house of Jesse Womack of Fort Bibb by the managers whose names are therein to subscribed from which it plainly appears that Jesse Womack is duly elected. Witness our hand and seal the 8th day of August in the year 1820.

                     James Wallace
                     Micajah Wade
                     William Lee

1. Compiled from "Alabama Historical Society Quarterly".

GREENVILLE WHIG
Edited by John W. Womack
Published every Saturday morning by Thomas J. Judge

Only one issue of the Greenville Whig appears to have survived to the present day, and it is located in The Department of Archives and History in Montgomery, Alabama. This issue is dated July 11, 1835, and is Volume 1, No. 48. Newspapers printed in the early 1800s were quite different from those of today. They were for the most part literary publications. In an average four page spread the first two pages usually were filled with stories, serials, poetry and articles that appear to have been copied from encyclopedias. The last two pages were, for the most part, advertisements, probate announcements, with one or two obituaries and items of local interest, mostly political. Because of the scarcity of material available on Butler County during this period I have elected to mention everything printed relating to the county including advertisements.

"Demize--Mr. Nathan Talley formerly of Butler, but now of Dallas County, has since the 3d inst., lost, by sickness, three of his sons.
Died--at his residence in Butler county, on the 8th inst. Mr. Henry Jones, in the 30th year of his age. Also--Mr. Richard Warren on the 3d inst. in the 72nd year of his age."

There was an election to be held in August, 1835. The following people were shown as running for office.

CANDIDATES
For President
HUGH L. WHITE
of Tennessee

For Governor
Enoch Parsons, of Monroe
In favor of Hugh L. White
C. C. Clay, of Madison
Opposed to Hugh L. White, and in favor
of Martin Van Buren

Congress, 4th District
Dixon H. Lewis

Legislature
H. L. Henderson
John W. Womack

Running for the office of Sheriff of the County of Butler
David Rogers   W. C. Carr
Running for the office of Clerk of the Circuit Court of Butler County
James G. Tigner, for re-election
Running for the office of Collector of Taxes for the County of Butler
Thomas H. Briggs   James Howel   Silas N. _____

The friends who heard the Rev. Mr. Butler's discourse on Wednesday night, are respectively requested to attend at the Presbyterian Church tomorrow, at the usual hour of service.

God willing, A. Graham & J. A. Butler will hold forth the words of life, in Greenville, on Lords day (12th inst.) at 3 o'clock, and by Candle lighting--Omitting the appointment at 11 o'clock, for the accomodation of others, who wish to occupy at that hour.

"Error can never harm, whilst truth is left free to combat it." We do, out of the best motives of sincere hearts, invite our religious friends; particularly our Pulpit Brethren, to attend and show why sentence of death should be passed against us, by the Court of public opinion. Much has been said against our views; but nothing heretical proved. If the Teachers, of this vicinity, do not meet us, and investigate the points at issue--we think them bound to perpetual silence upon these subjects. July 5, 1835.

A Protracted meeting will be held in this place, by the Rev. Messrs. Rice & Holly, assisted by other ministers, commencing on Friday evening before the third sabbath in July. Friends and brethren from a distance, are invited to attend. Arrangements will be made to take care of them & their horses. June 10th, 1835.

ADMINISTRATORS NOTICE

Letters of Administration on the Estate of Thomas Boggan, deceased, were granted to the undersigned, by the Hon. the Orphan's Court of Butler County, on the 20th October last. All persons indebted to said Estate, are required to present them within the time prescribed by law, or they will be barred. Anderson Boggan, Adm'r. June 27, 1835.

LAW NOTICE

John W. Mann having located in Hayneville, Lowndes County, for the purpose of practicing Law, will take pleasure in attending to any business which his friends may confide to him. Hayneville, May 9, 1835.

John W. Womack, has removed to Greenville, Butler County. He will attend the Courts in the same Counties in which he has heretofore practiced. Sept. 5.

I. S. McMean, Attorney at Law, keeps his office on Commerce St. adjoining H. Pierce's store. Aug. 30th.

ADVERTISEMENTS

GREENVILLE MALE AND FEMALE SEMINARY. Mr. & Mrs. Martin, respectfully inform the inhabitants of Greenville and its vicinity, that their SEMINARY is now in successful operation, and that they are now prepared to receive pupils of both sexes, as they are both intending to devote considerable time to instruction. If assistance should be needed, that of the best character will be obtained. Mr. and Mrs. M. have both been educated, at some of the best institutions of our country, and in their labors to the improvement and discipline of the mind and the regular growth of all its faculties, to meet the opprobation of those who may become their patrons. Their next quarter will commence on the first Monday in April next.

Rate of tuition will be as follows--
For Spelling, Reading small Geography, introduction to Arithmetic
  (per qr.) $4.00
For Writing, E. Grammar, Arithmetic, Geography & History of the
  United States $5.00
For Rhetoric, General History, Composition, Chemistry, Natural
  Philosophy $6.50
For Moral & Intellectual Philosophy, Matthematics, French, Latin
  & Greek Languages $8.00
For Painting, with Theorems, principles of Music (additional
  charge) $2.00
For Contingent bill, for fuel, repairs, & for the winter qr. $0.50
Note: Board in respectable families can be obtained.   Dec. 20, 1834.

Isaac Pierce--For sale superior Irish linens.
Pierce's Corner--Barrels of Molasses for sale.
John C. Caldwell--requests the person who took a shot gun from his store with the upper Thimble broke off, to please return it without delay to him or James Homes.
J. C. Caldwell--General assortment of Men's & Boy's fur hats, palm leaf hats, Tuscan & openwork, Brogans & shoes, Ladies calf, seal, Morocco & Prunella shoes, broad cloths, Bombazines, Checks, Ticklenburgs, Linens, Gingham, Chambrays, London, French & Domestic Preniz, Printed & Checked Muslins, plain Jackonet & Mull, Figured Swiss & Book, Silks, Laces, white blond Veils, fancy Silk & Crepe Handkerchiefs, Bik Italian Crepe, Bandana, Flag & Pongee Hdkfs, Shell, Brazil & Horn Tuck & Side Combs, Parasols, etc. Also Crockery & Glass Ware, Hardware & Cutlery, Tobacco, Spices, Patent Medicine, etc.
Isaac Pierce--During my absence from the State Ezekiel H. Pickens is my authorized agent. James Davenport & M. W. Holman--The firm of Davenport & Holman is dissolved on June 9, 1835 in Hayneville by mutual consent. Mr. Davenport still has on hand a few hogsheads of Cincinnati Bacon for sale.
R. S. & J. K. Ware--Ready made clothing for sale in Manningham.
Gerrell & Rabun--Ready made clothing, dry goods, drugs & medicines, Hardware & Cutlery, Crockery & Glass Ware. Greenville.
A. M. Reid--Subscriber has purchased the Blacksmith Shop in Greenville, which formerly belonged to Major Ward Taylor, immediately on the street 70 yards north of the Court House. The same Smith will remain in the shop, that worked there during the last year & will be assisted by an able striker who has also worked at the Blacksmith trade during the past year. I intend keeping on hand a general assortment of Iron and Steel, and all those who may think proper to call, may rest assured that their work will be done in the best style, and at the shortest notice; and will be warranted so far as is customary. The Smiths have the advantage of a good Shop and Tools, suited to every branch of their business, and will attend punctually to all who may think proper to give them a call, and are well qualified to do any work in their line of business.   A. M. Reid   January 10.

LETTERS IN THE P. O. 1st JULY 1835

Peter Arrauk,	N. H. Craig, Esq.	George Eagerton
Sarah Baker	G. Cheatham	Benjamin Fuller
Edward Berry	Jacob Cravy	Jacob Futch
John Barlow	A. Cunningham	William Goodwin
Susan Barrineau	Theophilus Daniel	Marvel Gray
Jessee Cone	Thomas Daniel	Samuel Gingles
James Chesnut 2	Samuel Dunlap	James Gibson
Hurbert Carter	Thomas Eason	Rutledge Hatcher

Rev. Peter Haskew	Charles Peavy	Isaac Smith
Daniel Hall	David Phillips 2	William G. Smith
Willis Hobbs	Daniel D. Patterson	Henry Terry
Francis W. Jones	John Payne	Moses Veal
J. D. Kirkpatrick	Own Paton	Thomas B. Windham
J. Kirkpatrick, Esq.	James Pool	J. W. Womack
Amos Little	David Rogers	F. A. B. Wheeler
H. Lundy	Ja's Shaw	Henry Weatherly
J. H. M'Daniel	John Smyth	Daniel Wright
Brittian Meeks	William T. Streety	John Wethers
James Merritt	James Stuart	James Wright
S. F. Miller, Esq.	E. L. Sanderson 2	E. P. Wright
Ja's M'Ceanne	Capt. G. W. Ship	Robert Welch
Dukel Mulles	William Skain	Henry R. Ward
Largent M'Corley	Ambrose Smith	Sandford Walker

A. McKellar, P. M.
Greenville, July 4, 1835

The law office of the Hon. Anderson Crenshaw located on the Ridge.

Fort Dale Cemetery.

CHAPTER 3

BUTLER COUNTY MEN IN THE REVOLUTIONARY WAR[1]

Autrey, George
Garner, John (Moved to Wilcox Co.)
Gary, Thomas
Goodwin, Theophilus
Gandy, Brinckley
Linton, John
Martin, Benjamin
Perry, Abraham
Petty, Theophilus, Sr.
Skanes, Adam
Sheppard, Andrew
Thomas, William
Wagster, William
Wheddon, Noah

PENSIONERS OF THE WAR OF 1812[1]

Bond, Robert
Bransford, Nathan
Brooks, John Z.
Buill, Parker
Dowling, Zacheus
Fleming, John
Fuller, Thomas
Hatcher, Rutledge
Lee, Hillary
Lowery, James
Perritt, Needham
Pickens, John C.
Pickens, Nathan C.
Pruett, Richard W.
Rabun, Richard
Rhodes, Jared
Wilkerson, William

CREEK WAR 1836-7[2]
HENDERSON'S COMPANY, SMITH'S ALABAMA MOUNTED VOLUNTEERS

Pvt. Benjamin Allday
Pvt. Tillman Barlow
Pvt. Anthoney Bevoley
Pvt. Thomas Branton
Pvt. James Brassell
Pvt. John Brassell
Capt. Thomas Briggs
Pvt. Allen Coleman
Pvt. Jackson Correll
Pvt. Andy Criswell
Pvt. Phillip Daves
Pvt. Edward Deming
Pvt. James Duglass
Pvt. D. M. Duncand
Capt. William A. T. Dunklin
Pvt. John B. Ellis
Pvt. Marshall Federick
Pvt. Daricus Fogerson
Pvt. G. A. Garett
Pvt. Isaac Green
Pvt. Richard Haile
Pvt. James K. Hamond
Pvt. James Hatley
Pvt. Allen Hawkins
Pvt. Jesse Hays
Capt. H. L. Henderson
Pvt. Simeon Hester
Pvt. John Holaday
Pvt. G. W. Homes
1 Sgt. Daniel B. Hough
Pvt. Sims Howell
Pvt. Ely Hutson
Pvt. William Jackson
Pvt. Greaf Jones
Pvt. Isaac Jones
Sgt. Thomas J. Judge
Pvt. Arnold Kent
Pvt. William Maning
Pvt. William McCune
Pvt. Shadrack McCormich
Pvt. John McCoy
Pvt. James Miller
Pvt. William Moore
1 Lt. James Neal
Pvt. John Otts
Pvt. John A. J. Page
Pvt. John Quinley (?)
Pvt. William Raborn
Pvt. Wiley Ray
Pvt. James Reeves

1. Obtained from the Department of Archives & History in Montgomery, Al.
2. "Index to Compiled Service Records-Ala. Units-Creek War 1836-1837" Benjamin Achee & Margery Wright. 1971

Pvt. John Seales
Pvt. Ransom Seales
Pvt. Thomas Shepheard
Pvt. Arter Sims
Pvt. Stephen Sims
Pvt. Willey Sims
Pvt. James D. Smith
Pvt. Benjamin Taylor
Pvt. Daniel Thomas
Pvt. James Tigner

Pvt. Thomas Winsley
Pvt. John H. Wallis
Pvt. Robert Wealch
Pvt. F. W. Williamson
Pvt. G. W. Winderwood
Pvt. Thomas Windham
Pvt. John W. Wommack
Pvt. Feddon Wood
Pvt. Thomas Wood
2 Lt. James Wright

On September 28, 1850 an act was passed entitling men who fought in the war to forty acres of bounty land and then again on March 3, 1855 another act was passed entitling these men to additional property. A copy of the papers of the men who fought the Indians can be ordered from Washington showing when they applied for this bounty land. On the service record of Stephen Sims of Butler County the following names appear: H. L. Henderson, Arthur Sims, Thomas Sheppard/Shepheard, Edward Lee, Justice of the Peace, J. Mirot, Commissioner, A. F. Posey, Esq., Samuel J. Bolling, Judge of Probate, D. A. W. Patterson, Justice of the Peace and John A. Jackson, Judge of Wilcox Co.

THE WAR BETWEEN THE STATES
COMPANY C 17TH ALA. REGIMENT

The Greenville Advocate   April 30, 1903

The following is a roster of Company "C" as organized and marched to the front, the copy bearing date of September 25, 1861.

Walter D. Perryman, Captain
John Bolling, 1st Lieutenant
John Payne, 2nd Lieutenant
L. W. Trawick, 3rd Lieutenant
C. C. Lloyd, 1st Seargent
Robert Perry, 2nd Seargent

Peter Goodson, 3rd Seargent
J. W. Wallace, 4th Seargent
W. R. Peterson, 1st Corporal
Edward Stevens, 2nd Corporal
J. W. Skipper, 3rd Corporal
Henry O. Seale, 4th Corporal

Privates

Marion J. Andrews
Theophilus Atkinson
George W. Bailey
B. F. Burton
Henry J. Boggs
Jonah Cater
William H. Conner
Sidney S. Creech
John W. Driver
James F. Dukes
James Dugan
Alfred Davis
Buford W. Dendy
James Ernest
Josiah Frost
Henry Frost
Thomas G. Gafford
Daniel E. Hester
Louis A. Hester
Isaiah H. Henderson
William Herndon

Henry S. Harper
Tapley Hendrix
John A. Harrison
Moses J. Harrison
John D. Howard
James W. Jay
J. T. Johnson
James H. Johnson
Andrew J. Kelley
John H. Kelley
Lewis M. Lard
LaFayette Lany
Jacob C. Milton
Isaiah G. Miller
John A. McCrary
John D. McCormick
Shadrick Nichols
Ira E. Payne
James Perry
Thomas Phylyaw
William H. Powell

Gardner E. Parker
William B. Pace
Thomas E. Pace
Frank M. Pierce
James A. M. Petty
Neal A. Ramsey
Richard Rayburn
William R. Smith
Thomas J. Sanders
Thomas S. Smith

Robert M. Sims
John F. Spurlock
Andrew C. Smyth
John J. Thompson
Solomon Troutman
Newton Troutman
Littleton Talley
James Willis
William J. Williamson

The following names are of the men who joined the company after that date.

J. R. Alford
M. Armstrong
H. C. Armstrong
S. D. Belton
W. E. Braden
James Boggus
J. T. Bailey
J. Bell
L. M. Brooks
S. S. Creech
F. L. Creech
O. Cox
A. Cheatham
D. H. Cheatham
J. E. Chambers
Frank Chambers
Andy Chambers
A. B. Cooley
J. W. Driver
L. A. Dendy
Bill Dendy
Elijah Dodson
Nate Dodson
J. D. Flowers
James Frost
W. H. Frost
J. T. Ganus
W. A. Graydon
H. S. Graydon
Ed Harrison
B. Hall
D. J. Holland
Dick Herbert
Alex Johnson
R. Kendrick
B. Kite
J. Lowery

R. B. Lowery
G. Lowery
H. B. Lowery
W. H. Leven
D. J. Mash
Seth Mercer
John W. Morgan
J. A. Morgan
J. W. Morgan
James W. Morgan
T. Miller
J. W. Mapes
William Milton
C. C. Nickles
Eb Pollard
T. B. Pollard
W. B. Perry
Ben. Perry
G. W. Posey
J. H. Perdue
W. H. Powell
D. M. Powell
W. J. L. Peterson
Tom Peterson
W. M. Pierce
Russell Pace
G. W. Rhodes
J. Rhodes
Yancey Rhodes
Wesley Rogers
H. D. Rogers
W. D. Rogers
W. P. Rouse
J. Rives
S. Rives
S. T. Russell
James B. Stanley

Charles D. Stanley
Seth Smith
J. Smith
J. S. Skipper
George Skipper
James K. Seale
Hamp Seale
Al Seale
J. A. Smith
W. C. Spradley
Thomas Spradley
J. E. Spradley
J. W. Skipper
A. T. Stringer
G. Stringer
J. F. Sims
John Sapp
D. M. Stewart
Hillary Stewart
J. Q. Stuckey
J. A. Thompson
C. C. Thompson
J. Tranum
K. H. Thornton
R. J. Traweek
A. J. Thagard
Josiah Talley
W. R. Thagard
W. H. Thagard
J. R. Vice
J. Wallace
J. Weaver
W. A. Walton
G. W. Wyche
R. Wyche

The above are all the names of the Company that could be thought of by the following members of the company to whom we are indebted for assistance in getting them up: Messrs. J. J. and C. C. Thompson, Eb. Pollard and F. L. Creech. There are others who were members of the company, but whose names have escaped those who have tried to get them all, and we will gladly publish them if anyone who reads this will notify us.

A number of the above recruits who entered the army after the company first went out, were elected to office. The following are some of the changes in the official roster: Capt. Perryman resigned and John Bolling was promoted. After the battle of Nashville where Capt. Bolling was captured the Regiment was consolidated with the 33rd and 26th, and J. L. Powell was promoted to the Captaincy. Lieutenant Payne died and Lieutenant Traweek resigned and John A. Harrison was elected lieutenant as was also Watt Dendy. Harrison was killed and William Pace was elected lieutenant."

REPORT OF ALABAMA HISTORY COMMISSION 1900. MISCELLANEOUS COLLECTIONS. VOLUME 1. CONFEDERATE WAR RECORDS

Thirty-third Regiment, Infantry. Organized at Greenville, March, 1862. Col. Samuel Adams. The muster rolls on file are of companies, without history of letter, as follows:

M. C. Kinney	Captain	T. G. Pou	Captain		
R. E. Ward	Captain	Needham Hughes	Captain		
David McKee	Captain	H. H. Norman	Captain		
A. H. Justice	Captain	James H. Dunklin	Captain		
R. J. Cooper	Captain	William J. Lee	Captain		

THE GREENVILLE OBSERVER

Jno. S. Davies, Editor   April 22, 1865

"EXTRA EXTRA
GLORIOUS NEWS
SURRENDER OF LEE
COMPLETE ROUT OF FORREST'S ARMY

Major G. W. Martin, 2nd Maine Cavalry, Lieuts. Coffinberry and Coghland, Co. G and Messrs. Mason, Runyan, Strickland, Maurice, Maxwell, Co. B., McMurtry, Co. G, 40th Mo. Vols. and Barrett, Co. F, 95th Ill. Vol. return their thanks to Mr. Jno. S. Davies, Editor and Publisher of the Greenville (Ala.) Weekly Observer, for courtesies extended them in the use of his press and materials for the publication of this Extra to their friends in Alabama, greetings. This is, perhaps, the first opportunity the citizens of Butler County and Central Alabama have had of reading the true state of affairs between the late opposing armies of the two sections of the Union - North and South.

The Occupation of Greenville

The occupation of Greenville to Federal troop took place yesterday, April 20. The citizens of Greenville were surprised by the entrance of Spurling's Cavalry Brigade: the people were pursuing their usual avocations, and the few officers and soldiers were unconscious of danger, and scattered about town, when Col. Spurling at the head of one hundred of his cavalry dashed upon them, capturing nine commissioned officers and eighty enlisted men, exclusive of three medical officers and two captains. Many of the citizens took to the swamps and escaped, but the greater part of them were taken prisoners, and afterwards released. All that remained at home were not molested, but those that attempted to run were arrested. Amid the confusion, many beautiful ladies came in the streets, imploring protection, and in a short time the gallant and dashing Spurling was surrounded by a bevy of beauties handsome enough to soften the sternest heart. As the cavalry were dashing down one of the streets the Stars and Stripes were unfurled from a neat little cottage, when the troop halted and gave three times three for that glorious Flag for which we have fought so long. We have heard of three American flags displayed from houses in this city and are informed that several more would be flying in the Southern breeze if they could be obtained.

Since the occupation of Greenville by the Federal troops, we have not heard of any depredations being committed by the soldiers and many have expressed their surprise at the good conduct of the enemy, as they expected that their houses would be pillaged and burned and any manner of depredations committed but to their agreeable astonishment not a single house has been destroyed, and the town is quiet and orderly. The citizens have treated us cordially and kindly, and we shall long remember our stay in Greenville as an oasis in the soldier's rough life.

As we were passing a group of citizens standing at a street corner yesterday we heard one inquire the name of the very determined looking man riding by at the moment. We informed them that he was no other than Major General A. J. Smith, the commander of this army, the hero of a hundred battles. 'Twas Gen. Smith's corps which formed the rear of Gen. Bank's army in the retreat from the Red River campaign. 'Twas Gen. Smith's corps that saved Thomas at Nashville a few months ago and played such havoc with Hoop's army. 'Twas McArthur's division of this army which made the terrible charge at Nashville, causing a panic in the rebel army, and winning stars for his brigade commanders and a second star for himself. In the catalogue of fighting Generals developed by this war the name of Major General A. J. Smith will be found among the first.

During the siege of Spanish Fort several officers rode down one day to take a look at the works, but getting somewhat close, were selected by some of the rebel sharpshooters for target practice, which, not being to their fancy, caused a slight advance to the rear in hot haste. On arriving at camp and being interrogated in regards to the adventure, one of the number remarked that he had been informed that there were quite a number of Secessionists in the Fort, and from the investigations, he had no doubt of the correctness of the report.

****

The following order has been received at Headquarters, 3d Division. It speaks for itself:
           HEADQUARTERS 17th ARMY CORPS
           GREENVILLE, ALA. APRIL 22, 1865
Brig. Gen. E. A. Carr, Commanding 3d:
    The Major General commanding directs that under the orders of the Secretary of War, and in compliance with General Field Orders No. 22, Headquarters Army and Division West Mississippi, April 15th, 1865, in honor of the surrender of Gen. Lee and the Army of Northern Virginia to the forces of the United States, under the command of Lieut. Gen. Grant, a salute of 200 guns will be fired at 3 o'clock p.m. this day under the direction and immediate supervision of Capt. J. W. Cowell, Chief of Artillery.

    I am, very respectfully,
                                  Your obedient servant,
                                  J. Rough,
                            Lieut Col. and A. A. G.

****

On entering town yesterday morning, we were not a little surprised to observe such a large number of beautiful ladies. Perhaps some allowance may be made for soldier boys who have been compaigning through the pine woods of Alabama for a couple of months, but we think we can safely swear that for pretty girls, Greenville stands unrivalled. If Gen. Smith could only be persuaded that the interests of the services demanded a delay at Greenville for a week or fortnight we are sure that some of these ladies would entertain a different opinion of the Yankee soldiers than they now do. Col. Spurling has received a number of notes from the citizens thanking him for the gentlemanly manner with which the soldiers have conducted themselves. It seems to have been a general belief that with the entry of the Union army a series of outrages too horrible to mention would begin. We observe the happy disappointment on every side. But we must be "marching along." We promise ourselves another visit to Greenville, when the white wings of peace shall cover the land.

In the meantime, may this goodly town enjoy its former prosperity, and the "busy hum of industry" find again its channel in this community. The dead must bury its dead. This beautiful town like too many others, still only regret the cruel destiny which like an avenging Nemesis drove it into the whirlpool of Secession.

With communication again established by rail and by river, between Mobile and Montgomery, we shall congratulate the community upon an opening dawn of prosperity such as has not been witnessed for years past. Brush the dust from your coffee cups and bring out the sugar bowl. This style of crockery is again in fashion, for the precious kernels are coming - Again, goodbye, city of pretty girls and spacious hospitals. 'Tis a lucky shot that disables a soldier boy, temporarily in this vicinity.[1]

****

ATTENTION SPORTSMEN!!

Just run the Blockade! 30,000 English Waterproof Percussion Caps and for sale, cheap from Josiah Rhodes.

Greenville, March 6, '65.

****

GREENVILLE FEMALE ACADEMY.   Mrs. J. S. Davies, Principal. Rates of Tuition: For the Session of ten months $150.00, to be paid monthly. No deductions made for absences caused by protracted sickness."

CONFEDERATE VETERANS REUNION

The following committee has been appointed to solicit baskets for the Reunion dinner of the Confederate Veterans Reunion which will be in Greenville on August 21st, 1897. These ladies are asked to send baskets even if they are unable to attend and to see that all the old Veterans in their beats are requested to attend the Reunion at the Fair Grounds. (The Living Truth, August 12, 1897)

1. This issue was obtained from The American Antiquarian Society.

Beat 1.
Mesdames Wiley Powell, John Harvell, Jessie Owens, John A. Vickery, Wash Leysath.

Beat 2.
Mesdames S. B. Griffin, John Herron, W. H. Norris, Alf Cook, Mattie Rhodes, F. E. Whittle, P. D. Rigsby.

Beat 3.
Mesdames John Crittenden, J. H. Shines, Richard Hughes, Marion Lee, J. M. Boan, James Johnson, Reuben Stallings.

Beat 4.
Mesdames J. W. Halso, Henry Hughly, J. J. Garrett, West Pierce, Rufus Shell, John Hinson.

Toluka.
Mesdames E. R. Howard, Herbert Howard, C. G. Jones, T. A. Kettler, Will Summerford, Mal Warren.

Beat 5.
Mesdames J. W. Brown, Eli Lester, J. B. Taylor, John H. Thompson.

Beat 6.
Mesdames Alex Whitten, S. K. McCormick, William McBride, Miss Mattie V. Newton.

Beat 7.
Mesdames T. A. King, W. A. Graydon, W. F. Cheatham, James Richards, Wiley Penn, J. A. Morgan, J. I. Williamson.

Beat 8.
Mesdames John Harrison, William Bush, Charles Heaton, Asy Hinson, Mack Barganier, W. H. Cheatham, W. A. Norsworthy, Gus Pierce, John Bush.

Beat 9.
Mesdames F. E. Heaton, W. C. Simmons, James Harper, B. L. Pierce, J. E. Brown, F. W. Crenshaw, Sr., Henry Crenshaw, Collidge Brown, John Peagler.

Beat 10.
Mesdames Robert Donald, James Yeldell, T. H. Barge, W. R. Luckie, T. P. Kendrick, S. R. Kendrick, Janie Atkins, Erskin Donald, J. E. Till, C. H. Crane.

Butler Springs.
Mesdames H. E. Carter, James Henderson, A. A. Sims, W. J. Jones, Amanda F. Murphy.

Forest Home.
Mesdames J. T. Moncrief, W. N. Watt, Joseph Benson, J. A. Smith, C. Wall, J. H. Lyman, C. C. Thompson, George Lazenby.

Beat 12.
W. P. Rouse, B. J. Newton, J. A. Rhodes, E. Pollard, W. R. Thagard, J. E. Smith, L. C. Hawkins, J. W. Wilson, H. C. Creech, F. L. Creech, J. S. Hartley, J. M. Whitehead, C. C. Lloyd, E. I. Norris, E. P. Watkins, J. B. Lewis, E. W. Cheatham, E. P. Roper, R. Y. Porter, H. G. Perry, R. E. Corry, J. Bealand, Reney Mercer, J. C. McQueen, Miss Ida Thagard.

Beat 13.
Mesdames J. W. Darley, W. J. Nicholson, Cout Barnes, B. B. McKenzie, H. L. Hobbs.

Beat 14.
Mesdames W. T. Smith, E. A. Vinson, Jno. M. Sims, G. P. Heard, A. L. Palmer, E. S. Pilley, G. A. Morrow, D. D. Bennett, N. M. Bazer, T. M. G. Porter, Wash Powell.

Beat 15.
Mesdames Robert Perry, J. A. Smyth, J. A. Sturges, W. P. Graham.

Beat 16.
Mesdames J. R. Sirmon, Sr., W. A. Baggett, Thomas McPherson, George A. Mathews.

Beat 17.
Mesdames D. P. Jernigan, A. C. Van Pelt, J. S. Russell.

Beat 18.
Mesdames J. J. Flowers, George W. Wallace, T. S. McCall, Andrew Barden, J. D. Flowers.

Beat 19.
Mesdames G. W. Lee, David Majors, J. J. Huggins.

DECORATION DAY[1]

The schedule for Decoration Day, May 10, 1872 is as follows: Procession to the Old Graveyard near the Methodist Church with the band playing.
1. Vocal music by Choirs
2. Prayer by Rev. J. Barker.
3. Music by the Silver Cornet Band of Greenville
4. Decoration of Soldiers' graves while the Choir sings.
5. Benediction by Rev. J. W. Jordan.

Marshall of the Day
CAPTAIN A. C. GREEN
Assistant Marshalls

J. P. Hodnett	Isaac Long	R. A. Payne
Capt. Ed Crenshaw	E. J. M. Padgett	John Watson
James S. Womack	Dr. Jno. Berney	John Mallett
Jno. E. Knight	D. B. Taylor	W. J. Dunklin
Hick Perdue	Jack Thagard	William McKenzie
Peter Sutherlin	Don Porter	Leo Frank
James Thames	Mally Riley	

Msrshall & Assistants will be mounted on horseback and wear the usual badge, viz: a white sash worn diagonally across the breast from left shoulder with a sprig of evergreen on the breast, each carrying a white baton decorated with black.   D. G. Dunklin, Chrm.

Members of the band: Prof. Battenhoussen, B. M. Archer, Meyer Frank, Abe Frank, Thomas Thames, Henry Lichten, James Johnson, Joseph T. Krahm, John W. Clarke, John Drake, Lonnie Blalock.

1. Greenville Advocate, 9 May 1872.

THE METROPOLITAN RIFLES [1]

In the latter half of the nineteenth century military units were formed in Butler County which probably operated in much the same fashion as the National Guard does today. In times of emergencies the members could be called on for assistance.

One of the earliest of these organizations was the Metropolitan Rifles of Greenville. It's membership was composed of some of the best material in Greenville. Their soldierly appearance and accurate manuevers made them the pride of the community. The citizens felt secure from the threats of any disturbance or riots with the formation of this company. In the period following the War Between the States the white population still lived in fear of retaliation from the negro citizenry. Captain Watson and Lieutenant Wimberly of the Metropolitan Rifles discovered on a trip to Montgomery to arm and uniform their men that the negroes of Butler County had already made application for 400 stand of arms and that they had formed companies sufficient to use them.

The officers elected in the Rifles in June, 1874 were: J. H. Dunklin, Commandant; D. J. Watson, Captain; J. H. Goolsby, 1st Lt.; M. W. Wimberly, 2nd Lt.; J. M. Steiner, 3rd Lt.; O. F. Webb, O. S.; W. O. Parmer, 2nd Sgt.; W. C. Foster, 3rd Sgt.; W. T. Kendrick, 1st Corp.; Ed Kirkpatrick, 2nd Corp.; Jack Steiner, 3rd Corp.; J. R. Jones, Q. M.; W. E. Payne, Color Bearer.

LIGHT GUARDS _____ BUTLER RIFLES [2]

Another military circle was the Greenville Light Guards which was organized before 1880. Due to some dissatisfaction among the members of the unit a large number of the members made the decision to resign and form their own organization. The recruiting officers of the Light Guards got busy and were able to present the names of 12 men for active membership at the first meeting following the division. This brought their total number of active members to 57 with 6 honorary members in addition.

The following non-commissioned officers elected to fill vacancies were as follows: T. W. Peagler, 1st Sergt.; Patton Burnett, 2nd Sergt.; J. H. Wilson, 3rd Sergt.; D. H. Rouse, 4th Sergt.; R. A. Lee, 5th Sergt.; W. B. Barrow, 1st Corpl.; T. J. Judge, 2nd Corpl.; N. E. Hamilton, 3rd Corpl.; J. R. Burnett, Jr., 4th Corpl. And the following gentlemen were elected to membership: Kingsbury Thames, John Gamble, Jr., T. W. Lee, J. P. Reynolds, G. H. Thigpen, C. A. Thigpen, S. L. Pinney, B. B. Hudson, J. R. Porterfield, William Pierce, J. D. Cook, and W. P. Routen.

The resigned members of the Light Guards immediately went to work setting up a new company, and in only a very short time they had accomplished their purpose. The names of 52 men were enrolled and authority to organize was obtained. The name of the Butler Rifles was chosen in honor of one of the most gallant companies in the War Between the States. The following officers were elected: A. Steinhart, Captain; M. W. Wimberly, 1st Lieut.; J. J. McMullan, 2nd Lieut.; J. B. Kendrick, 1st Sergt.; J. S. McMullan, 2nd Sergt.; D. G. Judge, 3rd Sergt.; Jos. Lichten, 4th Sergt.; Dan Knight, 5th Sergt.; J. B. Powell, 1st Corpl.; S. E. Parmer, 2nd Corpl.; Bartow Wimberly, 3rd Corpl.; Milton Park, 4th Corpl.; Solomon Patrick McCall, Color Bearer.

1. Greenville Advocate, 2 July, 1874. 2. Greenville Advocate, August 1884

GREENVILLE RIFLE COMPANY [1]

Still another military unit was the Greenville Rifle Comapny. In the election of officers in 1896 T. A. Broughton was re-elected Captain without opposition. The other officers serving with him that year were Charles Stewart, 1st Lt.; Clarence Seawright, 2nd Lt.; Seigfred Long, Jr., 3rd Lt.; W. S. Gramlin, M. D., surgeon; W. W. Wright, re-elected 1st Sgt.; H. H. McCall, 2nd Sgt.; Stanley Massey, 3rd Sgt.; Harry Dey, 4th Sgt.; Jasper Knight, 1st Corp.; Frank Jones, 2nd Corp.; Henry Brown, 3rd Corp.; Jack Thaggard, 4th Corp.; Seigfred Long, Secretary and W. J. Dunklin, Treasurer.

FATHER RYAN CHAPTER U.D.C. [2]

The Father Ryan Chapter of the United Daughters of the Confederacy was organized October 12, 1899. At the first meeting held on October 18th Mrs. H. Z. Wilkinson was elected President, Mrs. E. R. Adams, Director, Mrs. J. F. Stallings, Treasurer, Mrs. M. W. Wimberly, Corresponding Secretary and Mrs. Robert A. Lee, Recording Secretary. Out of the 12 members enrolled 6 attended the first meeting. Initiation fees of $1.00 were established with annual dues being set at 45¢. In 1903 the dues were raised to 50¢, with National and State dues being paid out of this amount along with the Soldiers' Tax leaving a surplus of 20¢ per member in the treasury to be used as the Chapter saw fit. With such a small amount of money to work with, but with a lot of determination and inspiration this group of women was able to move mountains in spite of their moments of discouragement.

On January 3, 1900 the members decided that they needed a specific purpose in view.to work for, to get the home people interested in their organization and to prove the sincerity of their cause. After an earnest discussion they decided to work for funds to erect a memorial stone over the last remains of the noble soldiers who shed their blood for their country and whose remains were left unmarked in Magnolia Cemetery. These soldiers had previously been interred in what was referred to as Greenville's Soldiers Graveyard. This cemetery property many years after the War had been used for the expansion of the Cedar Works and at that time the remains of the patriots who had been buried there were moved to Magnolia Cemetery and placed in a single grave. This grave was at first located in the back part of Magnolia in the center of one of the circular areas in the driveway, but was later moved near the entrance. The slab is inscribed simply "Our Confederate Dead, 1861-1865".

The next project of this organization was the erection of the Confederate Statue across from the City Hall. A Mr. Rammage, who was associated with a marble company in Columbus, came to a meeting on December 6, 1902 to present plans of a statue for their consideration. It was to be 16 feet high, including the base, foundation, stone steps and the statue. The cost of the monument would be $750.00 including all extra expenses, such as shipping, erection of the statue and all bricks to be used. Of this amount $500.00 would be due when the statue was erected and the balance to be paid as funds became available. After a discussion the women decided to accept the plans; the contract was drawn up and signed by the President. The monument was to be completed by Memorial Day if no serious hinderances prevented.

1. Greenville Advocate, 22 January 1896.
2. First Minute Book of the Father Ryan Chapter.

By April 9, 1903 the inscription to be engraved on the monument was agreed upon, as follows:

> To memory of Butler County's Confederate Soldiers
> 1861-1865
> Erected by the Father Ryan Chapter
> United Daughters of the Confederacy
> Our Confederate Dead
> Dead but his spirit breathes
> Dead but his heart is ours
> Dead but his sunny & sad land wreaths
> His crown with tears for flowers.
> Father Ryan.

Various committees were appointed to make plans for the following Memorial Day events. For decorating the Pavilion: Mrs. Clara Beeland, Chairman, Miss Salome Wilkinson & Mrs. Abe Lehman. Music committee: Mrs. Gaston, Chairman, Miss Gertie Ehlbert, Mrs. Arthur Gamble & Miss Effie Pilley. Committee for furnishing the Pavilion: Mrs. Jeff Beeland, Chairman, Mrs. J. C. Kendrick, Mrs. R. E. Corry. Committee on flowers: Mrs. Kate Herbert Judge, Miss Ailene Powell, Miss Ethel Stanley. Committee on Crosses: Mrs. R. Y. Porter, Mrs. R. A. Lee, Mrs. Kirkpatrick. Committee on Cleaning the Lot at Cemetery: Mrs. R. E. Corry, Mrs. Charles Stewart. Committee on invitations to schools: Miss Irene Stanley and Miss Georgie Ashford.

On May 20, 1903 a meeting was called for the purpose of arranging a program for the unveiling of the monument which was due to take place in June. The selection of the speaker for the occasion was discussed and the matter placed in the hands of Mr. Hamilton, who promised either to give the program himself or provide a speaker. The Minutes make no mention of the speaker selected or the outcome of the unveiling, but it can be assumed that all went as planned so carefully by the ladies. The Minutes do reveal that a Major Screws returned a check to the chapter which had been given to him for his expenses in attending the unveiling.

In September following the Memorial Day events we find that the work of these dedicated women had only begun. Several years were to pass before all indebtedness of their project was paid--years in which many fund-raising projects were executed. Among these were a Young Ladies Minstrel under the direction of Prof. Julius Membo on Nov. 30, 1903 at the Opera House. Tickets went on sale for 25¢, 50¢ and 75¢. The total collection made was $183.75 out of which the Chapter cleared $85.25. Soon after this the ladies put on another Minstrel in Fort Deposit and cleared $26.50. An unusual money raising project of the President was the sale of 1,000 "guesses". No explanation was made of just what this project entailed, but her endeavors stirred her chapter members to praise her efforts with a standing ovation. Another interesting project was the sale of a diamond broach which after considerable time had passed was finally sold to Mrs. R. A. Lee of Dothan for $100.00. Among other donations to help clear the indebtedness were a check for $5.00 from the Catholics, $6.00 from Mrs. Fred Crenshaw and $2.50 from George Lazenby of Forest Home.

With the statue finally paid for the ladies turned their efforts to the beautification of the grounds surrounding the monument. Different committees were organized to canvass the town for funds wherewith to work and to soon have their little park "A thing of beauty and a joy forever." Although a nice little sum was given or promised they still had to work like Turks to realize enough to carry out their plans. A landscape gardener was employed to take charge of the work, and believing that he would be happier working with a man, the ladies solicited Maj. T. W. Peagler to act as special treasurer and manager of the undertaking. However, as the Major found his hands full at the time he recommended Dr. Whittington who graciously accepted the task placed before him. Plans on beautifying the park were long delayed due to the extensive remodeling being executed on the Methodist Church which had created piles of debris in the park area. Their plans included the planting of several hundred bushes which were to be used as a hedge and the placement of many trees to provide shade. As one passes the block today and sees the many lovely camellias and azaleas it is apparent how well planned the landscaping job was. The park has truly become the heart of Greenville and is indeed "a thing of beauty and a joy forever".

CONFEDERATE MONUMENT
Greenville

THE OPERA HOUSE

CHAPTER 4

CEMETERY RECORDS OF PEOPLE BORN BEFORE 1850

This alphabetized listing has been compiled from cemetery censuses collected by members of the Butler County Historical Society. From obituaries taken from nineteenth century newspapers additional information has been utilized to fill in some of the gaps left by headstones that no longer exist. In some instances more complete names, birthplaces, etc., have been added to existing headstone inscriptions to make the information thereon more meaningful. It will be readily noticed that the statistics have been presented in a certain format for continuity and are not necessarily as inscribed. At the end of each inscription there is a number which indicates the cemetery in which that person was interred. For identification refer to the list at the end of the cemetery records.

Abrams, H. S., Lt., d. 15 Aug. 1867, CSA (Obit). 68.
   Joseph R., b. Georgetown, S.C. 1 July 1831; d. 5 Oct. 1898. 44.
   Laura E. Porter, wife of Joseph R., d. 16 Aug. 1903. 44.
Acreman, J. H., b. 29 Apr. 1848; d. 31 Dec. 1905. 2.
Adams, A. J., b. 25 Apr. 1828; d. 5 Feb. 1910. 41.
   Elizabeth, b. 12 May 1809; d. 6 June 1893. 22.
   Florence J., wife of James, d. 21 Dec. 1861, aged 23 yrs. 49.
   Gatsie, wife of A. J., b. 23 Nov. 1844; d. 25 Sept. 1929. 41.
   M. E., wife of Thomas R., b. 19 Nov. 1832; d. 10 May 1904. 64.
   Samuel, Col., b. 5 Mch. 1829; d. 21 July 1864, killed in battle, 33rd Ala. Rgt., CSA. 68.
   Thomas R., b. 3 Jan. 1826; d. 18 Aug. 1906. 64.
Alexander, Ann Louisa, consort of M. L., dau. of S. B. & Mary Brookins, b. Milledgeville, Ga. 14 Sept. 1840; d. 6 July 1860. 67.
Allbritton, Clara, wife of R. A., b. 22 Aug. 1807; d. 12 July 1903. 44.
Allen, D., CSA. 97*.
Allmon, Dora Evans, b. 13 Feb. 1846; d. 23 May 1925. 63.
   J. E., Dr., b. 3 Mch. 1840; d. 3 Apr. 1902. 63.
Amerine, C.S. Lee, wife of M.H., b. 10 May 1847; d. 17 July 1889. 44.
   J. P. W., Col., b. 21 Apr. 1824; d. 11 May 1876. 44.
   Miles Henry, Capt., son of Col. J. P., b. 21 Apr. 1847; mar. Lena Lee 21 Mch. 1867; d. 15 Feb. 1914. 44.
Amos, James Milton, b. 6 Feb. 1830; d. 22 Mch. 1879. 44.
   J. M., Mrs., d. 15 Sept. 1892. (Obit). 64.
Anderson, Annie Porter, b. Aug. 1847; d. Aug. 1930. 68.
   Samuel J., b. 31 July 1846; d. 24 Jan. 1938. 55.
   Seborn, d. Greenville in May 1869, aged 45 yrs. (Obit).
Andress, F. M., b. 1 Nov. 1849; d. 10 Sept. 1923. 1.
   Harriett C. McKenzie, wife of William J., b. 11 Jan. 1829; d. 16 Jan. 1902. 59.
   Sallie J., wife of S. F., b. 8 Mch. 1827; d. 25 Mch. 1909. 1.
   Stephen F., b. 22 Mch. 1824; d. 25 Apr. 1908. 1.
   William J., b. 18 June 1819; d. 13 Jan. 1897. 59.
Anthony, Thomas B., b. 23 Feb. 1812; d. 10 May 1886. 25.
Arant, Barbara, relict of Rev. Jacob, d. 15 July 1882. (Obit).
   C. L., b. 7 May 1833; d. 19 Feb. 1907. 85.

Callie, wife of C. L., (No dates). 85.
Archer, B. M., b. 24 June 1845; d. 21 June 1888. 44.
    M. T., Mrs., d. 30 June 1887. (Obit).
    Williamson, b. near Columbia, S. C. 1 Jan. 1800; d. 3 May 1878. 44.
Ardis, Archibald M., son of Rev. John & Martha, b. 28 Aug. 1818; d. 2
    May 1859. 68.
Armstrong, Charles Jacob, b. 3 Apr. 1834; d. 17 Dec. 1892. 44.
    E. J., wife of John Wesley, b. 27 Oct. 1818; d. 8 Aug. 1887. (Obit).
    W. H., d. 13 Feb. 1920, aged 72 yrs. 44.
Arnold, Minerva Moore, wife of S. C., b. 3 Sept. 1832; d. 24 Apr. 1924. 63.
Ashford, George R., b. S.C. 12 Mch. 1838; d. 29 Aug. 1866. 68.
    Lucinda Herbert, wife of Wm. R., b. 25 July 1830; d. 8 Aug. 1908. 68.
    Mary Abbie, dau. of Wm. F. & Martha J. Hartley, wife of Geo. R., d.
        29 Mch. 1883, aged 37 yrs. 10 mos. 27 days. 68.
    William R., b. 11 Feb. 1828; d. 22 June 1890. 68.
Atkins, James O., b. 3 Nov. 1825; d. 23 June 1882. 48.
Autrey, Urias, b. 17 Mch. 1839; d. 4 June 1906 (CSA Iron Cross). 24.
Awtrey, James L., b. Stewart Co., Ga. 1831; d. 30 Mch. 1860. (Obit)
Bailey, Mathew James, b. 22 Oct. 1832; d. 1 May 1901. 44.
Baisden, Harriet Elizabeth Hubert, wife of Z. T., b. 4 Mch. 1847; d.
    18 Oct. 1923. 44.
    Z. T., b. 5 Aug. 1845; d. 27 Jan. 1916. 44.
Baldwin, John A., d. 19 Aug. 1836, aged 49 yrs. 85.
    Margaret N., wife Dr. J. A., d. 20 Aug. 1846, aged 40 yrs. 79.
Barganier, Elizabeth Laura, wife of M. H., b. 16 Mch. 1848; d. 1 July
    1930. 44.
    Jesse M., b. 9 Aug. 1843; d. 11 Jan. 1863, aged 19 yrs. 5 mos. 2
        days. 35.
    John F., Capt., b. 17 Jan. 1834; d. 17 Feb. 1897. 44.
    M. H., b. 23 Nov. 1846; d. 19 Feb. 1911. 44.
    Martha Jane, b. 12 Sept. 1847; d. 9 Feb. 1935. 2.
    Sarah Elizabeth, wife of J. F., b. 23 Mch. 1847; d. 22 Apr. 1918. 44.
Barge, Edward, Dr., d. 11 Aug. 1854, aged 24 yrs. 10 mos. 8 days. 48.
    Elizabeth, d. 14 Dec. 1862, aged 50 yrs. 11 mos. 19 days. 48.
    Ellie C., wife of L. T., b. 25 Dec. 1827; d. 3 Dec. 1910. 67.
    John, Dr., d. 4 Mch. 1846, aged 55 yrs. 3 mos. 25 days. 48.
    Josiah Theodore, b. 23 Nov. 1833; d. 11 Apr. 1904. 44.
    Lewis T., b. 31 Oct. 1825; d. 21 Mch. 1896. 67.
    Sallie Powers, b. 17 Oct. 1841; d. 25 Nov. 1901. 44.
    Talitha Traweek, wife T. H., b. 6 July 1841; d. 21 Oct. 1928. 48.
Barker, William, CSA. 68*.
Barnes, Alfred, b. 1842; d. 19 May 1898, aged 56 yrs. 5.
    Elizabeth, b. 26 Dec. 1844; d. 18 Mch. 1913. 41.
    M. R., b. 12 Apr. 1838; d. 17 Mch. 1904. 25.
Barrett, Elizabeth, wife of Joshua, mar. 1818; d. 12 Apr. 1881, aged
    84 yrs. (Obit).
    Nathaniel W., b. 5 Jan. 1836; d. 21 Aug. 1862, 1st Sgt. Co. D,
        Hilliard's Ala. Legion, CSA. 65.
Barrow, Harriet Amelia, 1830-1918. 44.
    Robert Benjamin, b. 1832; d. 6 Mch. 1887. 44.
Bass, Elizabeth J., wife of Willis, b. Feb. 1842; d. Oct. 1923. 92.
    W. P., d. 20 June 1885 in Oaky Streak, aged 45 yrs. (Obit).
    Willis, b. 24 Feb. 1846; d. 19 Sept. 1904. 92.
Bates, Anderson, (No dates) Co. 1, 45 Ala. Inf., CSA. 8.
    Emily, wife of W. T., b. 10 Mch. 1831; d. 28 Oct. 1900. 8.
    James J., (No dates), Co. 1, 45 Ala. Inf., CSA. 8.
    Jane E., b. 16 Nov. 1835; d. 10 Aug. 1912. 8.
    William Thomas, b. 30 May 1830; d. 1 Jan. 1916. 8.
Baylol, E. W., CSA. 97*.
Beasley, Fannie, 1st wife of J. H., b. 6 July 1834; d. 24 Feb. 1923. 22.

Beaston, A., CSA. 97*.
Beckworth, J. N., b. 4 Aug. 1849; d. 20 Aug. 1898. 29.
Beeland, J., b. 15 Feb. 1835; d. 22 Feb. 1920. 44.
   Leah Frances Thomas, wife of Jeptha, b. 23 Apr. 1844; d. 21 July 1881. 44.
Beesley, James, b. 7 Mch. 1849; d. 1 Dec. 1879. 85.
   Jeston, b. 1 Aug. 1807; d. 1 Feb. 1852. 79.
   Mary Elizabeth, b. 6 July 1834; d. 24 Feb. 1923. 85.
Bell, Ed, b. Sumpter Co., S. C. 13 June 1802; d. 2 Sept. 1889, aged 87 yrs. 7 mos. 20 days. 63.
   Georgiana, wife of J. E., b. New Orleans, La. 23 Sept. 1834; d. 28 Oct. 1876, aged 42 yrs. 1 mo. 5 days. 63.
   J. E., Rev., b. 17 July 1830; d. 13 Mch. 1894. 63.
   M. H., wife of T. W., b. 1 Apr. 1840; d. 21 Nov. 1917. 64.
   Thomas W., b. 19 Feb. 1830; d. 30 Dec. 1898. 64.
Bennett, Caroline, b. 11 Oct. 1834; d. 15 Dec. 1877. 6.
   D. D., b. 1 June 1848; d. 4 Feb. 1905. 63.
   Joseph, b. 1842; d. 18 Jan. 1881 near Starlington (Obit)
   Mary Ellen Clark, 1847-1918. 67.
   T. B., b. 7 Apr. 1830; d. 19 Apr. 1914. 6.
   Walter C., 1847-1943. 63.
Benson, Joseph Preston, 1834-1929. 23.
   James K., b. 20 Apr. 1780; d. 28 Aug. 1867, aged 88 yrs. 7.
   Lucy Penelope, d. 12 Sept. 1858, aged 28 yrs. 1 mo. 6 days. 7.
   Lucy Drake, wife of James K., b. 26 Mch. 1790; d. 16 Jan. 1864, aged 74 yrs. 7.
   Mary Eliza, 1841-1925. 23.
   Sarah Patton, b. 8 Nov. 1819; d. 3 May 1905. 23.
Berdeaux, M. E., b. 14 Feb. 1842; d. 7 Feb. 1916. 53.
Bethena, Sallie, b. 3 Apr. 1849; d. 18 Dec. 1921. 71.
Betterton, Elizabeth, wife of A. D., b. 7 Dec. 1833; d. 24 Nov. 1916. 53.
   S. A., b. 15 Apr. 1836; d. 20 Aug. 1901. 53.
Bilbray, John, b. Dec. 1792; d. 28 July 1870. 83.
Binion, William H., b. 8 June 1818; d. 28 Jan. 1888. 79.
Black, Andrew M., (No dates), Co. D, 61 Ala. Inf., CSA. 68.
   E. L., b. 12 Dec. 1841; d. 2 Apr. 1905. 71.
   Elizabeth, b. 13 Jan. 1846; d. 11 June 1831. 50.
   Frances S., b. 24 Jan. 1836; d. 29 Jan. 1893. 39.
   Hugh L., father of T. M., d. 9 Nov. 1888 (Obit)
   John Calhoun, b. 9 Sept. 1844; d. 14 May 1884. 18.
   Mary A., b. Edgefield Dist., S. C., d. 8 May 1884, aged 83 yrs. (Obit)
   Mary M., b. 22 Sept. 1836; d. 27 Mch. 1928. 18.
   Mary Susan, b. 26 Mch. 1845; d. 29 Feb. 1896. 18.
   Robert L., b. 10 Oct. 1848; d. 2 Nov. 1937. 50.
   Thomas E., Sr., b. 21 Aug. 1833; d. 10 May 1909. 18.
Blackman, Anna Mariah, b. 17 Mch. 1813; d. 27 Oct. 1878. 49.
   L. D., b. 7 May 1827; d. 28 Mch. 1909. 43.
Blalock, James Armstrong, d. 24 June 1904, aged 63 yrs. 39.
   Prudence, b. 1799; d. 8 Aug. 1879. 64.
Blaum, Stephen J., Dr., b. 27 Dec. 1820 in Ger.; d. 4 July 1885. 44.
Blackmon, James, Sr., b. 1804; d. 6 Jan. 1896. 12.
Blythewood, Eliza Traweek, wife of Dr. D. H., d. 5 May 1903, aged 69 yrs. 48.
Boan, J. M., b. 25 Oct. 1829; d. 13 July 1918. 43.
Boggan, James P., b. 20 Sept. 1827; d. 5 Oct. 1896; mar. 9 Dec. 1852. 81.
   Mary Coleman, Mrs., d. 18 Feb. 1899, aged 64 yrs. (Obit).
   Pickett, emig. Butler before 1835; d. Nov. 1875. (Obit).
   Sarah Smith, wife of James P. b. 5 Dec. 1830; d. 31 Dec. 1896. 81.
Boland, Sallie E., wife Rev. J.M., b. 26 Oct. 1833; d. 12 Jan. 1881. 44.
Bolding, Mary, wife of John, b. 8 May 1813; d. 25 May 1901. 41.

Bolling, John, b. 1778 Petersburg, Va.; d. 1863, a descendant of Robert
    Bolling who came to Va. from England in 1660. 68.
  John, Capt., son of Samuel Jackson & Mary Ann Ewing, b. 1841; d. 6
    May 1898. Gentleman, Soldier, Lawyer. 44.
  Mary Ann Ewing, b. 1818; d. 5 July 1860, aged 42 yrs. 5 mos. 26
    days. 68.
  Samuel Jackson, son of John, b. 29 Feb. 1816 in Greenville, S. C.;
    Moved to Butler Co. 1819; d. 27 Nov. 1891. 68.
  Samuel Jackson, b. 14 Aug. 1849; d. 12 Apr. 1932. 44.
  Sarah Raburn, wife of John, 1773-1842. 68.
Booker, Martha, wife of W. J., 1847-1922. 69.
  W. J., 1843-1914. 69.
Boswell, J. J. (Jack), d. Pigeon Creek Jan. 1930, aged 82 yrs. (Obit) 70.
Boutwell, Burton, d. 15 Dec. 1901, aged 73 yrs. 44.
  Fannie Simmons, 1847-1929. 81.
  Henry, 1833-1911, (Masonic Emblem). 23.
  J. C., b. 5 Jan. 1847; d. 6 June 1929. 23.
  J. D., b. Lowndes Co.; d. 30 Oct. 1928. (Obit). 39.
  Lonnie B., (No dates) Co. M., 6 Ala. Inf., CSA, aged 109 (Died in
    1935). 39.
Bowden, Eliza, wife of William B., b. 1 May 1829; d. 8 Nov. 1902. 77.
  William B., b. 20 Nov. 1823; d. 8 June 1901. 77.
Bowin, Abi E., b. 27 Jan. 1804; d. Mch. 1869. 68.
  Edward, Col., b. 4 Oct. 1796; d. 21 Sept. 1874. 68.
Bowman, Joseph, b. 17 Jan. 1848; d. 14 May 1924. 22.
Boyd, Julia Ann King, b. 28 Dec. 1836; d. 30 Dec. 1917. 36.
  Mary Marina, wife of W. W., b. 8 Jan. 1838; d. 12 Apr. 1902. 44.
Boyle, James, b. Donagal Co., Ireland 1843; d. 29 Nov. 1899. 44.
Bozeman, James Daniel, d. 28 June 1896, aged 71 yrs. (Obit)
  J. D., Mrs., d. near Greenville 20 Dec. 1895, aged @ 60 yrs. (Obit).
Braden, A. M. T., b. 10 Apr. 1849; d. 8 Apr. 1925. 3.
Bradley, Anstine, 1820-1905. 92.
  Joe, b. 1845; d. 19 June 1890. 77.
  Sarah E., 1829-1926. 92.
Bragg, Catherine C., d. 19 Dec. 1838, aged 44 yrs. 10 mos. 1 day. 11.
  Elizabeth, b. 28 Aug. 1802; d. 11 Oct. 1870. 68.
  Martha, (Infant's grave), d. 10 Dec. 1832. 11.
  T. M., d. 10 Apr. 1899, aged 63 yrs. 44.
  Thomas M., Dr., b. Spartanburg, S. C. 28 Dec. 1793; d. 28 Nov.
    1882. 44.
  Zebulin, d. 3 May 1849; d. 21 yrs. 7 mos. 15 days. 11.
Braswell, Kisiah, b. 26 May 1838; d. 29 Nov. 1922. 53.
  Mary Fost, b. Richland Dist., S. C. 12 Oct. 1792; mar. James Brown
    1809; mar. James Braswell 1837; d. 9 July 1875. (Obit).
  William, b. 14 Sept. 1831; d. 17 Aug. 1899. 53.
Brooks, Edward P., d. 25 June 1860, aged 33 yrs. 18 days (Obit)
  Felix, 1807-1850. 79.
  Marion Taylor, b. 6 June 1848; d. 5 June 1925. 55.
  Phill, d. 17 July 1927, aged 78 yrs. 6.
  Rachael, b. 25 Dec. 1811; d. 2 Feb. 1898. 79.
Broughton, Elizabeth Stewart, wife of John A., b. 1 May 1841;
    d. 15 Nov. 1925. 44.
  J. T., Dr., b. 25 Apr. 1830; d. 29 Aug. 1913. 44.
Brown, Austen, Co. C, 20 Ala. CSA. 97*.
  Evelyn Stevens, wife of Jack, b. 13 Sept. 1840; d. 7 May 1923. 92.
  G. W. L., b. 24 Jan. 1824; d. 8 Aug. 1894. 58.
  Margaret Coleman, b. 31 Aug. 1840; d. 23 June 1908. 92.
  Mary A., b. 2 Jan. 1834; d. 23 Sept. 1923. 3.
  Sophronia, Mrs., step-sister of Geo. Buckhaults, d. 13 Nov. 1899
    (Obit) 24.
  William Coolidge, b. 15 Aug. 1828; d. 28 Feb. 1908, Co. I, 53 Ala.

Partison Rangers, CSA. 92.
Bruner, Elizabeth M. Moorer, wife of P. A., b. 2 Jan. 1835; d. 4 Mch. 1895. 44.
   J. F., Rev., b. 22 Feb. 1841; d. 1 May 1891. 48.
   M. C., wife of A. F., b. 31 Dec. 1839; d. 14 July 1869. 91
   James F., b. 1804; d. 6 Jan. 1896. 12.
   Mary M., wife of Rev. J. F., d. 18 Dec. 1915, aged 70 yrs. 48.
Brunson, Laura F., 1849-1936. 63.
   Samuel A., 1846-1929. 63.
Bryan, Calvin, b. Twiggs Co., Ga. 17 Jan. 1818; d. Georgiana 7 Mch. 1882. (Obit).
   Elizabeth J., b. 13 Sept. 1830; d. 6 Sept. 1899. 63.
   J. Oliver, b. 24 Dec. 1846; d. 27 Mch. 1923. 44.
   John A., b. 10 Mch. 1821; d. 28 Dec. 1904. 63.
Buck, J. W., b. 15 June 1817; d. 13 May 1872 (Masonic Emblem) 44.
Buckhaults, George R. C., b. 4 Aug. 1829; d. 19 June 1899. 24.
   Martha, b. 30 Oct. 1836; d. 8 Apr. 1906. 24.
Buell, David, b. 3 May 1836; d. 18 Nov. 1884. 68.
   Flora Herbert, dau. of Thomas E. & Dorothy Young Herbert, wife of James, b. 30 Oct. 1845; d. 2 May 1916. 68.
Burch, Delilah J. Murphy, b. 26 Aug. 1828; d. 26 Aug. 1903. 63.
   James S., b. 20 June 1829; d. 4 July 1884. 63.
Burkett, Alford S., b. 20 June 1826; d. 6 Sept. 1890. 79.
   Arenna, Mrs., b. 11 Apr. 1808; d. 11 Feb. 1894. 71.
   Elizabeth, wife of Levi, b. 1 Sept. 1831; d. 25 Mch. 1907. 92.
   Frances L., b. 11 Feb. 1845; d. 6 Feb. 1928. 71.
   Ivan, b. 2 July 1824; d. 20 Sept. 1905. 83.
   James M., b. 26 June 1847; d. 10 Jan. 1944. 71.
   Sallie Bethena, b. 3 Apr. 1849; d. 18 Dec. 1921. 71.
Burnett, Alexander, b. 17 Mch. 1800; d. 18 Feb. 1878. 44.
   Alma Florence, inf. dau. of William & Catherine, b. 21 Mch. 1843; d. 12 May 1845. 68.
   Ann L., b. 21 Sept. 1830; d. 2 June 1889. 68.
   Catharine, b. 10 Sept. 1806; d. 18 Oct. 1857. 68.
   Francis M., b. 20 Feb. 1828; d. 24 Dec. 1860. 68.
   Harriet C., wife of Alexander, b. Washington Co., Ga. 21 Dec. 1822; d. 19 Apr. 1897. 44.
   James R., b. 1 Mch. 1830; d. 15 Dec. 1887. 44.
   Jane, b. June 1822; d. Aug. 1908. 44.
   Juliett A., wife of J. R., b. 17 Dec. 1834; d. 13 Feb. 1882. 44.
   Martha C., b. May 1828; d. Sept. 1914. 44.
   Thomas Jeff, Maj., son of Wm. & Catharine, b. 30 Aug. 1826; d. 8 Oct. 1887. 68.
   Walter Reid, son of Wm. & Catharine, b. 30 Apr. 1840; d. 25 Mch. 1853. 68.
   William, b. 10 Jan. 1794; d. 26 Sept. 1856. 68.
Busbey, William, b. 22 June 1822; d. 29 Sept. 1897. 25.
Busby, W. M., b. 28 Feb. 1826; d. 25 Apr. 1909. 25.
Bush, Anna J. Harbin, wife of Richard, b. 3 Sept. 1844; d. 6 Apr. 1923. 49.
   C. G., b. 13 Nov. 1833; d. 9 Dec. 1894, mar. Mary Wilcox 10 Feb. 1850. 64.
   Lucinda Winzer, b. Stewart Co., Ga. 30 Jan. 1834; mar. John Bush Jan. 1857; d. 21 Sept. 1883. (Obit).
   Millie, b. 5 Dec. 1840; d. 21 Nov. 1914. 64.
   Nancy, wife of R. H., b. 17 July 1829; d. 11 Nov. 1879. 49.
   Richard H., b. 19 Feb. 1829; d. 20 Feb. 1887. 49.
Butler, Alexander K., b. 24 Mch. 1848 in Spartanburg, S. C.; d. 5 Apr. 1936. 58.
   M. J. (nee Glenn), b. 4 Nov. 1815; d. 3 Sept. 1887. 23.

Whitmill, b. Edgefield Dist., S. C. 2 Aug. 1791; d. 2 Feb. 1874. (Obit)
William, Capt., native of Va., pioneer settler of Butler Co. for whom the county is named. Massacred by Indians near Butler Springs 18 Mch. 1818. 68.
Caine, James M., Co. C, 33 Ala. Inf., CSA. 64.
Caldwell, Elizabeth M., relict of J. C., b. 7 Apr. 1800; d. 4 Mch. 1872. 68.
John C., b. 5 June 1801; mar. 1820; d. 6 June 1871. 68.
Calhoun, Aurelia Herbert, wife of W. B., b. 13 Apr. 1836; d. 16 Aug. 1868. 68.
Charles W., b. 10 Nov. 1830; d. 28 Feb. 1901. 68.
Calvin, Carolina Malvina, dau. of Willis & Amanda Chiles Crenshaw, wife of Joseph Hadden, b. 22 July 1831; d. 18 June 1899. 17.
Camp, Elizabeth H., wife of Thomas Manning, b. Milledgeville, Ga. 5 Apr. 1809; d. 5 July 1898. 44.
Foster P., b. 31 Oct. 1849; d. 14 Aug. 1874. 44.
Thomas M., d. 12 July 1851, aged 52 yrs. 8.
Campbell, John F., (No dates) Ala. Pvt., Co. G, 9 Regt. Ala. Inf., CSA.68.
Ketler, 1823-1893. 10.
Martha Kite, wife of J. Frank, b. Fayette Co., Ga. 14 Sept. 1838; d. 10 Jan. 1885. 68.
Mary E., wife of W. B., b. 9 Apr. 1848; d. 2 Feb. 1922. 77.
W. B., b. 10 Feb. 1845; d. 14 Jan. 1923. 77.
Carlow, Mary Ellen, dau. of Andrew & Ellen E., d. 4 June 1849, aged 4 yrs. 2 mos. 21 days. 68.
Sylvester, d. 2 June 1855, aged 53 yrs. 68.
Carpenter, Charity, b. 30 May 1849; d. 1 July 1922. 22.
Elizabeth, wife of Bailey, b. 31 Aug. 1838; d. 17 Jan. 1924. 85.
Carter, David, b. 3 Sept. 1788; d. 31 Jan. 1856. 14.
Fannie, dau. of Wm. & Lucinda, b. Jan. 1826; d. Feb. 1851. 14.
Francis, Mrs., d. 14 June 1860, aged 65 yrs. 8 mos. 14 days. (Obit).
John, b. 25 Mch. 1791; d. May 1851. 14.
Margaret, wife of Thomas, b. 27 Oct. 1827; d. 9 Feb. 1851. 14.
Martha Leona, wife of Euphronius, b.11 Mch. 1832; d. 18 June 1854. 14.
Nancy, dau. of Wm. & Lucinda, b. 1 Oct. 1833; d. 10 Aug. 1851. 14.
Thomas L., b. 9 Sept. 1827; d. 20 Jan. 1851. 14.
Cates, Josiah, b. 17 Mch. 1886, aged 63 yrs. 10 mos. 16 days. (Obit).
Chancellor, Martha A., 1839-1905. 23.
Chandler, Mahala, d. Greenville June 1860, aged @ 62 yrs. (Obit).
Chappell, A. H., b. 16 Dec. 1840; d. 1 Aug. 1902. 74.
Francis L., b. 22 May 1849; d. 6 Feb. 1913. 74.
Cheatham, Melinda, b. 20 Nov. 1810 in Twiggs Co., Ga; d. 12 Nov. 1862. 24.
William F., Co. K., 17 Ala. Inf., CSA. 49.
Nancy M., wife of W. F., b. 26 July 1849; d. 5 Oct. 1907. 49.
Peter, b. 20 Oct. 1805 in Edgefield Dist., S. C., d. 15 Sept. 1867. 24.
Susan A., b. 12 Mch. 1821; d. 28 Dec. 1916. 39.
W. H., (No dates) Co. C, 33 Ala. Inf., CSA. 24.
Childers, C. A., Mrs., d. Apr. 1881, aged 72 yrs. (Obit).
Chumby, J. W., Co. K, 54 Ala., CSA. 97*.
Claghorn, Jack, b. 1 June 1823; d. 18 July 1905. 77.
Clark, (No first name listed), CSA. 77*.
J. P., 1820-1875. 67.
Mary Ellen, 1847-1918. 67.
Susan, 1824-1879. 67.
Cole, James Madison, b. 17 Sept. 1847; d. 9 Feb. 1924. 80.
Mary Amanda, b. 25 Sept. 1845; d. 17 Sept. 1909. 80.
Coleman, Thomas Bragg, Co. C, 33 Ala. Inf., CSA. 23.
Colley, Allen, b. 6 May 1813; d. 25 Feb. 1891. 39.
Elizabeth, d. 5 July 1822. 52.
Mary, b. 23 May 1813; d. (blank). 39.

Colvin, James G., b. 7 July 1885, aged 58 yrs. (Obit) 68.
Condon, Charles D., Sr., b. 30 Jan. 1837; d. 19 Nov. 1891. 44.
　Leona A., b. 5 Aug. 1839; d. 17 Nov. 1924. 44.
Cone, F. M., Co. A, 4 Ala. Cav., CSA. 2.
Conner, Harriet, b. 27 Aug. 1822; d. 9 Mch. 1901. 39.
　Michael, b. 1800; d. 8 May 1861. 39.
Conway, William Chestley, b. 31 Jan. 1825; d. 28 Oct. 1886. 24.
Cook, Alonza D., b. 3 Feb. 1844; d. 5 Aug. 1907. 20.
　B. M., b. 6 Feb. 1838; d. 8 July 1913. 16.
　Daniel, b. 1 Mch. 1800 in S. C.; d. 30 Jan. 1859. 59.
　Sopha, wife of Daniel, (No dates). 59.
　Emma Herbert, wife of George M.; dau. Thomas E. Herbert, b. 22 Sept. 1838; d. 23 Mch. 1860. 68.
　George M., b. 5 Dec. 1830; d. Va. 31 May 1862, 6 Ala. Regt., CSA. 68.
　Mary Catherine Kettler, wife John P., d. 9 Feb. 1856, aged 28 yrs. 34.
　Joe, d. 11 Apr. 1887, aged 52 yrs., erected by sons, J.A. & F.C. 54.
　Joseph D., 1848-1910. 44.
　P. H., b. 28 June 1849; d. 10 July 1880. 23.
　Rebecca, wife of Alonza, b. 5 Jan. 1848; d. 23 Dec. 1896. 20.
　U. H., Dr., b. Nov. 1815; d. 15 May 1884. 64.
Cooper, Louis, b. Two Rivers, Manitowoc, Wis.; d. 7 Jan. 1892, aged 47 yrs. 7 mos. 71.
Corry, Eliza, wife of Robert Emmett, b. 22 Feb. 1837; d. 3 July 1919. 44.
　Robert Emmett, b. 19 Mch. 1829; d. 7 Dec. 1913. 44.
Cowart, Effie Turner, 1831-1908. 44.
Cox, George, CSA. 97*.
Coxwell, Mark, b. 15 Apr. 1847; d. 12 Sept. 1892. 41.
Coyne, H. F., d. in Greenville 12 Feb. 1868. (Obit).
Craig, James, Mrs., b. Abbe. Dist., S. C. 5 Mch. 1780; d. 14 Apr. 1860. 20.
　James P., b. 4 Oct. 1830; d. 14 Jan. 1835. 20.
　Jency Elizabeth, wife of W. G., b. 5 Mch. 1811; d. 21 May 1885. 20.
　John T., b. 3 Oct. 1831; d. 11 Feb. 1835. 20.
　John Fleming, son of James & Rosey, b. 22 Apr. 1818; d. 8 Dec. 1821. 20.
　Rachel L., dau. of Wm. G. & Jency E., b. 12 Aug. 1843; d. 18 May 1859. 20.
　Robert A., son of Wm. & Jency, b. 24 May 1846; d. 8 July 1859. 20.
　Rosey, wife of James, b. 20 Oct. 1780; d. 20 Apr. 1852. 20.
　William G., b. 5 Apr. 1806; d. 20 Apr. 1855. 20.
Crane, Charles H., b. 1 Jan. 1830; d. 17 Apr. 1903. 48.
Creath, Chaplain, CSA, 68*.
Creech, Amanda E., b. 7 Sept. 1820; d. 9 Sept. 1909. 76.
　Francis L., b. 29 Nov. 1845; d. 24 May 1926, Co. C, 17 Ala. Inf., CSA. 31.
　Henry C., b. 22 Dec. 1843; d. 18 Oct. 1921. 76.
　Josephine, b. 15 Nov. 1840; d. 22 Feb. 1920. 76.
　Margaret, b. 23 Mch. 1848; d. 21 Jan. 1920. 76.
　William C., b. 14 Jan. 1810; d. 23 Feb. 1892. 76.
Crenshaw, Anderson, Chancellor State of Alabama, b. Newberry Dist., S.C.; migrated Ala. 1819; d. 31 Aug. 1847, aged 65 yrs. 17.
　Edward, b. 29 Aug. 1842; d. 9 Sept. 1911. 44.
　Elmira Caroline, dau. of J. L. & Agnes E. Womack, b. 28 Aug. 1832; mar. F. W. 19 Dec. 1850; d. 3 Nov. 1867. 17.
　Frances, 1847-1864. 17.
　Frances S. Crews, b. 5 Aug. 1838; d. 27 May 1925. 92.
　Frederick William, son of Anderson & Mary, b. 9 Feb. 1824; d. 4 Aug. 1902. 17.
　Henrietta, dau. of Thomas C. & Lucinda. d. 19 Nov. 1849, aged 5 yrs. 17.
　Howell, b. 19 July 1832; d. 10 Feb. 1926. 92.
　Lucinda Womack, wife of Thomas Chiles, 1825-1870. 17.

Mary, wife of Anderson; dau. of Thomas Chiles, b. 25 Jan. 1790; mar. 13 Sept. 1816 in S. C.; d. 29 Nov. 1873. 17.
Sarah Anderson, wife of Walter H., b. 14 Apr. 1825; d. 11 Nov. 1895. 44.
Sarah Lewis, wife of Frederick W., b. 26 Jan. 1842; d. 5 Sept. 1911. 17.
Thomas Chiles, b. 25 Dec. 1818; d. 10 Nov. 1899. 17.
Walter R., son of Thomas C. & Lucinda, d. 22 Oct. 1849, aged 7 yrs. 3 mos. 17.
Walter Henry, b. 17 July 1817; d. 7 Dec. 1878. 17.
Crittenden, Caroline E. Stoneham, wife of John, b. 24 June 1820; d. 12 Feb. 1898. 64.
John, b. 8 May 1810; d. 1 Oct. 1897. 64.
Oliver, b. 22 Aug. 1842; d. 9 Feb. 1895. 64.
Cross, James R., b. 28 Mch. 1831; d. 17 Dec. 1922. 16.
Crew, E. D., b. 6 Mch. 1843; d. 17 Dec. 1901. 87.
Crum, Frederick, d. 1 Nov. 1842, aged @ 66 yrs. 91.
Mary, d. 17 Sept. 1845, aged @ 60 yrs. 91.
Curington, M. A. E., b. 19 Aug. 1842; d. 23 Dec. 1939. 77.
Cumbie, Narcisca, b. Oct. 1836; d. 8 Apr. 1911. (Obit)
Curtis, Anna B., consort of James H., d. 22 May 1848, aged 27 yrs. 68.
Dampier, Maggie Harrell, d. in Greenville May 1886, aged @ 40 yrs. (Obit).
Daniel, Christopher Columbus, b. 18 Aug. 1843; d. 18 Dec. 1920. 63.
J. G., b. 22 May 1843; d. 14 Apr. 1931. 44.
Thomas F., b. 6 Nov. 1847; d. 10 Nov. 1936. 86.
Darby, James W., b. 25 Jan. 1840; d. 26 June 1912. 25.
Darley, Henry Clay, b. 19 Sept. 1833; d. 3 Nov. 1907. 44.
Lucinda, wife of H. C., b. 8 June 1842; d. 22 Jan. 1917. 44.
Dash, Elizabeth, 1825-1873. 38.
Davison, Amanda I., wife of R. C., b. 4 Sept. 1833; d. 21 Apr. 1887. 48.
R. C., b. Union Dist., S. C. 22 Dec. 1817; d. 13 June 1897. 48.
Davis, Amanda, b. 1 Mch. 1843; d. 16 July 1905. 22.
Elizabeth, Mrs., d. 13 Oct. 1914, aged 66 yrs. 23.
Ella Grace, wife of A. Z. & dau. of John & Eliza S. R. Rudulph, b. 13 Oct. 1847; d. 1 Nov. 1875. 68.
Harriet P., wife of K. L., b. 2 Sept. 1834; d. 14 Sept. 1909. 47.
J. H., b. 25 Sept. 1843; d. 22 June 1909. 22.
Janie M., consort of Robert, b. 16 Aug. 1788 in Edgefield Dist., S.C. 1 June 1873, aged 78 yrs. 9 mos. 15 days. 20.
Kincy L., b. 11 Sept. 1828; d. 17 Mch. 1912. 47.
Martha P., b. 10 Feb. 1814; d. 23 May 1861. 20.
Robert, d. 4 July 1832, aged @ 50 yrs. 20.
Temperance Elizabeth, wife of W. R., b. 1838; d. 13 Sept. 1895. 57.
W. R., b. 15 Jan. 182(?); d. 12 June 1893. 57.
Dawson, Nancy Ann, b. 31 Oct. 1845; d. 13 Apr. 1920. 2.
Day, John T., b. 5 July 1830; d. 19 Apr. 1820, Co. C, 1 Ala. Inf., CSA. 2.
Mary L., b. 26 May 1849; d. 17 Dec. 1925. 59.
Nancy Elizabeth, b. 12 Jan. 1848; d. 4 May 1927. 2.
Sallie, b. 19 May 1814; d. 21 Jan. 1888. 66.
Dean, Delilah, wife of W. H., 1840-1874. 41.
Elizabeth A., wife of John, b. 12 Apr. 1840; d. 17 June 1909. 56.
Mary Ann, wife of Thomas, b. 14 Jan. 1823; d. 24 Oct. 1868. 59.
Minerva, wife of Thomas, b. 27 Dec. 1825; d. 30 Jan. 1905. 59.
Thomas, b. 25 Feb. 1806; d. 30 May 1887. 59.
Dees, C. H., Eld., b. 23 May 1844; d. 26 Dec. 1919. 44.
James, Co. C, 33 Ala. Inf., CSA. 2.
Nancy Ophelia, (No dates), aged 83 yrs., wife of James. 2.
Deming, Ezra, son of Simeon & Mary, b. 3 Feb. 1833; d. 18 Oct. 1858. 68.
Mary, Mrs., d. 26 Nov. 1875, aged 86 yrs. (Obit)
Simeon, Jr., b. 2 June 1819; d. 13 Nov. 1858. 68.
Simeon, Sr., d, 5 Jan. 1858, aged 72 yrs, 4 mos. 27 days. 68.

Walter, son of Simeon & Mary, b. 3 May 1828; d. 29 May 1849. 68.
William, son of Simeon & Mary, b. 1 Nov. 1812; d. 17 Sept. 1836. 68.
DeShields, Eugene M., b. 2 Dec. 1824; d. 24 Sept. 1910, Ala. Pvt. Co. H., 1 Regt., Ala. Inf., CSA. 2.
Tobitha, d. 15 Aug. 1853 (Same stone as E. M.) 2.
Dewberry, Eliza Caroline Bennett, wife of Thomas, b. 13 Feb. 1844; d. 26 Oct. 1918. 47.
Thomas, b. 22 Oct. 1830; d. 29 Feb. 1917. 47.
Dickerson, Sarah T., b. 16 Jan. 1838; d. 8 Oct. 1911. (Near Manningham)
Dickirson, J. A., CSA. 97*.
Dismuke, William L., b. 5 June 1848; d. 21 July 1931. 86.
Dohrmeier, Charles August Hermann, b. Germany 19 Feb. 1834; d. 16 May 1882. 44.
Mahela Isabella, wife of H., b. 6 Oct. 1844; d. 19 Jan. 1913. 44.
Donald, Eugenia Steen, 2nd wife of Dr. James Glenn, dau. of Perry R. & Martha Steen, b. 5 June 1845; d. 11 Feb. 1906. 52.
James Glenn, Dr., b. Cedar Springs, S. C. 2 Aug. 1826; d. 5 June 1893. 52.
Douglas, B. F., b. 16 Aug. 1841; d. 10 Dec. 1919. 94.
Elizabeth E., wife of B. F., b. 7 Sept. 1840; d. 23 Jan. 1924. 94.
Dowd, James, b. 15 Apr. 1799; d. 25 Dec. 1868. 44.
Margaret, wife of James, b. 18 Sept. 1826; d. 15 May 1873. 44.
Mary E., b. 18 Oct. 1849; d. 23 Apr. 1897. 44.
Dowling, Zaccheus, Rev., son of John, b. Darlington Dist., S. C. 29 July 1792; d. 18 June 1885. A veteran of War of 1812. 39.
Drake, Albin J., b. 20 June 1847; d. 18 Dec. 1915. 41.
Martha, wife of P. H., d. 9 May 1876, aged 70 yrs. 1 mo. 1 day. (Obit)
Duke, L. O. S., b. 6 Dec. 1825; d. 20 May 1905. 3.
Mary, wife of L. O. S., b. 1833; d. 30 Apr. 1904. 3.
Dulin, Adam B., b. 28 Feb. 1844; d. 20 Apr. 1893. 44.
Dunklin, Abbie S. Reid, wife of James H., b. 12 Mch. 1838; d. 25 June 1860. 68.
Anna P., 1839-1896. 68.
Catharine, b. 19 Jan. 1782; d. 1 Apr. 1862. 68.
D. G. "Papa Dan", b. 28 Oct. 1823; d. 14 Sept. 1895. 68.
Hannah P., b. 16 Oct. 1839; d. 19 June 1896. 68.
James, b. 24 June 1779; d. 10 Apr. 1827. 68.
James Hilliard, b. 15 Nov. 1834; d. 20 May 1877. 68.
James L., b. 12 Mch. 1816; d. 8 Feb. 1887. 68.
John Hendricks, son of Wm. & Ann, 1803-1824. (Isolated grave)
Joseph, b. Greenville, S. C. 22 Aug. 1804; mov. Ala. 1819; d. Montg. 17 Dec. 1885. 68.
Lillie Eskew, b. 15 Dec. 1847; d. 1 Oct. 1920. 44.
Mary A., dau. of William & Catherine Burnett, wife of James L., b. 18 Mch. 1821; d. 20 July 1879. 68.
Mary Christian Judge, wife of Joseph, b. 14 July 1813; d. 23 Jan. 1847. (Isolated grave)
Mary Greenville, dau. of William & Ann, b. 4 Oct. 1820; d. 23 Feb. 1823 (Isolated grave).
Susan Catherine, wife of D. G., b. 9 Nov. 1829; d. 28 June 1862. 68.
Walter Edward, son of W.A.T. & Mary H., b. 5 Feb. 1845; d. 21 May 1853. 68.
William Turner, b. 1 June 1843; d. 13 Dec. 1922. 44.
Dunn, W. J., CSA. 68*.
Durr, H. M., CSA. 97*.
Ealum, Matilda, wife of Solomon, b. 2 June 1833; d. 14 Nov. 1901. 16.
Solomon, b. 15 Sept. 1825; d. 4 Mch. 1893. 16.
Echols, Estellar T., b. 28 May 1833; d. 14 July 1885. 94.
Susan Palmer, wife of E. T., b. 10 July 1847; d. 3 Sept. 1879. 94.
Ehlbert, Clara, wife of Marcus, b. Davendorf, Elsas, France, 13 Nov. 1841; d. 18 July 1912.
Markus, b. Hassloch, Rheinpfalz, Bayern; d. Selma 12 Aug. 1918. 44.

Ernest, Mary J., b. 9 Nov. 1835; d. 13 May 1900. 44.
Eskew, M. M., relict Rev. Isaac R., dau. Rev. John Milner, d. Greenville 21 June 1881, aged 60 yrs. (Obit)
Evans, Adonier E., wife of Rev. Uriah, b. 26 Sept. 1820; d. 17 Oct. 1886. 39.
    Fielden, son of Uriah & Adonier, b. 20 Jan. 1847; d. 15 Sept. 1866. 39.
    Mary Jane, b. 17 Oct. 1836; d. 19 Aug. 1906. 52.
    Rachel D., wife of Joshua, b. 26 Sept. 1818; d. 25 May 1860. 72.
    Rufus H., son of Uriah & Adonier, b. 16 Jan. 1845; d. 20 July 1867. 39.
    Uriah, b. 15 May 1816; d. 2 Oct. 1900, aged 84 yrs. 5 mos. 11 days. 39.
Ewing, M. C. E., b. 7 Nov. 1833; d. 7 Dec. 1911. 76.
    Mary K., b. 9 June 1827; d. 26 Jan. 1891. 8.
Fail, John J., b. 23 Dec. 1847; d. 29 Oct. 1929. 80.
    Martha S., Mrs., d. 28 Mch. 1882, aged 66. (Obit).
    Nancy, b. 31 Mch. 1848; d. 2 Jan. 1929. 80.
    Barbra Schuler, b. 30 Sept. 1832; d. 4 Nov. 1918. 8.
Fails, Elsbery, b. 17 Nov. 1821; d. 19 Sept. 1901. 29.
Fallaw, A. J., b. 22 July 1830; d. 4 Dec. 1890. 63.
    Elizabeth, b. 25 Feb. 1832; d. 17 Jan. 1912. 63.
Farrior, Anna Maria, b. 29 June 1849; d. 25 Sept. 1866. 44.
    James S., 1847-1903. 44.
    John, b. N. C. 23 Jan. 1809; d. 26 Dec. 1871. 44.
    Sarah S., b. Ga. 23 Dec. 1821; d. 10 Jan. 1891. 44.
Feagin, Caroline Elizabeth Martin, wife of Henry Jones, b. 1 Apr. 1837; d. 16 Sept. 1921. 63.
    Henry Jones, b. 2 June 1835; d. 26 Sept. 1919. 63.
Ferguson, Jacob, b. 26 Mch. 1782; d. 25 Nov. 1852. 81.
Fife, James, Dr., b. 20 Nov. 1797 Abbeville Dist., S. C.; d. 14 Dec. 1871. 59.
    John, husb. of Sarah, d. 24 Aug. 1882. 20.
    John H., b. 20 Oct. 1845; d. 1 Oct. 1921. 20.
    Mary A., wife of J. H., b. 16 Mch. 1848; d. 4 Sept. 1894. 20.
    Sara, wife of John, b. 29 Apr. 1808; d. 22 Aug. 1876. 20.
Finch, Ann, b. Sumpter Dist., S.C. 3 Nov. 1794; d. 11 Apr. 1869. 68.
Findley, William, Eld., b. 17 July 1805; d. 20 Feb. 1870. 36.
Florence, Toliver, d. Forest Home 3 Jan. 1887, aged @ 55. (Obit).
Flowers, Carrie T. Wood, wife of F. A., b. 25 Dec. 1848; d. 7 Nov. 1892. 44.
    Sarah T., wife of W. H., b. 18 Apr. 1819; d. 7 Oct. 1885. 44.
    Sarah T., Jr., dau. of W. H. & Sarah T., b. 17 Aug. 1848; d. 24 June 1862. 44.
    Sophronia E., b. 17 Oct. 1848; d. 10 Mch. 1888. 44.
    William Hampton, b. Darlington Dist., S. C. 7 Jan. 1818; d. 24 Aug. 1899. 44.
Foster, Ann Eliza, mother of D. N., d. Greenville 3 Oct. 1882. (Obit) 63.
    David N., b. 8 May 1841 in Ga.; d. 8 Jan. 1892. Co. G, 2 Bn. Ala. Cav., CSA. 63.
    Susan A., wife of John T., b. 23 Nov. 1834; d. 3 Nov. 1890. 36.
    Thomas L., d. 30 Sept. 1882, aged 35 yrs. (Obit).
    William, b. 23 Aug. 1819; d. 28 Aug. 1877. 44.
Fowler, J. T., CSA. 97*.
Franklin, Benjamin, b. 15 Jan. 1813; d. 10 Nov. 1894. 51.
    Nancy, b. 18 Nov. 1841; d. 4 May 1922. 51.
    Richard, b. 28 Oct. 1828; d. 6 Mch. 1893. 51.
    Susan, b. 15 Aug. 1837; d. 17 Jan. 1926. 51
Freeman, John F., b. 8 Dec. 1847; d. 24 Apr. 1935. 87.
Frost, Tamer, b. 14 Apr. 1817; d. 2 Nov. 1889. 87.
Funderburke, I. G., d. 7 Apr. 1883, aged 64 yrs. (Obit).
Fussell, Mandy, wife of B. A., b. 20 Sept. 1847; d. 12 Feb. 1904. 3.
Gafford, Edward Eugene, inf. son of Stephen F. & Elizabeth G., d. 23 Oct. 1849, aged 11 mos. 29 days. 68.

Elizabeth G., wife of Stephen F., b. 2 Jan. 1827; d. 30 Nov. 1855. 68.
Felix L., b. 21 July 1832; d. 8 Aug. 1854. 68.
James Lee, d. 24 Jan. 1881, aged @ 70 yrs. (Obit)
James M., b. 22 Sept. 1810; d. 5 Sept. 1882. 24.
Jeremiah, b. 6 Sept. 1795; d. 6 July 1844. 68.
Jeremiah W., b. 26 Dec. 1829; d. 30 Sept. 1859. 68.
John P., Co. H, Conf. Inf., CSA. 2.
Joseph M., d. 13 Oct. 1882, aged 58 yrs. (Obit). 68.
Josiah Milton, b. 19 Aug. 1840; d. 11 July 1870. 87.
Mabel A., wife of Frank, b. 4 Feb. 1837; d. 12 Feb. 1898. 68.
Mary L., wife of J. P., b. 18 Aug. 1849; d. 3 Apr. 1894. 2.
Nancy Z., wife of Josiah M., b. 9 Sept. 1831; d. 24 Oct. 1859. 68.
Stephen Franklin, b. 15 May 1822; d. 2 Feb. 1877. 68.
Walter J., b. 26 Mch. 1844; d. 11 Oct. 1910. 2.
Gallagher, Frank, b. Castlelogery Co., Donegan, Ireland, d. 9 Jan. 1927, aged 80 yrs. 44.
Gamble, John, b. 2 Aug. 1833; d. 27 Dec. 1896. 44.
Permelia, b. 18 Oct. 1839; d. Dec. 1907. 4.
S. H., b. 30 Sept. 1836; d. Aug. 1906. 4.
Sarah Ann Bond, wife of John, b. 21 Sept. 1842; d. 23 May 1878. 44.
Gandy, Alford, b. S. C. 20 Dec. 1810; mar. A. E. Kinnebrew 5 Apr. 1840; d. 29 May 1876. 44.
Elizabeth A., b. 9 Dec. 1830; d. 19 Aug. 1900. 52.
Phebe, wife of Oxford, b. 2 Oct. 1805; d. 9 Dec. 1863. 9.
W. M., b. 15 May 1842; d. 16 Sept. 1922. 43.
Ganus, M. F., wife of T. J., b. 31 Dec. 1842; d. 1 Mch. 1898. 25.
Thomas J., Co. O, 17 Ala. Inf., CSA. 25.
Gardner, James S., b. 10 May 1849; d. 2 Dec. 1952. 84.
Julius, b. 31 Aug. 1837; d. 23 Mch. 1875. 44.
Lou Brooks, b. 17 July 1840; d. 13 Oct. 1914. 44.
Garner, Selena, b. 13 May 1830; d. 8 Apr. 1905. 26.
Garrett, J. J., b. 13 June 1847; d. 23 June 1917. 77.
Gary, Rebecca, wife of Thomas; dau. of Charles Jones, b. S. C. 15 Dec. 1764; d. 16 May 1826. 24.
Thomas, son of Charles, b. 11 Aug. 1764 in S. C.; d. 23 Apr. 1818 (DAR marker). 24.
Gaston, Lucius G., b. 22 Sept. 1826; d. 23 Sept. 1905. 44.
Gibson, Mary Janes, wife of Henry T., 1829-1897. 2.
Giddens, Annie, b. 1847; d. 21 Oct. 1923. 27.
Callie, b. 4 May 1838; d. 20 Jan. 1940. 27.
Gilbert, James H., 1829-1888. 18.
L. G., 1805-1908. 18.
Gilchrist, Dorinda, 1829-1904. 8.
John, b. 28 Aug. 1827; d. Nov. 1887, 2 Lt. 60 Ala. Inf., CSA. 8.
Gillion, William T., b. 7 Oct. 1843; d. 23 Mch. 1928, Ala. Pvt. Co. I, 60 Regt., CSA. 8.
Gillespie, Lucy, b. Lincoln Co., Ga. 8 Oct. 1824; d. 7 Aug. 1887. 44.
Gipson, John, b. 27 June 1839; d. 26 Dec. 1895. 43.
Minerva B., wife of John, b. 21 Sept. 1849; d. 5 Oct. 1913. 43.
Glasgow, J. R., Dr., d. 14 May 1881, Capt., Hilliard's Legion, CSA (Obit)
John, Capt., b. Green Co., N.C.; d. 18 Oct. 1867, 59 & 60 Ala. Inf., CSA (Obit). 28.
Susanna E., wife of J. J., b. 15 Oct. 1836; d. 18 Feb. 1884. 28.
Glenn, Abraham N., b. 23 Dec. 1845; d. Feb. 1922. 63.
Joseph E., b. 10 Aug. 1828; mar. Martha A. Little 5 Sept. 1868; d. 3 Oct. 1897, CSA (90.
Sarah A., b. 4 May 1836; d. 24 Feb. 1904. 23.
Margaret B., b. 25 Dec. 1849; d. June 1933. 63.
S. T., b. 4 Jan. 1825; d. 23 July 1899. 23.

Godwin, Frank, b. 11 June 1849; d. 24 Feb. 1929. 21.
   Wells, d. 31 Apr. 1873, aged @ 82. (Obit)
Gohlson, Matilda, Mrs., one of oldest citizens in the county, d. 22 July 1892. (Obit).
Goldsmith, James M., son of William Hale & Zilpha Kornegay, b. 2 Apr. 1826; d. 11 Mch. 1895. 44.
   Margaret A. Stow, dau. of Thomas M. & Elizabeth Kornegay Stow, wife of James M., b. 29 Jan. 1837; d. 5 June 1907. 44.
Gomillian, F. M., b. 20 Aug. 1836; d. 10 Jan. 1901. 22.
   F. M., Mrs., b. 12 Oct. 1838; d. 21 June 1906. 22.
Goodwin, Henry J., Co. F, 63 Ala. Inf., CSA. 24.
   Silvestion H., 1841-1929. 4.
   Simpson, d. 9 Feb. 1898, aged 81 yrs. (Obit).
   T. J., b. June 1810; d. 9 July 1890. 4.
Goodwyn, Louisa, wife of T. J., b. 21 Nov. 1822; d. 28 July 1879. 4.
Goolsby, Henry R., b. 2 Sept. 1830; d. 22 Aug. 1908. 68.
Grace, Sarah Frances, wife of K. C., d. 14 Feb. 1858. 55.
Graham, E. C. W., wife of James A., b. 2 May 1820; d. 22 Nov. 1877. 44.
   James A., b. 1 May 1811; d. 18 Sept. 1878. 44.
   Louisa M., wife of W. P., b. 18 Oct. 1835; d. 4 Mch. 1900. 94.
   M. H., b. 24 July 1808; d. 11 Feb. 1882. 94.
   S. N., b. 21 Aug. 1797; d. 18 Feb. 1880. 94.
Gramling, Adam Clark, b. 12 Nov. 1843; d. 17 June 1878. 44.
Grant, E. A., b. 22 Feb. 1840; d. 7 July 1912. 44.
   I. M., b. 22 Oct. 1842; d. 29 Nov. 1922. 24.
   John W., b. 3 July 1849; d. 22 Aug. 1899. 44.
   Laura Josephene, 1849-1942. 8.
   Mary Elizabeth, b. 26 July 1844; d. 25 Sept. 1912. 24.
   Mary Jane, b. 6 July 1845; d. 8 July 1886. 24.
   Matilda, Mrs., b. 1 Apr. 1805; d. 15 June 1872. 8.
Graves, E. E., 1835-1892. 49.
Gray, Drakeford, Co. I, Ky. Mtd. Inf., CSA. 35.
Graydon, Nan, b. 17 May 1840; d. 31 Mch. 1908. 87.
   Henry S., 1837-1908, Co. C, 17 Ala. Inf., CSA. 2.
   Jane E., b. 5 Apr. 1845; d. 10 Sept. 1929. 87.
   John Clinton, b. 15 Apr. 1830; d. 11 Jan. 1892. 87.
   Sarah Ann Mercer, wife of J. C., b. 26 Aug. 1828; d. 10 July 1895. 87.
   William A., b. 12 Mch. 1828; d. 2 Jan. 1902. 87.
Green, Fariba Jane, 1837-1930. 39.
   Rolla Alonza, b. 14 Mch. 1807; d. 16 Aug. 1850. 68.
Greene, Augustus C., b. 11 June 1831; d. 28 July 1873. 44.
   Mary, wife of A. C., d. 8 Mch. 1861, aged 26 yrs. 67.
Gregory, Johnathan, b. 26 May 1831; d. 7 Nov. 1893. 66.
   Martha, wife of Johnathan, b. 15 Mch. 1841; d. 5 Nov. 1893. 66.
Griffin, B. J., b. 1 June 1843; d. 24 Mch. 1929. 22.
   Catherine, wife of M. H., b. 27 June 1836; d. 18 Aug. 1914. 3.
   Ellen P., wife of B. J., b. 11 Dec. 1848; d. 5 Feb. 1935. 22.
   H. H., b. 6 Sept. 1835; d. 18 Oct. 1918. 3.
   Jeremiah M., Co. A, 2 Ga. Cav., CSA. 80.
   Joseph Clyde, b. 17 Jan. 1841; d. (blank). 43.
Griffins, M. E., b. 5 Apr. 1848; d. 18 Feb. 1930. 92.
Hagerman, Tap, CSA. 68*.
Hagood, John M., b. 8 Mch. 1848; d. 19 Sept. 1887. 44.
   Susan Elizabeth Merriweather, wife of John M., b. 7 Aug. 1845; d. 10 July 1922. 44.
Hall, M. C., b. 1837; d. 2 July 1920. 88.
   Malissie, b. 26 Oct. 1848; d. 18 Mch. 1927. 94.
   Martha E., b. 29 June 1843; d. 18 July 1933. 92.

Robert H., b. 1845; d. 21 July 1893. 94.
Halso, Damaris, wife of J. W., b. 17 Dec. 1827; d. 5 Feb. 1905. 77.
   Elizabeth, Miss, sister of J. W., d. Butler Co. 22 July 1874. (Obit).
   J. W., b. 23 June 1823; d. 24 Oct. 1918. 77.
Ham, A. L., Mrs., b. 27 Oct. 1841; d. 9 Nov. 1909. 56.
Hamil, Augustus F., b. 26 Feb. 1840; d. 14 Mch. 1898. 44.
Hamilton, Catherine, 1842-1934. 12.
   Hollis, 1835-1880. 12.
Hammonds, Larkin R., d. 10 Sept. 1877, aged 68 yrs. (Obit).
   Mary M., d. 13 Oct. 1881 in Three Runs, aged 57 yrs. (Obit).
   Nancy Johnson, b. N. C.; mov. Ala. 1839; d. near Georgiana 23 Dec. 1886, aged 88 yrs. (Obit).
Hamner, Mary James, wife of Wesley, b. 25 Apr. 1813; d. 6 Feb. 1895. 94.
   Wesley, b. S. C. 19 Mch. 1812; mar. 7 Oct. 1833; d. 11 Jan. 1886. 94.
Hamrick, John M., d. Mch. 1900, aged 63 yrs., 17 Ala. Regt., CSA (Obit)
   Sarah E. Smith, wife of Jno. M., b. 20 Jan. 1842; d. 4 Apr. 1888. 44.
Hancock, Sarah A., b. 28 Nov. 1830; d. 4 May 1902. 76.
Harbin, Elizabeth Coburn, wife of G. W. O., 1812-1879. 68.
Harris, Florence L. Murphy, wife of Peterson, d. 17 June 1896, aged 50 yrs. (Obit).
   Wiley J., b. 20 Nov. 1822; d. 11 Sept. 1869. 68.
Harrison, Abbie, dau. of W. & D. Mosley, wife of Levi, d. Sept. 1868.49.
   Amanda Elizabeth, wife of W., b. 16 Apr. 1818; d. 5 Aug. 1890. 30.
   Caroline, b. 25 July 1806; d. 21 Aug. 1877. 18.
   Daniel, b. 3 Apr. 1842; d. 23 Apr. 1909. 49.
   Delany, b. Darlington Dist., S. C. 3 June 1790; d. 18 Feb. 1836. 30.
   Elizabeth Tillery, b. 7 Jan. 1822; d. 14 May 1884. 35.
   Fannie, wife of J. M., b. 27 Dec. 1848; d. 19 Jan. 1923. 2.
   George David, b. 18 Feb. 1842; d. 8 May 1920. 71.
   Henry, b. 10 Feb. 1808; d. 20 Sept. 1873. 21.
   J. H., Maj., 1804-1883. 18.
   James, b. Montgomery Co., Ga. 14 Oct. 1788; d. Covington Co., Ala. 5 Nov. 1848. 30.
   John, b. 19 Jan. 1823; d. 2 Feb. 1907. 35.
   John, b. Dale Co., Ala. 27 Feb. 1820; d. 5 May 1838. 30.
   John A., Lt., d. 28 July 1864 near Atlanta, aged 24 yrs. 2 mos. 29 days. 30.
   Joseph, Dr., son of Nathaniel & Sarah Smith, b. Newcombe Co., N.C. 22 Feb. 1828; mar. Mary Louise Tomblinson in Carrolton, Ga. 26 Dec. 1854; d. 7 Sept. 1898. (Obit). 68.
   M. E., b. 23 Oct. 1848; d. 31 Aug. 1910. 30.
   M. J., d. 30 Nov. 1864 in Franklin, Tenn, aged 20 yrs. 7 mos. 8 days, Co. O, 17 Ala. Vol., CSA. 30.
   Rhodia M., b. 12 Oct. 1844; d. 25 Aug. 1926. 71.
   Richard Henry, b. 10 Aug. 1849; d. 20 Nov. 1909. 51.
   Siddie E., wife of Daniel, b. Lowndes Co. 4 Aug. 1842; d. 26 Aug. 1899. 49.
   Williamson, b. 1 Dec. 1814 Wilkinson Co., Ga.; d. 1 Mch. 1887. 30.
   William Green, b. 15 June 1847; d. 16 May 1940. 59.
Harrold, Louis, Capt., d. 26 June 1896, aged 74. (Obit).
Hartley, Agnes G., b. 5 May 1836; d. 2 Mch. 1839. 24.
   A. C., Mrs., b. 12 Aug. 1847; d. 9 July 1918. 44.
   Anderson Comer, b. 30 Dec. 1832; d. 2 Aug. 1913. 44.
   Ann Wathen, dau. of William F. & Martha J., b. 12 Dec. 1842; d. 22 Feb. 1844. 68.
   Georgia J., dau. of W. F. & M. J., d. 19 June 1889, aged 41 yrs. 68.
   Henry G., b. 16 Apr. 1808; d. 27 Apr. 1881. 24.
   Hillary H., b. 10 Mch. 1839; d. 4 Sept. 1840. 24.
   John R., b. 5 Mch. 1799; d. 1 June 1864. 24.
   John R., b. 16 Mch. 1835; d. 5 Dec. 1870. 24.

    Joseph, b. 22 Aug. 1779 in N.C.; d. 13 Oct. 1849. 24.
    Joseph G., d. 6 Sept. 1913, aged 66 yrs., CSA. (Obit).
    Joseph S., b. 13 Sept. 1831; d. 11 Feb. 1910. 31.
    Lucinda Gafford, wife of J. S., b. 24 Nov. 1833; d. 23 Nov. 1877. 24.
    Martha, b. 10 Jan. 1838; d. 16 July 1881. 24.
    Martha Jane, dau. of Dr. Hillary & A. B. Herbert, wife of W. F., b. 16 Apr. 1822; d. 5 Sept. 1885. 68.
    Mariah W., b. 16 Oct. 1799; d. 2 Aug. 1874. 24.
    Mary, wife of Joseph, b. 1777; d. 14 Mch. 1863. 24.
    Mary S., wife of J. S., b. 28 Apr. 1838; d. 12 Nov. 1909. 31.
    Nancy S., widow of H. G., b. 16 Sept. 1812; d. 25 Jan. 1882. 24.
    Thomas Watts, b. 19 Mch. 1834; d.11 Apr. 1881. 24.
    W. F., b. 24 Feb. 1819; d. 6 June 1900. 68.
Hartsfield, Catherine Palmore, wife of Richard, b. 28 Dec. 1838; d. 1 Apr. 1901. 78.
Harvill, David A., d. 15 Jan. 1908, aged 74 yrs. 9 mos. 14 days. 67.
Hawkins, A. N., wife of William, b. 7 Jan. 1818; d. 28 Dec. 1896. 2.
    Mary, d. 5 Nov. 1908, aged 84 yrs. 49.
    Mary, b. 13 June 1832; d. 25 Oct. 1898. 12.
    Mathew C., b. 10 Mch. 1848; d. 21 Mch. 1937. 44.
    Stephen, d. in Manningham 18 Mch. 1875, aged 87 yrs. (Obit).
    William, b. 1 Jan. 1800; d. 12 Mch. 1871. 2.
    William, Mrs., b. 7 Jan. 1818; d. 28 Dec. 1896. 2.
Hawthorne, Adoniran J., b. 25 May 1834; d. 26 Aug. 1877. 44.
    Clara E., b. 2 Jan. 1835; d. 9 Oct. 1908. 44.
    Kedar, Rev., b. 15 May 1797; d. 28 Aug. 1877. 44.
    Lydia, 1838-1926. 23.
    Martha, wife of Rev. K., b. 26 Oct. 1799 in Ga.,.d. 17 Sept. 1872 44.
Hayes, Jane, 1846-1928. 90.
    W. H., d. 16 Dec. 1908, aged 70 yrs. 90.
Hays, Eliza Perkins, wife of Sunsbury, b. 25 July 1827; mar. 17 Dec. 1846; d. 28 June 1895. 44.
    (First name unreadable), b. 21 Mch. 1801; d. 1888. 9.
Heartsill, Abner T., b. 14 Feb. 1842; d. 19 Dec. 1914, Co. G, 59 Tenn. Mtd. Inf., CSA. 36.
    Elizabeth, wife of A. T., b. 2 Jan. 1845; d. 6 Jan. 1882. 36.
    Martha, Mrs., b. 19 June 1840; d. 4 Sept. 1911. 36.
    N. H., b. 5 Jan. 1845; d. 24 Dec. 1921. 36.
Heaton, Frank E., b. 23 Dec. 1849; d. 5 Dec. 1932. 45.
    Lewis, b. 29 Sept. 1834; d. 23 Mch. 1899. 44.
Henderson, S. M., b. 14 Nov. 1835; d. 5 July 1915. 12.
Hendrix, Mary Elizabeth, wife of N. A., b. 6 Apr. 1844; d. 16 Apr. 1892. 44.
    Nathan A., d. 1866, aged 65 yrs. 44.
Henry, Cecil, CSA. 68*.
    J. Elvira, wife of Judge J. K., d. 4 Apr. 1900, aged 79 yrs. (Obit)
    Miles, 1847-1914. 44.
    G. L., Capt., CSA. 68*.
    J. T. W., Col., 1824-1876. 44.
Herbert, Abigail Bolling, wife of Hillary, b. 12 Oct. 1797; d. 5 Mch. 1857. 68.
    Abigail Wathen, dau. of Hillary & Abigail B., b. 13 Apr. 1828; d. 30 Aug. 1837. 68.
    Ann Wathen, consort of George B., d. 27 Dec. 1839, aged 37 yrs. 7 mos. 30 days, a member of the Methodist Church 12 yrs. 68.
    Dorothy T., d. 4 Feb. 1851, aged 15 yrs. 68.
    Elizabeth, 1769-1830. 68.
    George Hillary, M. D., b. 29 June 1826; d. 9 Oct. 1851. 68.
    Hillary, M. D., b. S. C.; mov. Ala. 1819; d. 19 Dec. 1854, aged 66 yrs. 68.

James Dunklin, b. 12 Dec. 1824; d. 4 Dec. 1851. 68.
Mary C., dau. of C. B. & A. W., d. 27 Oct. 1849, aged 9 yrs. 11
    mos. 24 days. 68.
Mary Eliza, wife of James D., b. 19 Apr. 1828; d. 27 July 1852. 68.
Thomas E., b. Newberry Dist., S.C. 26 Feb. 1804; d. 5 Nov. 1868. 68.
Herlong, D. A., wife of Elisha G., b. 4 Aug. 1833; d. 26 Oct. 1916. 8.
Daniel E., b. 15 May 1825; d. 13 Sept. 1863. 8.
Elihu F., b. 1 July 1826; d. 24 July 1872. 8.
Elisha G., b. 17 Feb. 1822; d. 18 Oct. 1887. 8.
James A., b. 3 Dec. 1842; d. 23 Feb. 18(?)7. 8.
Missoura A., b. 27 Nov. 1842; d. 22 July 1923. 8.
William F., b. 7 Nov. 1827; d. 26 July 1862. 8.
Hester, Jasper N., b. 10 Apr. 1832; d. 9 Sept. 1907. 22.
Winnie Beesley, wife of J. N., b. 19 Sept. 1838; d. 19 May 1924. 22.
Hickman, Joseph M., b. 23 Aug. 1825; d. 27 Dec. 1888. 77.
Sarah A., wife of Joseph M., b. 25 May 1825; d. 27 July 1904. 77.
Sarah M., b. 23 Aug. 1823; d. 27 Dec. 1888. 77.
Hicks, Annie M., b. 22 Mch. 1835; d. 29 Mch. 1874. 4.
Enoch J., d. 4 Apr. 1891, aged 52 yrs. CSA (Obit).
J. A., b. 4 Mch. 1839; d. 15 May 1892. 60.
Josiah A., b. 24 Jan. 1836; d. 20 June 1899. (Obit).
Saphronia, b. 5 Nov. 1847; d. 23 Nov. 1929. 60.
Higdon, John H., b. 16 July 1848; d. 17 Sept. 1915. 22.
Hightower, Bettie, b. 14 Jan. 1845; d. 11 Sept. 1882. 68.
F. D., wife of H., b. 9 Aug. 1817; d. 20 Apr. 1860. 68.
Lou, d. 25 June 1892, aged 49 yrs. 6 mos. 22 days. 68.
Hildreth, Benjamin, Rev., 1808-1868. 68.
Hill, Josiah, b. 13 Sept. 1787; d. 6 Sept. 1840. 52.
Pamelia, d. 1 June 1840, aged @ 40 yrs. 52.
Hinson, Asa E., b. 22 Sept. 1824; d. 25 Aug. 1900. 24.
Emily J., wife of D. D., b. 27 July 1847; d. 31 May 1926. 43.
J. H., b. 9 Oct. 1844; d. 20 Sept. 1884. 24.
John W., b. 15 May 1838; d. 26 Nov. 1908. 74.
M. E., b. 11 Apr. 18__(stone broken); d. 20 Sept. 1884 (Same stone
    as J.R. & died same day). 24.
Mary Ann Martin, wife of W. E., b. 18 Oct. 1844; d. 13 Nov. 1920. 2.
S. A., b. 24 Mch. 1842; d. 6 June 1915. 74.
Sallie H., b. 6 July 1820; d. 24 Feb. 1905. 24.
V. C., b. 20 Jan. 1848; d. 1 Sept. 1925. 24.
William E., b. 9 Jan. 1845; d. 18 July 1935. 2.
Hitson, John Wesley, 1839-1923, Co. B, 18 Regt. Ala. Inf., CSA. 12.
Holcomb, Martha, b. 25 Mch. 1821; d. 7 Jan. 1876. 39.
Holcombe, J. G., Mrs., b. S.C.; d. 2 Dec. 1885, aged @ 73 yrs. (Obit).
Holloway, Rachael, d. 31 Mch. 1892, aged 72 yrs. 3 mos. 16 days. (Obit).
Holmes, David, 1828-1880. 25.
Hook, Mary C., wife of Peter L., b. 19 Apr. 1814; d. 30 Dec. 1889. 8.
Hornday, George N. A., b. 13 May 1841; d. 11 Oct. 1871. 61
Howard, Elbert, b. 30 Nov. 1826; d. 8 June 1914. 63.
Elizabeth Rebecca, b. 15 Jan. 1837; d. 22 Feb. 1924. 33.
John W., b. 5 Dec. 1822; d. 24 Mch. 1875. 33.
Martha Ann, wife of Elbert, b. 8 Oct. 1837; d. 2 June 1914. 63.
Howell, Martha, b. 12 Dec. 1824; d. 4 July 1913. 83.
Hudson, Martha Hamner, wife of N.B., b. 6 Feb. 1841; d. 7 Mch. 1909. 94.
Huggins, Columbus M., b. 19 Nov. 1848; d. 13 Mch. 1919. 71.
J. B., Rev., b. 28 Feb. 1830; d. 30 July 1873. 85.
Sarah, wife of J. B., aged 83 yrs. 85.
Hughes, Alma Bray, b. 15 Jan. 1815; d. 10 Nov. 1887. 16.
Elizabeth, b. 28 Feb. 1841; d. 23 Feb. 1929. 16.
Elizer, b. 14 Mch. 1826; d. 22 Sept. 1897. 16.
Emily L., b. 16 Oct. 1845; d. 2 Aug. 1911. 16.
George D., d. Dec. 1883, aged 47 yrs. (Obit).

James B., b. 5 Sept. 1847; d. 24 Feb. 1929. 16.
Jiles J., b. 8 Apr. 1849; d. 17 Feb. 1940. 16.
Louezar N., Mrs., b. 7 Mch. 1836; d. 9 Oct. 1920. 94.
Mahalia, b. 13 Mch. 1849; d. 11 Aug. 1924. 16.
Richard, Eld., b. 13 Feb. 1830; d. 24 Jan. 1912. 16.
T. M., b. 7 Jan. 1828; d. 24 Sept. 1906. 94.
Wilson, b. 12 Mch. 1812; d. 30 Apr. 1886. 16.
Hughston, Laura Owens, dau. of Thad Owens, 1845-1928. 44.
   Elisha Milton, son of John & Mary, b. Spartanburg, S. C. 4 May 1836; d. 27 Oct. 1874. 44.
Huguley, George, b. 1833; d. 24 Oct. 1863, 1 Regt. Ga. Inf., CSA. 68.
   George, 1846-1908. 68.
Hunt, J. A., d. Greenville 18 Jan. 1892, aged 50 yrs. (Obit).
Hutchinson, Elizabeth Steen, wife of James D., dau. of Perry R. & Martha Steen, b. 25 Dec. 1828; d. 24 Apr. 1914. 52.
   James D., b. 9 Apr. 1814; d. 16 May 1880. 52.
   Thomas J., b. 12 June 1845; d. 14 July 1903. 44.
Hutto, Mary G., b. 25 Nov. 1840; d. 19 Feb. 1928. 47.
Hutton, Mary Thames, Mrs., b. 19 Mch. 1843; d. 20 Sept. 1892. 68.
Ingram, Louisa F., b. 30 Oct. 1835; d. 10 Nov. 1912. 64.
Ivez, Elizabeth, Mrs., d. 21 Mch. 1898, aged 79 yrs. 18 days. (Obit).
Jackson, Henry, b. 21 Mch. 1832; d. 28 Aug. 1902. 2.
   John R., 1841-1919. 63.
   Lucy Adams, 1841-1919. 63.
   Mary A., b. 22 Sept. 1835; d. 11 Dec. 1913. 2.
   Simeon D., son of A. & M., b. 19 Aug. 1832; d. 4 Oct. 1862. 68.
Jennings, Mary Jane, b. Baltimore, Md. 12 Aug. 1811; mar. Dr. J. M. Apr. 1844; d. Greenville 11 Jan. 1885. (Obit).
Jernigan, John W., b. 20 May 1832; d. 1 Dec. 1887. 51.
   Lewis J., Co. G, 33 Ala. Inf., CSA. 51.
   Martha J., b. 12 Sept. 1847; d. 29 Nov. 1926. 94.
   Marvin, d. 19 Nov. 1926, aged 79 yrs. 94.
   Narcissus L. Ellis, wife of John W., b. 25 Mch. 1844; d. 16 May 1929. 51.
   Sarah Jane, b. 7 Apr. 1843; d. 17 May 1941. 64.
   William, b. 10 Dec. 1846; d. 11 Jan. 1919. 94.
Johnson, Asbury B., b. 12 July 1841; d. 18 May 1861. 94.
   Eliza, wife of G. W., b. 1814; d. 18 Apr. 1891. 41.
   Francis E. McGehee, dau. of J. H. & M. A. McGehee, b. 27 Sept. 1843; mar. J. H. 28 Mch. 1860; d. 7 Aug. 1891. 44.
   H. V., b. 18 Dec. 1842; d. 7 Nov. 1882. 16.
   Henry V., b. 5 Feb. 1838; d. 30 Dec. 1930. 16.
   J. S., b. 23 July 1846; d. 14 Dec. 1878. 24.
   James H., b. 26 Feb. 1836; d. 30 June 1905. 44.
   L. J., b. 18 Oct. 1830; d. 4 Aug. 1917. 57.
   Mary A., b. 13 June 1821; d. 6 Dec. 1893. 94.
   Mary C., wife of J. C., b. 31 Dec. 1833; d. 24 Dec. 1903. 85.
   Robert W., b. 1845; d. 25 Aug. 1881. 21.
   Timothy M., b. 12 Feb. 1820; d. 1 Jan. 1864. 94.
Johnston, John, b. 12 July 1831; d. 13 May 1899. 64.
   Sarah S. C., consort of John, b. 3 May 1830; d. 28 Jan. 1877. 64.
Jones, Andrew, b. N. C. 1777; emig. Ala. 1819; d. 1822. 24.
   Caroline Kettler, wife of Amos, b. 23 Dec. 1825; d. 26 Sept. 1874. 34.
   Charles G., b. 14 Aug. 1848; d. 12 Oct. 1914. 18.
   Civility Josephine, 1822-19__. 55.
   Elizabeth A., consort of Joseph, b. 11 Sept. 1820; d. 11 Nov. 1853. 24.
   Henriette Tarver, b. 27 July 1833; d. 15 Feb. 1914. 44.
   Henry, Co. K, 25 Ala. Inf., CSA. 51.
   Henry, d. 8 Nov. 1835, aged 30 yrs. (Obit).

James, d. 31 Aug. 1842; aged 38 yrs. (Isolated grave near Bragg).
Joseph, b. 11 July 1818; d. 15 Dec. 1857, aged 39 yrs. 5 mos. 4
   days. 24.
Kate D., 1848-1922. 29.
Mary M., b. 30 Aug. 1840; d. 30 July 1912. 51.
Mary M., Dean, b. 23 Jan. 1832; d. 4 Aug. 1916. (Near Old Bethel).
Sarah, consort of Andrew, b. N.C.; emig. Ala. 1819; d. 26 Oct.
   1851, aged @ 73 yrs. 24.
Thomas, aged gentleman died Greenville 19 July 1900. (Obit).
Thomas Edgar, inf. son of Joseph & Elizabeth, b. 15 Feb. 1849; d.
   14 June 1851. 24.
William Pleasant, son of Joseph & Elizabeth A., b. 23 Dec. 1845; d.
   16 Oct. 1850. 24.
William T., b. 9 Apr. 1829; d. 14 Apr. 1859. 80.
Jordan, Esther A., relict of Rev. Joshua A., b. 1825; d. Apr. 1892. 44.
   Joseph, Co. G, 21 Texas Cav., CSA. 39.
   Joshua W., Rev., B. N.C. 19 Mch. 1815; d. 12 Oct. 1887. 44.
   Malinda Lowhorn, wife of Membrane, b. 25 Dec. 1813; d. 22 Feb.
      1912. 23.
   Samuel R., b. 9 Aug. 1849; d. 26 Apr. 1907. 70.
Josey, James S., Ala. Cav., CSA. 16.
Joyner, H. E., wife of W. H., b. 19 Sept. 1847; d. 20 Mch. 1926. 57.
   James L., b. 8 Aug. 1832; d. 17 Sept. 1906. 25.
   Mary A., b. 10 Aug. 1834; d. 24 Jan. 1907. 25.
   Mary A., wife of Jessie L., b. 18 Feb. 1829; d. 22 June 1918. 3.
   William H., Eld., b. 31 Jan. 1848; d. 7 Feb. 1906. 57.
Judge, Thomas J., Statesman, Jurist, Judge, b. 1 Nov. 1815; d. (?). 44.
   Thomas, Mrs. (nee Graves), d. 18 Nov. 1890, aged @ 73 yrs. (Obit).
Keebler, Mary A., wife of J. J., b. 14 Sept. 1835; d. 20 Jan. 1901. 25.
Keith, Sarah H., b. 23 Apr. 1827; d. 2 July 1908. 77.
Kellam, Mattie, wife of Robert, b. 4 June 1836; d. 21 May 1900. 44.
Kelly, John, d. May 1884, aged 68 yrs. (Obit).
   Sallie Wimberly, dau. of Mack & Rocela; wife of W. D.I., b. 23
      Oct. 1832; d. 23 June 1864. 44.
Kendrick, A. T., b. 21 July 1848; d. 24 July 1930. 44.
   A. Tom, b. 22 Jan. 1808; d. 12 Aug. 1892. 44.
   Ann Elizabeth Riviere, wife of Dr. J. C., b. 28 Dec. 1833 Warren
      Co., Ga.; d. 22 Sept. 1896. 44.
   Lettie, wife of S. R., b. 22 Sept. 1841; d. 1 Sept. 1876. 52.
   Mary Susan, wife of T. P., dau. of John B. & Susan Scott, b. 21 Jan.
      1846; d. 17 May 1933. 52.
   S. R., b. 30 Nov. 1837; d. 28 Nov. 1933. 52.
   T. P., b. 1 Aug. 1839; d. 15 Apr. 1928. 52.
Kennedy, Robert Hays, 1848-1909. 44.
Kent, James K., d. 1 Jan. 1902, aged 55 yrs. 81.
Kern, Rachel Elizabeth, b. 2 May 1832; d. 6 Feb. 1926. 44.
   Simon Moses, b. Boechingen, Ger. 10 Apr. 1820; d. 21 Nov. 1904. 44.
Kersey, Annie R., b. 2 Oct. 1849; d. 15 Mch. 1899. 87.
Kettler, Charles L., b. 7 Aug. 1829; d. 30 May 1856. 34.
   Hetty, wife of T. S., d. 1 Jan. 1859, aged 63 yrs. 10 mos. 4 days. 34.
   Mary Elizabeth, b. 23 Dec. 1848; d. 15 July 1903. 34.
   Peter, son of Thomas S. & Hetty B., d. 15 Feb. 1856, aged 20 yrs.
      11 mos. 7 days. 34.
   Ruby Ann Jones, wife of T. F., b. 28 Jan. 1828; d. 28 Nov. 1915. 34.
   Sarah J., b. 16 Mch. 1831; d. 2 June 1856. 34.
   Thomas Franklin, b. 27 Aug. 1821; d. 19 Dec. 1872. 34.
   Thomas Stubbs, b. 1790 in Va.; d. 1870. 34.
Keys, Sallie Ann Menifee, dau. of R. H. & M. R. Rivers, b. 29 Oct.
   1837; d. 24 Aug. 1883. 44.
Kilgore, Abigail G. Moorer, wife of B. F., b. 1 Oct. 1846; d. 21 Aug.
   1899. 44.
   Benjamin F., b. 4 Mch. 1832; d. 26 Nov. 1896. 44.

Kimmons, J. M., 1837-1910. 29.
Kinball, Theodore H., Capt., d. Greenville 22 Feb. 1874, CSA (Obit).
King, John M., b. June 1800; d. Jan. 1879. 36.
    Joseph O., b. 20 July 1840; d. 9 Jan. 1885. 25.
    L. H., widow of Jacob W.; mother of Clara, Stella & Charles M., b. 10 May 1822; d. 10 July 1904. 44.
    Mary A., wife of Thomas M., b. 11 Jan. 1830; d. 15 Feb. 1906. 36.
    Thomas C., 1832-1907. 44.
    Thomas M., b. 30 Mch. 1817; d. 9 Aug. 1892. 36.
Kingsbury, John b. Vermont 1820; d. 12 Dec. 1885. 37.
    M. A., b. Ga. 1820; d. (?) (marker broken). 37.
Kirkpatrick, Edward McCrea, b. 13 Nov. 1848; d. 17 Sept. 1927. 44.
Kirksey, D. J., b. 15 Sept. 1849; d. 22 Mch. 1938. 18.
    D. L., wife of Isaac, b. 16 May 1845; d. 10 Oct. 1911. 92.
    J. J., b. 13 June 1823; d. 26 Mch. 1893. 43.
    S. A., wife of J. J., b. 12 Feb. 1830; d. 8 May 1906. 43.
Knight, Catherine Priscilla, wife of Comer W., b. 10 Jan. 1834; d. 4 Mch. 1882. 44.
    Comer J., b. 19 Feb. 1838; d. 28 Dec. 1891. 44.
    Edwin, b. 15 Dec. 1805; d. 29 Jan. 1852. 52.
    Jessie, b. 4 Jan. 1828; d. 28 June 1862. 52.
    John Thomas, Capt., b. 23 Nov. 1832 in Ga.; d. 30 July 1903. 44.
    Kate, Mrs., b. 24 Sept. 1831; d. 13 Sept. 1916. 52.
    Laura Posey, b. 15 June 1831; d. 14 Jan. 1931. 44.
    Lewis J., b. 19 Aug. 1829; d. 11 Aug. 1863. 52.
    Martha, b. 6 May 1806; d. 7 May 1853. 52.
    Martha A., wife of T. A., b. 11 Aug. 1842; d. 15 Oct. 1876. 52.
    Mary E., b. 18 June 1839; d. 6 May 1930. 60.
    Missouri Hutchison, wife of J. T., b. 26 June 1839; d. 7 July 1907. 44.
    Permelia Routon, 1839-1885. 44.
    Thomas A., b. 2 May 1832; d. 11 Oct. 1887. 52.
    William, b. 18 June 1839; d. 9 Feb. 1887, Pvt. 33 Regt., CSA. 60.
    William, b. N. C. 15 Mch. 1811; emig. Ala. 1857; d. 15 Mch. 1887 on his 78th birthday. (Obit).
    Willis, b. 7 Aug. 1821; d. 19 May 1892. 53.
Knowles, Jefferson Rice, b. 14 Apr. 1848; d. 22 June 1911. 44.
Knox, William Henry, 1849-1935. 63.
Konklin, D., CSA. 97*.
Kram, J. T., d. in Greenville 5 June 1898, Union Army. (Obit).
Lampley, Caleb B., Dr., b. Rockingham, N.C. 22 July 1830; mar. 8 Oct. 1856; d. 16 Jan. 1885. 68.
    Thryza Rudulph, wife of Caleb B., 1836-1911. 68.
Lane, F. T., b. 17 Oct. 1833; d. 18 Apr. 1868. 68.
    Leonidas Mansfield, b. 29 Oct. 1846; d. 15 Jan. 1926. 44.
    Marcus G., b. 4 July 1825; d. 28 July 1876. 68.
Lansdon, John A., b. 3 Sept. 1846; d. 6 May 1922. 77.
    John M., b. Edgefield Dist, S.C. 1780; d. 14 Feb. 1874. 77.
    M. F., wife of John A., b. 24 July 1847; d. 12 May 1914. 77.
    W. J., b. 7 Oct. 1849; d. 5 July 1922. 94.
    Wiley, b. Edgefield, S.C. 1 Nov. 1800; d. 31 Mch. 1903, aged 102 yrs. 5 mos. (Obit). 77.
Larkin, Eleazar, b. 4 Jan. 1820; d. 27 Nov. 1901. 63.
Laseter, Mary Morris, b. 8 May 1847; d. 26 July 1930. 44.
Lawson, D. M., b. 10 Mch. 1833; d. 20 Nov. 1918. 47.
Layne, Wyatt, b. 16 July 1803; d. 18 Sept. 1877. 8.
Lazenby, Elias M., d. Forest Home in Aug. 1896, aged @ 69 yrs. (Obit).
    James G., b. 21 Sept. 1849; d. 10 Feb. 1908. 23.
    Martha J., wife of Elias M., b. 2 May 1821; d. 7 Apr. 1902. 23.
Leatherwood, T. M., d. 2 Jan. 1868. (Obit).

Ledlow, William, b. 13 Sept. 1849; d. 10 Apr. 1907. 22.
Lee, Andrew J., b. 4 Feb. 1831; d. 6 Mch. 1872, son of G. B. & M. J. 85.
   Caroline J., b. 16 June 1827; d. 20 Mch. 1876. 44.
   George W., Eld., b. 30 Oct. 1841; d. 6 May 1908. 22.
   Hilliary, b. 26 Apr. 1848; d. 2 Nov. 1929. 16.
   Jackson, b. 18 Dec. 1814; d. 27 Dec. 1895. 84.
   Joel, d. 19 July 1861, aged 47 yrs. 79.
   Mahulda, wife of S. A., b. 2 Aug. 1847; d. 5 Dec. 1916. 22.
   Martha A., b. 10 Apr. 1843; d. 7 Jan. 1925. 16.
   Rhoda A., wife of George, b. 13 May 1846; d. 5 Mch. 1900. 22.
   Robert S., b. 18 Mch. 1822; d. 7 May 1916. 44.
   William, b. Ga.; emig. Butler Co. 1818; d. 1824. (Obit).
Legriff, Sarah, Mrs., aged lady, d. 14 Feb. 1874. (Obit).
Leonard, C. W., d. 5 Feb. 1891, aged 71 yrs. (Obit).
   John M., d. 27 June 1884, aged 44 yrs. 44.
Lester, Eli, b. 22 Sept. 1844; d. 16 July 1902,Co. A, 2 Regt. Eng.
   Troop, CSA. 66.
   Callie J., b. 8 Feb. 1840; d. 24 Dec. 1917. 66.
   Jesse, son of John & Nancy, b. 2 July 1849; d. 1870. 66.
   John, b. 14 Apr. 1817; d. 2 Aug. 1898, CSA. 66.
   Nancy, b. 25 Mch. 1819; d. 22 Mch. 1899. 66.
Levingston, A., b. 14 Oct. 1782; d. 28 Mch. 1832. 96.
   William, b. 7 Apr. 1817; d. 12 Sept. 1833. 96.
Lewis, J. B., b. 6 Jan. 1840; d. 5 June 1918. 72.
   Katie J., b. 25 Sept. 1844; d. 10 May 1912. 44.
   Lucretia, wife of C. H., b. Mobile 1836; d. 5 July 1901. Marker
     placed by bro., Morris Williams of Pensacola. 44.
Leysath, Elvira, b. 30 Nov. 1830; d. 7 Dec. 1913. 38.
   John A., b. 2 Feb. 1829; d. 15 Jan. 1877. 38.
Linan, John B., Mrs., d. Forest Home 8 Nov. 1891,aged 80 yrs. (Obit).
Little, D. J., mother of J. H., d. 15 May 1911, aged 73 yrs. 23.
   Harriet M., wife of Amos A., b. 18 Aug. 1815; d. 15 Feb. 1890. 90.
   Joanna Palmore, wife of Pinkney, b. 28 Dec. 1842; d. 2 Sept. 1926. 23.
   John Goodwin, b. 3 Dec. 1825; d. 24 Apr. 1909. 44.
   Martha M., b. 18 Jan. 1838; d. 26 Jan. 1905. 90.
   Mary Hayes, 1848-1921. 44.
   P. H., b. 1 Apr. 1839; d. 10 Dec. 1895. 23.
   Permelia Thompson, wife of W. J., b. 11 Sept. 1833; d. 24 Feb.
     1906. 90.
   Saphronia Elizabeth Howell, wife of John G., b. 28 July 1828; d.
     10 Jan. 1892. 44.
   W. J., b. 7 Oct. 1830; d. 10 May 1884. 90.
Lloyd Benjamin, Sr., b. 6 Oct. 1804; d. 11 Jan. 1860. 40.
   C. C., Rev., b. 2 Apr. 1834; d. 8 Sept. 1917. 2.
   Eugene E., b. 26 May 1838; d. 4 July 1880. 40.
   J. C., b. 22 Nov. 1846; d. 19 Dec. 1892. 67.
   Julia A., b. 3 Nov. 1839; d. 7 Oct. 1915. 2.
   Milton S., b. 12 Aug. 1849; d. 29 Jan. 1874. 40.
   Naomi A., wife of Benjamin, b. 17 May 1814; d. 7 Aug. 1884. 40.
   Wylie W., Rev., b. 9 Apr. 1845; d. 4 Oct. 1873. 40.
Loche, J. W., Dr., d. Greenville 8 Mch. 1884. (Obit).
Locklear, Milley Jane Williams, b. in Greenville 1825; d. 26 May 1885.
   (Obit). 68.
Loe, Fulton B., b. 30 Apr. 1849; d. 23 Apr. 1935. 43.
Long, Benjamin L., Capt., b. 28 Nov. 1834; d. 15 July 1887. 44.
   John T., b. 13 Mch. 1829; d. 27 Nov. 1879. 68.
   Louise Thagard, wife of John T., b. 22 Nov. 1837; d. 29 Oct.1905. 68.
Lowe, J. T. H., 1840-1915. 94.
Lowery, Harriet McKay, 1814-1905. 29.
   J. F., b. Dublin, Ire.; mov. Butler @ 1863; d. 2 Oct. 1893. (Obit).

Julia Ann, wife of J. A., b. 5 Dec. 1838; d. 24 Apr. 1906. 20.
Martha J., wife of J. M., b. 17 Nov. 1848; d. 10 Apr. 1898. 12.
Mary, Mrs., d. Apr. 1, 1884, aged 40 yrs. (Obit).
W. W., b. 18 July 1839; d. 8 July 1914. 29.
Luckie, Alice J., wife of J. W., b. 17 Oct. 1848; d. 12 Oct. 1899. 52.
    Archibald Carter, son of E. Jackson & Margaret E., b. 20 Oct. 1845; d. 14 Apr. 1930, CSA. 52.
    E. Jackson, b. Montecello, Ga. 14 Mch. 1814; d. 15 Feb. 1892. 52.
    Icie Phena, b. 11 June 1849; d. 17 Jan. 1922. 23.
    J. Walker, son of E. Jackson & Margaret D., b. 4 Jan. 1848; d. 22 Sept. 1919. 52.
    Jackson, b. 14 Mch. 1814; d. 15 Feb. 1892. 52.
    James H., b. 24 Nov. 1842; d. 14 Aug. 1864 in Civil War, CSA. 52.
    Margaret D., wife of E. Jackson, b. 16 Sept. 1816; d. 17 July 1893. 52.
    Martha Drucilla, wife of William R.; dau. of Henry & Sarah Ann Smith, b. 16 June 1842; d. 1 Mch. 1914. 52.
    W. H. (Bee), 1844-1931. 23.
    William R., son of E. Jackson & Margaret D., b. 18 Feb. 1841; d. 13 Oct. 1927. 52.
Ludlam, Samuel P., Co. 1, 31 Ala. Inf., CSA. 63.
Lut, Thomas R., CSA. 97*.
McAlister, Susan Ann, b. 7 Sept. 1827; d. 4 Mch. 1900. 39.
McAllister, Andrew Morrow, b. Abbeville Dist., S. C. 9 Dec. 1836; d. 4 May (?). 44.
    Colin, d. Apr. 1856, aged 72 yrs. 68.
    Harriet Rebecca Brown, b. Sandersville, Ga. 25 July 1830; d. 19 Feb. 1903. 44.
McBride, d. East Butler Co. 8 Apr. 1892, aged 69 yrs. (Obit).
McCall, Daniel Terry, b. 7 Feb. 1817; d. 27 Feb. 1899. 44.
    Jesse, Capt., b. Ga.; d. 1 Dec. 1860 near Greenville. (Obit).
    Martha J., wife of D. T., b. 20 Sept. 1828; d. 8 Nov. 1871. 44.
McCane, Frances Kettler, b. Jan. 1837 Henry Co., Ga.; d. in 79 yr. 34.
    Jud T., b. 1 June 1843; d. 14 Aug. 1929. 92.
    Thomas A., Dr., b. 20 May 1834; d. 3 Apr. 1885. 34.
McCarter, James L., b. 15 May 1845; d. 16 Apr. 1918. 64.
McCaskill, F. R., Co. D, 33 Ala. Inf., CSA. 41.
McClure, Permelia, b. 12 July 1832; d. 27 Jan. 1894. 41.
McCombs, Emma Sarah, wife of Joseph Herkimer, b. 2 June 1829; d. 18 Feb. 1916. 44.
McCormack, Frances, wife of S. K., b. 29 Dec. 1844; d. 13 Jan. 1883. 59.
    Martha E., wife of S. K., b. 11 May 1844; d. 11 Sept. 1866. 59.
    Mary F., 3rd wife of S. K., d. 8 Mch. 1911, aged 65 yrs. 59.
    Samuel K., b. 26 Dec. 1836; d. 9 Feb. 1912. 59.
McCormick, Thomas, b. Galway Co., Ire; d. 17 Mch. 1887. Erected by children, Jos. & Catherine Fields. 44.
    William, Mrs., sister of T. F. Sims, b. Tallapoosa, Ga., d. 10 Feb. 1914, aged 68 yrs. (Obit). 44.
McCoy, John, d. Spring Hill 6 Feb. 1888, aged 77 yrs. (Obit).
    John, Mrs., d. Mch. 1891, aged @ 45 yrs. (Obit).
    Joseph V., b. 1 Nov. 1841; d. (blank). 42.
    Martha, b. 19 Mch. 1838; d. 28 June 1910. 42.
    Mary C., b. 27 July 1807; d. 20 Jan. 1893. 42.
    Mattie D. Cheatham, b. 18 Dec. 1847; d. 20 (?) 1897. 42.
    Sindarella R., b. 1 Mch. 1838; d. 2 June 1862. 20.
    Thomas H., b. 25 Apr. 1838; d. 19 June 1862. 42.
McCrory, John, b. 17 Dec. 1817; d. 4 Jan. 1894. 80.
    M. E., wife of T. M., b. 23 Jan. 1845; d. 24 Sept. 1907. 80.
    Margarete, b. 3 July 1818; d. 3 Feb. 1909. 80.
    T. M., b. 14 Feb. 1841; d. 30 Mch. 1925. 80.
    Ann, b. 13 Sept. 1810; d. 1 Dec. 1869. 80.

McCullough, Mary Ann Stephens, wife of J. W., d. 24 Sept. 1875, aged 55 yrs. (Obit).
McDaniel, Ennis, son of Thomas & Sarah, b. 29 June 1798; d. 22 Aug. 1831. 24.
   Eustatis P., wife of Ennis, b. 7 Sept. 1805; d. 14 Dec. 1878. 24.
   Julia A., wife of J. A., b. 13 Oct. 1838; d. 3 Oct. 1896. 8.
   Lucinda, wife of Daniel, b. 1829; d. 23 Sept. 1913. 44.
   P., wife of J. W., d. 16 Apr. 1882, aged 52 yrs. 3 mos. 26 days (Obit)
McDowell, Adell, b. 13 Jan. 1811; d. 25 Dec. 1863. 88.
McDuffie, F. Marion, b. Houston Co., Ga. 12 Nov. 1838; d. 3 Aug. 1874. 49.
McFerrin, James, b. 3 May 1822; d. 4 Feb. 1896. 63.
McGehee, Jacob Abner, b. 11 Oct. 1847; d. 28 Jan. 1919. 44.
McGlaun, Diademia B., Mrs., b. 6 Feb. 1836; d. 9 Nov. 1915. 94.
McKee, Hugh, b. Batecourt Co., Va. 9 Feb. 1801; d. 5 Sept. 1863. 48.
   Wilson M., d. 27 Jan. 1859, aged 18 yrs. 10 mos. 24 days. 48.
McKellar, Mr., CSA 68*.
   M. A., Mrs., dau. of William Caldwell; b. S.C.; mar. A. McKellar 1830; d. 24 Nov. 1890. (Obit).
McKenzie, Charlie, b. 11 July 1822; d. 11 Apr. 1900. 22.
   Elias G., b. 29 Apr. 1815; d. 17 Jan. 1895. 59.
   Emma Herbert, wife of W. F., b. 17 Sept. 1848; d. 11 Mch. 1923. 44.
   Narcisa Frances Brown, wife of Charlie, b. 11 Dec. 1844; mar. 12 Jan. 1873 in Leon, Al.; d. 14 Oct. 1936. 22.
   W. F., b. 5 Dec. 1847; d. 19 Nov. 1932. 44.
McKinney, M. D., b. 25 Oct. 1820; d. 18 Oct. 1900. 22.
   Victoria L., wife of J. F., b. 2 Aug. 1847; d. 5 Dec. 1916. 22.
McKinzie, James Henry, b. 3 Aug. 1845; d. 19 Jan. 1878, Pvt., Co. D, 61 Regt. Ala. Inf., CSA. (Two headstones. Death date on one was shown as 1879). 87.
   John, b. 9 Apr. 1789 in Darlington Dist., S.C.; d. 4 Nov. 1866. 59.
   Mary Ann, dau. of Minerva J., b. 23 Sept. 1849; d. 18 Sept. 1863. 59.
   Mary V., wife of James H., b. 5 May 1845; d. 31 May 1880. 87.
   Sarah Elizabeth, wife of Elias G., b. 28 Sept. 1823; d. 28 July 1871. 87.
McLain, Alafair, 1835-1870. 21.
   Wesley, d. 22 Sept. 1873. (Obit).
McMillian, C. C., b. 26 July 1839; d. 2 June 1923. 44.
   Susan B., b. 26 Feb. 1845; d. 1 May 1921. 44.
McMullan, Ann Judson, b. 4 May 1831; d. 22 June 1903. 44.
   John Seaborn, b. 20 Apr. 1816; d. 31 July 1877. 79.
McPherson, John F., b. 4 Mch. 1817; d. 30 Aug. 1887. 79.
   John, b. 7 June 1837; d. 4 June 1921. 39.
   Margret, b. 7 Mch. 1840; d. 15 June 1924. 39.
   Nancy P., 1st wife of W. S., b. 1833; d. Apr. 1886. 85.
   Sarah M., wife of J. F., b. 13 June 1823; d. 27 Aug. 1904. 79.
McPurifoy, Nancy Caroline, wife of Rev. M., b. 12 Sept. 1813; d. 19 Apr. 1895. 23.
McQueen, Bettie, wife of E. Y., b. 19 May 1849; d. 11 Aug. 1885. 87.
   Daniel, b. 14 Jan. 1814; d. 11 Aug. 1875. 59.
   E. Y., 1849-1929. 59.
   Eliza, Mrs., d. 13 Apr. 1860 in Reddock Springs. (Obit).
   Harriet Ashley, wife of J. C., b. 7 Aug. 1828; d. 8 Jan. 1904. 44.
   John C., b. S.C. 1821; d. 7 June 1900. (Obit).
   Melvina, b. 15 Jan. 1824; d. 26 Nov. 1896. 59.
McWhorter, John, 1819-1869. 52.
McWilliams, Daniel, b. 5 July 1803; d. 26 Sept. 1854. 52.
   Eleanor E., d. 17 Nov. 1857, aged @ 44 yrs. 52.
   John B., son of M. L. & Eleanor E., b. 27 Aug. 1840; d. 31 Oct. 1860. 52.

Lockwood A., b. 4 Mch. 1847; d. 24 Apr. 1851. 52.
Madison, Isaac, b. 8 June 1825; d. 14 Dec. 1906. 92.
Mahone, Georgia Johnson, wife of Stephen W., b. 7 July 1849; d. 18 Dec. 1936. 44.
   Stephen William, b. 20 Aug. 1842; d. 8 Feb. 1910. 44.
Majors, Benjamin, b. 27 Apr. 1830; d. 10 Mch. 1899. 60.
   David, b. 11 Dec. 1836; d. 15 Sept. 1914. 92.
   Elizabeth, wife of Benjamin, b. 2 Nov. 1833; d. 26 Sept. 1883. 60.
   Fannie, wife of S. D., b. 6 Sept. 1839; d. 19 Aug. 1915. 63.
   James E., b. 8 Feb. 1845; d. 6 Sept. 1899. 60.
   James Cornelius, Co. B, Ala. Inf., CSA. 60.
   John L., b. 14 Apr. 1849; d. 29 Mch. 1873. 60.
   Jonathan, b. Mch. 1793; d. Feb. 1863. 60.
   Margaret B., 1844-1920. 12.
   S. A., Mrs., b. 4 June 1840; d. 23 Feb. 1898. 92.
   Samuel D., b. 17 June 1817; d. 20 July 1908. 63.
   Sebena M., wife of John, b. 30 Mch. 1816; d. 12 May 1912. 18.
Mancil, M. A., b. Nov. 1831; d. 10 Aug. 1912. 18.
Manning, Martha, wife of S. J., b. 18 July 1844; d. 3 Jan. 1926. 22.
   S. J., b. 13 Oct. 1842; d. 1 Feb. 1926. 22.
Maraman, William, b. 11 Jan. 1846; d. 3 Feb. 1914. 63.
   Missouri Gillen, b. 29 July 1845; d. 27 July 1915. 63.
Marsh, M. S., wife of Rev. W. C., dau. of S. & K. J. Meriwether, d. 4 Sept. 1849, aged 28 yrs. 68.
Martin, A. M., wife of Peter, d. 1901, aged @ 70 yrs. 39.
   David, d. Georgiana 2 Apr. 1881, aged 74 yrs. 7 days. (Obit).
   John H., 1847-1918. 44.
   Katchern, b. 1823; d. 18 July 1889. 63.
   Loucinda Stallings, b. 1 Aug. 1837; d. 10 Mch. 1924. 24.
   Martha J., 1824-1911. 44.
   Nellie, b. 1821; d. 27 Mch. 1887. 49.
   Peter, b. 7 Jan. 1818; d. 22 July 1886. 49.
   R. G. W., b. 1822; d. 11 Sept. 1888. 49.
Mash, A., b. 10 May 1806; d. 5 Feb. 1893. 76.
   Celia Styles, wife of John, b. 17 Apr. 1839; d. 1 May 1893. 18.
   John S., b. 22 Sept. 1835; d. 19 Dec. 1928. 18.
   Mary Evans, wife of N., b. 29 Jan. 1810; d. 8 Apr. 1894. 76.
   Milton, b. 5 Oct. 1849; d. 15 May 1894. 76.
   Nathan, b. 10 May 1806; emig. Butler Co. 1856; d. 5 Feb. 1893. 76.
   Safronie M. Gholson, b. 22 July 1842; d. 16 Apr. 1917. 76.
   Surilda J., dau. of Nathan & Mary, b. 1 Nov. 1828; d. 23 Feb. 1871. 18.
   David J., b. 23 Feb. 1844; d. 1 Apr. 1905. 76.
   Susan E., b. 17 July 1838; d. 5 Aug. 1863. 18.
Mason, John Charles Lewis, b. Dublin, Ire.; d. 5 Mch. 1888, aged @ 65 yrs. 44.
   Mary Malinda, b. 2 Mch. 1836; d. 8 Apr. 1917. 23.
Mastin, John, Co. A, 56 Ala. Cav., CSA. 44.
Mathews, George A., Dr., b. 5 Mch. 1830; d. 8 Oct. 1912. 3.
   Mary E., wife of George A., b. 17 Jan. 1837; d. 17 Feb. 1919. 3.
May, James, b. 8 June 1832; d. 26 Apr. 1900. 39.
   S. S., aged citizen of Butler Co., d. 16 Dec. 1879. (Obit).
Maynard, Elizabeth Graham, b. 24 Oct. 1829; d. 23 Aug. 1896. 94.
   Georgia Ann Simmons, 1830-1915. 81.
Melton, Francis F., b. 25 May 1829; d. 25 Apr. 1850. 52.
Mercer, Catherine, wife of Noah, b. Darlington Dist., S.C. 1801; d. 7 Nov. 1869, aged 68 yrs. 87.
   Delilah, wife of William, b. 27 Jan. 1804; d. 30 May 1879. 77.
   Irena W. Fails, wife of Seth, b. 20 June 1829; d. 1 May 1899. 29.
   J. A., b. 5 May 1821; d. 12 Nov. 1911. 12.
   Noah, b. N.C. 31 May 1803; d. 16 Mch. 1874. 87.
   Seth, b. 13 Oct. 1826; d. 25 June 1912. 29.

William, b. 4 Sept. 1806; d. 8 Oct. 1878. 77.
Metcalf, Albert West, b. 2 Oct. 1841; d. 18 June 1921. 44.
   Jane Eugenie, wife of A. W., b. 2 Oct. 1844; d. 29 Nov. 1916. 44.
Middleton, Marion Wesley, b. 1 Nov. 1846; d. 23 Apr. 1925. 25.
Miller, Henry, b. 25 Dec. 1848; d. 7 Mch. 1916. 63.
   Hetty Elizabeth Cheatham, wife of I. G., b. 1 Jan. 1844; d. 19 July 1899. 72.
   Isaiah George, b. 6 Dec. 1843; d. 6 Mch. 1895. 63.
Mills, George H., b. 28 Apr. 1847; d. 30 July 1935. 44.
Milner, Anna, dau. of Rev. & Mrs. Pitt S., d. 1857. In honor of Anna & their home state of Ga., the city of Georgiana was named. Placed by the Kiwanis Club in 1971. 47.
   Elisha C., son of Rev. Pitt S., b. 4 Aug. 1831; d. 26 Mch. 1888, CSA. 47.
   Joseph B., Sgt., Co. K, 8 Ala. Inf., CSA. 47.
   Pamelia N., b. 8 Aug. 1814; d. 12 May 1878. 47.
   Pitt S., Rev., b. 31 July 1806; d. 30 Aug. 1873. 47.
   Willis J., b. Wilkes Co., Ga. 20 Feb. 1797; d. 15 Jan. 1864; mar. Elizabeth Turner & after her death, Mary Turner, who survives him. His children were: John Turner Milner, Ollie Milner Gibson, Benjamin Charles Milner, Bonita Milner Parker, Elizabeth Milner Caldwell, Willis J. Milner. 68.
Milton, J. M., Dr., b. 17 Sept. 1817; d. 28 July 1877. 18.
   Mary B., wife of Dr. J. M., b. 27 May 1819; d. 28 Nov. 1899. 18.
Miniard, J. T., b. 3 July 1848; d. 8 Jan. 1890. 85.
Minse, Mr., CSA. 97*.
Mitchell, R. M. J., b. 25 Jan. 1804; d. 1 Sept. 1890. 22.
   Rhoda A., b. 25 Apr. 1819; d. 11 May 1909. 22.
   Rollie, b. Feb. 1842; d. Jan. 1926. 22.
   Z. G., b. 21 Oct. 1846; d. 18 Feb. 1930. 22.
Mize, F. M., b. 5 Sept. 1826; d. 27 Dec. 1894. 23.
   Julia Ann, b. 26 June 1836 Sumpter Co., Ga.; d. 21 Jan. 1910. 23.
Moats, Martha, b. 1 Sept. 1837; d. 1912. 87.
Moodey, J. D., b. 22 Dec. 1848; d. 1 Oct. 1917, CSA Iron Cross. 8.
   Narcissa E. Williams, wife of Jno. A., b. 2 May 1847; d. 24 Jan. 1930. 8.
Moodie, Francis, Rev., b. 21 Oct. 1816; d. 21 May 1854. 68.
Moore, Acy, b. 19 July 1848; d. 25 July 1925. 12.
   Mattie J., b. 2 Aug. 1842; d. 24 Oct. 1898. 67.
   P. A., wife of S. P., b. 1847-1925. 63.
   Sarah, d. 6 Feb. 1871, aged 63 yrs. 44.
   Seaborn, Rev., b. 21 Jan. 1838; d. 6 Oct. 1903. 67.
   Teresa, wife of Louis, d. 7 July 1860, aged 88 yrs. 35.
Moorer, Carolina, d. 3 July 1848, aged @ 19 yrs. 52.
   Elizabeth, 1835-1895. 44.
   Nelson J., b. 3 Nov. 1823; d. 31 May 1898. 48.
   William D., b. 25 Apr. 1848; d. 27 June 1918. 90.
Morgan, Celia A., wife of James W., b. 12 Jan. 1835; d. 14 June 1918. 87.
   James W., b. 9 Nov. 1830; d. 13 Nov. 1919. 87.
   John A., b. 1 Aug. 1829; d. 15 June 1890. 87.
   Margaret, wife of John A., b. 30 Oct. 1834; d. 25 July 1868. 87.
   Arcary Mercer, wife of John A., b. 24 Jan. 1825; d. 5 May 1901. 87.
   Nancy Mariva Andress, b. S.C. 1803; d. 1890. 87.
   Thomas R., b. 5 May 1825; d. 14 Nov. 1890. 87.
   Thomas Richard, b. S.C. 1797; d. 1875. 87.
   W. W. b. 25 Aug. 1841; d. 9 May 1926, Co. C, 17 Ala. Reg., CSA. 87.
Morrill, Zenobia A., wife of E. W.; dau. of Dr. George B. & Elizabeth Herbert, d. 19 May 1869, aged 24 yrs. 68.
Morris, A. E., wife of W. L., b. 23 Apr. 1843; d. 13 Dec. 1915. 94.
   Ivy, d. 29 Jan. 1887, aged 74 yrs. (Obit).
   W. L., b. 15 Sept. 1838; d. 10 Feb. 1917. 94.

Morrow, Abraham, b. 28 Dec. 1794; d. 28 Sept. 1880. 21.
  Abraham Sidney, b. 5 Apr. 1842; d. 5 Nov. 1903. 21.
  James W., b. 6 Apr. 1837; d. 9 Mch. 1864. 21.
  Joseph Calvin, b. 17 Mch. 1846; d. 8 Jan. 1922. 50.
  Martha Ann, wife of Wm. C., b. 22 Jan. 1831; d. 3 Sept. 1888. 44.
  Mary, wife of A., b. 26 June 1805; d. 25 Dec. 1884. 21.
  Theodocia A. T., b. 23 Nov. 1848; d. 12 May 1917. 50.
Moseley, J. A., b. 23 Dec. 1848; d. 1 Oct. 1917, CSA Iron Cross. 8.
  Narcissa E. Williams, wife of Jno. A., b. 2 May 1847; d. 24 Jan. 1930. 8.
Mosley, Deletha, wife of W. M., b. 30 Apr. 1825; d. 11 Mch. 1894. 49.
  Missouria, b. 27 Dec. 1849; d. 21 Jan. 1917. 2.
  Nancy B., b. 9 Apr. 1827; d. 17 May 1911. 87.
  Sarah Ann, wife of J., b. 30 July 1813; d. 13 Apr. 1884. 1.
  William, b. 20 Sept. 1822; d. 21 Feb. 1899. 49.
  William, b. 30 Oct. 1842; d. 3 Aug. 1917. 2.
Mosely, Thomas M., b. 11 May 1846; d. 8 Oct. 1891. 12.
Murphy, Amanda Watts, wife of Augustus, b. 11 Apr. 1834; mar. 30 Jan. 1855; d. 2 Mch. 1906, youngest sister of Ex-Gov. Watts. 67.
Murtaugh, John, b. Co. Coscommen, Ire.; d. 21 Nov. 1904, aged 67 yrs. 44.
Myers, Elisha, b. Adams Co., Penna. 16 May 1813; d. 14 July 1886. 44.
  Mrs., mother of P.C., d. Apr. 1898, aged 87 yrs. (Obit). 44.
Myrick, Moses, b. 2 Mch. 1805; d. 3 Dec. 1886. 71.
Nall, S. B., b. 28 Nov. 1833; d. 13 Nov. 1868. 21.
Newcomer, Elizabeth J., 1843-1888. 44.
  John T., Capt., b. 1832; d. 18 Sept. 1884. Union Army. 44.
Newman, James M., d. 16 Dec. 1874, aged 74 yrs. A pioneer settler.(Obit)
  Margaret L., b. 3 Sept. 1841; d. 27 Sept. 1901. 44.
  W. D., b. 9 Jan. 1841; d. 12 May 1901. 44.
  William L., b. 3 Sept. 1844; d. 27 Sept. 1901. 44.
Newton, Abigail Sophronia, dau. of Caswell & Malinda, b. 17 Oct. 1838; d. 19 May 1927. 20.
  Amos, b. 18 Dec. 1819; d. 16 Dec. 1862. 20.
  Benjamin, b. 17 Mch. 1808; d. 19 Mch. 1883. 20.
  Benjamin J., b. 1 Aug. 1834; d. 10 Jan. 1899. 20.
  C. T., b. 30 Mch. 1840; d. 25 Aug. 1917. 51.
  Caswell, d. 10 Nov. 1901. 20.
  Eliza Jane, wife of Benjamin, b. Feb. 1817; d. 19 Feb. 1863. 20.
  Hanna, wife of W. H., d. Nov. 1877, aged 37 yrs. (Obit).
  Isabella B., wife of T. E., b. 13 May 1841; d. 15 Jan. 1929. 18.
  John I., b. 18 Aug. 1847; d. 19 June 1909. 47.
  Malinda, wife of Caswell, b. 30 Mch. 1818; d. 25 May 1901. 20.
  Margaret Ellen, wife of B. J., b. 16 Jan. 1843; d. 1 Oct. 1940. 20.
  Martha, wife of Thomas, b. 22 Jan. 1808; d. 23 June 1878. 20.
  Martha Jane, dau. of Thomas & Martha, b. 24 Sept. 1841; d. 21 May 1921. 20.
  Mary Ann Kirkland, dau. of E. J., b. 20 July 1840; d. 12 Aug. 1864. 20.
  Mattie M., b. 4 Oct. 1847; d. 5 Jan. 1920. 51.
  Robert E., son of B. & E. J., b. 16 Dec. 1837; d. 3 Sept. 1862. 20.
  Susan, wife of Angus, b. 18 June 1836; d. 11 Apr. 1897. 20.
  T. E., b. 2 Nov. 1839; d. 21 Jan. 1905. 18.
  Thomas, b. 18 Mch. 1810; d. 14 July 1888. 20.
  W. H., b. N.C. 3 Mch. 1842; d. 18 Nov. 1922. 29.
Nichols, Bettie, wife of D. R., b. 4 Mch. 1844; d. 6 Dec. 1927. 77.
  George W., CSA. 97*.
  Joel, b. 28 Sept. 1800; d. 27 May 1886. 46.
  John J., b. 18 Aug. 1847; d. 19 June 1909. 47.
  W. E., b. May 1825; d. 3 Dec. 1920. 77.

Nicholson, George W., 1811-1874. 25.
   Martha Ann, 1847-1925. 25.
   William James, b. 28 Jan. 1848; d. 15 Sept. 1912. 25.
Nix, Adam G., b. 25 May 1844; d. 10 July 1899. 64.
   Jane, wife of Edward, b. 30 Oct. 1820; d. 4 Jan. 1901. 64.
   Lucinda, b. 30 Oct. 1848; d. 4 May 1930. 64.
Norman, John J., b. 2 June 1830; d. 18 May 1891. 61.
   Mary Elizabeth Sheppard, wife of J. J., b. 11 July 1830; d. 5 Feb. 1905. 61.
Norris, Catherine, Mrs., d. 5 Aug. 1886 in Greenville. (Obit).
   D. I., b. 30 Jan. 1830; d. 1 Mch. 1913. 3.
   Martha A., b. 18 Apr. 1837; d. 19 Oct. 1915. 3.
   William Oliver, 1842-1929. 66.
Norsworthy, K. Elizabeth, b. 18 Jan. 1833; d. 6 July 1909. 24.
   William J., b. 18 Nov. 1828; d. 6 Mch. 1907. 24.
Oatis, Henry J., d. 12 Sept. 1881 in Georgiana, aged 42 yrs. (Obit).
O'Brien, Mike, d. 7 Apr. 1883, aged @ 82 yrs. (Obit).
Ockenden, Ina Porter, b. Mch. 1837; d. Feb. 1919. 68.
O'Connell, Morris P., b. Co. Cork, Ire.; d. 28 Mch. 1887, aged 63 yrs. 44.
Odom, A. I., b. 22 Nov. 1844; d. 14 Jan. 1920. CSA. 81.
   A. J., Sr., b. 28 May 1837; d. 3 Dec. 1885. 41.
   Jeanette A., wife of A. J., Sr., b. 27 Feb. 1832; d. 8 Dec. 1893. 41.
   Mary Ellen, wife of A. I., b. 1843; d. 11 June 1907. 81.
O'Gwynn, Eliza, wife of G., b. 22 Aug. 1832; d. 17 Mch. 1871. 89.
Oliver, Alice Purdon, dau. of Henry & Catherine, b. 17 Apr. 1846; d. 18 Apr. 1846. 68.
   Ann, consort of Rev. Samuel, d. 24 Feb. 1858, aged 60 yrs. 4 mos. 22 days. 68.
   Eleanor, 1800-1836. 68.
   Frances Louisa, dau. of Henry & Catherine F., b. 10 May 1848; d. 10 June 1849. 68.
   Henry P., son of Samuel & Eliza, b. 12 July 1833; d. 27 Mch. 1836. 68.
   Kate, wife of Henry P., b. Butler Co.; d. 3 Jan. 1898, aged @ 72 yrs. (Obit).
   Mary Catherine, dau. of Henry & Catherine, b. 17 June 1844; d. 5 June 1845. 68.
   Samuel, Rev., d. 19 Feb. 1865, aged 86 yrs. 68.
   Sarah, Mrs., d. Apr. 1884, aged 63 yrs. (Obit).
O'Neal, Sallie B., b. 29 Apr. 1841; d. 22 Sept. 1920. 63.
Ormand, Dr., d. Apr. 1867. (Obit).
Otts, S. B., d. 24 Dec. 1887, aged 75 yrs. (Obit).
   Willie, Lt., CSA. 68*.
Owen, Elizabeth Marsh, b. 28 Mch. 1830; d. 20 Nov. 1920. 53.
   Franklin, b. 15 Apr. 1821; d. 18 Dec. 1883. 53.
   Jane C., wife of John A., b. 26 Aug. 1833; d. 30 Nov. 1894. 44.
   Jesse W., Co. D, 34 Ala. Inf., CSA. 13.
   John A., b. Ga. 10 Apr. 1828; d. 16 Apr. 1900. 44.
   Robert E., Co. B, 17 Ala. Inf., CSA. 19.
Owens, Emily Elizabeth, dau. of Jared & Jane Dennard, b. 13 Feb. 1825 in Ga., d. 3 Oct. 1906. 44.
Padgett, Marjorie, wife of E. J. M., dau. of James L. Dunklin, b. 31 Aug. 1845; d. 10 Jan. 1874. 68.
Page, John Wesley, 1843-1916. 4.
   Martha Jane, 1843-1920. 4.
Palmer, A. L., Mrs., d. Georgiana 8 Nov. 1880. (Obit). 47.
   Amasa L., b. 8 Feb. 1839; d. 30 July 1913, Co. D, 33 Ala. Reg., CSA. 47.
   Emma J., b. 3 July 1849; d. 30 July 1916. 47.
   Sarah Rebecca, b. 3 Dec. 1840; d. 14 Sept. 1883. 94.
   Serena, wife of William W., b. 28 Aug. 1816; d. 14 Sept. 1871. 94.

William W., b. 19 Sept. 1810; d. 29 July 1868. 94.
Palmore, Mollie, d. 16 Apr. 1904, aged @ 60 yrs. 44.
Park, Thomas, d. 25 Apr. 1857, aged @ 66 yrs. 48.
Parker, Grace B., b. 30 Dec. 1826; d. 20 Aug. 1902. 49.
  Henry Clay, Lt., Co. B, 10 Cav., CSA. 63.
  James B., b. 11 Sept. 1848; d. 30 Nov. 1923. 69.
  Latha, wife of Columbus, b. 1 Jan. 1828; d. 20 Aug. 1895. 44.
  M. A., wife of Samuel, b. 11 Apr. 1848; d. 29 Mch. 1913. 12.
  Philip T., Co. E, 15 Cav., CSA. 43.
  Samuel, b. 27 Feb. 1843; d. 19 May 1926. 12.
  W. A., wife of P. T., b. 16 Feb. 1841; d. 16 Jan. 1908. 43.
Parkes, Elizabeth, wife of James D., b. 8 Apr. 1803; d. 16 Dec. 1879. 80.
  Elizabeth G., dau. of James D., b. 21 Dec. 1832; d. 11 Feb. 1865. 80.
  James D., b. 8 Apr. 1808; d. 30 Nov. 1880. 80.
  Permelie D., dau. of James D. & Elizabeth, b. 6 Feb. 1836; d. 7 Oct. 1860. 67.
  Tempy D., b. 25 Feb. 1831; d. 27 May 1904. 80.
Parkman, Margaret A. Crew, wife of J. B., b. 19 Jan. 1835; d. 15 May 1911. 3.
Parmer, Catharine Amanda, wife of J. M., b. 24 May 1812; d. 10 May 1853. 68.
  Clinton Dale, b. 16 Sept. 1831; d. 15 June 1873. 68.
  Eleanor Oliver, b. 5 June 1837; d. 7 Feb. 1877. 68.
  Ephraim, b. 10 Mch. 1786; d. 1 June 1853. 8.
  Henry Gus, b. 14 July 1839; d. 9 Feb. 1922. 2.
  Hilery C., b. 1 Mch. 1827; d. 12 Feb. 1908. 8.
  J. M., b. Jones Co. Ga. 24 Dec. 1808; mov. Greenville 1818; d. 18 Nov. 1862. 68.
  John M., b. 12 Jan. 1822; d. 25 Nov. 1897. 39.
  Josephine, dau. of J. & Nancy Ewing, b. 1 Mch. 1834; mar. William K. 27 Nov. 1849; d. 7 Feb. 1875. 44.
  M. A., b. Hawkensville, Ga.; d. 21 May 1884 in Greenville. (Obit).
  Mary Elizabeth, wife of Joseph M., b. 20 Feb. 1834; d. 17 Aug. 1908. 68.
  Nancy, b. 5 July 1820; d. 25 Nov. 1899. 8.
  William K., b. 2 Aug. 1816; d. 1 May 1886. 44.
  W. K., b. 25 Nov. 1846; d. 28 June 1935. 8.
Parritt, Lou Vicey Reaves, wife of Needham, d. 20 Sept. 1831. 53.
  Needham, b. 11 June 1794; d. 26 Nov. 1880, pensioner of War of 1812. 53.
Parson, Francis, wife of P. R., b. 8 Aug. 1847; d. 11 Feb. 1929. 64.
  P. R., b. 22 Sept. 1847; d. 17 Oct. 1929. 64.
Pascie, S., CSA. 97*.
Patillo, Rebecca J., dau. of J. E. & J., d. 12 Apr. 1858, aged 12 yrs. 4 mos. 23 days. 87.
Patrick, John, b. 25 Aug. 1833; d. 5 Jan. 1913, Pvt, 4 Ala. Cav., CSA. 69.
  N. Elizabeth, b. 29 Mch. 1842; d. 20 Jan. 1915. 69.
Patton, Ann J., wife of Matthew, d. 4 July 1858, aged 57 yrs. 68.
  Louisa Ann, consort of Matthew; dau. of Dr. John & Nancy Leake Coleman, b. 15 Apr. 1811; d. 16 Nov. 1841. 15.
  Matthew, Sr., d. 25 May 1860, aged 55 yrs. 3 mos. 20 days. 68.
  Matthew, b. 11 May 1832; d. 19 May 1901. 29.
Payne, Ann, b. 12 Sept. 1847; d. 1895. 54.
  Annie L., b. Richmond Co., Ga. 27 Jan. 1842; d. 14 Nov. 1871. 49.
  Frances G., wife of Jackson, b. 20 Sept. 1806; d. 12 June 1881. 31.
  Henry Clay, Co. B, 10 Ala. Cav., CSA. 63.
  Jesse D., son of Claiborn & Dorcas Payne, b. 15 Apr. 1843; d. 19 June 1857. 68.
  John, b. 4 Aug. 1798; d. (blank). 31.
  Latha, wife of Columbus, b. 1 Jan 1828; d. 20 Aug. 1895. 44.

Pete, b. 18 Feb. 1844; d. 22 Aug. 1934. 16.
Sarah Elizabeth, Mrs., d. 24 May 1858. 68.
Theodora Herbert, 1843-1890. 68.
Thomas J., b. 5 Nov. 1822; d. 13 May 1874. 87.
Peacock, R. A. R., wife of N. B., dau. of J. S. & Rebecca Brooks, b.
    Macon Co., Ga. 15 Mch. 1833; d. Garland 30 July 1890. 63.
Peagler, Absilla, wife of George S., b. 27 Oct. 1815; d. 8 Mch. 1878. 65.
    George S., b. Orangeburg Dist., S.C. 26 Jan. 1808; d. 28 May 1872. 65.
    Gideon J., b. 23 Oct. 1847; d. 30 Apr. 1931. 44.
    John, d. Manningham 15 Dec. 1899, aged 88 yrs. (Obit).
    Martin P., b. Orangeburg Dist., S.C. 1786; d. 8 Mch. 1872. 65.
    Martin Gray, b. Sept. 1841; d. 12 Dec. 1861. 65.
    Sarah Ann, b. 21 May 1826; d. 4 Nov. 1917. 3.
Pearce, John W., b. 11 July 1841; d. 29 Oct. 1911. 51.
Peaster, Matilda, b. May 1828; d. 10 Jan. 1897. 52.
Peavy, Abraham, b. 9 Apr. 1836; d. 9 June 1901. 60.
Peevy, Asa, b. 4 May 1813; 9 Jan. 1894. 85.
    Epsy M., wife of Asa M., b. 12 May 1820; d. 12 May 1890. 85.
Penn, Alice Janes, wife of Wiley M., 1849-1922. 2.
    Wiley M., b. 1 Sept. 1838; d. 19 Feb. 1936. 2.
Pentecost, L. M., Dr., d. 16 Aug. 1867. 68.
Perdue, Alexander Orren, b. 4 Dec. 1837; d. 14 Feb. 1919. 8.
    Catherine Golson, 1844-1872. 8.
    E. A., wife of J. E. W., b. 15 Dec. 1826; d. 28 Apr. 1912. 8.
    Foster W., son of J. A. & M. A. W., b. 1 Oct. 1846; d. 21 June
       1864. 66.
    J. E. W., b. 5 Mch. 1823; d. 10 Aug. 1889. 66.
    James H., 1827-1901. 44.
    Jane M., b. 24 Aug. 1834; d. 15 Nov. 1902. 44.
    John Newton, b. 10 Apr. 1848; d. 4 May 1908. 44.
    Joshua, son of J. A. & M. A. W., b. 19 Nov. 1848; d. 21 July 1849.
       (Isolated grave near Perdue).
    Joshua A., b. 19 Nov. 1817; d. 23 Jan. 1894. 66.
    M. A., wife of M. W., b. 25 July 1829; d. 26 Jan. 1909. 8.
    Martha A. W., wife of J. A., b. 13 Feb. 1821; d. 6 Feb. 1891. 66.
    Mary Camilla Giddens, wife of W. W., dau. of E. L. Womack & Ansley
       Giddens, b. 19 June 1834; d. 6 Aug. 1858. 8.
    Mary Emily, b. 28 July 1846; d. 1 Aug. 1881. 66.
    Payton, b. 11 June 1842; d. 24 Sept. 1898. 66.
    S. Tully, b. 24 Nov. 1836; d. 21 Nov. 1917, Co. K, 5 Ala. Inf., CSA
       1861-65. 44.
    Sovereign Tully, Sr., 1792-1863. 8.
    W. E., b. 30 Apr. 1849; d. 4 Aug. 1893. 8.
Perkins, Rossie Lee M., b. 15 Sept. 1818; d. 1 July 1906. 3.
    Sarah R. Little, wife of Thomas E., b. 16 July 1840; d. 8 Nov.
       1941. 90.
    Thomas E., b. 22 Oct. 1835; d. 17 Sept. 1921. 90.
Perry, Amanda, b. 10 May 1830; d. 1 Nov. 1882. 20.
    Arminta D. Tompkins, wife of J. T., b. Pike Co., Al. 27 Apr. 1848;
       d. Greenville 22 Sept. 1886; mar. 3 Nov. 1871. 44.
    Edna P., b. 10 Mch. 1843; d. 30 Aug. 1935. 20.
    Eldridge S., b. 17 May 1849; d. 12 Jan. 1933. 2.
    Elizabeth, wife of John, d. 14 Feb. 1833, aged @ 35 yrs. 20.
    Harriet A., b. 19 Jan. 1809; d. 26 Dec. 1883. 20.
    J. T., d. 24 June 1887, aged 44 yrs. 44.
    James, b. 21 Jan. 1822; d. 12 Oct. 1885. 20.
    Lucinda, b. 7 May 1826; d. 8 Feb. 1907. 76.
    Luvina, b. 27 July 1821; d. 18 Feb. 1901. 2.
    Martha Jane, dau. of Robert, d. 20 July 1891, aged 42 yrs. (Obit).
    Mary E., b. S.C. 1804; d. 5 July 1867. 44.

    Rebecca Jane, b. 5 Dec. 1838; d. 27 July 1916. 20.
    Robert, b. 24 Nov. 1840; d. 24 Jan. 1901. 20.
Peterson, Freeman F., b. 13 July 1847; d. 31 Jan. 1925. 18.
Petty, John E., d. Garland 9 Apr. 1900, aged 74 yrs. (Obit)
Phelps, Annie, wife of Edward A., b. Marlborough, S.C. 1823; d. 16 Oct. 1882. 59.
    Edward A., b. 3 Aug. 1826 Dallas Co.; d. 24 Feb. 1879. 59.
    Emmie, wife of James, b. 29 Oct. 1842; d. 12 May 1878. 18.
    G. W. T., b. 20 Mch. 1811; d. 3 June 1886. 18.
    J. A. J., b. 12 Jan. 1833; d. 5 Mch. 1895. 87.
    J. A. J., b. 10 Apr. 1836; d. 5 Mch. 1895. 87. (These two graves are 15-20 ft. apart & this information is as inscribed.)
    James A., b. 1 Oct. 1841; d. 23 Mch. 1918. 18.
    M. A., b. 29 June 1840; d. 22 Nov. 1912. 87.
    Martha, Mrs., b. 20 Mch. 1814; d. 10 Jan. 1893. 18.
    Samuel, d. 17 Nov. 1899, aged 69 yrs. 3.
    Sarah R. M., wife of John A., b. 27 Feb. 1845; d. 28 Mch. 1910. 18.
    W. E., 1811-1833. 18.
Pickens, Andrew, b. 28 Oct. 1770; d. 4 Sept. 1852. 68.
    Ezekiel H., b. 20 July 1798; d. 12 Mch. 1873. 68.
    Hannah, d. 18 Apr. 1880, aged 85 yrs. (Obit).
    Isabella, b. 4 Jan. 1776; d. 5 Oct. 1849. 68.
    Isabella, 1805-1885. 18.
    John A., b. 18 June 1834; d. 9 Dec. 1887. 71.
Pierce, Fannie Stubbs, b. 25 Sept. 1846; d. 3 Aug. 1907. 44.
    Frances Mason, 1849-1924. 44.
    Hiram, d. Greenville 27 June 1884, aged 68 yrs. (Obit).
    Ollie M., 1828-1933. 92.
    Philo Hubbell, son of Hubbell & Permelia, b. 6 Oct. 1831; d. 3 Aug. 1838. 68.
    Wesley, Mrs., d. 9 May 1886 Greenville, aged 40 yrs. (Obit).
    William R., b. 7 July 1831; d. 18 June 1890. 24.
Pierson, Frances J., wife of W. G., b. 10 June 1847; d. 9 Sept. 1910. 41.
Pilley, R. S., b. 29 May 1848; d. 26 Dec. 1912. 63.
    Sarah B., b. 16 Dec. 1816; d. 29 Oct. 1899. 94.
    Stephen F., Rev., b. 4 July 1805; d. 12 Nov. 1873. 94.
Pinkerton, Margaret, 1815-1895. 71.
Pitts, Greed, b. 6 Jan. 1831; d. 15 Mch. 1896. 16.
    Jack, d. 30 Jan. 1894, aged 60 yrs. 16.
Plant, Clara J., 1849-1935. 44.
    John W., 1846-1933. 44.
Pollard, Albert, b. 25 Oct. 1793; d. 6 Nov. 1878. 87.
    Andrew J., son of Albert & Margaret, b. 16 Mch. 1827; d. 12 Oct. 1852. 87.
    Everett, b. 6 Sept. 1830; d. 16 Nov. 1910. 18.
    Margaret, wife of Albert, b. 7 Aug. 1796; d. 21 June 1876. 87.
    Mary A., b. 28 Dec. 1841; d. 20 Aug. 1897. 76.
    Mary Jane, wife of E., b. 21 Mch. 1844;d. 21 Sept. 1873. 18.
    Mary L., dau. of Albert, b. 3 Jan. 1822; d. 11 Feb. 1850. 87.
    Roderick M., 1825-1863, Ala. Cav., CSA. 1.
    Susan, wife of Mack, b. 7 Feb. 1833; d. 20 Nov. 1924. 1.
    Thomas B., son of Albert, b. 26 Oct. 1835; d. 3 Apr. 1878. 87.
Pope, Kezekiah, b. 30 Dec. 1816; d. 12 July 1904. 12.
Porter, Benjamin F., b. S.C.; d. 4 June 1868, aged 60 yrs. (Obit) 68.
    Eliza T., relict of Judge Benjamin F., b. 17 Nov. 1808, Chester Co. S.C.; d. 30 Dec. 1883. 68.
    Ellen T., b. 3 Aug. 1838; d. 30 Nov. 1896. 68.
    James D., Rev., b. 24 Oct. 1839; d. 20 Nov. 1880. 68.
    John R., Lt., CSA. 68*.

Lucy Ann, b. 16 Sept. 1836; d. 14 Oct. 1913. 94.
Thomas M. J., b. 15 Feb. 1834; d. 29 Mch. 1901. 94.
Posey, Addison Francis, b. 4 Dec. 1820; d. 5 Jan. 1903, lived in Greenville 52 yrs. 68.
  Deborah, wife of J. T., d. 2 May 1875, aged 62 yrs. 52.
  Florella Young, wife of Addison F., b. 3 May 1827; d. 19 Apr. 1915. 68.
  John Trail, b. 8 Feb. 1805; d. 4 July 1891. 52.
Potter, Thomas Forbs, b. Georgetown, S.C. 3 Dec. 1822; d. 13 Apr. 1900. 44.
Powell, Barbara, b. 22 Aug. 1842; d. 26 Mch. 1879. 18.
  Henry Washington, b. 4 Aug. 1840; d. 4 Mch. 1928. 50.
  James Monroe, son of Susan Scott & Honorius, b. 1823; mar. Elizabeth Snell 5 Sept. 1844; d. 6 Oct. 1852. 52.
  Johnathan Louis, b. 11 Aug. 1837; d. 30 Nov. 1901. 44.
  Lucinda Elizabeth Bolling, wife of Johnathan Louis, b. 10 Dec. 1845; d. 3 Oct. 1892. 44.
  Mary Ann Scott, wife of Dempsey M., b. 29 Sept. 1840; d. 12 Apr. 1914. 57.
  Rebecca H., b. 28 Aug. 1841; d. 6 Jan. 1866. 91.
Powers, Amanda M., wife of William, b. 28 Aug. 1834; d. 31 July 1854. 52.
  James, b. 26 Feb. 1785; d. 13 Apr. 1859. 52.
  John S., b. 7 Nov. 1826; d. 7 Oct. 1902. 52.
  Josephine A., Mrs., b. 14 July 1835; d. 5 Sept. 1875. 52.
  Mary Warren, wife of James, b. 19 Nov. 1795; d. 15 Mch. 1874. 52.
  Richard, b. 1814; d. 25 Dec. 1888. 52.
  Robert, b. 20 Aug. 1834; d. 18 Jan. 1905. 48.
Price, D. P., Maj, b. Va.; d. 27 July 1896. (Obit).
  Mollie E., wife of D. P., 6 Apr. 1888, aged 48 yrs. 67.
Pride, Moses Herman, b. Greenfield, N.Y. 28 May 1841; d. Georgiana 1920 (Obit).
Prior, A. W., b. 28 Mch. 1794; d. 1 July 1883. 20.
  Allen Wade, Jr., b. 26 Sept. 1845; d. 10 Apr. 1920. 20.
  Patrick Henry, b. 15 Feb. 1842; d. 7 Nov. 1893. 20.
Pruett, Indiana, wife of S. T., b. 22 Nov. 1845; d. 10 Feb. 1916. 64.
  S. T., b. 25 Apr. 1842; d. 14 Mch. 1911. 64.
Pryor, Lizzie G., b. 23 Oct. 1802; d. 28 Apr. 1889. 44.
Pugh, Mastin B., d. 29 Jan. 1873, aged 78 yrs. (Obit).
Pulaski, John B., b. 22 July 1821; d. 14 Aug. 1898. 92.
  Sarah, b. 15 June 1838; d. 11 Dec. 1915. 92.
Purifoy, M. C., Rev., d. 7 Nov. 1859, aged 57 yrs. 67.
Raborn, Ansley, wife of William, b. 2 Jan. 1833; d. 17 June 1912. 18.
Rainer, J. J., b. 23 Apr. 1847; d. 17 Aug. 1923. 64.
  Martha A., b. 29 May 1832; d. 25 Mch. 1932. 64.
  Young S., b. 13 June 1849; d. 18 July 1876. 64.
Rains, Mary, b. 1799 Darlington Dist., S.C; d. 5 Oct. 1877. 59.
Ramage, Alexander Taylor, b. 22 June 1847; d. 19 Dec. 1915. 44.
Rape, Charlie, d. 1898, aged 70 yrs. 12.
  Cyntha, b. 12 Nov. 1812; d. 8 Sept. 1905. 12.
Rawls, Marina, wife of Moses, b. 12 Aug. 1813; d. 20 Apr. 1901. 77.
  Moses, b. 31 Dec. 1801; d. 9 Nov. 1876. 77.
  Susan, d. 12 Jan. 1881, aged 40 yrs. 77.
Reddoch, Alexander, d. 13 Feb. 1850, aged 76 yrs. 4 mos. 5 days. 72.
  Hetty, wife of Alexander & oldest dau. of John & Elizabeth Perdue, b. Maryland 30 June 1781; mar. 19 Mch. 1798; d. 8 Oct. 1846. 72.
Reese, Albert, b. 3 May 1831; d. 9 Nov. 1914. 49.
  Mary R., b. 8 Apr. 1828; d. 3 Aug. 1882. 49.
Reeves, Benj., d. Nov. 1875. (Obit).
Reid, A. M., b. Ga. 20 Jan. 1811; mov. Ala. 1822; d. 8 Oct. 1883. 44.
  Anna C., dau. of A. M. & E. A., d. 24 Sept. 1864, aged 21 yrs. 68.

Elizabeth A., dau. of Hillary Herbert, wife of A. M., b. S.C. 6
  Mch. 1818; d. 28 June 1881. 44.
Nellie, wife of Sam, d. 5 Mch. 1896, aged 55 yrs. 64.
Reynolds, C. C., Mrs., b. 10 Sept. 1836; d. 1 Apr. 1928. 8.
  Caroline F. Herndon, wife of R. R., d. 2 May 1887, aged 55 yrs. 87.
  Clarricie, dau. Wyatt Layne, wife of Elijah, 1836-1928. 8.
  Elijah, Capt., b. Coffee Co., Tenn. 24 Feb. 1830; d. 28 Jan.
    1877. 8.
  James, b. 12 July 1818; d. 1 Nov. 1899. 67.
  John C., b. 1 Dec. 1842; d. 30 Jan. 1916. 18.
  John P., b. 26 May 1847; d. 20 Apr. 1912. 44.
  Margaret Josephine, b. 30 Aug. 1849; d. 7 Mch. 1931. 44.
  Martha M., b. 23 May 1826; d. 10 Feb. 1919. 67.
  Seaborn Marion, b. 3 Jan. 1849; d. 16 July 1903. 39.
Rhodes, Amanda M., b. 22 July 1832; d. 12 May 1918. 29.
  Elizabeth A., wife of N. M., b. 29 Jan. 1831; mar. Nov. 1848; d.
    4 Aug. 1856. 85.
  J. H., 1848-1862. 18.
  L. J., 1830-1862. 18.
  Newton Marion, b. 23 Mch. 1829; d. 28 Aug. 1901. 74.
  Sarah A. Turner, wife of N. M., b. 1 Nov. 1835 Edgefield Dist.
    S.C.; d. 17 Feb. 1883. 74.
  (broken marker), d. 1856, aged @ 68 yrs. 74.
Richards, James, b. 14 Dec. 1832; d. 15 June 1912. 49.
  Lafayette L., b. 20 Mch. 1837; d. 21 Nov. 1855. 68.
  M. M., Mrs., dau. John Dannelly, d. near Forest Home 31 July
    1886, aged 77 yrs. (Obit).
  Mattie, b. 22 Jan. 1849; d. 26 Sept. 1908. 49.
  William, b. Maryland 7 Feb. 1799; d. 6 May 1855. 68.
Rigsby, Frances Arant, wife of P. D., b. 25 Apr. 1840; d. 27 Mch.
    1907. 94.
  P. D., b. 4 May 1841; d. 13 Nov. 1909. 94.
Riley, B. F., b. 15 Mch. 1847; d. 28 Dec. 1914. 74.
  G. A., b. 1 Nov. 1845; d. 6 Jan. 1932. 74.
  Henry C., b. 16 Aug. 1805; d. 5 Aug. 18(?)5. 74.
  James P., b. 13 Jan. 1837; d. 14 June 1893. 16.
  M. V., b. 14 Sept. 1845; d. 10 Nov. 1926. 74.
  Mary Johnson, wife of Capt. R. H., b. 14 Mch. 1838; d. 6 Sept.
    1915. 44.
  Nancy Caroline, b. 2 Feb. 1848; d. 15 Mch. 1926. 74.
  Sarah A., widow of H. C., b. 13 Aug. 1805; d. 5 Aug. 1876. 74.
  William J., b. 26 Jan. 1834; d. 4 Feb. 1894. 74.
Ringgold, William H., d. 15 Dec. 1850, aged 37 yrs. 75.
Riviere, W. W., b. Ga.; d. 29 Aug. 1891, aged 48 yrs. (Obit).
Roach, D. C., 1826-1895. 18.
  Elvira M., 1846-1879. 18.
  Henry Thomas, b. 4 Jan. 1838; d. 13 Feb. 1928. 18.
  Mary S., wife of H. T., b. 15 Dec. 1846; d. 21 June 1879. 18.
  Matilda, 1828-1911. 18.
Roberts, Ester, b. 11 Mch. 1822; d. 7 May 1861. 20.
Robinson, Carrie, wife of James R., d. 22 May 1919. 44.
  James R., b. 3 Aug. 1827; d. 12 June 1911. 44.
Robison, Frances W., b. 8 Jan. 1836; d. 7 May 1919. 23.
  Lodwick H., b. 8 May 1828; d. 13 Oct. 1882. 23.
Rodgers, Elizabeth A., b. 9 Jan. 1834; d. 22 Oct. 1909. 49.
  Jasper, b. 29 Sept. 1824; d. 9 Oct. 1899. 49.
Rogers, Eliza Majors, b. 12 Apr. 1819; d. 9 Aug. 1900. 62.
  Icy Saphronia, b. 5 Oct. 1830; d. 29 May 1911. 23.
  Margaret Ann, wife of R. D., b. Sumpter Dist., S.C. 13 June 1812;
    d. 14 May 1876. 64.

Margaret S. Benbow, wife of John G., b. 28 Dec. 1846; d. 28 Feb.
   1891. 64.
Mary Elizabeth, b. 21 Jan. 1848; d. 10 Dec. 1932. 64.
Robert D., b. 28 July 1807; d. 12 May 1890. 64.
Sarah Louise, b. 10 Jan. 1846; d. 16 Jan. 1928. 64.
William, b. 10 Mch. 1822; d. 20 Jan. 1912. 23.
Rollins, Sarah H., Mrs., b. Edgefield, Dist., S.C. 27 Feb. 1818; d.
   Montg. Co. 7 Dec. 1871. 49.
Roper, Eldridge Fleming, b. 6 Mch. 1824; d. 28 May 1906. 8.
   John M., d. Three Runs 24 June 1875, aged @ 80. (Obit).
   Permelia P., b. 16 May 1827; d. 3 May 1908. 8.
Roundtree, York, d. 28 July 1900, aged 75 yrs. 73.
Rouse, William P., b. N.C. 28 Oct. 1829; d. 4 Feb. 1901. 20.
Routon, Emma J., dau. Wm. P. & Sarah, d. Greenville 26 June 1860,
   aged 14 yrs. 2 mos. (Obit).
   Jeremiah P., 1832-1877. 44.
Royall, Theodora Herbert, b. 7 Feb. 1843; d. 30 Oct. 1890. 68.
Rudulph, Daniel Rambo, 1838-1862, CSA. 68.
   Eliza Rambo, b. 1814; d. Milledgeville Ga. 11 Apr. 1892. 68.
   John, b. Columbia, S.C. 21 Sept. 1803; d. 1 Mch. 1882. 68.
   John Seborn, 1842-1868, CSA. 68.
   Zebulon Jacob, b. 1833; d. 23 June 1865. 68.
Ruffin, John A., b. Jan. 1843; d. Oaky Streak 27 Oct. 1885. (Obit).
Russell, John S., b. 12 Feb. 1849; d. 29 Apr. 1919. 19.
   Laura A. Petry, wife of John S., b. 10 June 1849;-d. 24 Dec. 1920. 19.
   Mahaza E., b. 22 June 1832; d. 26 Apr. 1935. 77.
   Samuel T., b. 23 Oct. 1832; d. 25 Dec. 1907. 77.
   Sara Jane, wife of Henry, b. 8 Feb. 1835; d. 13 June 1920. 41.
Rutledge, M. A. V., widow of D. A., d. 27 Apr. 1894, aged 70 yrs. 11
   mos. (Obit).
Rye, Ammie, 1820-1890. 63.
   William S., 1813-1895. 63.
Salcher, George, Co. E, 29 Ala., CSA. 97*.
Salter, Harry C., d. 14 Sept. 1842, aged 63 yrs. 52.
   Mary, wife of H., d. 18 Aug. 1842, aged 30 yrs. 52.
   Samuel, d. 7 Jan. 1837, aged 50 yrs. 52.
   Samuel Crysuel, d. 28 Jan. 1834, aged 26 yrs. 52.
Sampler, Sophronia, wife of W., b. 17 Dec. 1840; d. 19 Nov. 1870. 44.
Sanders, John T., b. 3 Oct. 1835; d. 31 Dec. 1917. 49.
   Martha A., b. 29 Sept. 1842; d. 11 Nov. 1927. 49.
   Mary K., d. 7 July 1840, aged 11 yrs. 23 days. 52.
   Nancy, d. 11 Sept. 1847, aged 37 yrs. 6 mos. 21 days. 52.
   Sarah, d. 13 Oct. 1844, aged 13 yrs. 3 mos. 9 days. 52.
   Sarah, Mrs., b. 6 Apr. 1838; d. 18 Mch. 1934. 29.
Sapp, William, CSA. 68*.
Saucer, Elizabeth J., wife of B. F., b. 28 Feb. 1831; d. 7 Jan. 1901. 80.
   Mary, d. July 1889, aged 78 yrs. 80.
Sawyer, C., CSA. 97*.
   Lewis, b. 11 Oct. 1834; d. 2 Apr. 1912. 67.
   Marina, wife of Lewis, 1837-1919. 67.
Scarborough, Sarah, dau. Matthew Patton; wife of Lt. A.B., b. 9 Apr.
   1832; d. 20 May 1900. 44.
Schoolcraft, Laura, wife of Robert, b. Hardin Co. Ky; d. 22 Jan. 1890,
   aged 48 yrs. 44.
Scoggins, G. R., b. 9 Feb. 1837; d. 1 Sept. 1895. 69.
Scott, Amanda B., b. 9 Mch. 1830; d. 10 Aug. 1880. 23.
   Hester M., 1837-1898. 44.
   John B., b. 15 Dec. 1806; d. 9 July 1891. 52.
   Joseph M., Rev., b. 5 Feb. 1823; d. 29 Aug. 1899. 23.
   Leonard, 1782-1845. 52.
   Martha, dau. of John B., b. 26 Dec. 1822; d. 25 June 1903. 52.

Mary A., wife of John B., b. 26 Dec. 1822; d. 25 June 1903. 52.
Nathan L., b. 5 Feb. 1847; d. 11 Feb. 1921. 85.
Susan, wife of John B., d. 4 Oct. 1853, aged 41 yrs. 15 mos. 9 days. 52.
William D., b. 14 Feb. 1828; d. 9 Apr. 1862. 68.
Seale, Henry Oliver, b. 9 Dec. 1839; d. 29 Mch. 1913. 39.
  Ransom, son of Wm. & Rulincy Hilson, b. 27 June 1841; d. 9 Oct. 1885. 78.
  Rulincy, dau. of Aaron & Sarah Hilson, b. Milledgeville, Ga. 14 Nov. 1807; d. 22 Sept. 1883 at 9:00 A.M. 78.
  Susan Henderson, b. 22 July 1843; d. 21 Dec. 1915. 39.
  William, b. 28 Mch. 1807; d. 16 Apr. 1904. 78.
  Wilson Murphy, b. 18 Sept. 1829; d. 3 Apr. 1910. 48.
Searcy, Andrew J., b. 15 June 1841; d. 23 Dec. 1880. 18.
  Ann Eugenia, b. 2 Feb. 1848; d. 26 Dec. 1925. 44.
  Eliza, wife of Andrew J., b. 23 Aug. 1840; d. 30 Nov. 1899. 18.
  James Riley, b. 14 June 1843; d. 13 Aug. 1892. 44.
Seawright, George A., b. 1 Sept. 1843; d. 14 Dec. 1915, Ala. Sgt., Co. K, 17 Regt. Ala. Inf., CSA. 44.
Sellers, Calvin, son of William & Ellender, b. Brunswick Co., N.C. 20 Nov. 1818; mar. Elizabeth Talbot 1836; d. 23 June 1886, Pvt. 3 Bn., Ala. Res., CSA. 71.
  D. B., Sr., b. 10 Aug. 1832; d. 16 Apr. 1918, Pvt., Co. B, 17 Ala. Inf., CSA. 69.
  Duncan T., b. 9 Oct. 1844; d. 10 June 1919. 79.
  Julia A., b. Aug. 1835; d. 3 July 1900. 69.
  Martha A., wife of J. R. E., b. 8 Dec. 1841; d. 1 Sept. 1924. 56.
  N. E. Robinson, b. 8 Dec. 1849; d. 13 July 1867. 79.
  R., CSA. 97*.
Selman, Mary S. Pilley, wife of Rev. B. L., b. 2 Nov. 1841; d. 21 Feb. 1902. 63.
Shanks, W. L., b. 2 Mch. 1836; d. June 1922. 92.
  Margaret Mrs, d. Apr. 1884, aged 70 yrs. (Obit).
  William H., b. 15 Nov. 1849; d. 6 Feb. 1927. 23.
Sharp, Francis R., wife of J. C., b. 15 Nov. 1842; d. 12 May 1871. 36.
Shell, Delilah, b. 17 Jan. 1848; d. 6 June 1940. 77.
  Elizabeth, formerly the wife of George Herbert, b. 18 Aug. 1769; d. 10 Apr. 1830. 68.
  Fannie Crawford, wife of H. H., b. 23 Sept. 1845; d. 4 Apr. 1911. 12.
  George D., b. 18 Jan. 1846; d. 19 Mch. 1909. 77.
  Henry H., b. 22 Apr. 1840; d. 31 Oct. 1925. 12.
  Martha A., b. 22 Oct. 1826; d. 14 Sept. 1912. 77.
  Mary Ann, wife of Robert C., b. 6 May 1847; d. 26 Sept. 1885. 77.
  R. D., b. 19 July 1848; d. 23 Sept. 1922. 77.
Shepherd, Eliza L., b. 4 Apr. 1833; d. 1 Nov. 1891. 84.
  Frances, Mrs., b. 10 Jan. 1781; d. 14 Dec. 1861. 95.
  James, b. 1779; d. 29 Dec. 1863. 95.
  John Thomas, 1805-1863, among first settlers in Georgiana 1826. 21.
  John A., b. 5 Jan. 1831; d. 11 Feb. 1905. 63.
  Martha J., wife of John A. b. 4 Apr. 1838; d. 10 Dec. 1922. 63.
  Nancy Carr, b. 1810; d. 5 Mch. 1886. 21.
  Thomas, b. 1 Mch. 1812; d. 1 Nov. 1891. 84.
Sheppard, Alexander Reddoch, Dr., son of Francis & Sarah T., b. 15 June 1832; mar. Mary A. Gholson 10 Dec. 1857; d. 8 Jan. 1873. 61.
  Francis, b. 19 Aug. 1799; d. 15 Mch. 1869. 61.
  M. M., b. 22 Dec. 1833; d. 2 Feb. 1913. 61.
  Sallie, wife of Francis, b. 3 Sept. 1800; d. 3 Dec. 1885. 61.
Shine, Hilary R., b. 6 May 1842; d. 10 Sept. 1895. 64.
  Patience Long, wife of H. R., b. 11 Jan. 1844; d. 20 May 1934. 64.
  Stille Shines, b. 1822; d. 14 July 1903. 64.
  William Porter, b. 28 Aug. 1826; d. 2 May 1895; mar. Martha Hammonds 22 Aug. 1844. 64.

Shultz, Jeremiah, b. 8 Oct. 1825; d. 21 Feb. 1908. 80.
Simmons, Catherine J., b. Edgefield, Dist., S.C. 18 May 1825; d. 9
    Jan. 1903. 87.
  James A., b. 12 Oct. 1848. d. 28 May 1927. 82.
  Katie Irene, wife of James, b. 7 Nov. 1848; d. 26 Dec. 1887. 82.
  Mary Alice, wife of W. C., b. 27 Sept. 1836; d. 16 Aug. 1905. 81.
  W. C., Dr., b. 24 Nov. 1824; d. 29 Dec. 1914. 81.
Simpson, Jere B., b. N.C.; d. 12 Sept. 1888, aged 71 yrs. 10 mos. 11
    days. 44.
  M. Evelyn Ashcraft, wife of J. B., b. 28 Mch. 1836; d. 5 May 1888. 45.
Sims, A. C., Co. F, 18 Ala. Inf., CSA. 23.
  Alexander Theodore, Rev., son of Arthur C. & Sarah C. Austin. b.
    16 July 1849; d. 17 Sept. 1927. 63.
  Arthur C., b. S.C. 2 Aug. 1807; d. 14 Oct. 1881. 80.
  Dorcas A., wife of T. F., d. 11 Jan. 1893, aged 46 yrs. 9 mos.
    27 days. 44.
  F. N., d. Butler Springs 7 Aug. 1854, aged 54 yrs. 7 mos. (Obit).
  J., Mrs., d. 24 Dec. 1906, aged 70 yrs. 4.
  James Henry, 1848-1882. 9.
  James M., Sgt., Co. H, Ala., CSA. 63.
  Jim B., b. 11 Oct. 1849; d. 8 Jan. 1927. 53.
  John, b. 5 Jan. 1831; d. 11 Feb. 1905. 63.
  John W., 1848-1923. 53.
  Martha J., wife of John A., b. 4 Apr. 1838; d. 10 Dec. 1922. 63.
  Nancy A., wife of Rev. A. T., dau. of Pinkney & Anna Odom Hilson,
    b. 29 Oct. 1850; d. 5 Nov. 1903. 63.
  Sarah C., wife of A. C., b. 22 May 1822; d. 21 Aug. 1880. 80.
  Sherrod, Sr., Mrs., d. June 1881 near Starlington. (Obit).
Sirmon, John R., b. 9 Jan. 1834; d. 15 Aug. 1898. 67.
  Susan, b. 15 Oct. 1835; d. 18 Mch. 1910. 67.
Skinner, Ariss, b. 6 May 1829; d. 7 Nov. 1916, CSA. 39.
  Asa, Rev., b. 30 June 1808; d. 9 July 1888. 39.
  Mary S., dau. of Rev. Asa & Rachel, b. 23 May 1842; d. 5 Aug.
    1866. 39.
  Rachel, b. 3 May 1808; d. 31 Jan. 1895. 39.
  Sarah M. Wiggins, 1832-1892. 39.
Skipper, Ora Goins, b. 27 Jan. 1849; d. (?). 92.
Smith, Amanda, b. 23 Mch. 1833; d. 26 Aug. 1853. 20.
  Ambros, b. Jefferson Co., Ga. 7 Apr. 1797; emig. Ala. 1824; d. 25
    Mch. 1885. 20.
  Annie A., b. 31 Dec. 1835; d. 8 Oct. 1879. 20.
  Barbra, 1809-1889. 18.
  Betty J., b. 29 Mch. 1849; d. 11 Oct. 1937. 76.
  Charles A., b. 27 Feb. 1832; d. 20 Apr. 1914., Co. E, 17 Regt.
    Ala. Inf., CSA. 13.
  Daniel L., b. 24 July 1830; d. 25 Feb. 1879. 20.
  Drucilla, Mrs., b. 1794; d. 11 Sept. 1865. 52.
  Eliza Jane, dau. of Ambros & Margaret Duke, b. 15 Dec. 1839; d. 2
    Feb. 1876. 20.
  F. C., b. 10 Apr. 1846; d. 9 May 1902. 44.
  Henry G., b. 20 Feb. 1824; d. 6 Aug. 1899. 64.
  Harrison, son of Henry & Sarah A., b. 5 Oct. 1841; d. 2 Oct. 1844. 52.
  Henry, b. 15 Apr. 1792; d. 29 July 1873. 84.
  Henry, b. 5 July 1814; d. 21 June 1857. 52.
  Horace, b. Savannah, Ga. 4 July 1838; d. 1 Dec. 1885. 44.
  I. A., wife of H. G., b. 24 Apr. 1835; d. 30 Nov. 1912. 64.
  Isabel C., wife of Henry, b. 18 May 1804; d. 28 Oct. 1861. 84.
  J. A., elderly gentleman, b. Pike Co.; d. Sept. 1900. (Obit).
  J. S. M., b. 30 Apr. 1842; d. 8 Aug. 1890. 44.
  Emily, Mrs., d. Apr. 1884, aged 72 yrs. (Obit).

James A., d. Sept. 1900, Co. H, 13 Ga. Inf., CSA.   44.
James B. R., 1807-1878.   18.
James Robert, b. Ga. 9 July 1829; d. 11 July 1884; mar. Lucy Ann,
    31 Oct. 1850; Co. E, 56 Regt. Ala. Cav., CSA.   80.
Johnnie Thornton, CSA.   21.
Julia Ann, wife of J. A., b. 15 Apr. 1842; d. 8 Feb. 1927.   53.
Lucy Ann, 1835-1915.   13.
Margaret, wife of Ambros, b. 18 Sept. 1803; d. 6 Mch. 1880.   21.
Martha A., wife of S. T., b. 3 Jan. 1830; d. 19 Mch. 1914.   64.
Martha E., b. 4 Jan. 1833; d. 27 Aug. 1907.   56.
Martha W., b. 23 Jan. 1828; d. 7 Oct. 1836.   20.
Mary, b. 24 Dec. 1774; d. 14 Dec. 1862.   20.
Mary A., wife of W. J., b. 23 July 1845; d. 21 Mch. 1926.   71.
Mary Elizabeth, dau. of J. B. R. & B. E., b. 19 May 1836; d. 7 Feb.
    1894.   18.
Mary J., wife of Thomas, b. 23 Mch. 1825; d. 5 May 1878.   52.
Megaren Sophronia, b. 25 Oct. 1844; d. 11 Dec. 1911.   44.
Nancy, b. Nov. 1841; d. 26 June 1914.   56.
Robert J., b. 19 Dec. 1843; d. 19 Jan. 1916.   18.
Samuel Thomas, b. 26 Oct. 1821; d. 11 Sept. 1863.   64.
Sarah A. E., b. 9 May 1832; d. 30 Dec. 1893.   84.
Sarah Ann Steen, wife of Henry, dau. of Perry R. & Martha, b. 18
    July 1823; d. 25 Dec. 1898.   52.
Sarah Jane, b. 29 Jan. 1823; d. 10 Nov. 1908.   71.
Selia A., d. 2 Aug. 1894, aged 64 yrs.   63.
Seth, d. 13 Jan. 1839, aged @ 56 yrs.   52.
Tempy Elizabeth, b. 23 Oct. 1848; d. 27 Nov. 1919.   80.
Thomas, b. 20 June 1817; d. 1 Feb. 1891.   52.
Thomas Seth, b. 2 Feb. 1844; d. 1 May 1862.   52.
W. J., b. 24 July 1845; d. 28 Aug. 1902.   71.
William, b. 3 Oct. 1815; d. 15 May 1864.   52.
William P., b. 18 Aug. 1843; d. 27 Jan. 1915.   56.
William T., b. 28 Sept. 1822; d. 24 Jan. 1862.   84.
Smyth, J. A., b. 3 July 1833; d. 4 June 1908.   53.
  Matilda, b. 10 Mch. 1822; d. 27 Oct. 1847.   73.
  Sarah Elizabeth, dau. of William & Mary Wright, b. 2 July 1839;
    mar. Robert B. 31 Aug. 1851; d. 21 Sept. 1855.   68.
Smythe, Lou F. Harrison, wife of Robt. B., Sr., b. 29 Dec. 1839; d.
    17 Mch. 1908.   18.
  Rosanah A., wife of R. J., Sr., b. 8 Feb. 1849; d. 17 Sept. 1895.   18.
Soleer, Robert, CSA.   97*.
Spann, Sarah Cornelia, b. 2 Oct. 1843; d. 3 Sept. 1923.   94.
Speir, Mary A., b. 12 Oct. 1846; d. 18 Nov. 1934.   44.
Spivey, Amos, b. Sept. 1830; d. 1904, Pvt, Co. C, 46th Ala. Inf.,
    CSA.   12.
Stabler, J. J., Mrs., b. 20 Nov., 1849; d. 30 June 1928.   29.
Staggers, J. H., b. 27 Mch. 1842; d. 6 Oct. 1899.   66.
  Lauretta, wife of James H., b. 20 Oct. 1844; d. 21 May 1924.   66.
Stallings, Archie Reid, b. 12 Jan. 1831; d. 18 May 1898, CSA.   24.
  James T., b. 30 Jan. 1826; d. 1 Apr. 1883.   64.
  Lenora Ann, wife of Reuben R., b. 25 Feb. 1831; mar. 24 Dec. 1851;
    d. 11 Nov. 1897.   64.
  Lucy Thompson, b. Mch. 1840; d. 4 July 1919.   44.
  Mary, dau. of Jesse, d. Apr. 1900, aged 72 yrs. (Obit).   62.
  Mary, wife of Jesse, d. 2 Dec. 1879, aged 84 yrs. (Obit).
  Mary Patrick Thompson, wife of Archie Reid, b. 5 Sept. 1843; d. 6
    Aug. 1917.   44.
  Nancy C., wife of Archie, dau. of Peter & Melinda Cheatham, b. 8
    Oct. 1840; d. 26 Apr. 1882. (Obit).
  Nancy F., wife of James T., b. 27 Feb. 1827; d. 15 May 1899.   64.

Nannie Cheatham, b. 15 Nov. 1834; d. 2 Dec. 1884. 24.
Reuben R., b. 1 Apr. 1830; d. 20 Sept. 1908. 64.
Thomas D., Dr., b. 12 Jan. 1836; d. 16 Nov. 1870. 24.
Stamps, Britton, b. 13 Dec. 1792; d. 17 Dec. 1868. 88.
Sallie, b. 20 Feb. 1811; d. 28 Sept. 1867. 88.
Stanford, A. J., b. 30 Sept. 1830; d. 10 Dec. 1899. 3.
Nancy A., wife of A. J., b. 30 Aug. 1830; d. 7 Nov. 1911. 3.
Stanley, Emma Stone, wife of B. H., b. Paris, France 1810; d. 8 Sept. 1892. 44.
James Berney, b. 9 Aug. 1844; d. 9 Dec. 1934. 44.
Lula C., wife of James B., dau. of A. M. & E. A. Reid, b. 21 Mch. 1848; d. 23 May 1886. 44.
Mattie, b. 3 Nov. 1840; d. 21 June 1905. 44.
Robert H., b. Columbia, S.C. 29 Feb. 1808; d. 21 Nov. 1880. 44.
Steele, John Wesley, b. Augusta, Ga. 1840; d. 7 Nov. 1883, CSA. 44.
Martha Stanley, b. Columbia, S.C. 12 May 1812; d. 26 Dec. 1889, DAR Marker. 44.
Steen, Curtis, b. 29 May 1803; d. 21 Dec. 1828. 91.
Curtis, Jr., d. 31 Dec. 1873, aged @ 36 yrs. 52.
Franata A., wife of James, b. 6 Apr. 1828; d. 1 July 1860. 93.
J. Wingate, d. 12 Apr. 1895, aged @ 60 yrs. 52.
James, d. 1838, aged @ 60 yrs. 52.
Josephine, dau. of Perry R. & Martha, d. 25 Dec. 1842, aged 3 yrs. 11 mos. 26 days. 52.
M. E., Mrs., b. 8 June 1812; d. 14 Aug. 1876. 91.
Martha, consort of Perry R., dau. of Robert & Margery Yeldell, b. Abbeville Dist. S.C. 1805; mov. Ala. 1818; d. 21 July 1864. 52.
Permelia M. A., b. 19 Mch. 1831; d. 28 Mch. 1878. 52.
Perry B., Jr., b. 20 Sept. 1842; d. 10 Aug. 1863. 52.
Perry R., son of James & Sara H., b. 2 Apr. 1800; d. 13 July 1887. 52.
Prudence, wife of James, d. 22 July 1850, aged 20 yrs. 2 mos. 10 days. 93.
Robert, b. 10 Feb. 1826; d. 26 Jan. 1913. 52.
Sara H., mother of Perry R., d. 1834, aged @ 55 yrs. 52.
Steiner, Joseph b. 25 Dec. 1826; d. 3 Jan. 1889. 44.
Margaret M. Camp, wife of Joseph, b. 6 Feb. 1829; d. 7 May 1904. 44.
Stevenson, Eliza Ann, wife of R. Y., b. 24 May 1829; d. 21 Aug. 1856. 52.
Robert Y., b. 18 Dec. 1822; d. 28 Dec. 1868. 52.
Steward, Alexander, b. 2 Nov. 1810; d. 17 July 1874. 52.
E. M. E., wife of J. W., b. 7 May 1836; d. 18 Sept. 1925. 94.
J. W., b. 22 Nov. 1833; d. 22 Apr. 1902. 94.
Stewart, Jacob A., b. 7 Apr. 1848; d. 3 Sept. 1884. 85.
John A., b. 2 Feb. 1835; d. 24 Mch. 1879. 44.
Louis C., b. 18 Aug. 1837; d. 6 Feb. 1887. 85.
W. A., Co. E, 56 Ala. Partison Rangers, CSA. 67.
Stinson, Annie E., b. 29 Nov. 1849; d. 14 Nov. 1937. 71.
James Leander, Rev., b. 15 Aug. 1849; d. 7 Aug. 1933. 71.
John C., b. 19 Oct. 1846; d. 9 Aug. 1910, Pvt., Ala. Co. A, 1 Bn. Ala. Arty., CSA. 71.
Nancy, b. 17 Feb. 1826; d. 25 May 1886. 71.
Stockton, M., CSA. 97*.
Stokes, Amanda, b. 12 June 1838; d. 5 Mch. 1907. 25.
Stott, Abdiel, son of David & Mary, d. 19 May 1866, aged 32 yrs. 3 mos. 11 days. 89.
David, d. 19 Nov. 1867, aged 72 yrs. 89.
John R., b. 11 July 1845; d. 18 Apr. 1890. 47.
Josie E. Stamps, wife of J. R., b. 16 June 1847; d. 7 May 1893. 47.
Lena M., widow of Ira W., d. Georgiana 28 June 1885. (Obit).
Mary, wife of David, d. 10 Sept. 1866, aged 71 yrs. 6 mos. 21 days. 89.
Stringer, Charlie, b. 22 Mch. 1847; d. 14 Apr. 1921. 67.
John Ashley, b. 21 Dec. 1818; d. 13 Dec. 1895. 86.

Margaret Frances, wife of J. H., Sr., b. 22 Aug. 1844; d. 22 Dec. 1931. 86.
Nancy A., wife of John A., b. 13 Dec. 1827; d. 15 July 1894. 86.
Stringfellow, Ann McCrory, wife of Reuben, b. 13 Sept. 1810; d. 1 Dec. 1869. 80.
Jefferson W., b. 6 Jan. 1830; d. 13 Nov. 1897. 80.
Martha A. Byrd, wife of J. W., b. 16 Dec. 1832; d. 15 Nov. 1919. 80.
Stuart, Ann Louiza, wife of W. A. Stewart, d. 30 Mch. 1912, aged 73 yrs. 4 mos. 12 days. 67.
Anna, b. S.C. 24 Apr. 1812; mar. 1830; d. 24 Apr. 1882. (Obit) 85.
Frances Palmer, wife of W. D., b. 8 Dec. 1844; d. 6 Aug. 1869. 94.
Stuckie, N. L., d. 30 Dec. 1874, aged 57 yrs. (Obit).
Sweatt, J. M., b. 23 Mch. 1847; d. 3 May 1933. 29.
Tallant, Rebecca V., wife of Samuel, b. Wilcox Co. 8 Feb. 1839; mar. 1865; d. South Butler 5 May 1882. (Obit).
Talley, Henry W., b. 17 Sept. 1847; d. 9 Jan. 1928. 49.
John, 1811-1895. 49.
Martha, b. 9 Oct. 1836; d. 28 Mch. 1902. 39.
Mary Day, 1822-1879. 49.
Taylor, Bethenia, Mrs., b. 15 Jan. 1848; d. 12 Jan. 1901. 3.
Dunklin Bonner, Capt., b. 10 Mch. 1840; d. 25 Aug. 1899. 63.
H. H., b. 7 Oct. 1848; d. 13 Nov. 1932. 8.
Louisa Hinson, b. 18 Oct. 1833; d. 31 May 1891. 81.
Lucinda, d. 25 Mch. 1868, aged 56 yrs. 68.
Margaret Ann, Mrs., d. 24 Feb. 1896, aged 70 yrs. 39.
Margery Catherine Herbert, wife of Hubbard Bonner, b. 20 Feb. 1820; d. 24 May 1902. 68.
Sallie, b. 11 Nov. 1847; d. 28 Nov. 1932. 8.
Sarah L., b. 23 June 1836; d. 20 Feb. 1872. 68.
Wesley Berry, b. 1 Apr. 1835; mar. Louisa H. 9 Jan. 1859; d. 21 June 1919, Co. 1, 53 Ala. Partison Rangers, CSA. 81.
William, CSA. 97*.
Teal/Teel, Elizabeth, b. 10 Dec. 1829; d. 28 Jan. 1908. 53.
Jesse H., b. 16 Oct. 1828; d. 19 Nov. 1899. 53.
Teat, Mary, b. 26 Aug. 1808; d. 22 Apr. 1906. 81.
Terrell, Sarah A., b. Pike Co., Ga. 23 Aug. 1835; d. 29 Oct. 1914. 44.
William A., b. 25 Nov. 1832; d. 6 Sept. 1904. 44.
Terry, M. Z., son of Thomas Edmonson, b. Muscogee Co., Ga. 11 June 1838; mar. Lizzie Morrison 1857; d. 16 Sept. 1898. (Obit). 29.
Thagard, A. J., b. 4 Oct. 1845; d. 13 July 1897. 18.
E. F., wife of A. J., b. 2 June 1846; d. 2 Nov. 1869. 59.
Elizabeth J., wife of W. R., b. 5 Mch. 1839; d. 29 Oct. 1880. 18.
Mary E. Reese, wife of T. S., b. 12 Sept. 1837; d. 23 July 1892. 76.
Sarah Permelia, wife of W. R., b. 8 Mch. 1846; d; 24 Dec. 1900. 44.
Thomas S., b. 23 Jan. 1831; d. 21 Sept. 1899. 76.
Warren R., b. 25 Apr. 1833; d. 27 Oct. 1911. 44.
Thaggard, George, b. N. C. 1 July 1798; emig. Ala. 1822; d. 26 Sept. 1860. (Obit).
Thames, Bethany, wife of J. G., b. 13 Aug. 1818; d. 1 July 1860. 68.
Hullena, wife of N. B., b. 23 Dec. 1835; d. 28 Dec. 1884. 2.
J. G., b. 10 Jan. 1817; d. 2 Sept. 1863. 68.
Joel Flanagan, Co. A, 1 Ala. Cadets, CSA. 44.
Mary Eskew, wife of Thomas J., b. 9 July 1849; mar. 1871; d. 18 Nov. 1896. (Obit).
N. B., b. 11 Feb. 1835; d. 11 Mch. 1908. 2.
Susan Florence Dunklin, wife of Joel F., b. 28 Nov. 1847; d. 7 Aug. 1914. 44.
William H., b. Henry Co., Ga. 6 Nov. 1827; d. 11 Aug. 1871. 37.
Thigpen, Gray, b. 15 Aug. 1824; d. 19 Dec. 1884. 37.

    Henry, d. Apr. 1851, aged 62 yrs. 52.
    Hester M. Scott, wife of J. M., b. 24 Aug. 1837; d. 16 Feb. 1896. 44.
    Job, b. 26 July 1828; d. 1 Feb. 1894. 44.
    John, b. 13 Oct. 1775; d. 30 Nov. 1858. 52.
    Joseph M., Sr., b. 20 Apr. 1836; d. 15 Oct. 1894. 44.
    Martha Farrior, b. 30 Dec. 1838; d. 18 July 1919. 44.
    Martha Watts, wife of Job, b. 11 May 1844; d. 27 Aug. 1888. 44.
    Mary A., d. 5 Apr. 1885, aged 64 yrs. (Obit).
    Prudence Watts, 1844-1922. 63.
    Susanah, wife of John, b. 20 Sept. 1781; d. 11 Nov. 1850. 52.
    William, d. Manningham 11 July 1885, aged @ 60 yrs. (Obit).
Thomas, Benifoyd, son of W. & S., b. 2 July 1849; d. 6 Aug. 1858. 59.
    Daisy B., b. 14 Oct. 1814; d. 21 May 1851. 59.
    James T., b. 29 Jan. 1824; d. 15 Mch. 1860. 9.
    Richard S., d. 15 Apr. 1860, aged @ 30 yrs. (Obit).
    Sarah, wife of Eld. William, b. 17 Feb. 1812; d. 2 July 1891. 59.
    Susanna R. Cook, wife of William A., b. Fairfield Dist., S.C. 20
        Sept. 1826; d. 5 May 1876. 44.
    W. D., Co. H, 50 Ala. Inf., CSA. 59.
    William, Eld., b. 21 Dec. 1803; d. 30 June 1858, first preacher and
        gave the land for the church & cemetery. 59.
    William Adams, b. Marlborough Dist., S.C. 21 June 1820; d. 17
        Sept. 1879. 44.
Thompson, C. C., b. 25 Apr. 1844; d. 23 Apr. 1917. 90.
    Frank W., b. 12 Mch. 1837; d. 28 Oct. 1883. 90.
    G. W., b. 28 Mch. 1837; d. 28 Dec. 1915. 56.
    John P., b. 15 Jan. 1815; d. 17 Nov. 1898. 66.
    Linna S., b. 8 July 1838; d. 15 Mch. 1880. 66.
    Mary, wife of Warren A., b. 6 June 1806; d. 16 Feb. 1884. 90.
    Mary A., d. 6 Sept. 1849, aged 29 yrs. 66.
    Mary Ann Chancellor, wife of James A. who was lost in Civil War,
        b. 20 Dec. 1841; d. 23 May 1925. 23.
    Mary L., b. 16 Mch. 1838; d. 1919. 90.
    Mary L., wife of C. C., b. 28 Jan. 1848; d. 18 June 1919. 90.
    Mary Theodocia, wife of J. F., b. 16 Mch. 1845; d. 21 May 1910. 66.
    P. M., b. 16 Oct. 1846; d. 2 Nov. 1926. 90.
    Samuel E.. Dr.. b. 11 Feb. 1826; d. 21 Feb. 1885. 87.
    Sarah J., wife of Dr. Samuel E., b. 5 Dec. 1841; d. 2 Feb. 1900. 87.
    T. J., dau. of Bennett Duncan, wife of J. P., b. 29 Dec. 1849; d.
        10 Dec. 1914. 59.
    Warren A., b. 10 May 1802; d. 4 July 1891. 90.
Thornton, Eli, b. 22 Mch. 1804; d. 27 Apr. 1873. 18.
    Hannah, widow of Jacob, b. 29 Sept. 1798; d. 27 July 1875. 18.
    Jacob, b. Edgefield Dist., S.C. 22 Aug. 1798; d. 24 Aug. 1870. 18.
    Jacob A., b. 30 Oct. 1826; d. 30 Jan. 1920, Co. E, 8 Ala. Inf.,
        CSA. 86.
    Julia A. Murphy, 1846-1898. 24.
Thrower, Elizabeth, b. 15 Jan. 1820; d. 12 July 1895. 77.
Till, Daniel G., b. 22 Apr. 1838; d. 10 May 1928. 57.
    Hampton, b. 3 Mch. 1826; d. 7 June 1905. 48.
    M. E. Luckie, wife of Hampton, b. 26 Dec. 1836; d. 27 Dec. 1902. 48.
    Maria Louise Garrison, wife of Jacob G., b. 21 Feb. 1844; d. 19
        June 1925. 44.
    Nancy A., b. 24 Apr. 1842; d. 21 Feb. 1925. 57.
Tillery, Herbert Cary, b. 20 Aug. 1840; d. 12 Apr. 1911. 25.
    J. S., b. 2 Nov. 1845; d. 3 Nov. 1907. 44.
    J. W., b. 23 June 1831; d. 9 Sept. 1862, erected by dau. Jimmie
        Tillery. 61.
    Ophelia Sheppard, Mrs., b. 15 Oct. 1842; d. 8 Mch. 1920. 44.
    Rebecca Catherine, b. 12 Jan. 1849; d. 27 Nov. 1922. 25.

William, b. Edgefield Dist., S.C. 1 Aug. 1808; emig. Ala. 1818; d.
    16 Oct. 1885. (Obit).
Traweek, Ira Yeldell, b. 11 Nov. 1843; d. 11 Oct. 1911., Jeff Davis
    Arty. Jackson's Corp., CSA. 44.
  Lewis O., b. 28 May 1839; d. 26 July 1859. 48.
  Louisa Simpson, b. 25 Jan. 1839; d. 1 Oct. 1927. 80.
  Martha A., wife of Ira Y., b. 8 Oct. 1846; d. 27 Apr. 1880. 48.
  Mary M., d. 2 Feb. 1869, aged 21 yrs. 10 mos. 9 days. 48.
  Sallie L., 1849-1933. 48.
  Sarah, wife of W. H., b. 12 Jan. 1811; d. 14 Mch. 1856. 48.
  Sarah B., wife of W. H., b. 26 Sept. 1827; d. 20 Oct. 1880. 48.
  T. M., b. 25 Nov. 1834; d. 9 Feb. 1900. 80.
  William H., b. 6 Jan. 1811; d. 18 Nov. 1896. 48.
Turk, Clem, b. 16 Sept. 1814; d. 22 Dec. 1911. 94.
Turner, John B., 1798-1875. 68.
Uhink, Lucius Eugene, d. Greenville 21 June 1860, aged 16 yrs. 7 mos.
    1 day. (Obit).
Van Pelt, A. C., b. 22 Aug. 1826; d. 6 Aug. 1900. 19.
  J. S., b. 21 Mch. 1821; d. 20 Apr. 1891. 63.
  M. L., b. 19 Dec. 1841; d. 22 Apr. 1907. 19.
  Sarah A., b. 10 Nov. 1827; d. 23 Aug. 1897. 63.
Vann, Harriet A., dau. of Rev. Asa & Rachel Skinner, b. 31 Dec. 1834;
    d. 14 July 1869. 39.
Vickery, George, b. 27 May 1848; d. 5 Dec. 1926. 69.
Vinson, Charles Moses, b. Wilkerson Co., Ga. 23 Feb. 1813; d. 7 Feb.
    1895. 63.
  Sarah Wright, wife of C. M., b. 6 May 1819; d. 8 Apr. 1908. 63.
Walker, Amelia A., wife of C. S., b. 12 July 1842; d. 22 Jan. 1896. 23.
  D. E., b. 19 Dec. 1830; d. 20 Nov. 1912. 74.
  Felix G., b. 17 July 1833; d. 17 Dec. 1911. 74.
  Isaiah, b. 8 Oct. 1847; d. 28 Feb. 1917. 3.
  James Franklin, b. 14 Aug. 1845; d. 10 Jan. 1915. 81.
  Mary Elizabeth, b. 29 Dec. 1849; d. 25 July 1921. 81.
  William M., Rev., b. 21 July 1831; d. 26 Apr. 1895. 63.
Vurnon, M. Jane, d. 16 Jan. 1920, aged @ 80 yrs. 52.
Wall, Conrad, Dr., b. 22 Sept. 1829; d. 25 Dec. 1898. 23.
  Cornelia Elizabeth, b. 3 June 1844; d. 7 Dec. 1904. 23.
Wallace, E. G., wife of S. G., b. 3 Feb. 1844; d. 24 Apr. 1901. 20.
Waller, L. S., 1801-1877. 27.
  N., 1805-1895. 27.
  R., 1822-1900. 27.
Walton, Frances, b. 13 Nov. 1835; d. 28 Nov. 1868. 18.
  W. A., Dr., b. 3 May 1838; d. 19 Mch. 1879. 18.
Ward, Mary, b. Ireland; d. 28 June 1910, aged 75 yrs. 44.
Wardlaw, David, b. Abbeville Dist., S.C. 3 Dec. 1774; d. 3 June 1840. 52.
Warley, Charles Henry, b. Bristol, Eng. 7 Mch. 1845; d. 7 Jan. 1894. 44.
  Elizabeth Dukes, b. 18 Mch. 1829; d. 6 July 1881. 44.
Warren, Richard, d. 3 July 1835, aged 72 yrs. (Obit).
Warrick, Martha, b. 16 Mch. 1836; d. 29 May 1918. 22.
Waters, Levi M., b. 14 Dec. 1810; d. 18 Jan. 1870. 58.
  Martha M., b. 22 Aug. 1822; d. 23 June 1899. 58.
  S. A., wife of P. R., b. Apr. 1816; d. Oct. 1873. 68.
  Wilkes B., b. Newberry Dist., S.C. 28 Feb. 1773; emig. to Ala.
    1829; d. 19 Aug. 1849, aged 67 yrs. 96.
Watford, Frank, b. 14 Feb. 1840; d. 9 July 1935. 12.
Watkins, Ezra P., d. 2 Nov. 1898, aged 81 yrs. 1 mo. 26 days. 44.
  Mary, wife of E. P., b. 19 Mch. 1821; d. 30 Mch. 1891. 44.
Watson, A., d. 9 Oct. 1833, aged 38 yrs. 49.
  A. J., b. 19 Feb. 1837; d. 29 Oct. 1915. 92.
  A. M., b. 1 Mch. 1845; d. 20 July 1905. 92.

E. A., wife of W. F., b. 17 May 1843; d. 1 Jan. 1883. 52.
Elisabeth, 1822-1906. 92.
Eliza, wife of Wileby, b. 1 Oct. 1824; d. 3 Feb. 1907. 92.
Elizabeth Jane, wife of William M., b. 8 Jan. 1827; d. 1 Sept. 1891. 52.
Floyd M., b. 10 Mch. 1824; d. 9 Dec. 1894. 52.
Gilbert, 1789-1885. 92.
M. H., d. 27 Apr. 1875, aged 50 yrs. 52.
Martha F., wife of J. T., b. 7 Nov. 1845; d. 7 Sept. 1873. 64.
Mary, wife of A. J., b. 21 Nov. 1837; d. 29 Jan. 1928. 92.
Nancy Proctor, wife of Gilbert, 1801-1868. 94.
Wileby, aged 88 yrs. 92.
William F., son of W. M. & E. J., b. 9 Apr. 1849; d. 26 May 1884.52.
William G., 1831-1916. 92.
William M., b. 1 Sept. 1822; d. 4 June 1883. 52.
Watt, Charles P., b. Jones Co., Ga. 27 Jan. 1827; d. 19 May 1874. 48.
Sarah Frances Ely, b. Muscogee Co., Ga. 27 Aug. 1836; d. 11 Apr. 1882. 48.
Watts, Augustus C., b. 16 Mch. 1836; d. 7 Dec. 1858. Erected by his dear wife, Sarah Watts. 93.
Henry P., b. 19 Sept. 1848; d. 19 Apr. 1922. 24.
J. H., Jr., d. 15 July 1850, aged 29 yrs. 7 mos. 22 days. 93.
John H., b. 2 Apr. 1781; d. 20 Oct. 1841, War of 1812. 93.
Mary, 1822-1908. 44.
Mary F. Carter, wife of T. C., b. 16 June 1840; mar. 23 Feb. 1860; d. 27 Mch. 1876. 44.
Theodore, son of John H. & Prudence, b. 17 Aug. 1841; d. 15 Dec. 1858. 93.
Vinson T., b. 3 Oct. 1812; d. 24 July 1883. 44.
Wyley T., b. 26 Mch. 1820; d. 27 Aug. 1853. 52.
Weathers, J. A., Rev., b. 27 Mch. 1830; d. 12 July 1901. 63.
Martha E., b. 20 Mch. 1844; d. 31 Aug. 1928. 63.
Webb, Benjamin F., b. 26 July 1848; d. 18 Oct. 1893. 44.
Caroline Elizabeth, b. Dallas Co., Ala. 1 Oct. 1830; d. 28 Nov. 1888. 44.
Foster Cornelius, M.D., b. Charles City, Va. 25 Jan. 1814; d. 2 Apr. 1888. 44.
Wells, J. E., b. 5 Sept. 1845; d. 28 Mch. 1918. 16.
Wesley, Martha, b. 16 Nov. 1827; d. 19 Apr. 1911. 39.
Peter, b. 22 Nov. 1817; d. 7 Feb. 1871. 39.
West, Christian Sylvester, b. 24 Oct. 1849; d. 31 Dec. 1921. 29.
Thomas K., d. 7 Jan. 1899, aged 56 yrs. 16.
Whiddon, David, 1793-1862. 18.
White, Hugh L., b. 22 Dec. 1837 Decatur Co., Ga.; d. 28 Sept. 1896. 59.
Mary, b. 17 Jan. 1822; d. 2 Apr. 1903. 57.
Mary Law, wife of H. C., b. Monroe Co. 17 July 1840; d. 5 Nov. 1862. 44.
Susan M., wife of Calvin, b. 14 Mch. 1829; d. 21 Jan. 1923. 57.
Susan Jane, wife of Hugh L., b. 19 Apr. 1839; d. 19 July 1883. 59.
Whitehead, James Madison, Col., b. 21 Feb. 1839; d. 30 Aug. 1898. 44.
Mary J. Bailey, wife of J. M., b. Baker Co., Ga. 18 May 1839; d. 19 Apr. 1885. 44.
Whittington, B. H., Dr., b. 4 Jan. 1848; d. 18 June 1936. 44.
J. T., b. 12 Dec. 1842; d. 25 Nov. 1921. 12.
William M., b. 21 Dec. 1848; d. 21 Aug. 1936. 32.
Whittle, Auguston F., b. 27 Feb. 1823; d. 7 July 1898. 43.
P. J., b. 18 Aug. 1828; d. 17 Jan. 1919. 43.
Wiggins, Francis, wife of W. A., b. 29 June 1848; d. 24 Aug. 1897. 69.
Joshua, b. 1818; d. 7 Dec. 1879. 85.
Lucinda, wife of Joshua, b. 27 Nov. 1818; d. 3 Oct. 1895. 85.
W. A., b. 1 Mch. 1846; d. 27 Nov. 1921, Co. F, 2 Res. Inf., CSA. 69.

Wilkerson, D.P., b. 16 May 1847; d. 6 Aug. 1914. 94.
  Emily M., wife of D. P., b. 26 Mch. 1846; d. 6 Dec. 1891. 94.
Wilkinson, Elizabeth Jane Vinson, wife of W. W., b. 22 Sept. 1839; d. 20 May 1919. 44.
  William W., b. 4 June 1828; d. 23 July 1894. 44.
Williams, Andrew, b. 1800; d. 15 May 1873. 85.
  Burten, b. 14 Mch. 1817; d. 29 Feb. 1892. 84.
  David Harry, b. 4 Apr. 1848; d. 19 Oct. 1911. 8.
  David, 1793-1862. 18.
  Elizabeth A., b. 29 Dec. 1823; d. 1 July 1879. 84.
  F. M., husband of Nancy Jane, b. 9 Apr. 1839; d. 25 Nov. 1933. 24.
  Jane, d. 18 May 1848, aged 80 yrs. 52.
  Martha, wife of E. R., b. 14 Feb. 1828; d. 25 May 1900. 94.
  Mary, d. 29 Oct. 1883, aged 67 yrs. 6 mos. 80.
  Nancy Jane, wife of F. M., b. 16 Nov. 1844; d. 29 Apr. 1905. 24.
  Philip, 1822-1912. 54.
  Rebecca, wife of Auston, b. 25 Nov. 1839; d. 31 Aug. 1898. 18.
  Rebecca, 1832-1908. 54.
  Sarah Jane Bowen, b. 12 July 1849; d. 8 July 1936. 8.
Williamson, Augusta, 1826-1916. 49.
  John W., b. 31 Jan. 1847; d. 6 Aug. 1927, Co. B 17th Ala. Inf., CSA, 64.
Willis, Annie, Mrs., b. 2 Feb. 1819; d. 25 Feb. 1909. 2.
  Sam, d. Butler Springs Sept. 1891, aged 50 yrs. (Obit).
  William, b. Marlborough Co., S. C. 8 Feb. 1813; d. 7 Dec. 1893. 2.
Wilson, David R., b. 9 May 1825; d. 22 May 1910. 81.
  Elizabeth S. V., b. Georgetown, S.C. 5 Oct. 1823; d. 20 Jan. 1893. 68.
  Julia Ann, b. 25 July 1825; d. 28 Sept. 1915. 44.
  Matilda Ann, b. 4 Feb. 1831; d. 19 May 1910. 81.
  S. Annie, 1846-1936. 68.
  Stephen Mazyck, b. Charleston, S.C. 13 July 1820; d. 5 Oct. 1880. 68.
Wimberly Bartow, b. 20 Oct. 1847; d. 3 Sept. 1891. 44.
  Mack, Sr., b. Ga. 19 Aug. 1808; d. 17 May 1885. 44.
  Rocela Langley, wife of Mack, b. 29 Sept. 1811; d. 21 Aug. 1864. 44.
  Samuel Houston, son of Mack & Rocela, b. 11 Apr. 1836; d. 21 July 1861 in 1st battle of Manassas, 4 Regt. Ala. Vol, CSA. 44.
Windham, A. L., b. 23 Apr. 1843; d. 29 May 1926, Ala. Pvt., Eufaula Lt. Arty., CSA. 44.
Winkler, August G., b. 14 Apr. 1839; d. 6 Dec. 1912. 44.
Winn, Mary Elizabeth, Mrs., d. 4 July 1898, aged 71 yrs. (Obit).
Winslow, William Augustus, b. 16 Sept. 1833; d. 16 Sept. 1906. 44.
Wirthen, Margaret Ann, wife of Thomas, b. 4 Sept. 1833; d. 31 Mch. 1859. 53.
Womack, A. M., b. 3 Feb. 1809; d. 14 Feb. 1856. 96.
  Adelia, dau. of J. L. & A. E., b. 25 July 1830; d. 28 Oct. 1833. 96.
  Agnes E., wife of Jacob L., b. 2 Oct. 1809; d. 25 May 1890. 17.
  Elizabeth L., b. 23 Jan. 1813; d. 14 Nov. 1833. 96.
  Jacob L., b. 4 Aug. 1806; d. 19 Mch. 1877. 17.
  Lewis, son of W. N. & A. J., b. 26 Feb. 1841; d. 30 Dec. 1845. 96.
  Mansel, b. 14 June 1770; d. 11 Dec. 1826. 96.
  Mary M., b. 25 Feb. 1773; d. 12 Feb. 1855. 96.
  Mattie E., wife of Thaddeus, b. 10 Feb. 1835 in LaGrange, Ga.; d. 2 Feb. 1882. 44.
  N. B., Miss, d. 14 Sept. 1876, aged 49 yrs. (Obit).
  Sarah E., b. 7 June 1831; d. 1836. 96.
  Wiley, b. LaGrange, Ga. 25 July 1839; d. 1 Mch. 1877. (Obit).
Wood, James S., b. 9 Oct. 1819; d. 26 Sept. 1871. 44.
  Mary L., wife of J. S., b. 17 June 1825; d. 19 Oct. 1886. 44.
  Richard L., b. 13 Aug. 1849; d. 28 Feb. 1882. 77.
Woodruff, Mary M. Sellers, b. near Raleigh, N.C. 17 Nov. 1817; d. 17 Oct. 1906. 44.

Wrash, Lenard, 1823-1893. 10.
Wright, Emily E., b. 11 Feb. 1838; d. 5 Dec. 1923. 44.
   Helen Mar, wife of W. A., b. 29 Dec. 1839;mar. 8 May 1856; d. 8 Feb. 1872. 68.
   J. T., b. 15 June 1836; d. 3 Sept. 1913. 44.
   James Nenan, b. 2 Jan. 1833; d. 20 Sept. 1901, Pvt., Co. A, 17 Regt. Ala. Inf., CSA. 44.
   John J., b. 27 Sept. 1836; d. 21 Oct. 1900. 44.
   John Sharp, son of William & Mary, b. 18 Nov. 1826; d. 28 Feb. 1858. 68.
   Margaret Melvina, wife of W. T., b. 30 Jan. 1839; d. 7 July 1902. 44.
   Nathan, d. 31 Oct. 1883, aged 71 yrs. (Obit).
   Rebecca, Mrs., b. 23 Apr. 1821; d. 29 Oct. 1895. 68.
   Robert R., b. 8 Feb. 1822; d. 22 May 1879. 68.
   Stephen M, d. 31 Dec.1882, Co. C, 17 Ala. Inf., CSA. 44.
   W. A., Dr., d. 6 Sept. 1876. (Obit).
   William, b. Washington Co., Ga. 15 Oct. 1797; d. 22 July 1866. 68.
   William P., b. 1 Sept. 1812; d. 15 June 1900. 51.
Yeldell, David L., son of J. A. & C. M., d. 14 Oct. 1819, aged 6 mos. 91.
   Eliza, wife of J. M., b. Abbeville Dist., S.C. 17 Nov. 1818; d. 7 May 1847. 52.
   Frances E. Powers, consort of Robert, dau. of James & Mary W. Powers, b. 30 June 1830; d. 22 May 1860. 52.
   James Leonides, b. 11 Oct. 1844; d. 6 Nov. 1846. 52.
   Joseph A., d. 10 Sept. 1856, aged 43 yrs. 5 mos. 17 days. 91.
   Lettye, dau. of Robert & Margery, d. 4 June 1852, aged 44 yrs. 52.
   M. O., wife of R. W., 1836-1859. 52.
   Margaret L., dau. of J. A. & C. M., d. 18 Jan. 1839; aged 2 yrs. 91.
   Margary E., dau. of Robert & Elizabeth, d. 10 Sept. 1855, aged 30 yrs. 52.
   Margery, wife of Robert, d. 27 May 1851, aged 78 yrs. 52.
   Mary E. Knight, wife of W. A., 1848-1897. 48.
   Robert, d. 29 July 1854, aged 76 yrs. 52.
   Robert, d. 18 Jan. 1835, aged 40 yrs. 52.
   Robert, b. Nov. 1800; d. 7 July 1865. 52.
   Susan M., b. 22 June 1805; d. 11 Aug. 1840. 52.
   W. A., b. 1 Oct. 1842; d. 19 Sept. 1906. 48.
Young, Benjamin H., Co. E, 23 Ala. Inf., CSA. 23.
   C. M., b. 13 Nov. 1849; d. 8 July 1940. 41.
   James Mason, b. S.C. 27 Jan. 1846; killed at Resaca, Ga. 15 May 1864, 33 Ala. Regt., CSA. 68.
   Mary Ann, wife of B. H., b. 1 Mch. 1839; d. 19 Apr. 1882. 80.
Zeigler, D. A., b. 16 Dec. 1822; d. 16 June 1862. 61.
   Elizabeth, d. 6 Mch. 1859, aged 74 yrs. 87.
   John Calhoun, b. 18 Nov. 1848; d. 25 June 1928. 87.
   John M., b. Orangeburg Dist., S.C. 11 Oct. 1809; d. 30 Jan. 1860. 87.
   Rachael R., wife of John M., b. Orangeburg Dist., S.C. 1 Nov. 1813; d. 1 Dec. 1886. 87.
   Sallie, dau. of John & Rachel, b. 28 Apr. 1845; d. 1 Feb. 1916. 24.
   W. H., Capt., b. Orangeburg Dist., S.C. 11 Oct. 1834; d. 20 Aug. 1894. 87.

<u>LOCATIONS OF BUTLER COUNTY CEMETERIES.</u>

1. <u>Andress Cemetery</u>. On Hwy 65 three miles North of intersection with Hwy. 10. Tsp. 10 N, Rng. 15 B, Sec. 13.
2. <u>Antioch East Church Cemetery</u>. One & one-half miles NE of Greenville on <u>Hwy 31</u>, turn North on <u>Hwy 61</u>. Cemetery located two miles from intersection on West side of road by the church. Tsp. 11 N, Rng. 15 E, Sec. 32.
3. <u>Antioch West Church Cemetery</u>. Three miles West of Bolling on North side of Hwy 28. Tsp. 9N, Rng. 13 E, Sec. 22.

4. <u>Barnes Cemetery</u>, Three & one-half miles West of intersection of Hwy 16 & I-65. Located in field on North side of rd., west of Georgiana. Tsp. 8 N, Rng. 12 E, Sec. 2.
5. <u>Barnes-Hunter graves</u>. Located in NE Butler Co. on Hwy 31 two & one-half miles So. of Hwy. 75 turn West on dirt road & follow road to end. Graves located in field on North side of road where it dead-ends at I-65. Tsp. 11 N, Rng. 15 E, Sec. 9.
6. <u>Bennett Cemetery</u>. On Hwy 16 one-half mile west of intersection with Hwy 15 turn South on Dirt road. Cemetery about one-half mile on East side of road. Tsp. 8 N, Rng. 12 E, Sec. 35.
7. <u>Benson Cemetery</u>. These graves are located near Pine Flat Methodist Church in a location not easily accessible. No road to the site. Tsp. 10 N, Rng. 12 E.
8. <u>Bethel Methodist Church Cemetery</u>. On Hwy 31 at Butler-Lowndes Co. line turn East on county road. Cemetery two & one-half miles on North side of road by the church. Tsp. 11 N, Rng. 16 E, Sec. 5.
9. <u>Old Bethel Cemetery</u>. At site of the old church on Hwy 106 just inside the Butler-Conecuh Co. line on North side of road. Tsp. 8 N, Rng. 12 E, Sec. 6.
10. <u>Bolling Cemetery</u>. One mile SW of Bolling on South side of Hwy. 28. Tsp. 9 N, Rng. 13 E, Sec. 25.
11. <u>Bragg Cemetery</u>. About twelve miles NW of Greenville on Hwy 42 across road from Bragg Hill Church. Tsp. 11 N, Rng 13 E, Sec. 30.
12. <u>Brushy Creek Cemetery</u>. Two miles East of East Chapman on Hwy 37 turn North on McGowin Lake Road. Cemetery located on both sides of road one-fourth mile from intersection. Tsp. 8 N, Rng. 14 E, Sec. 8.
13. <u>Butler Springs Baptist Church Cemetery</u>. Fifteen miles West of Greenville on Hwy. 10 turn South on Hwy 11 for three miles. Cemetery behind church on East side of road. Tsp. 10 N, Rng. 12 E, Sec. 33.
14. <u>Carter Cemetery</u>. Located in the woods about two miles South of Pine Flat Methodist Church on Hwy 10. No road to cemetery. Tsp. 10 N, Rng. 12 E, Sec. 30.
15. <u>Coleman Cemetery</u>. One-half mile NE of Manningham in the woods. No road to cemetery which has been destroyed by vandals. Only one marker left. Tsp. 11 N, Rng. 13 E, Sec. 27.
16. <u>Consolation Primitive Baptist Church Cemetery</u>. Located on unnumbered county road one mile North of Oaky Streak Church in extreme SE Butler Co. Tsp. 11 N, Rng. 15 E, Sec. 22.
17. <u>Crenshaw Cemetery</u>. Ten miles NW of Greenville on Hwy 42. Tsp. 11 N, Rng. 13 E, Sec. 29.
18. <u>Damascus Cemetery</u>. Seven miles East of Greenville on Hwy 10. Tsp. 9 N, Rng. 16 E, Sec. 6.
19. <u>Ebenezer Cemetery</u>. In Pigeon Creek Community across road from Post Office on Hwy. 59. Tsp. 8 N, Rng. 15 E, Sec. 13.
20. <u>Ebenezer-Craig Cemetery</u>. Three miles SE of Greenville on Hwy 65 @ one-fourth mile North of Halso Mill Rd., Tsp. 10 N, Rng. 15 E, Sec. 31.
21. <u>Ebenezer West Missionary Baptist Church Cemetery</u>. Two miles North of Georgiana on Hwy 25 turn West at end of blacktop onto dirt road. Cross over I-65 & turn left onto cemetery road. Tsp. 8 N, Rng. 13 E, Sec. 9.
22. <u>Elizabeth Cemetery</u>. One mile North of McKenzie. Tsp. 7 N, Rng. 13 E, Sec. 24.
23. <u>Forest Home Cemetery</u>. One block East of intersection of Hwy 7 & 46 in Forest Home. Tsp. 10 N, Rng. 12 E, Sec. 2.
24. <u>Fort Dale Cemetery</u>. Three miles North of Greenville on West side of Hwy.185. Tsp. 11 N, Rng. 14 E, Sec. 28.
25. <u>Garland Cemetery</u>. One & One-half miles North of Garland on East side of Hwy 15. Tsp. 7 N, Rng. 12 E, Sec. 14.
26. <u>Garner Cemetery</u>. Seven miles NW of Garland in field on West side of Hwy 5. Tsp. 8 N, Rng. 12 E, Sec. 30.

27. Giddens Chapel Cemetery. Four miles West of Greenville on South side of Hwy 42. Tsp. 10 N, Rng. 14 E, Sec. 8.
28. Glasgow graves. Six miles SE of Hwy 31 on Hwy 59 turn East at paved intersection. Graves two miles from intersection behind a house. Tsp. 9 N, Rng. 15 E, Sec. 23.
29. Gravel Hill Baptist Church Cemetery. On West side of Hwy 41 one-half mile South of Hwy 31 by church. Tsp. 9 N, Rng. 14 E, Sec. 2.
30. Harrison Cemetery. Five & one-half miles East of Greenville on Hwy 10 turn North on Hwy 65. Cemetery located one-half mile on right. Tsp. 10 N, Rng. 15 E, Sec. 26.
31. Hartley Cemetery. Two miles North of Greenville on Hwy 45 on West side of road. Tsp. 10 N, Rng. 14 E, Sec. 1.
32. Hopewell Church Cemetery. Five miles NE of East Chapman on Hwy 37 by Church. Tsp. 8 N, Rng. 14 E, Sec. 3.
33. Howard Cemetery. On South side of Hwy 10 one mile from Butler-Crenshaw Co. line. Tsp. 9 N, Rng. 16 E, Sec. 16.
34. Kettler Cemetery. Eleven miles East of Greenville on Hwy 10 turn South onto unnumbered county road. Cemetery two & one-half miles on West side of road. Tsp. 9 N, Rng. 16 E, Sec. 29.
35. Kilgore Cemetery. On East side of Hwy 185 about one & one-half miles South of Butler-Lowndes Co. line. Tsp. 11 N, Rng. 14 E, Sec. 11.
36. King Cemetery. Nine miles NE of Hwy 31 on Hwy 62 turn East on County road for one mile. Inside Butler-Crenshaw Co. line. Tsp. 11 N, Rng. 16 E, Sec. 9.
37. Kingsbury Cemetery. In Greenville behind home two blocks West of intersection of Hwys 185 & 10. Tsp. 10 N, Rng. 14 E, Sec. 14.
38. Leysath Cemetery. On Hwy 106 at Pine Level Church turn North onto dirt road. Cemetery @ two miles on East. Tsp. 9 N, Rng. 12 E, Sec. 30.
39. Liberty Methodist Church Cemetery. One-fourth mile South of Hwy 10 in Liberty Community. Tsp. 10 N, Rng. 14 E, Sec. 29.
40. Lloyd Cemetery. On East side of Hwy 185 two & one-half miles North of Greenville. Tsp. 10 N, Rng. 14 E, Sec. 3.
41. McClure Cemetery. On South side of Hwy 5 two miles East of Garland. Tsp. 7 N, Rng. 13 E, Sec. 19.
42. McCoy Cemetery. On Hwy 75 one & one-half miles NW of Hwy 31 near I-65. Tsp. 11 N, Rng. 15 E, Sec. 3.
43. Macedonia Cemetery. Three miles South of Industry on East side of Hwy. 45. Tsp. 7 N, Rng. 14 E, Sec. 14.
44. Magnolia Cemetery. In Greenville on Hwy 10 two blocks West of Hwy 185. Tsp. 10 N, Rng. 14 E, Sec. 22.
45. Manningham Cemetery. In Manningham Community eight miles NW of Greenville on South side of Hwy 54. Tsp. 11 N, Rng. 13 E, Sec. 34.
46. Marsh Cemetery. Three miles West of Pigeon Creek Community on un-numbered dirt road. Tsp. 8 N, Rng. 15 E, Sec. 22.
47. Milner Cemetery. In Georgiana. Tsp. 8 N, Rng. 13 E, Sec. 27.
48. Monterey Cemetery. In Monterey Community, four miles NW of Forest Home on West side of Hwy 7. Tsp. 11 N, Rng. 12 E, Sec. 29.
49. Moriah Church Cemetery. Five miles North of Greenville on Hwy 31 turn West on Hwy 64 & cross I-65. Turn North on Hwy 45. Cemetery two miles by church. Tsp. 11 N, Rng. 15 E, Sec. 7.
50. Morrow Cemetery. Three miles West of Georgiana North of Hwy. 106. Tsp. 8 N, Rng. 13 E, Sec. 17.
51. Mt. Carmel Church Cemetery. Seven miles SE of Greenville East of Hwy 59. Tsp. 9 N, Rng. 15 E, Sec. 23.
52. Mt. Moriah Baptist Church Cemetery. Four miles North of Forest Home on Hwy 7 turn West on Hwy 52. Cemetery two miles on North side of road on Butler-Wilcox Co. line. Tsp. 11 N, Rng. 12 E, Sec. 18.
53. Mt. Olive East Cemetery. On Hwy 45 four & one-half miles North of Hwy 106. Tsp. 9 N, Rng. 15 E, Sec. 31.
54. Mt. Olive Methodist Church Cemetery. On Hwy 50 one mile East of Hwy 10 in a pasture. Tsp. 10 N, Rng. 15 E, Sec. 21.

55. **Mt. Olive West Cemetery.** In Grace Community three miles West of I-65 on Hwy 5. Tsp. 7 N, Rng. 12 E, Sec. 5.
56. **Mt. Pisgah Church Cemetery.** Seven miles West of Greenville on Hwy 10 turn SE on Hwy 38. Go eight miles & turn South onto Hwy 11. By Church three & one half miles from intersection. Tsp. 9 N, Rng. 12 E, Sec. 28.
57. **Mt. Pleasant Baptist Church Cemetery.** Fifteen miles South of Greenville on Hwy 45. Tsp. 8 N, Rng. 14 E, Sec. 24.
58. **Mt. Zion Methodist Protestant Church Cemetery.** Ten miles NW of Greenville on Hwy 54. Tsp. 11 N, Rng. 13 E, Sec. 32.
59. **Mt. Zion Primitive Baptist Church Cemetery.** On Hwy 65 one & one-half miles North of Hwy 10 & @ six miles West of Greenville. Tsp. 10 N, Rng. 15 E, Sec. 23.
60. **New Prospect Cemetery.** Eight miles East of Georgiana on Hwy 106 turn North on Hwy 45. Turn East in one-half mile & cemetery located about five miles on East of road. Tsp. 8 N, Rng. 15 E, Sec. 8.
61. **Oak Bowery Primitive Baptist Church Cemetery.** Turn East on Hwy 31 one mile from Butler-Lowndes Co. line onto dirt road. Cemetery @ two miles on South of road in field. Tsp. 11 N, Rng. 16 E, Sec. 18.
62. **Oak Grove Cemetery.** Three miles East of Georgiana on Hwy 16 turn North on Hwy 37. Cemetery one-half mile on West of road by church. Tsp. 8 N, Rng. 13 E, Sec. 25.
63. **Oak Wood Cemetery.** In Georgiana. Tsp. 8 N, Rng. 13 E, Sec. 27.
64. **Oaky Streak Methodist Church Cemetery.** Twenty miles SE of Greenville on Hwy 59. Tsp. 7 N, Rng. 15 E, Sec. 27.
65. **Peagler Cemetery.** NW of Greenville on Sherling Lake Road. Graves located in the woods in a remote area. Tsp. 11 N, Rng. 14 E.
66. **Perdue Cemetery.** Three miles North of Greenville on Hwy 31 turn East on Hwy 62. Five miles from intersection. Tsp. 11 N, Rng. 16 E, Sec. 31.
67. **Pine Flat Cemetery.** Sixteen miles West of Greenville on Hwy 10. Tsp. 10 N, Rng. 12 E, Sec. 17.
68. **Pioneer Cemetery.** In Greenville across street from First Methodist Church. Tsp. 10 N, Rng. 14 E, Sec. 23.
69. **Pleasant Hill Cemetery.** Two & one-half miles West of McKenzie on Hwy 6. Tsp. 7 N, Rng. 13 E, Sec. 28.
70. **Pleasant Home Church of Christ Cemetery.** On Hwy 46 one mile North of Hwy 10 West of Greenville. Tsp. 10 N, Rng. 13 E, Sec. 14.
71. **Providence Methodist Church Cemetery.** On Hwy 15 three miles North of Hwy 106 West of Georgiana. Across road from church. Tsp. 9 N, Rng. 13 E, Sec. 26.
72. **Reddoch Cemetery.** In Liberty Community four miles West of Greenville on Hwy 10. Tsp. 10 N, Rng. 14 E, Sec. 20.
73. **Rhodes Cemetery.** On West side of Hwy 45 two miles South of Hwy 31. Tsp. 9 N, Rng. 14 E, Sec. 1.
74. **Riley Cemetery.** Five miles East of Georgiana on Hwy 16 turn South on dirt road. At first intersection turn East. Cemetery located one mile on right. Tsp. 7 N, Rng. 14 E, Sec. 9.
75. **Ringgold-Sirmon Cemetery.** To North of Hwy 46 ten miles West of Greenville. Tsp. 10 N, Rng. 13 E, Sec. 5.
76. **St. Paul Methodist Church Cemetery.** Five miles East of Greenville on Hwy 10. Tsp. 10 N, Rng. 15 E, Sec. 28.
77. **Sardis Baptist Church Cemetery.** Twelve miles SE of Greenville on Hwy 59. Tsp. 8 N, Rng. 15 E, Sec. 12.
78. **William Seale Cemetery.** Three miles West of Hwy. 185 on Hwy 42 turn South on first dirt road past Giddens Chapel. In field at end of road. Tsp. 10 N, Rng. 14 E, Sec. 18.
79. **Sellers Cemetery.** Three miles South of Georgiana. Tsp. 7 N, Rng. 13 E, Sec. 9.
80. **Shackleville Cemetery.** On North side of Hwy 38 six miles SW of Hwy 10 in Shackleville. Tsp, 9 N, Rng. 12 E, Sec. 2.

81. <u>Shiloh Primitive Baptist Church Cemetery</u>. Five miles NE of Greenville on Hwy 42 at intersection with Hwy 54. Tsp. 11 N, Rng. 13 E, Sec. 36.
82. <u>Simmons graves</u>. Across road from Shiloh Primitive Church. Tsp. 11 N, Rng. 13 E, Sec. 36.
83. <u>Sims Cemetery.</u> Three miles West of Georgiana on Hwy 106 turn North on Hwy 15. Cemetery two & one-fourth miles on West of road in woods. Tsp. 9 N, Rng. 12 E, Sec. 26.
84. <u>Smith Cemetery</u>. Two miles North of Georgiana on East side of Hwy 25. Tsp. 8 N, Rng. 13 E, Sec. 15.
85. <u>South Butler Cemetery</u>. One & one-half miles North of McKenzie & West of Hwy 31. Tsp. 7 N, Rng. 13 E, Sec. 24.
86. <u>Spring Creek Missionary Baptist Church Cemetery</u>. Turn East off Hwy 31 at Butler-Lowndes Co. line onto unnumbered road. Go three miles to end of road & turn South on Hwy 62. In two miles turn East & cemetery by church. Tsp. 11 N, Rng. 16 E, Sec. 21.
76. <u>Springhill Methodist Church Cemetery</u>. In Springhill Community by church. Tsp. 11 N, Rng. 15 E, Sec. 27.
88. <u>Stamps Cemetery</u>. On Hwy 15 one mile from Hwy 106 on West of road. Tsp 8 N, Rng. 12 E, Sec. 14.
89. <u>Stott Cemetery</u>. Two & one-half miles NW of Chapman on West of road. Tsp. 8 N, Rng. 13 E, Sec. 2.
90. <u>Thompson Cemetery.</u> Two miles North of Forest Home on Hwy 7 turn East for one-half mile. Cemetery on West of road. Tsp. 11 N, Rng. 12 E, Sec. 27.
91. <u>Traweek Cemetery</u>. On West side of Hwy 7 two & one-half miles North of Monterey. Tsp. 11 N, Rng. 12 E, Sec. 9.
92. <u>Union Cemetery</u>. Two miles East of Georgiana on Hwy 106. Tsp. 8 N, Rng. 14 E, Sec. 30.
93. <u>Watts Cemetery</u>. Fourteen miles West of Greenville on Hwy. 10 in Pine Flat Community. Tsp. 10 N, Rng. 13 E, Sec. 16.
94. <u>Wesley Chapel Methodist Church Cemetery</u>. On North of Hwy 16 five miles East of Georgiana. Tsp. 8 N, Rng. 14 E, Sec. 34.
95. <u>Giles Williams Cemetery</u>. At end of Hwy 25 North of Georgiana turn West onto dirt road and Cross I-65. Cemetery one mile from Hwy on right of road in woods. Tsp. 8 N, Rng. 13 E, Sec. 4.
96. <u>Womack Cemetery</u>. On North side of Hwy 54 sixteen miles NW of Greenville. Tsp. 11 N, Rng. 13 E, Sec. 19.
97. <u>Greenville's Soldiers Graveyard</u>. This cemetery no longer exists. It was destroyed at the time of the expansion of a factory and the remains of all the soldiers were placed in a common grave in Magnolia Cemetery.
* The inscriptions followed by an asterisk were obtained from an article written by Mrs. I. M. P. Henry on May 2, 1872 in The Greenville Advocate. All of these men so designated were Confederate Soldiers, and were interred in either Pioneer, Magnolia or Greenville's Soldiers Cemeteries.

UNITED STATES PATENT OFFICE
Joseph R. Abrams, of Greenville, Alabama
Improvement in Grave-Mounds

Specification forming part of letters Patent No. 151,070, dated May 19, 1874: application filed March 21, 1874.

To all whom it may concern:
    Be it known that I, Joseph R. Abrams, of Greenville, in the county of Butler, in the State of Alabama, have invented a new and improved Grave-Mound; and I do hereby declare that the following is a full, clear, and exact description of the same, reference being had to the accompany-

ing drawings forming a part of this specification, in which-
Figure 1 is a side elevation partly broken out. Fig. 2 is a bottom view, one elliptical ring being attached to the dome.

The invention related to means whereby the dome of a grave-mound may be adapted to graves of different length and size by fitting thereto successively increasing elliptical pieces, as hereinafter fully described, and pointed out in the claim.

"A" represents the dome of a grave-mound, and "B" subjacent and elliptical supporting pieces, which are made independent and of different size, but all bearing a definite shape relatively to the said dome and to each other. I case the dome with inner lugs "a a", placed preferably, but not necessarily, at the ends, and also case each size of the elliptical pieces "B" separately, and with corresponding lugs "b b". By means of these lugs and the clamp screws "C", several sections are attached firmly together. A party has thus only to select the particular design or pattern of dome which pleases his taste and by connecting these with more or less of the subjacent elliptical pieces, the mound is readily adapted to the size of grave required for the deceased. Ordinarily various sizes of dome and subjacent pieces were necessarily required in order to meet the public demand.

My invention constitutes an improvement in grave-mounds, which is not only convenient and much less expensive to the dealer in articles of the kind, but equally so to the public.

Having thus described my invention, what I claim is--
1. A grave-mound, having dome "A" and different sized subjacent elliptical pieces "B", all independent of each other, but relatively arranged as and for the purpose described.
2. The combination of dome, lugs "a a", and corresponding lugs "b b" of pieces "B", as and for the purpose described.

Witnesses:

Solon C. Kemon
Chas. A. Pettit

Grave of an infant in Oak Wood Cemetery, Georgiana, Ala. Made by J. R. Abrams and inscribed Pat'd. Oct. 7 & May 19, '74.

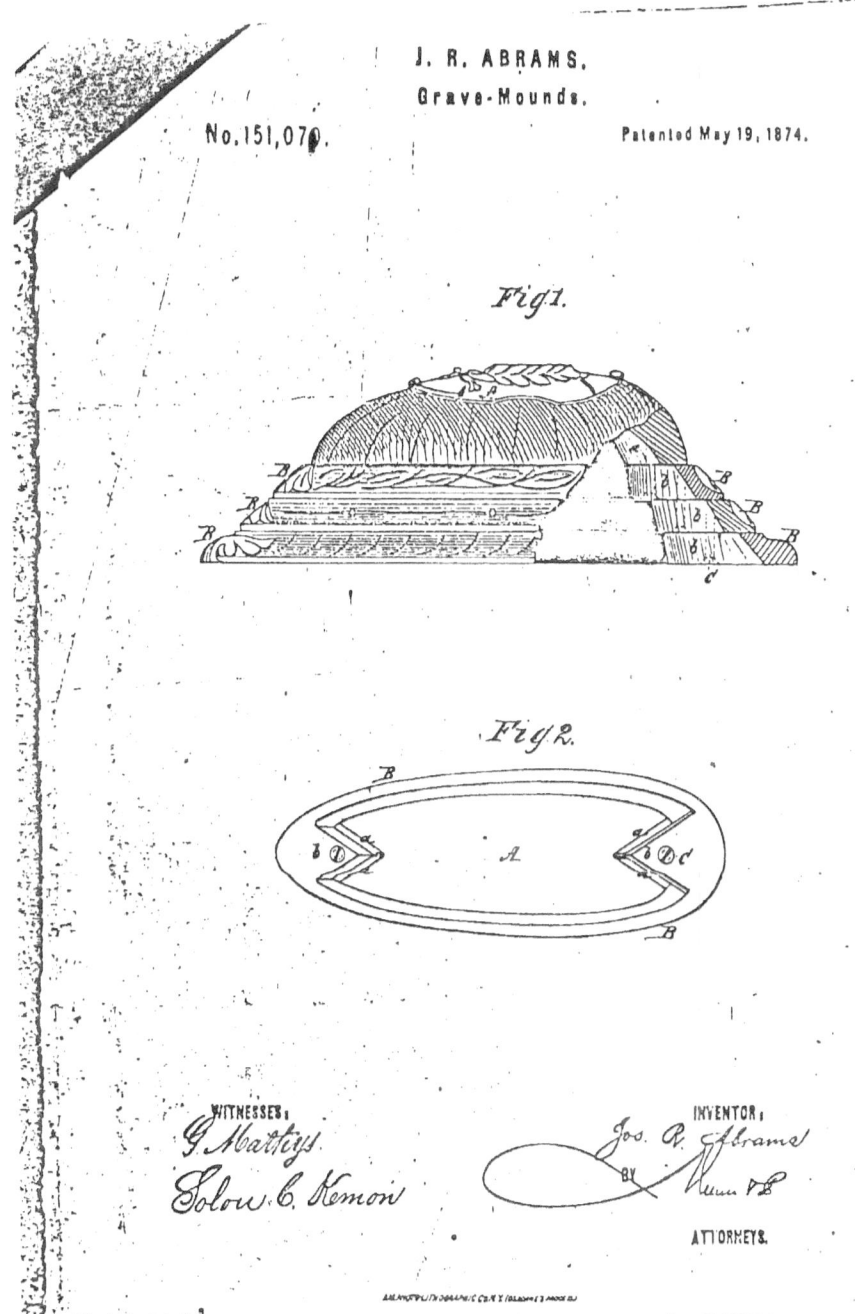

CHAPTER 5.

INCOME TAX FOR 1865-66

The Internal Revenue Act of July 1, 1862 was intended to "provide Internal Revenue to support the Government and to pay interest on the Public Debt." Monthly specific and ad valorem duties were placed on manufactures, articles and products ranging from ale to zinc. Monthly taxes were levied on the gross receipts of transportation companies; on interest paid on bonds; on surplus funds accumulated by financial institutions and insurance companies; on gross receipts from auction sales; and on sales of slaughtered cattle, hog and sheep. Annual licenses were required for all trades and occupations, and annual duties were placed on carriages, yachts, billiard tables and gold and silver plate. All income in excess of $600 was taxed. This tax list was prepared for microfilming by John Fawcett.

Following the name of the person being taxed is the place of residence, reason for being taxed and the amount of tax paid.

Arms, E. B., Garland, Retail Dealer, $10.00
Ardis, W. H., Greenville, Retail Dealer, $10.00
    Common Carrier, $10.00
Ashcraft, John, Manningham, Miller, $10.00
Abrams, J. R. & G. H., Greenville, Wholesale Dealer, $50.00.
    Gross Receipts, $16,000 @ 1%, $160.00.
Batcheller, W. C., Greenville, Retail Dealer, $10.00.
Bedell, W. H., Greenville, Hotel Keeper, $900 rentals, $45.00.
Benbow, A., Greenville, Miller, $10.00
Bragg, T. W., Greenville, Physician, $10.00.
Bement & Burbank, Greenville, Cotton, 7 bales, 3,390 tons @3¢ $101.70.
    Wholesale Dealer, $50.00.
    Gross Receipts, $2,290 @ 1% $22.90.
Bell, I. E., Greenville, Common Carrier, $10.00.
Brown, Ed, Manningham, Farmer, $10.00.
Bear, Lewis, Greenville, Retail Dealer, $10.00.
Burnett & Smith, Greenville, Wholesale Dealer, $50.00.
    Cotton, 10 bales, 5,136 tons @ 3¢, $154.08.
Braunner, C. C., Greenville, Retail Dealer, $10.00.
Barge, T. H., Monterey, Retail Dealer, $10.00.
Broughton, J. T., Greenville, Physician, $10.00.
Busby & Porter, Greenville, Manufacturing, $10.00.
Bear, David, Greenville, Sugar Manufacturer, 12,500 lbs. @ 4¢, $500.00.
Bail, David, Greenville, Lawyer, $10.00.
Brown, J. G. & Co., Manningham, Retail Liquor Dealer, $25.00.
Burnett & Smith, Greenville, Gross Receipts, $20,000 @ 1%, $200.00.
Brinkman, Frank, Greenville, Retail Liquor Dealer. $25.00.
Cook, W. H., Greenville, Physician, $10.00.
Chandler, H. B. & Co., Greenville, Retail Dealer, $10.00.
Campbell, B. C., Greenville, Common Carrier, $10.00.
Crenshaw, W. H., Greenville, Lawyer, $10.00.
Cannon, C. F., Greenville, Photographer, $10.00.

Caldwell, H. H. & Co., Greenville, Apothacary, $10.00.
Cook, R. F., Greenville, Lawyer, $10.00.
Cushing, I. R., South Butler, Physician, $10.00.
Colvin & Payne, Greenville, Retail Dealer, $10.00.
Chambliss, D. E., Greenville, Physician, $10.00.
Dotzheimer, W., Greenville, Retail Liquor Dealer, $25.00.
Dunklin & Steiner, Greenville, Wholesale Dealer, $50.00.
    Patton, $97.00 @ 3%, $2.91.
    Gross Receipts, $32,000 @1%, $320.00.
Donald, J. G., Greenville, Physician, $10.00.
Dunklin, J. H., Greenville, Apothacary, $10.00.
Duncan, J. W., Greenville, Wagon Mfg., $300.00 @1%, $15.00.
Dulin, A. B., Greenville, Cotton, 17 bales, 7,835 lbs. @3%, $225.05.
Dunklin & Steiner, Greenville, Gross Receipts, $24,500 @1%, $245.00.
Dotman, C. W., Greenville, Labor Agency, $10.00.
Dendy, W. M., Greenville, Builder & Contractor, $10.00.
Day, Joseph, Greenville, Manufacturing, $10.00.
Evans, Teat & Co., Manningham, Wholesale Dealer, $50.00.
    Manufacturer, $10.00.
Frear, J. B. & Co., Greenville, Retail Dealer, $25.00.
    Retail Dealer, $10.00.
Franklin, Benjamin, Greenville, Wholesale, $66.00 @2%, $1.32.
    Farmer, $10.00
    Shoes, 143 pair, @5¢, $7.15.
    Leather, 27 lbs. @5%, $1.35.
Flood, Thomas, Greenville, Retail Dealer, $25.00.
Farris, Kamp & Co., Greenville, Retail Liquor Dealer, $16.67.
    Apothacary, $6.67.
Finch & Melton, Greenville, Retail Liquor Dealer, $16.67.
Ferguson, D. T., Manningham, Leather, 30 lbs. @5%, $1.50.
Ford, W. A., Greenville, Mfg., $10.00.
Gregory, Henry, Greenville, Common Carrier, $10.00.
Gaffney, S(?). F., Greenville, Eating House, $10.00.
Gamble, John, Greenville, Lawyer, $10.00.
Gibson, W. & C., Greenville, Keeper Stallion, $10.00.
Giles, Erwin, Greenville, Gross Receipts, $178.00 @2%, $3.56.
Gray, Richard H., Greenville, ___ Dealer, $5.00.
Gass, D. John, Greenville, Cotton, 48 bales, 24,248 lbs. @3¢, $727.44.
Herbert, H. A., Greenville, Lawyer, $10.00.
Hightower, J. R., Greenville, Retail Dealer, $10.00.
Henry, George L., Greenville, Lawyer, $10.00.
Hutton, J. M., Greenville, Common Carrier, $10.00.
Hawkins, Thomas, Greenville, Miller, $10.00.
Hartley, J. S., Greenville, Miller, $10.00.
Hendrix, W. A., Greenville, Retail Dealer, $10.00.
Herbert, C. B., Greenville, Physician, $10.00.
Hyde, James, Monterey, Mfg., $10.00.
Hamil, J., Greenville, Contractor & Builder, $6.67.
Hawthorn, A. J., Greenville, Retail Liquor Dealer, $14.58.
Hightower, J. R., Greenville, Retail Liquor Dealer, $7.50.
Harrison & Payne, Greenville, Builder & Contractor, $7.50.
Harris, J. W., Greenville, Mfg., $7.50.
Hamill, A. A., Greenville, Builder & Contractor, $7.50.
Jefcoat, W. J., Sal Soda, Mfg., $10.00.
Johnson, W. M., Greenville, Livery Stable, $10.00.
Jones, Rebecca, Mrs., Greenville, Shoes, 28 pr. @5¢, $1.40
    Mfg., $10.00.
    Leather, 147 lbs. @5%, $7.35.
Jones, J. A., Greenville, Retail Dealer, $25.00.
Jones, J. A. & Co., Greenville, Retail Dealer, $10.00.
    Billiard Table, $10.00.

Jordan & Knight, Greenville, Retail Dealer, $10.00.
Joyner, J. L. & Co., Garland, Retail Dealer, $10.00.
Jones & Pullam, Georgiana, Retail Dealer, $10.00.
Jordan, & McPherson, Greenville, Mfg., $5.00.
Jones & Trawick, Monterey, Retail Liquor Dealer, $12.50.
Keating, W. W., Middville, Mfg., $10.00.
Kelley & Cole, Manningham, Mfg., $10.00.
Keefer, Jas., Greenville, Mfg., $10.00.
Kirpatrick, T. N(?)., Georgiana, Retail Liquor Dealer, $20.00.
Knight, L. W., Greenville, Peddler, $7.50.
Knight, C. W., Greenville, Wholesale Liquor Dealer, $50.00.
Lloyd, C. C., Greenville, Physician, $10.00.
Leatherwood & Stanley, Greenville, Printers, $10.00.
Lyman & Goldsmith, Greenville, Gross Receipts, $15,000 @ 1%, $15.00.
    Gross Receipts, $17,000 @1%, $17.00.
    Wholesale Liquor Dealer, $50.00.
Lane, M. C., Greenville, Lawyer, $10.00.
Luckie, E. J., Monterey, Mfg., $10.00.
Lewis & Wade, Greenville, Retail Dealer, $10.00.
Locklear, W. W., Greenville, Mfg., $7.50.
Lanier, F. M., Greenville, Real Estate Dealer, $7.50.
Mallett, Dewing and Co., Greenville, Wholesale Liquor Dealer, $37.50.
Mallett, Demming & Co., Wholesale Dealer, $50.00.
Mallett, J. M., Greenville, Hotel Keeper, $500.00., $35.00.
Milner, J. T., Greenville, Wholesale Dealer, $50.00.
    Mfg., $10.00.
Miller, W. J. & Co., Greenville, Wholesale Dealer, $50.00.
McMullen, J. D., Greenville, Real Estate Agent, $10.00.
    Common Carrier, $10.00.
Morris & Wright, Greenville, Mfg., $10.00.
    Increased Value, $636.00 @5%, $31.80.
Murphy, R. J., Greenville, Physician, $10.00.
Mills, Thomas H., Greenville, Physician, $10.00.
Mills, R. M., Greenville, Mfg., $10.00.
McKensie, Charles, Greenville, Mfg., $10.00.
Milner, B. C. & Co., Greenville, Wholesale Dealer, $33.33.
    Mfg., $6.67.
McCan & Perry, Greenville, Butcher, $3.33.
May, W. P., Greenville, Retail Liquor Dealer, $10.42.
Morgan, David, Greenville, Saddler, $192.00, $9.60.
Norrell, J. M., Greenville, Retail Dealer, $25.00.
O'Connor, J., Greenville, Tailor, $10.00.
Owens & Anderson, Greenville, Retail Liquor Dealer, $25.00.
Owens, Randolph, Greenville, Butcher, $10.00.
Owens & Burns, Greenville, Mfg., $10.00.
O'Connor, M., Greenville, Mfg., $10.00.
O'Brien, M. & Co., Georgiana, Retail Dealer, $25.00.
Padgett, J. A., Greenville, Retail Dealer, $10.00.
Payne, S. C., Greenville, Keeper of Stallion, $10.00.
Posey, A. F., Greenville, Claim Accounts, $4.17.
Pryor, W. C., Oakey Streak, Physician, $10.00.
Perkins, J. M., Greenville, Common Carrier, $10.00.
Perry, J. F., Greenville, Retail Liquor Dealer, $12.50.
Perkins, J. L., Greenville, Retail Dealer, $10.00.
Potter, T. F., Greenville, Mfg., $10.00.
    Tin Ware, $29.00 @5%, $1.45.
Parmer, W. F., Greenville, Retail Liquor Dealer, $25.00.
Parmer, D. B., Greenville, Lawyer, $10.00.
Porter, Benj. F., Greenville, Lawyer, $10.00.
Peagler, Isaac, Greenville, Mfg., $10.00.

Powell, J. L., Greenville, Lawyer, $10.00.
Pentticost, L. M., Greenville, Physician, $10.00.
Powers & Etheridge, Greenville, Retail Dealer, $25.00.
Parmer & Webb, Greenville, Apothecaries, $10.00.
Parmer, D. C., Greenville, Physician, $10.00.
Parmer, T. J., Greenville, Physician, $10.00.
Perry, Robert, Greenville, Butcher, $3.33.
Potter, I. F., Greenville, Tin Ware, $175.00 @ 5%, $8.75.
Potts, George C., Greenville, Increased Value, $1,765 @ 5%, $88.25.
Potter, F. T., Greenville, Tin Ware, $125.00 @ 5%, $6.25.
Robertson, I. W. & Co., Greenville, Retail Dealer, $10.00.
Rhodes, John, Garland, Retail Dealer, $10.00.
Rushton, O. C., Fullers Cross Rds., Retail Dealer, $10.00.
Robinson & Powell, Georgiana, Retail Dealer, $10.00.
Reid, A. M. & Co., Greenville, Wholesale Liquor Dealer, $66.67.
      Cotton, 10 bales, 4,788 lbs. @ 3¢, $143.64.
      Cotton, 16 bales, 7,597 lbs @3¢, $227.91.
Rhodes, William, Greenville, $2.50.
Riley & Cooley, Greenville, Builder & Contractor, $7.50.
Rouse, Daniel, Greenville, Mfg., $7.50.
Sherwood, J. J., Greenville, Retail Liquor Dealer, $25.00.
Shally (?), M. S., Greenville, Butcher, $5.00.
Stanley, R. H., Greenville, Retail Dealer, $10.00.
Simons, J. R., Manningham, Mfg., $10.00.
Stallings, Thomas D., Greenville, Physician, $10.00.
Simpson, J. B., Manningham, Retail Dealer, $25.00.
Sheppard, A. R., Greenville, Physician, $10.00.
Smith, P. M. & E. C., Georgiana, Retail Dealer, $10.00.
Seawell, W. B. & Co., Greenville, Auction Sales, $5.61.
Stewart, J. H., Greenville, Retail Liquor Dealer, $12.50.
Shuster, Jno. B., Greenville, Auctioneer, $10.00.
Tulin, A. B. & Co., Greenville, Retail Dealer, $10.00.
Tonaf (?), G. & Co., Greenville, Retail Dealer, $25.00.
Thames, W. H., Greenville, Farmer, $10.00.
Thigpen, Job, Monterey, Physician, $10.00.
Trawick, T. M. G., Monterey, Mfg., $10.00.
Tompson, W. A., Monterey, Mfg., $10.00.
Thames, W. H., Greenville, Leather, $76.00 @5%, $3.80.
Teague, A. A. & Co., Greenville, Cotton, 9,226 lbs. @ 2%, $276.68.
Thames, W. C., Greenville, Leather, $193.00 @ 5%, $9.65.
Wood, W. J. & J. S., Greenville, Wholesale Dealer, $50.00.
Webb, F. C., Greenville, Physician, $10.00.
Wright & Rouse, Greenville, Mfg., $10.00.
Wall, D. C., Monterey, Physician, $10.00.
Walton, W. A., Greenville, Physician, $6.67.
Wilkinson, W. W., Greenville, Retail Liquor Dealer, $22.92.
Wright, W. M., Greenville, Retail Liquor Dealer, $12.50.
Yeldell, J. R., Monterey, Mfg., $10.00.
Yeldell, J. W., Monterey, Retail Dealer, $25.00.
Yeldell, A. R. & Co., Greenville, Retail Dealer, $10.00.

Examined and found correct by A. C. White, Deputy Collector,
                     Theo. H. Kimball
                     S. W. Lanier, Assistant Assessor
                     A. M. McDowell, Assessor

A compilation of the months in 1866.

Following each name is the community lived in, the article taxed, value of article and amount of tax paid.

Abrams, Henry S., Greenville, piano, $200.00, $2.00.
    Carriage, $100.00, $1.00.
    Income, $2,595, $129.75.
    Gold watch, $100.00, $1.00.
    2 Buggies, $200.00, $2.00.
Ardis, John, Greenville, 2 carriages, $400.00, $1.00.
Andrews, Jeremiah, Greenville, carriage, $100.00, $1.00.
Andrews, S. F., Greenville, buggy, $100.00, $1.00.
Ardis, W. H., Greenville, buggy, $100.00, $1.00.
    Watch, $100.00, $1.00.
Archer, W., Greenville, buggy, $100.00, $1.00.
Abrams, J. R., Greenville, income, $2,595, $129.75.
    Buggy, $200.00, $2.00.
    Watch, $200.00. $2.00.
Abram, H. S., Greenville, Income, $2,595, $129.75.
Butler, Edmond, Ft. Deposit, Carriage, $100.00, $1.00.
Barrett, Joshua, Greenville, buggy, $100.00, $1.00.
Barrett, A. J., Greenville, buggy, $100.00, $1.00.
Binion, Elizabeth, Garland, buggy, $100.00, $1.00.
Brooks, John, Garland, buggy, $100.00, $1.00.
Bowdon, Edward, Greenville, carriage, $200.00, $2.00.
Bowden, W. B., Greenville, buggy, $100.00, $1.00.
Baugh, Edward, Greenville, carriage, $200.00, $2.00.
    Watch, $100.00, $1.00.
Blackmond, William, Starlington, carriage, $100.00, $1.00.
Bishop, S., Greenville, carriage, $200.00, $2.00.
Butts, Benjamin, Manningham, buggy, $100.00, $1.00.
Bedgood, R., Greenville, buggy, $100.00, $1.00.
Broughton, J. T., Greenville, buggy, $100.00, $1.00.
    Watch, $100,00, $1.00.
    Piano, $200.00, $2.00.
Burnett, T. J., Greenville, buggy, $100.00, $1.00.
    Carriage, $300.00, $3.00.
    Watch, $100.00, $1.00.
Brent, Thomas W., Greenville, silver plate, 145 ozs., $7.25.
    Watch, $100.00, $1.00.
Bolling, S. J., Greenville, 2 carriages $400.00, $4.00.
    Gold watch, $200.00, $2.00.
    Income, $36.00, $1.80.
Bowen, Edward, Manningham, 2 carriages, $400.00, $4.00.
    Income, $1,180.00, $59.00
    Buggy, $100.00, $1.00.
    Watch, $100.00, $1.00.
Bennett, T., Greenville, carriage, $200.00, $2.00.
    2 Watches, $200.00, $2.00.
    Piano, $500.00, $6.00.
Barge, J. T., Greenville, income, $900.00, $45.00.
    Watch, $100.00, $1.00.
Bear, Lewis, Greenville, income, $115.00, $.75.
Barge, T. H., Greenville, watch, $100.00, $1.00.
Bronner, C. C., Greenville, watch, $100.00, $1.00.
Burke, H. F., Georgiana, watch, $100.00, $1.00.
    Buggy, $100.00, $1.00.
Crenshaw, F. W., Manningham, income, $127.78, $6.39.
    Carriage, $100,00, $1.00.
    2 Watches, $200.00, $2.00.
    Piano, $200.00, $2.00.

Crenshaw, W. H., Georgiana, carriage, $100.00, $1.00.
    Watch, $100.00, $1.00.
    Piano, $200.00, $2.00.
    Income, $80.00, $4.00.
Crenshaw, Mary, Mrs., Manningham, buggy, $100.00, $1.00.
Crittenden, John, Oaky Streak, carriage, $200.00, $2.00.
    Income, $3,243.88, $162.19.
Crews, A. M., Greenville, income
Collen, Ross, Greenville, carriage, $100.00, $1.00.
Carter, Frances, Mrs., Butler Springs, buggy, $100.00, $1.00.
Carter, Alfred W., Butler Springs, buggy, $100.00, $1.00.
Cheatham, Peter, Greenville, buggy, $100.00, $1.00.
    Watch, $100.00, $1.00.
Cheatham, N. A., Mrs., Greenville, buggy, $100.00, $1.00.
Carter, R. W., Greenville, carriage, $300.00, $3.00.
Caldwell, A. M., Greenville, buggy, $100.00, $1.00.
    Watch, $100.00, $1.00.
    Piano, $400.00, $4.00.
Cook, J. B., Greenville, buggy, $100.00, $1.00.
Cook, R. W., Greenville, buggy, $100.00, $1.00.
Crenshaw, Thomas, Manningham, income, $640.00, $32.00.
    Buggy, $100.00, $1.00.
    Watch, $200.00, $2.00.
Caldwell, J. C., Greenville, income, $4,400.00, $220.00.
    Income, $3,711.50, $371.15.
Dunklin, Joseph, Greenville, watch, $200.00, $2.00.
    Davidson, C., Greenville, buggy, $100.00, $1.00.
    Watch, $100.00, $1.00.
Day, Joseph, Greenville, carriage, $200.00, $2.00.
Donald, J. G., Monterey, watch, $100.00, $1.00.
Dukes, J. G., Monterey, watch, $100.00, $1.00.
Dean, J. J., Garland, buggy, $100.00, $1.00.
Demming, John, Greenville, buggy, $100.00, $1.00.
    Watch, $100.00, $1.00.
    Income, @75.00, $13.75.
Dunklin, D. G., Greenville, watch, $100.00, $1.00.
    Buggy, $100.00, $1.00.
Ellsworth, E. L., Greenville, 2 Watches, $200.00, $2.00.
    Piano, $400.00, $4.00.
    Silver plate, 76 ozs., $3.80.
    Carriage, $200.00, $2.00.
Evans, J. W., Forest Home, income, $244.00, $12.20.
    Buggy, $100.00, $1.00.
    Carriage, $200.00, $2.00.
Evans, Holden, Forest Home, income, $244.00, $12.20.
    Watch, $100.00, $1.00.
Fail, W., Greenville, buggy, $100.00, $1.00.
Florence, T., Oakey Streak, carriage, $200.00, $2.00.
Failes, E., Oakey Streak, buggy, $100.00, $1.00.
Ferrell, D. B., Greenville, buggy, $100.00, $1.00.
Flowers, J. J., Greenville, buggy, $100.00, $1.00.
Fickling, Isabella, Mrs., Greenville, $100.00, $1.00.
Freeman, Newton, Greenville, income, $300.00, $15.00.
    Buggy, $100.00, $1.00.
Farrer, J., Greenville, income, $2,684.45, $134.22.
    Watch, $100.00, $1.00.
    Piano, $200.00, $2.00.
Flood, Thomas, Greenville, watch, $100.00, $1.00.
Golson, I. (or J.), Ft. Deposit, buggy, $100.00, $1.00.
Graydon, A. S., Graydon's X Rd., buggy, $100.00, $1.00.

Graham, W. P., South Butler, buggy, $100.00, $1.00.
Gamble, J., Greenville, watch, $100.00, $1.00.
Goldsmith, Isabella, Mrs., Greenville, carriage, $200.00, $2.00.
Gaffney, D. F., Greenville, watch, $100.00, $1.00.
    Buggy, $100.00, $1.00.
Goldsmith, W. H., Greenville, income, $3,929.00, $196.45.
Glasgow, John R., Greenville, piano, $400.00, $1.00.
    Watch, $200.00, $2.00.
Gibson, Robert C., Greenville, buggy, $100.00, $1.00.
Graham, J. A., Greenville, carriage, $200.00, $2.00.
    Piano, $400.00, $4.00.
Gailliard, J., Three Runs, buggy, $100.00, $1.00.
Goldsmith, J. M (W?)., Greenville, 2 Watches, $200.00, $2.00.
    Piano, $200.00, $2.00.
    Income, $831.50, $41.58.
Gibson, H. T., Greenville, income, $85.00, $4.25.
    Piano, $200.00, $2.00.
    Watch, $200.00, $2.00.
Gregory, Susan, Mrs., Greenville, income, $2,198.00, $109.50.
    Buggy, $100.00, $1.00.
    Silver Plate, 32 ozs., $1.60.
    Piano, $200.00, $2.00.
Goldsmith, M. C., Ft. Deposit, buggy, $100.00, $1.00.
Gafford, A. F., Greenville, buggy, $100.00, $1.00.
Gandy, A., Garland, income, $1,741.00, $87.05.
    2 Buggies, $400.00, $4.00.
    Piano, $200.00, $2.00.
    Watch, $100.00, $1.00.
Gibson, W. L., Graydon's X Rds., buggy, $100.00, $1.00.
Goldsmith, J. B., Greenville, 2 buggies, $400.00, $4.00.
    Watch, $100.00, $1.00.
Gafford, S. F., Greenville, buggy, $100.00, $1.00.
    Watch, $200.00, $2.00.
Goldsmith, G. M., Greenville, buggy, $100.00, $1.00.
Gildcrist, John, Greenville, buggy, $100.00, $1.00.
Gholson, Jno., Ft. Deposit, buggy, $100.00, $1.00.
Gasgon, Jno., Greenville, buggy, $100.00, $1.00.
Golay, Albert, Greenville, watch, $100.00, $1.00.
    Piano, $200.00, $2.00.
    Income, $831.50, $41.58.
Garthy, J. Y., Greenville, watch, $100.00, $1.00.
Garrison, J. W., Mrs., Greenville, buggy, $100.00, $1.00.
Harrison, W., Greenville, buggy, $100.00, $1.00.
Hartley, J. S., Greenville, watch, $100.00, $1.00.
Harrold, L., Greenville, buggy, $100.00, $1.00.
Harrison, M. A., Mrs., Greenville, buggy, $100.00, $1.00.
Hayley, W., Greenville, buggy, $100.00, $1.00.
    Watch, $100.00, $1.00.
Hudson, E., Greenville, buggy, $100.00, $1.00.
Henry, J. R., Greenville, carriage, $200.00, $2.00.
    Watch, $100.00, $1.00.
    Piano, $200.00, $2.00.
Holland, James, Greenville, carriage, $100.00, $1.00.
Hulong, E. F., Greenville, carriage, $100.00, $1.00.
Hartley, W. F., Greenville, watch, $100.00, $1.00.
Howard, J. W., Greenville, buggy, $100.00, $1.00.
Herbert, C. B., Greenville, buggy, $100.00, $1.00.
Herbert, H. A., Greenville, buggy, $100.00, $1.00.
    Watch, $100.00, $1.00.
    Piano, $200.00, $2.00.

Henry, George L., Greenville, watch, $100.00, $1.00.
Hawkins, Jefferson, Greenville, buggy, $100.00, $1.00.
Hutchins, T. W., Greenville, buggy, $200.00, $2.00.
Josey, E. S., Greenville, buggy, $100.00, $1.00.
Jones, Rebecca, Mrs., Greenville, buggy, $100.00, $1.00.
    Watch, $100.00, $1.00.
Jones, J. A., Monterey, watch, $200.00, $2.00.
Kirkpatrick, T. L., Greenville, buggy, $200.00, $2.00.
    Piano, $400.00, $4.00.
Kirkpatrick, R. W., buggy, $100.00, $1.00.
Kettler, Thomas S., Greenville, buggy, $100.00, $1.00.
    Watch, $100.00, $1.00.
Kingsbury, Jno., Greenville, buggy, $100.00, $1.00.
    Watch, $100.00, $1.00.
King, T. C., Greenville, buggy, $100.00, $1.00.
Knight, E. T., Mrs., Monterey, watch, $100.00, $1.00.
    Carriage, $200.00, $2.00.
Lane, M. C., Greenville, buggy, $100.00, $1.00.
    Watch, $100.00, $1.00.
    Piano, $200.00, $2.00.
Ley, R. S., Greenville, buggy, $100.00, $1.00.
Lyman, P. C., Greenville, buggy, $100.00, $1.00.
    Watch, $100.00, $1.00.
Layseth, J., Greenville, buggy, $100.00, $1.00.
Lockhart, J. C., Greenville, buggy, $100.00, $1.00.
Lowry, Jas., Greenville, buggy, $100.00, $1.00.
Luckie, E. J., Monterey, watch, $100.00, $1.00.
Milner, J. T., Greenville, 2 buggies, $200.00, $2.00.
    4 Watches, $200.00, $4.00.
    Piano, $200.00, $2.00.
McMillen, J. S., Greenville, watch, $100.00, $1.00.
McQueen, J. C., Greenville, buggy, $100.00, $1.00.
    Watch, $100.00, $1.00.
    Piano, $200.00, $2.00.
Mash, J. S., Greenville, buggy, $100.00, $1.00.
McDaniel, A., Ft. Deposit, buggy, $100.00, $1.00.
Murphy, Wilson, Sr., Greenville, income, $174.04, $8.70.
    Buggy, $100.00, $1.00.
    Watch, $100.00, $1.00.
Mash, Nathan, Greenville, buggy, $100.00, $1.00.
Milner, E. C., Starlington, buggy, $100.00, $1.00.
Martin, Green, Greenville, buggy, $100.00, $1.00.
McFarland, A. A., Greenville, buggy, $100.00, $1.00.
McTier, J. C., Greenville, buggy, $100.00, $1.00.
McKee, J. P., Admn., Monterey, buggy, $100.00, $1.00.
    Carriage, $300.00, $3.00.
Mallett, J. W., Greenville, buggy, $100.00, $1.00.
    2 Watches, $200.00, $2.00.
Miller, W. A., Greenville, buggy, $100,00, $1.00.
    Watch, $100.00, $1.00.
McCann, A., Greenville, buggy, $100.00, $1.00.
Murphy, Wilson, Jr., Greenville, buggy, $100.00, $1.00.
    Piano, $200.00, $2.00.
Newton, Thomas, Greenville, buggy , $100.00, $1.00.
Newton, L. C., Greenville, buggy, $100.00, $1.00.
Owens, T. C., Greenville, buggy, $100.00, $1.00.
Oglesby, G. T., Greenville, buggy, $100.00, $1.00.
    2 Watches, $200.00, $2.00.
Oliver, A. P., Greenville, watch, $200.00, $2.00.
    Income, $44.26, $2.21.

Perkins, E. A., Greenville, watch, $200.00, $2.00.
Payne, T. J., Greenville, piano, $200.00, $2.00.
Perryman, W. R., Greenville, carriage, $200.00, $2.00.
    Watch, $200.00, $2.00.
Posey, A. F., Greenville, piano, $200.00, $2.00.
Peagler, A., Manningham, buggy, $200.00, $2.00.
Parmer, T. W., Greenville, buggy, $100.00, $1.00.
Farmer, T. J., Greenville, watch, $100.00, $1.00.
    Buggy, $100.00, $1.00.
    Income, $119.35, $5.97.
Palmore, M., Monterey, carriage, $100.00, $1.00.
Payne, J. S., Greenville, carriage, $100.00, $1.00.
Perdue, J. A., Greenville, carriage, $100.00, $1.00.
    Watch, $100.00, $1.00.
Perry, Robert, Greenville, buggy, $100.00, $1.00.
Peagler, D. S., Greenville, buggy, $100.00, $1.00.
Peagler, M., Manningham, buggy, $100.00, $1.00.
    Watch, $100.00, $1.00.
Pryor, W. D., Oaky Streak, watch, $100.00, $1.00.
Pryor, A. W., Greenville, buggy, $100.00, $1.00.
    Watch, $100.00, $1.00.
Perkins, J. S., Greenville, income, $200.00, $10.00.
Perkins, J. A., Greenville, buggy, $100.00, $1.00.
Presley, Allen, South Butler, buggy, $100.00, $1.00.
Perritt, A., Greenville, buggy, $100.00, $1.00.
Porter, B. F., Greenville, piano, $200.00, $2.00.
Rudolph, Jno., Greenville, buggy, $100.00, $1.00.
    Watch, $200.00, $2.00.
    Piano, $200.00, $2.00.
Rodgers, Joseph, Greenville, Carriage, $200.00, $2.00.
Reed, H. H., Greenville, watch, $100.00, $1.00.
Roberts, L. C., Greenville, watch, $100.00, $1.00.
Rhodes, A., Greenville, $100.00, $1.00.
Riley, T. D. N., Greenville, buggy, $200.00, $2.00.
Rhodes, A. N., Greenville, buggy, $200.00, $2.00.
Sims, W. A., Greenville, piano, $200.00, $2.00.
Simpson, Thos. S., Greenville, buggy, $100.00, $1.00.
Stallings, Jesse, Greenville, buggy, $100.00, $1.00.
Stanley, R. H., Greenville, watch, $100.00, $1.00.
Smith, E. J., Greenville, carriage, $200.00, $2.00.
Stallings, Daniel, Greenville, buggy, $100.00, $1.00.
Simpson, J. B., Manningham, carriage, $100.00, $1.00.
Stanley, J. C., Greenville, watch, $100.00, $1.00.
Sheppard, T., Greenville, buggy, $100.00, $1.00.
Small (Sewell or Sowell--Name had been written over & hard to read)
    Greenville, Carriage, $100.00, $1.00.
    Carriage, $200.00, $2.00.
    Watch, $100.00, $1.00.
Sheppard, A. R., Three Runs, buggy, $100.00, $1.00.
    Watch, $100.00, $1.00.
Saunders, J. T., Ft. Deposit, buggy, $100.00, $1.00.
Steiner, Joseph, Greenville, buggy, $100.00, $1.00.
Smith, C. W., Mrs., Greenville, buggy, $100.00, $1.00.
Stamps, Britton, Garland, watch, $100.00, $1.00.
    Buggy, $200.00, $2.00.
Smith, Ambrose, Greenville, buggy, $100.00, $1.00.
Thompson, Jno. P., Three Runs, buggy, $100.00, $1.00.
Teat, W. T., Greenville, buggy, $100.00, $1.00.
    2 Watches, $200.00, $2.00.
Thorton (Thornton?), Jacob, Manningham, buggy, $100.00, $1.00.

Thigpen, Gray, Jr., Greenville, watch, $100.00, $1.00.
Thigpen, J. M., Greenville, buggy, $100.00, $1.00.
    Watch, $100.00, $1.00.
Thigpen, Job, Manningham, buggy, $100.00, $1.00.
    Watch, $100.00, $1.00.
Thigpen, E. T., Butler Springs, buggy, $100.00, $1.00.
Thigpen, L. Gray, Sr., Manningham, buggy, $100.00, $1.00.
Tate, T. C., Greenville, watch, $100.00, $1.00.
Trawick, L. W., Monterey, buggy, $100.00, $1.00.
    Carriage, $200.00, $2.00.
    Watch, $100.00, $1.00
Thomas, E. D., South Butler, carriage, $100.00, $1.00.
Van Pelt, A. C., Pigeon Creek, carriage, $100.00, $1.00.
    Watch, $100.00, $1.00.
Van Pelt, E. S., Pigeon Creek, piano, $200.00, $2.00.
Wade, A., Greenville, carriage, $200.00, $2.00.
    Piano, $200.00, $2.00.
    Watch, $200.00, $2.00.
White, M. E., Mrs., Greenville, buggy, $100.00, $1.00.
Ward, A. R., Monterey, buggy, $100.00, $1.00.
Watts, T. C., Greenville, watch, $100.00, $1.00.
Wall, C., Monterey, carriage, $300.00, $3.00.
    Watch, $100.00, $1.00.
Watts, M. M., Monterey, carriage, $100.00, $1.00.
Womack, E. L., Manningham, carriage, $500.00, $6.00.
    Carriage, $300.00, $3.00.
Well, T. C., Greenville, buggy, $100.00, $1.00.
    Watch, $100.00, $1.00.
    Piano, $200.00, $2.00.
Wood, G. W., Ft. Deposit, watch, $100.00, $1.00.
Williams, D. B., Georgiana, buggy, $100.00, $1.00.

1886 GAZETEER OF ALABAMA BUSINESSES

BOLLING

On the L&N RR. 133 miles from Mobile, eight from Greenville, the county seat, and fifty-six from Montgomery.
Brooks, W. W., general merchandize.
Milner, Caldwell & Flowers, steam saw and planing mill.
Sutton, Salvador, Lumber and Shingles.
Farmers--W. J. Warden, T. G. Bush, J. E. Long, D. Wright, W. E. Kervin, John Stanford, A. J. Stanford.

BUTLER SPRINGS

This is a small place, taking its name from a small spring located 25 miles South of Greenville, the county seat. It has a tributary population of about 100.
Levy, M., general merchandize.
Farmers--J. T. Carter, S. M. Reynolds.

FOREST HOME

Is 15 miles from Greenville, the seat of justice, via which it is 60 miles to Montgomery and 136 from Mobile. Greenville is the nearest shipping point; it has telegraph and express offices. Mails daily by horseback.
Barge, Thomas, general merchandize.

Campbell, S. J., shoemaker.
Florence, T. F., justice of the peace.
Forest Home Academy.
Glenn, T. L., general merchandize.
Lazenby, E. M. & Son, Elias M. & George S., general merchandize, druggists, school books, etc.
Rodgers & Florence, saw mill and cotton gin.
Sims, A. C., saw mill and cotton gin
Smith, J. A., saw and grist mill.
Wall, C., Physician.
Wright, J. J., blacksmith, grist mill and cotton gin.
Farmers--T. Florence, J. A. Rogers, William Rogers, B. T. Ansley, G. A. Gillespie, J. W. Northcut, J. H. Simmons, Isaac Sims, A. C. Sims, B. Boutwell, Henry Boutwell, W. H. Boutwell, F. M. Boutwell, Dr. C. Wall, G. S. Lazenby, E. M. Lazenby, H. D. Lazenby, J. G. Lazenby, J. P. Benson, M. Wright, W. W. Wright, S. Moore, W. H. Watt, J. Bryson, B. Bryson, W. A. Bryson, C. S. Walker, S. T. Glenn, J. N. Glenn, F. M. Mize, F. C. Mize, R. E. Whittle, R. Hawkins, W. H. Hawkins, J. P. Vickery, T. M. McCrary, J. N. Griffin.

GARLAND

M&M RR., Located in a pine region on the above railroad, 22 miles SW of Greenville and 113 from Mobile; has a population of 150 and contains one white Baptist church and one colored, several saw mills and cotton gins, Western Union Telegraph and Southern Express offices. Naval stores and timber constitutes the leading business. Mails daily.
Andrews, H. F., general merchandize.
Anthony, Thomas, physician.
Baldwin, ____, physician.
Binion & Bro., lumber.
Darby, J. W., general merchandize and school books.
Darby, O. C., general merchandize and school books, etc.
Darby, Willis, general merchandize.
Fountain, James T., general merchandize.
Howell, J. J., steam mill and cotton gin.
Jones, T. C., general merchandize
Kendrick, S. & Co., general merchandize, school books, etc.
King, J. O., timber agent and general merchandize.
King, J. S., general merchandize.
McKenzie, B. B., saw mill.
Nicholson, W. J., steam mill.
Peacock, N. B., physician.
Robinson, M. E. B., general merchandize.
Sawyer, C. J., saloon.
White, A. G., boot and shoe maker.
Spratling, Edwards & Avery, mill.
Farmers--E. R. Amos, R. P. Barnes, D. D. Bennett, Jos. Bennet, W. C. Bennett, Wm. Busby, J. Chancellor, J. Cheppen, Robt. Cheppen, Geo. T. Chule, Jas. W. Darby, Thos. Duberry, N. B. Felton, J. J. Howell, Henry Huson, P. Huson, W. D. Huson, J. Keeble, Samuel P. Keeble, Geo. & John McClure, Jas. McClure, Jonathan McClure, T. McCorkle, John McPherson, Samuel McPherson, Mary Thomas, Mrs. E. E. Mills, A. J. Oden, W. G. Peason, Dr. N. B. Peacock, George W. Pressley, H. S. Pressley, Estate of Thompson, W. Wiggins, Charles Young.

GEORGIANA

L&N R.R. A lively little place of some 300 inhabitants, on the Mobile and Montgomery division of the L&N R.R.; is 16 miles South of Greenville, the county seat; 126 from Mobile and 60 from Montgomery.

Allen, J. E., drugs and physician.
Barfield, S. M., general merchandize.
Barrow & Son, general merchandize.
Barrow, R. B., general merchandize.
Bayzer & Adams, mill.
Beck, W., saloon.
Burk, R. W., general merchandize.
Davis, K. L., saw mill.
Easley, C. A. M., general merchandize.
Feagin, A. H., druggist.
Foster, W. C. & Co., general merchandize.
Heard, George P., general merchandize.
Hervey & Weirick, saw mill.
Holt, John R., grocer.
Ibell, W. F., general merchandize.
McMillan, C. C., general merchandize.
Milner, E. C., general merchandize.
Rhodes & Graham, grist mill.
Sellers, J. M. Y., general merchandize.
Sims, James M., general merchandize
Sims & Bayzer, general merchandize and saw mill.
Touart, Joseph, general merchandize.
Vinson, U. C. & Co., general merchandize.
Webb, B. F. & Son, general merchandize.
Wimberly, M., general merchandize.

GREENVILLE

L&N R.R. County seat; is beautifully situated on the Montgomery & Mobile division of the L&N combination, 141 miles NE of Mobile and 45 South of Montgomery, the State capital. The climate is pleasant and healthful, and the soil, though light, is fertile, producing good crops of cotton and corn. Pine forests are also extensive. The population of Greenville is about 3,000 and it has a number of good church edifices and school buildings as well as the public building and business houses, some of which are quite imposing. The Greenville Female College, located here is as high a grade as any in the State, the course of study as extensive and the teaching as thorough. Connected with this establishment is a Male Institute. The new buildings, which have just been completed, are very handsome, commodious, well arranged, and in every way suitable for the purpose of a first-class Female College and Male Institute. The cost of building was $30,000. The South Alabama Female Institute also commends itself to the public and is in a flourishing condition. Greenville has two hotels, the leading of which is the Perry House, several mills and cotton gins, carriage shop, two weekly newspapers, and a goodly number of large business houses that would do credit to much larger places. The shipments in cotton amount to about 7,000 bales. Mails received daily.

Ardle & Moore, confectioners.
Advocate Job Printing Office, J. B. Stanley, proprietor.
Bailey, M. J., gunsmith.
Barrow, W. B., broker.
Bear, D., general merchandize.

Beck, W., saloon.
Blaum, S., dentist
Blaum, M. A., Mrs., millinery.
Boling, S. L., lawyer.
Boling, S. J., Jr., saloon.
Bragg, Thomas M., Jr., gunsmith.
Brooks & Stalling, lawyers.
Broughton, J. T., physician.
Brown, George B., upholsterer.
Bryan & Carrol, saloon.
Buell & Lane, lawyers.
Burnett, J. D., carriages, wagons.
Burnett, J. R., furniture, harness, saddles, carriages & wagons.
Clark, Mrs. & Co., millinery and fancy goods.
Cory & Flowers, mill.
Crawford, F. M., grocer.
Crenshaw & Posey, lawyers.
Crenth & Brewster, booksellers.
Daniel & Smith, grocers.
Davison, P & Z, general merchandize.
Dixon, S. A., butcher.
Dohmieir, M., Mrs., Confectioner and baker.
Dunn & Ezekiel, general merchandize.
Dunklin & Son, general merchandize.
Elhbert, M., Mrs., hotel.
Etheridge, H. & Co., saloon and billiards.
Farrior, A. E., Mrs. & Sister, private school.
Farrior, R., general merchandize.
Flexner & Lichten, general merchandize.
Flowers, W. M., saw mill.
Foster, R. Z., general merchandize.
Foster Brothers, general merchandize.
Gambling & Boling, lawyers.
Gantt, H. & Son, general merchandize.
Garrett, Mary, Mrs., private school.
Garrett, T. G., cotton buyer and general merchandize.
George, Heyward, shoemaker.
Glenn, J. R., county tax assessor.
Goldsby, H. R. & Co., hardware.
Greenville Advocate, J. B. Stanley, proprietor, L. J. Walker, editor.
Greenville Collegiate Institute, Rev. R. S. Holcome, president, Rev. R. W. Erwin, principal.
Greenville Female College, Rev. R. S. Holcome, president, Miss Jennie Moffatt, principal.
Greenville Oil and Grist Co.
Hamilton, Clarence, physician.
Harper, P. O., lawyer.
Harrison, F. M., proprietor Perry House.
Herbert, C. B., physician.
Harrison, William F., physician.
Henry, George L., Mrs., private school.
Henry, J. K., general merchandize.
Hicks & Martin, general merchandize.
Hinson, A. T. & Bro., general merchandize.
Holzer, Benjamin, butcher.
Howell, W. C., general merchandize.
Hunt & Owen, grist mill and cotton gin.
Jackson & Co., hardware.
Johnson, Peter, barber.
Johnson, Thomas, barber.

Jones, J. R. & Co., saloon.

Kendrick, J. C., physician.
Kendrick, W. T., physician.
King, C. W., coroner and lawyer.
Kingsbury, J., contractor and builder.
Knight, E., warehouseman.
Lee, Robert T., contractor and builder.
Lehman, A., general merchandize.
Lehman, A. & H., confectioner.
Leonard, J. M., cotton buyer.
Levy, M., general merchandize.
Lichten & Co., druggists.
Long, B. L., saloon.
Long & Greenhut, general merchandize.
McKellan, M. E., Mrs., millinery.
McKenzie, J. M., grocer.
McKenzie & Co., grocers and saloon.
McKenzie, W. F., china, glass, etc.
McMillan, L. G., watchmaker and jeweler.
McMullen, C., photographer.
Martin, A. B. & Co., general merchandize.
Martin, W. B., saloon.
Mason, J. C., carriage and wagon manufacturer.
Mertief, H., general merchandize.
Metcalf, A. W., insurance agent.
Milner, J. T. & Co., steam saw.mill.
Morris, E. A., contractor and builder.
Morris, J. L., shoemaker.
Morrow, Mrs., hotel.
Moseley, W. C. T., general merchandize.
Murphy, William, barber.
Neumann, C., general merchandize.
Norman, J. M., tinner.
Norvell, J. M., painter.
Palmer, T. J., physician.
Parmer, E. & Co., livery.
Patillo, S. V., confectioner.
Payne, R. A., druggist.
Peagler, G. J., general merchandize.
Perry House, F. M. Harrison, proprietor.
Perry, J. T., general merchandize.
Persons, F. S., bookseller.
Pierce, H., mayor and superintendant city schools.
Pierce, H. & Co., furniture, etc.
Pierce, William, grocer.
Potter, H. H., stoves, etc.
Potter, T. F., stoves and tinware.
Pou, T. G., dentist.
Pryor, G. W., general merchandize.
Reid Bros. & Co., druggists.
Reid, J. A. & Co., hardware.
Richardson, J. C., lawyer.
Roberts, M. M., Mrs., confectioner.
Roberts, M. & J., general merchandize.
Rouse & Thaggard, saw and grist mill.
Seale, J. K., grocer.
Searcy & Perry, general merchandize.
Shine, J. T., general merchandize.
Singer Manufacturing Co.
Skipper, J. W., grocer.
Smith, H., general merchandize.
South Alabama Female Institute, J. M. Thigpen, president.

Southern Express Company, J. F. Maddox, agent.
Stanley, J. B., proprietor Greenville Advocate.
Stiner, J. M. & Co., hardware.
Stiner, J. & Sons, bankers.
Stiner & McGhee, general merchandize.
Stephens, Misses, millinery.
Stewart & Peagler, drugs.
Stouse & Steinhardt, general merchandize.
Teague & Newman, livery stables.
Thames, J. F., warehouseman.
Thames, K. J., furniture.
Thigpen, Job, physician.
Walker, J. F., general merchandize.
Walker, L. J., editor Greenville Advocate.
Walton, E. P., grocer and confectioner.
Weatherly & Barron, harness and saddles.
Webb, F. C., physician.
Wellborn, Nelson, dentist.
Whitehead, J. M., lawyer.
Whitehead, J. M. & Son, steam saw and grist mill.
Wilkerson, W. W., warehouseman and general merchandize.
Williams, C., carriage manufacturer.
Williams, H., grocer.
Wimberly, B. & Co., general merchandize.
Wimberly, M., contractor and builder.
Wimberly, W. M., general merchandize.
Winler, A. G., general merchandize.
Farmers--F. M. Andress, F. S. Andress, W. J. Andress, W. C. Arant, M. S. Barganier, A. J. Barrett, S. J. Bolling, George Buckhaults, G. R. G. Buckhaults, J. B. Burnett, B. Burns, R. Bush, R. H. Bush, J. T. Butler, N. T. Butler, Josiah Cales, W. F. Cheatham, W. H. Cheatham, W. O. Chiles, N. V. Clopton, James B. Cook, D. Craig, W. C. Creech, M. P. Davis, Charles Driver, W. S. Dryess, D. G. Dunklin, J. L. Dunklin, C. Ellington, E. Fail, John Fife, John Freeman, J. J. Flowers, A. M. Gafford, A. P. Gafford, Jessie Gafford, J. M. Gafford, J. C. Graydon, W. C. Graydon, John Harrison, H. Hartley, W. F. Hartley, M. C. Hawkins, Charles Heaton, A. E. Hinson, A. T. Hinson, D. B. Jones, J. S. Kirkpatrick, M. Kirksey, J. J. McBride, S. R. McCormick, A. McKellar, J. T. McPherson, J. A. Martin, R. G. W. Martin, Seth Mercer, W. Mosely, J. Murphy, E. T. Newton, J. A. Owen, R. R. Pace, Robert Perry, D. T. Phelps, L. D. Phelps, J. A. Pickens, E. Pollard, J. A. Porterfield, S. Powell, Joseph Raiburn, A. Reese, J. O. Rhodes, M. P. Roper, W. P. Rouse, George R. Searcy, G. R. Seawright, J. R. Sermon, R. Shanks, Asa Skinner, N. Skipper, A. Smith, J. Q. Smith, J. R. Smith, Sr., J. A. Smith, Joseph Steiner, S. A. Stubbs, Joseph Tally, A. J. Thagard.

MONTERY

This little place has a population of 400, and is situated in some of the finest lands in the State. It is 18 miles West of Greenville, the seat of justice, which is also its nearest telegraph, express and shipping point. Mails tri-weekly.

Barge & Powers, general merchandize.
Campbell, S. J., justice peace.
Cross, Thomas, physician.
Donald, J. M., general merchandize.
Donald & Donald, blacksmith and wheelwrights.
Donald, J. G., physician.
Donald, J. M., general merchandize.
Knight & Rantyn, general merchandize.

Luckie, A. C., general merchandize.
Myrick, A. M., shoemaker.
Moore, John, private school.
Seale, W. M., shoemaker.
Trawick, T. W. & Co., general merchandize.
Farmers--J. Benson, J. T. Brown, J. M. M. Brown, J. N. Carter, S. Carter, S. C. Carter, S. H. Crane, T. Crews, N. Davison, R. Donald, J. F. Gaston, L. R. Glenn, C. Green, J. M. Gray, B. F. Hale, N. P. Harris, James Hutchison, William Hutchison, J. P. Kendrick, S. R. Kendrick, J. W. Kendrick, C. J. Knight, George A. Knight, John E. Knight, T. A. Knight, James Lewis, N. Lewis, M. Lewis, J. F. Little, A. C. Luckie, E. J. Luckie, J. W. Luckie, W. R. Luckie, N. J. Moore, D. M. Murphy, L. Murphy, J. T. Posey, J. F. Powell, R. Powell, R. Y. Powell, W. H. Powell, R. Powers, J. N. Ragsdale, J. B. Scott, Joseph Scott, J. M. Smith, R. H. Smith, S. A. Smith, Thomas Smith, P. R. Steen, R. C. Swindle, E. M. Thigpen, Robert Thigpen, C. C. Thompson, F. W. Thompson, W. A. Thompson, J. Y. Trawick, S. W. Trawick, W. H. Trawick, W. M. Watts.

OAKEY STREAK

Just a small place and a postoffice for the convenience of a thickly settled community; is 21 miles South of Greenville, 14 miles from Georgiana, the nearest shipping point on the Mobile & Montgomery Railroad, via which it is 144 miles from Mobile and 74 from Montgomery. Receives mail daily except Sunday.

Bass, W. P. justice of the peace.
Crittenden, G. S., general merchandize.
Crittenden, John, cotton gin.
Crittenden, Joseph, blacksmith.
Hughes, R. S., Rev., Baptist.
Hughes, W., grist mill and cotton gin.
Jernigan, William, constable.
Kendrick, W. T., physician.
Morris & Jones, cotton gin.
Pryor, W. D., physician.
Rawles, J. H., wagon maker and cooper.
Shine, J. H., justice of the peace.
Webb, F. G., general merchandize.
Farmers--J. W. Payne, T. P. Payne, John Crittenden, R. S. Hughes, L. B. Wilson, S. J. Jones, W. L. Morris, Wilson Hughes, J. F. Rogers, Joseph H. Shine, W. P. Shine, H. C. Smith, James Jones, T. R. Adams, C. T. Pitts.

SEARCY

A small place on the Mobile & Montgomery R.R. with some 200 inhabitants. Is 6 miles North of Greenville, the county seat, 38 from Montgomery and 142 from Mobile.

Barganier, H. W., sewing machine agent and constable.
Cheatham, William, justice of peace.
Hamilton, W. C., physician.
Hinson, William, justice of peace.
Roughton, J. F., physician and druggist, school books, etc.
Searcy, J. R., general merchandize, cotton gin and saloon.
Snyder & Roughton, general merchandize.
Farmers--H. W. Barganier, J. Barganier, John Barganier, M. S. Barganier, R. Bush, W. Bush, S. Cheatam, J. Colvin, H. G. Day, J. Elington, T. Frost, J. Gafford, M. Gafford, H. Garrett, ____ Grant, T. Hall, Daniel Harrison, John Harrison, G. W. Hawkins, Charles Heaton, J. M. Holliday,

H. Jackson, T. C. King, Robert Kates, F. McCoy, John McCoy, W. M. McCoy, George Martin, G. Moseley, W. M. Moseley, E. L. Norris, W. Porterfield, Robert Pace, A. B. Reese, James Reese, J. R. Searcy, John Waters, L. W. Waters, E. White, F. Williams, J. Wooldridge.

SHACKLEVILLE

Is located on Pine Barren Creek, 13 miles SW of Greenville, the county seat, and 53 from Montgomery.

Barge and Shanks, general merchandize.
Crane, D., grist mill and cotton gin.
Coley, J., constable.
Donald, _____, physician.
Dunklin, D. B., banker.
Florence, B., justice of peace.
Lazenby & Son, general merchandize.
Levy, _____, general merchandize.
Murphy, J., constable.
Peters, Nathan, justice of peace.
Seale, H. T., carriage and wagon manufacturer, shoemaker, etc.
Seale, D. T., Rev.
Sellers, E., justice of peace.
Smith & Simmons, grist mill and cotton gin.
Vickery, J., justice of peace.
Farmers--J. D. Baker, J. Y. Blackman, M. Blackman, J. Carter, William Carter, R. Cole, William Fail, R. Hainesworth, J. M. McCoy, J. McCrary, M. McCrary, J. Murphy, J. M. Pickens, W. Phillips, M. M. Reaves, A. C. Sims, A. T. Sims, M. Sims, H. Thomason, F. Vickery, T. Vickery, W. W. Walker, M. R. Watts.

SOUTH BUTLER

See Georgiana.
Rhodes & Graham, general merchandize.

The home of Henry Simmons, Jr. near the Ridge

CHAPTER 6.

LAND OFFICE REMOVAL

Greenville Advocate, November 8, 1893.   Addison Francis Posey

"There is an episode in the history of Greenville entitled to be known, and only myself and another could ever have given a full explanation, and the other is now dead, the late Hon. J. S. McMullan. It may look like vanity in me as the chronicler, considering the part I bore in it; but I am beyond the period of vanity, and when I look back over the more then seventy years I have lived and realize how much less I know than I once thought I did, and how much less I have accomplished than was due from me, vanity, if I possessed it, would be paralyzed into nonentity.

It will be remembered by those of sufficient age that in 1854 Congress passed what is known as "The Graduation Act", reducing the price of lands according to the time government lands had been in market and not disposed of. It allowed each purchaser for actual settlement, to take up 320 acres in one body, or for the use of adjoining farms. Most of the lands in Butler, and the lower end of the land district, was at 50 cents per acre, and some at 12½ cents. Then came a rush to enter lands, and the streets of Greenville often presented a scene of passers like pilgrims on their way to Mecca, and the few men who had money to lend had to entertain scores hearing papers with the endorsement-- "Samuel J. Bolling."

The land office was then at Cahaba, Alabama. Vast quantities were being entered, valuable for timber, and much in the southern portion for farming purposes.

Judge Henry, Col. Abrams and others started papers and obtained signatures by the thousand, including mine as a signer and no more, for removal of the land office to Greenville, which they sent to Hon. Eli S. Shorter, who was met and defeated by Hon. Percy Walker, of Mobile, in whose district Cahaba then was. Walker was not armed with long lists of petitions against removal, but with the protest of all Cahaba, and with its hotel and bar room influences and its Goliahs of mental, social and political power, Greenville went down at the first round and was lying there.

In the winter of 1855-6 I happened to visit Montgomery during legislative session, when J. S. McMullan was then one of the representatives of Butler. He told me he had seen Hon. Ben Fitzpatrick, on his way to Congress, and asked his aid for removal, but was assured that Shorter and Walker would have to fight it out, that he could not interfere unless he knew sufficient reasons for removal, and evidence of it being to the interest and in accordance with the desire of the people. I and Mack then arranged a program. I made a map of the land district and obtained the data of lands most contiguous to each place. I expected to find big point in lands nearer Greenville but ascertained in that it was about equal. I drew up a paper for the signatures of senators and representatives so each could state for those they represented.

Senator Bob Hatcher, of Dallas, while admitting the force, begged off from signing, as it would offend his Cahaba friends, and as the government owned but forty acres in Dallas, and that in the middle of a frog pond. I obtained the signatures of senators and representatives of Autauga and Bibb, that while there was much land in their counties subject to entry, the land was stony, barren and of but little value, even for timber, and that they did not believe their people would object to removal. I obtained the milk and water endorsement of representives of Monroe. I piled up the agony for Butler, Lowndes, Pike, Coffee, Covington and Conecuh, and they signed with a wim, emphasizing as facts that, "the entrees in Perry, Autauga, and Bibb were planters who rode in carriages, (all had to appear in person) for timber on hills, for the use of rich bottom land while the entries in Butler and below, were by farmers on horse back, some on side saddle, some on foot, for actual settlement and cultivation; and that if Cahaba owned the location as a birthright, the loan of it to Greenville for the ensuing ten years would be an act of justice and generosity."

The only hostile opponent I met was Senator Jack Cocke, of Perry, who said he would write and fight against removal, laughed at me, said it couldn't be done, and if so he would owe me the finest hat to be had.

I sent the papers to Shorter, he obtained the endorsement of Ben Fitzpatrick, invited Percey to meet him again (as welcoming Cumberland's steed to the shock) before Commissioner General Land Office, the contest was short, and victory perched on the standard of Greenville.

I telegraphed Cocke that I wore 7 1/8, to which he never responded."

HENRY-BEELAND-STANLEY House - c-1850
Built by Judge John K. Henry

PROBATE RECORDS

The Butler County Court Houses burned 12 Apr. 1853. In a Special Term some transactions were re-recorded in the Probate Court, some of these referring to events that occurred as much as ten years prior to that time. This Special Term lasted through the summer following the fire.

Estate of James D. Herbert, deceased. John R. Hartley, Administrator of Estate, produced a Bill of Sale dated 27 Mch. 1852 to Thomas D. Gafford for $607.00 for Real Estate. On 11 Dec. 1851 Mr. Hartley was appointed Administrator and produced bond in the amount of $7,000. He was also appointed Administrator of the Estate of Mrs. Mary E. Herbert, deceased.

Estate of H. O. Wilson, deceased. George W. Esselman appointed Administrator of Estate on the __ day of __ 1851.

Estate of Isabella M. Phelps, deceased. Andrew W. Black appointed Guardian of minor heir, James S. Phelps on __ day of __ 18__.

Estate of Thomas Butts, deceased. Jesse B. Knight and Thomas J. Butts, Executors. Gave account of property of Estate sold in Feb. 1851.

Estate of Jacob Ferguson, deceased. Darius J. Ferguson produced Letters Testamentary. Made bond in amount of $1,000. William H. Ferguson, John W. Armstrong, Abram Hutchinson, E. H. Ferguson, R. H. Ferguson, Matthew Patton and Jacob L. Womack, Securities. Property sold 1 Feb. 1853.

Estate of William Davis, deceased. James L. Thagard appointed Guardian of John, Henry & Allen Davis, minor heirs. George W. Thagard, Security.

Estate of David Roach, deceased. James Roach appointed Administrator 8 July 1851. E. H. Pickens, Security.

Estate of George Vickrey, deceased. George W. Vickrey appointed Guardian on 10 Jan. 1853 of John, Napoleon D., Nancy & Jackson Vickrey, minor heirs. Bond made with Franklin & E. L. Vickrey, Thomas McCrory, James M. Black and James B. Sheppard, Security.

Estate of Eli Walton, deceased. Daniel G. Boggan appointed Guardian in 1852 of John Walton, minor heir. Substitute account entered.

Estate of Reuben Stringfellow, Sr., a lunatic. Reuben Stringfellow appointed as Guardian in 1852.

Estate of Daniel B. McDonald, deceased. James Norman appointed Administrator with Francis Sheppard, Security. Property sold 11 Jan. 1853.

Estate of George H. Herbert, deceased. Hillary Herbert appointed Administrator of the Estate 15 Dec. 1851. Bond made in amount of $6,000. Property sold on 29 Jan. 1852.

Estate of Thomas Seale, deceased. Wilson Murphy appointed Guardian of John Wilson, William and Thomas Seale, minor heirs.

Estate of Henry Powell, deceased. Wm. Powell appointed Administrator of Estate 3 July 1852. Security: Joseph W. Atkins. Property sold 17 August 1852.

Estate of Rolla A. Green, deceased. Robert R. Wright, Administrator Ex-officio as Sheriff.

Estate of Pinkney W. Hillson, deceased. Anna Hillson appointed Administratrix-Estate and Guardian of Martha Ann, Aaron H., Lucinda Ann & Sarah N. Adelia, minor heirs. Daughter, Rutha, wife of George W. Vickery, named. Security, Wilson Murphy. Account current filed on 21 Mch. 1853.

Estate of Andrew Pickens, deceased. Ezekiel H. Pickens appointed Administrator of Estate in October 1852.

Estate of Nathaniel Y. Fife, deceased. Benjamin Newton appointed Administrator.

Estate of Benj. Miller, deceased. Ezra Miller appointed Guardian 16 Sept. 1848 of Allen, Samuel & William Miller, minor heirs of Benjamin Miller, dec'd & heirs at law of James Miller, Sr., deceased. H. L. Henderson and John R. McQueen, Security.

Estate of James D. Boggan, deceased. In 1852 George W. Thagard was appointed Administrator.

Estate of Henry Richardson, deceased. George W. Thagard, Administrator, reapplied for sale of negro property.

Estate of Desdamonia Carter, deceased. Edward Bowin appointed Administrator of Estate 18 Nov. 1851. Had inventory of money in hand on 16 June 1852 of $220.00.

Estate of Jarrett Carter, deceased. Edward Bowin appointed Guardian of Jefferson, Martha & William Carter, minor heirs on 18 Nov. 1851. Edward & George Carter were distributors of Estate.

Estate of John Thomas, deceased. Jack Thornton, Guardian of John Thomas, minor heir.

Estate of George Lewis, deceased. Jacob L. Womack, appointed Guardian 26 Aug. 1846 of George W. & Sarah E. Lewis, minor heirs. Account on hand 12 Dec. 1846 $1,493.88 from hire of negroes and balance due from 1847 to present.

Estate of William W. Reddoch, deceased. Sarah M. Reddoch & Uriah Evans were appointed Administrators of Estate 20 Dec. 1852. Joseph Stiner, Joshua W. Evans, Alexander B. Evans & Young H. Frost, Security.

Estate of Daniel Gafford, deceased. James M. Gafford appointed Guardian of Maria L. Gafford, minor heir, in 1843. Jesse Stallings, Security.

Estate of Elizabeth Simmons, deceased. G. W. Thaggard, Sheriff appointed Administrator in 1853.

Estate of Mary K. Walton, deceased. Watkins Salter, appointed Administrator of Estate 19 Jan. 1852. Also for Estate of Eli W. Walton.

HENRY WEST ESTATE

In the J. Hubert Scruggs Collection in the Department of Archives & Manuscripts of the Birmingham Public Library one Probate Packet has been located pertaining to the settlement of the Estate of Henry West of Butler County. This packet was probably in the lawyer's office at the time the Court House burned, otherwise it would have been destroyed also. Hopefully by the time this extensive collection has been catalogued in its entirety other papers on early Butler County will be discovered.

It is to be remembered that almost all business in the early 1800s was conducted on credit with bills being paid when the crops came in. Therefore, when a man died it took a considerable amount of time for all claims against his Estate to be examined and settled.

On August 21, 1837 Margaret E. West was appointed the Administrator of her husband's Estate by Judge Herndon L. Henderson. Samuel J. Bolling, later to become a Judge, was Clerk of the County Court at that time. William Wallace, George W. Shipp, Jeremiah Watts, and later on William P. Routon were named as Security in the amount of $35,000.

In December, 1839, the Court ordered the sale of the real estate owned by West in order that the Estate be equally divided among his heirs. One Richard West is named, but his relationship to the Deceased is not stated. The property to be sold was in Cahawba, Dallas Co., and in Butler County with S. J. Bolling, Richard Lynn and Thomas B. Windham appointed to auction the property at the Court House in Greenville. The Butler County properties to be sold were in Sections 1 and 13 in Township 7 and Range 12, which are located due north of Garland.

Claims against this Estate were as follows:

James D. Craig, note and interest	$1,041.31
William Whitted, note and interest	689.29
McElroy & Hunter, note and interest	82.77
P. Walter Herbert, claim and interest	47.87
Gayle & Bower, account and interest	2,349.52
Perine & Crocheron, note and interest	1,773.57
J. B. Clark, note and interest	121.33
W. P. Watson, account and interest	4.55
Trustees Farmers Academy, account & interest	48.00
Starling (Sterling) Parker, account & interest	101.36
Nelson & Bates, account and interest	4.00
Alen Chittey, account and interest	81.81
Edward Bowen, account and interest	120.60
J. Hardy, account and interest	6.00
T. J. Frow, account and note and interest	62.10
Charles C. Langdon, account	6.00
Judges & Clerks fees (Henderson, Bolling, Windham and Lynn)	19.18
Comm. for selling land	6.50
	$6,565.76
Receipts from sale of property and cotton	$8,589.08

The Estate was ordered to pay these debts on the third Monday in November 1841; P. B. Waters, Sheriff of Butler Co. The case was appealed by Cook & Evans, attorneys for Mrs. West and was taken to the Supreme Court in Tuscaloosa where the decree was reversed. William T. Streety and E. H. Pickens were also listed as Clerks in Butler County and James B. Wallace as Clerk of the Supreme Court. The final date shown was May 3, 1848.

A copy of this Probate Packet has been placed in the Court House in Greenville, Alabama.

EARLY COUNTY MARRIAGES

The Court House fire of April 12, 1853 destroyed all marriage records. The first marriage recorded after the fire was dated May 8, 1853. The following marriage records have been obtained from biographies, obituaries, Bible records and from descendants of the people named and are all believed to have taken place in Butler Co., Alabama.

Armstrong, John Wesley married E. J. Ferguson 21 Mch. 1833.

Austin, Davis Washington married Amanda Seals 3 Feb. 1847 at the home of Benjamin Rhodes with James K. Benson officiating.

Benson, John Wesley married Haseltine Yeldell 8 Aug. 1850.

Benson, William Drake married Ann C. Chapman 2 Jan. 1832.

Bloxom, Washington married Luveny Powell 7 Jan. 1830.

Bolling, Samuel Jackson married Mary Ewing, dau. of Jonathan in Greenville in 1838.

Bonner, Henry Hubbard married Sarah Homes in 1829 in or near Greenville.

Branton, Thomas Hillery married Mary Jane McCann in 1848.

Bush, C. G. married Mary Wilcox 10 Feb. 1850.

Camp, Manning married Elizabeth____ in Runville in 1826.

Cook, John H. married Cloea Eliza Benson 15 Jan. 1832.

Crenshaw, Frederick William, son of Anderson & Mary, married Elmira Caroline Womack, daughter of J. L. & Agnes, 19 Dec. 1850.

Crenshaw, Thomas Chiles, son of Anderson & Mary, married Lucinda Womack in 1841.

Davenport, David married Martha Mosely Stallings 21 Mch. 1838.

Davidson, R. C. married Nancy J. McKee 28 Dec. 1851.

Deming, John married Josephine Armanda Payne 22 Mch. 1853.

Dunklin, Daniel D., son of James & Catherine Lee Dunklin, married Susan C. Burnett 19 Jan. 1847.

Dunklin, James J. married Mary A. Burnett in Jan. 1841.

Dunklin, Joseph married Mary C. Judge 23 Dec. 1829. Rev. Benjamin Dulaney officiated.

Gafford, James married Lucinda Gafford Stallings 7 Nov. 1832.

Gafford, Stephen Franklin married Elizabeth G. Caldwell, dau. of John C. in 1846.

Griggs, John married Sarah Ann Hodge, dau. of Lewis & Dorothy on 3 Aug. 1852.

Henry, John Kelly married Jane Elvira Caldwell, dau. of John Calhoun & Elizabeth Black Caldwell in Greenville 22 Mch. 1836.

Herbert, Edward Hampton, son of Thomas Sharpe & Elizabeth Hampton Herbert married Martha Womack, dau. of John & Sarah Lewis Womack in 1824.

Herbert, Dr. George married Annie Dunklin in Feb. 1819, John Cook, J. P. officiating.

Hilson, Pinkney W. married Anna E. Odom 7 Feb. 1832.

Lazenby, Elias M. married Martha J. Benson 14 Dec. 1848.

Lea, Benjamin married Lucinda Powell 22 Dec. 1831.

Lea, Lovard married Matilda Powell 30 Sept. 1824.

Luckie, E. Jackson married Margery D. Yeldell, dau. of Robert, Sr. of Monterey in May 1840.

McKellar, Alexander married M. A. Caldwell, dau. of William, in Greenville in 1830.

Morrow, Abraham married Polley Powell 23 Feb. 1823.

Parmer, William married Josephine Ewing, dau. of Jonathan & Nancy on 27 Nov. 1849.

Payne, Daniel Gafford married Lucinda Emmett in Feb. 1850.

Payne, John Jackson married Mary Frances Gafford 20 Sept. 1820.

Payne, William Walker married Emily Catherine Wright in 1850.

Poole, Calvin married Francis L. Davidson 28 Apr. 1848.

Posey, Addison Francis married Florella Young 1 July 1847.

Powell, D. P. married Lona Ann Yeldell 7 Jan. 1836.

Powell, Henry married Martha Butts 4 Dec. 1829.

Powell, John married Frances Yeldell 18 Nov. 1835.

Powell, Moses married Salley Bloxom 15 Dec. 1831.

Powell, William married Mary Ann Yeldell 10 June 1824.

Powell, Zachariah married Charlott Powell 27 Dec. 1839.

Powers, Richard married Rebecca A. Benson 2 May 1835.

Price, James married Martha Hobbs in 1839.

Reid, Archibald M. married Elizabeth Ann Herbert, dau. of Hillary, 20 Jan. 1835.

Reynolds, James, son of John, married Martha M. Barge, dau. of Abel & Martha 7 Mch. 1846 in Pine Flat.

Reynolds, L. Berry (Littlebury) married Nancy P. Benson 20 Dec. 1849.

Seale, Allen B., son of Ransom Seale & Ellen Murphy married Elizabeth Sarah Stallings 1 Apr. 1852.

Seale, William married Rulincy Hilson, dau. of Aaron & Sarah 26 Nov. 1826 at the home of Reuben Davis.

Sellers, Calvin K. married Elizabeth Talbot in 1836.

Shine, William Porter married Martha Hammonds 22 Aug. 1844.

Sims, Wiley married Luvina Reddoch in 1841.

Smith, James D. married Clarrisa W. Shine 16 Oct. 1838.

Stallings, Reuben Reid married Lucinda A. Ferguson, dau. of Jacob & Elizabeth of Manningham 10 Sept. 1850.

Stallings, Reuben Reid married Leonora Ann Brogden 24 Dec. 1851 at Oaky Streak.

Stevenson, Thomas married Margarette E. Wyrosdick in July 1838.

Swanson, Francis married Celia Ann Stallings 2 Oct. 1845.

Thompson, Warren A. married Mrs. Mary Danvis dau. of Thomas Hays 19 Dec. 1829.

Wiggins, Joshua A. married Lucinda Presley 2 May 1839.

PROBATE NOTICES
FROM THE SOUTHERN MESSENGER

Toliver Adams. Sheriff's Sale. Auction of negro woman, Polly, aged 40 and negro man, Jupiter, aged 45 in Lowndes Circuit Court. 6/22/1859.

Archabal M. Ardis Estate. Letters Administration granted to Isaac Ardis. 6/22/1857.

Rhoda Berry Estate. Harry T. Berry appointed Administrator. Auction of property, household, kitchen furniture, 1 lot farming tools, 25 head hogs, 1 yoke oxen, milch and dry cattle, property. 4/27/1859.

Daniel G. Boggan Estate. A. B. Scarborough and D. V. Boggan appointed Administrators. 7/13/1859.

Thomas Boggan Estate. Letters Administration granted to Anderson Boggan. 6/27/1859.

John N. Boggan and Thomas B. Boggan, minors. A. J. Caldwell, Guardian. Annual settlement. 3/14/1860.

Joseph J. Boggan and Mary E. Boggan, minors. A. B. Scarborough, Guardian. Annual settlement. 10/17/1860.

Edward P. Brooks Estate. Administrator: D. W. Brooks. 8/1/1860.

Francis M. Brown vs. S. Deming & Co. Sheriff's sale of property by virtue of execution in favor of S. Deming & Co. 3/30/1859.

John Burkett Estate. Aurena Burkett appointed Administratrix. 11/16/1859.

John Bush Estate. House to be sold on East Sparta Road 11 miles from Greenville by William P. Bush, Administrator. 3/28/1860.

G. Chancellor and Joshua Green vs. C. M. Yeldell. Sheriff's sale. Case settled in favor of Yeldell. 6/23/1859.

Gilbert Chancellor Estate. Jack Chancellor applied for Admistration of Estate. Heirs: Gilbert C., Reuben C., William C. Chancellor and Peggy Hardy, wife of Kindred Hardy, Levi M. Bloxom and Martha J Bloxom. 7/27/1859.

Daniel Cook Estate. Letters of Administration granted on 3/3/1859 to W. J. Wilson. 4/13/1859.

William G. Craig Estate. Robert R. Wright, Guardian for Teletha J., William H., George M. and David A. Craig, minors. Annual settlement. 3/14/1860.

E. H. Daily Estate. Mrs. Ellen Daily appointed Administratrix. Minor heirs: William S., Margarett C., Rachael E. and Christian E. Daily. 5/11/1859.

Moses Davidson vs. Henry G. Parker. Sheriff's Sale. Auction of property in case settled in favor of Parker. 6/22/1859.

Simeon Deming, Jr. & Ezra Deming Estate. Auction of Steam Saw and Crist Mill and 640 acres of pine land. 3/16/1859.

James A. Ellington Estate. Davis F. Holland appointed Administrator. 5/4/1859.

Maria L. Gafford Estate. James M. Gafford, Administrator. Settlement to be made in April 1859. 3/16/1859.

R. Gentry vs. Joseph Rogers. Sheriff's Sale. Auction to settle case in favor of Rogers. 6/22/1859.

Louisa A. Gideon Estate. Robert R. Wright, Guardian. Minors: James L., Laxy and William T. Gideon, Leroy S. Seaborn, Martha F., Ireland and S. H. Hix and Asa F. Holloday, minor heir of Martha Holloday, dec'd. Final settlement. 3/14/1860.

John P. Gholson Estate. Alexander B. Evans, Guardian. John S. Gholson, minor heir. Annual settlement. 3/16/1859.

Margarett Glanton Estate. A negro woman, Clo, and child, Dolly, to be sold by Administrator, Robert Smith. 3/14/1860.

James D. & Mary E. Herbert Estate. John R. Hartly, Guardian of James Ennis, minor heir. 7/13/1859.

Dennis Hodge Estate. Mrs. Lydia Vernell filed for Administrator of Estate. 9/28/1859.

Josiah Houson vs. A. J. W. Page. Sheriff's Sale. Case settled in favor of Page. 6/22/1859.

James H. & Elizabeth J. Johnson, minors. Mrs. Lavinia Alexander, Guardian. Final settlement. 9/28/1859.

James F. Jones, minor heir. John B. Lewis, Guardian, annual settlement. 4/6/1859.

Dr. Joseph Jones Estate. 22 likely negroes to be sold, including Depse, good blacksmith and wood workman, and Maria, good cook, washer and ironer. 2,000 bushels corn, 15,000 lbs. of fodder, 12 mules, a wagon and harness, 2 yoke oxen, meat, hogs, plantation tools, piano, 1 dentist chair, 2 gins. 11/16/1859.

Levi Jones vs. Joseph Harrison. Sheriff's Sale. Case settled in favor of Harrison. 6/22/1859.

W. K. Jones vs. Joseph Henderson. Sheriff's sale. Case settled in favor of Henderson. 6/22/1859.

William T. Jones Estate. Mary R. Jones appointed Administratrix. 4/27/1859.

John Jordan Estate. Joseph Steiner, Administrator. Final settlement. 6/22/1859.

Sarah E. Lewis, minor heir. John B. Lewis, Guardian. Annual settlement. 4/6/1859.

Thomas H. Lowery Estate. Arnold Kent, Guardian of J. D. James, Thomas and George Lowery. Annual settlement. 3/14/1860.

F. W. Mims Estate. Sale of negro girl, Rinda, 16 yrs. To be divided between Foster J. and John A. Mims, Ema and Newton Freeman. 4/4/1860.

Michael S. Morgan Estate. Thomas R. Morgan, Sr., Administrator. 11/16/1859.

Patience McCoy Estate. Odom Cox, Administrator filed for sale of property. 10/17/1860.

Ebbin Odom Estate. Mary Odom, Levi S. Waller and Benjamin Odom signed the Executor's Bond. 4/29/1861.

James W. Odom Estate. James Odom, minor, aged 5 yrs., Mrs. Annie J., Sarah and William Odom, heirs. 1/8/1868.

John Odom Estate. Margaret Odom, widow, 3 minor children. Odom died 2/10/1865.

Robert and Mary T. Owen, minors. Alford Gandy, Guardian. Annual settlement. 3/16/1859.

Pascal P. Park Estate. Administrators sale, Mary A. Park, Administrator. 11/16/1859.

Eliza R. Patton Estate. Will filed by Wiley Duberry. 6/27/1860.

John Patton Estate. James L. Davis, Administrator, filed for sale of property. 10/3/1860.

James H. Petty vs. John Bolling. Sheriff's auction. Case settled in favor of Bolling. 5/4/1859.

Sarah Pitts Estate. David W. Pitts, appointed Administrator. 10/24/1860.

Rachael F., William L. and John H. Reddoch, minors. Dr. W. C. Webb, Guardian. Annual settlement. 4/18/1860.

Sarah Reddoch Estate. W. C. Reddoch, Administrator. William C. Reddoch and Wilson M. Seale produce Last Will & Testament. William and Rulincy Seale, George W. and Ruth Vickery, E. H. Pickens, Guardian for Martha Ann, Aaron H., Lucinda and Sarah N. Adelia Hillson, minor heirs. Residence of W. C. Reddoch for sale for 12 months credit on 6/11/1859, household, kitchen furniture, 4 milch cows and calves and 3 yearlings to be auctioned. 5/18/1859.

William C. Reddoch Estate. Sarah M. Reddoch and Uriah Evans, Administrator. Final settlement. 3/30/1859.

Charlotte Rhodes Estate. Kincheon Rhodes, Executor. Annual settlement. 3/16/1859.

Mrs. Aannah (Hannah?) Seale Estate. Richard H. Williams, Administrator. 5/25/1859.

James Seale Estate. Will filed by Ransom and Anderson Seale. 3/14/1860.

Rulincy and William Seale vs. W. C. Reddoch et al. Affidavit filed on Levina Sims, wife of Wiley Sims of Texas. 5/9/1860.

F. W. Sims Estate. Letters of Administration filed by Newton Freeman. 3/14/1860.

James Sims Estate. John R. Deen, Administrator. Auction at home of Dr. William F. Allen. 8/10/1859.

Joseph B. G. Sims Estate. Annual settlement. Edna D. Sims, Guardian of Julius F., Walter C., Erastus P. and J. V. G. Sims, minor heirs. 3/14/1860.

William Sims Estate. Damarius Sims, Guardian of Thomas J. & Ashley L., minors. Annual settlement. 3/14/1860.

Stephen Sims Estate. Sherod Sims filed as Administrator of Estate. Requests the dower interest of Rhoda Sims, widow be assigned to her in real estate as described in petition. Sale of land requested for equal distribution. 10/12/1859.

Thomas Skains Estate. Letters testamentary, Charner T. Skains, Executor. 3/16/1859.

Mary Skipper Estate. G. B. Wyche, Administrator. Filed for sale of property. 10/3/1860.

Robert Smith vs. S. Deming, E. Deming, T. M. Bragg & G. W. Ormand. Sheriff's auction. 5/4/1859.

John Smyth Estate. Robert B. Smyth, Administrator. Partial settlement. 3/21/1860.

John Thigpen Estate. James J. Thigpen, Administrator. Sale of property in Monterey adjoining William Sturdivant, Dr. Allison & Yeldell.

James Thompson Estate. Partial settlement. W. D. Perryman, Administrator. 3/14/1860.

Richard Tillery Estate. Will filed by William Tillery. 10/17/1860.

Susan Troutman Estate. W. D. Perryman, Administrator. 8/31/1859.

Augustus C. Watts Estate. Wilson Murphy, Administrator, entered appraisement bill. 2/8/1859.

Wiley T. Watts Estate. Mary M. Watts, Administrator. Final settlement. 10/19/1859.

Noah Whiddon vs. John S. McMullen. Sheriff's auction. Case settled in favor of McMullen. 5/4/1859.

Jethro S. Williams, Guardian of Madison M. and William S. Williams, minors. Lot auctioned for settlement with A. Gugenheim & Co. Final settlement. 5/25/1859.

Thomas Williams Estate. James S. Farrior, Administrator. Settlement set for July 1, 1874. 5/18/1874.

J. B. Wicks vs. Seth S. May. Sheriff's auction. 5/4/1859.

J. L. Womack, Guardian of Victory F. Womack. Annual settlement. 4/18/1860.

Martha Womack. Slave, Will, to be auctioned to satisfy execution of L. M. Pruitt. 5/30/1860.

William Wyrick Estate. Administration granted to J. R. Benson. 7/14/1860.

A REMINISCENCE OF OVER 40 YEAR AGE[1]
By Addison Francis Posey   From Vicksburg, Mississippi

   Today is the 44th anniversary of the first touching of my foot to the soil of the city, then the town, or village of Greenville, although it was four years later before I became a citizen, which I still am, though temporarily absent. My mind running back upon the date first named and its incidents, is crowded with items too numerous to mention. I then lived in a distant State and where railroads had no more than starts and no connections. The stage coach and private conveyance were the only modes of transit between distances. I came all the way, 400 miles, in the best outfit of that day, the newest, nicest and tonest buggy that money could buy and drawn by a "3-40 on the dirt",

1. Greenville Advocate. May 20, 1891

by "Jerry-go-nimble" of precious memory. I spent the last night before I made my debut in Greenville at "uncle Jake Thornton's" on Pigeon, eight miles east. He asked me many questions, all of which I answered without evasion, except one, towit: "Why do you come so far to visit so poor a place as Greenville? Have you relatives there?" I can't now call to mind what words I used, but they were about as satisfactory as the small boy's "jist Kase", and for what Tallyrand said was the proper use of language--to hide out and misconvey. I didn't tell him I was in quest of extending my relationship, and that there was such uncertainty about it, that after his delicious supper and on a downy bed under his hospitable roof I passed a sleepless night, and the cause of it.

I crossed tanyard branch about 10 o'clock on a bright morning and stopped on the west side for the sun to dry my buggy wheels, which done I wiped tire, spokes and hub with a $2 silk hankerchief. I then made my way up the hill and passed the square and halted in front of a shanty-store on the spot now occupied by R. A. Lee & Co. where a lot of young fellows were being regaled by the long yarns of Rube Bonner, (a Dunk Taylor sort of a man.) I had temporary palpitation of the heart and had to succeed after an effort to inquire: "Gentlemen, can you tell me where Mr. Thomas Herbert resides?" Rube promptly gave directions and I saw a twinkle in his eye as he spoke and I noticed all eyes followed me until lost in the distance. There was also a tell-tale that I had come from afar, in my horse showing evidence of travel and a trunk covered with an $8 bear skin. Rube afterwards told me that he remarked to Jeff Burnett and others after I had passed: "That man means business, which may interfere with the calculations of some of you young fellows".

The records of your court, had they not been burned, would show the object and success of my mission to Greenville, dating July 1st, 1847. I sold my buggy to Tom Watts and sent Jerry to an old friends at Wetumpka, who kept him until he had a chance to send him east of Savannah River. I and my new relative on the 13th of July 1847 took passage on stage coach to railroad, and from railroad to stage coach and from stage coach to railroad and from railroad to stage coach and by stage coach to where I belonged and near her former home.

Greenville, as I first saw it, and four years later became a citizen, was not then what it is now, and when I think of the change I can scarcely realize it as covering the same soil. The houses occupied by Dan Dunklin, Tom Bragg and the Deming house are the only land marks of old Greenville. It was then a small and "finished town", according to Judge Dougherty's compliment to old Sparta, in Conecuh--"looked like new plank and paint had gone out of use there". When I compare myself with the now and then I can scarcely realize it as the same person: and when memory calls back the citizens of that day who were my seniors, dead or gone, save one.

> "I feel like he who treads alone
> Some banquet hall deserted."

Nearly every householder was my senior. Where are they? Harvey Harrington, Dr. T. M. Bragg, William Burnett, John Caldwell, A. McKellar, Ezekiel Pickens, John Bolling, P. B. Waters, Sheriff John K. Henry, J. F. Johnston, Milton Parmer, David Parmer, Bill Goodall, Williamston Williams, Jim Williams, W. F. Streety, Reuben Bonner, J. W. Mallett, Sim Deming, Junior and Senior, Frank Gafford, John Bowen, James J. Dunklin, H. P. Oliver, Rev. Moody, Hubb Taylor, Pat Little, Thomas E. Herbert, S. J. Bolling. All were my seniors and now only one remains, the last named. I would put Dan Dunklin ahead of me, but he might deny it, and I would accept it and challenge to a comparison of which looks the older. I found him in 1847 and 1851 "quartering on the enemy", his father-in-law. Will Williams was living in Texas ten years ago, and later than that Rube Bonner; also in 1882 John Bowen, as I know from a letter I had from him from his dear Tenn., to which he had returned. He was a blacksmith and occupied an humble position, but he was a man of excellent sense, and as good a man and fellow as ever lived in the town. I helped to make him a mason, and he made the prayer for himself, a thing I never knew any other to do.

Greenville wives of 40 years ago exist in greater number, of whom I call to mind, Mrs. McKellar, Mrs. Henry, Mrs. Oliver, Mrs. Taylor, Mrs. Johnston, Mrs. Mallett, Mrs. Posey, Mrs. Ashford (then Abney).

I know and appreciate the dislike of females to being made the subject of age-gossip, but in these cases it can be only an unmeaning prejudice, an instinct, as I am sure none of the disengaged ever expect, or desire to change their present condition; only one remains her incumbrance. Their youthful bloom has passed away, the dross of earth consumed leaving instead the mellowness and purity of age, a life-giving influence and odor necessary to the young. God's work contains no mistakes, nor useless arrangements.

There are some incidents of persons and things of Greenville as I knew her (or it) before her new birth of 1858, produced by the railroad, which may be of interest to younger persons then of that day and this, and new comers, which I may "dot", I don't promise if leisure and inclination should join hands and you promise more careful proof reading than in the past."

From Vicksbury, May 17, 1891.

Yours truly,
A.F.P.

LOOKING AT THE ECLIPSE THROUGH SMOKED GLASS
A total eclipse occurred on 28 May 1900 when it was completely dark in Greenville for ninety seconds. Mrs. E. L. Cook is in the center of the picture above (without a hat) and H. P. Martin on the extreme right.

CHAPTER 7.

BUTLER SPRINGS

BUTLER SPRINGS HOTEL

One of the most popular and best known places in the county in the 1800s was Butler Springs. Soon after the medicinal value of the water was discovered in the early 1840s the pilgramage began to this small community which was to last over half a century. It was visited not only by those who were ailing, but by people of all ages who went solely for the purpose of enjoyment.

Some of the owners of this property have been John Ubanks, F. Nathaniel Sims, John Eddy, Capt. T. A. Knight, Alph Carter, James Benson, John Carter, William S. Sims, S. D. Wilson, William Jones and W. S. and J. C. Gramling.

Butler Springs was once considered the Saratoga of South Alabama with as many as 500 regular boarders staying at the springs at one time, either in the hotel or one of the many cottages. The water contained magnesium, iron and sulphur while the water in nearby Reddock Springs, had only magnesium and sulphur. The third spring in the area. Roper Springs had all three qualities with many more besides. At one time when Roper Springs was owned by W. W. Wilkinson it was bottled and sold on the market under the name of the Matchless Mineral Water. According to Dr. J. T. Broughton, "An analysis shows it to be well adopted to every grade of disease where the blood in emaciated and the constitution protracted and dibilitated from a wasting of all the tissues. Helpful in many cases of dyspepsia, accompanied with chronic diarrhea, skin diseases, ring worms, tetters, old ulcers, etc. Having specialized in female diseases for many years he found it helpful for gleet, vaginitis, inflamation of the vaginal portion of the woman and etc." Reddock and Roper Springs never were developed to the extent that was Butler Springs, however, because of its easy accessability to Greenville, Reddock Springs did enjoy quite of bit of popularity.

Several hotels have been on the site of the springs in Butler Springs, the first one being built by John Ubanks. In June 1852 while under the proprietorship of Nat Sims the following rates were advertised for those who wished to stay at the hotel: By the month, $20.00; by the week, $7.00; by the day, $1.25. Children and servants, Half price. Horses, $15.00 per month.

Mr. S. D. Wilson first leased the property in 1873. At that time the only things remaining of the splendor of the antebellum days were the ball room, storehouse and 18 or 20 cabins. The large hotel which had entertained so many people under its roof, had fallen to the ground. However, the water could still work its wonderous cures and Mr. Wilson immediately made plans to rebuild. By July, 1874 the rates were being advertised for $30.00 a month; $8.00 a week and $2.00 a day. These rates were considered to be very reasonable in comparison with other hotels in the State. For many years Butler Springs was a popular place to take a summer vacation of two or three weeks, and year after year the same people would return giving testamony either to the healing qualities of the water, good food, the society of congenial folks or a combination of all three. The crowds of people congregated in this small place drew politicians like flies or ants to a picnic and no doubt many races for office were won or lost as the result of a Fourth of July debate on the porch of the hotel. This was also a favorite rendevous spot for the young ladies and gentlemen with more than a few marriages resulting from introductions made within the confines of the community.

In the March 18, 1914 Greenville Advocate we learn the hotel burned nearly six years prior to that date and was never rebuilt. Up to then there had been hardly a time when a hotel had not been there for at least the past 20 to 30 years. The property was purchased by two former Butler County boys, W. S. & J. S. Gramling who planned a corporation and it was understood that before many years passed there would be a great modern hostelry built, equipped with all the modern conveniences and with everything in the way of sports from swimming pools to golf and tennis.

This, of course, never materialized and in driving past the site of the springs there is no evidence left today that anything had ever been built on the site. Nature has completely reclaimed the land.

KOLB CITY, INC.[1]

Kolb City was incorporated two miles North and South and one mile East and West with H. C. Darley, Mayor; C. S. Dowd, Marshall; S. C. Whitehead, City Attorney; J. A. Rhodes, C. T. Reid, W. A. Gafford, W. P. Bodiford and D. L. Bradley, Councilmen; Seth Mercer, Sec. and Treas.; R. E. Peagler, Tax Collector and J. M. Johnson, Street Overseer.

1. The Living Truth, 8 July 1897.

GEORGIANA[1]

Georgiana had its founding several years before the railroad passed through this section. The present site of the city was picked out by Pitt S. Milner, a Baptist minister, who came there from Pike County, Ga. to establish his homestead. He settled on the location now known as the "old Milner place" in 1855, and established a postoffice the same year, naming it Georgiana, the name being a combination of Georgia and Anna, the latter for his little daughter.

In later years when the railroad established a depot, it was named Pittsville for the reverend gentleman, but he objected to the name, and had it called Georgiana, the same as the postoffice. At that time, several people lived in the surrounding country; the oldest settler, named John Sheppard and also from Georgia, lived about two and one-half miles north of what is now Georgiana, having moved there in 1824.

In 1858, Rev. Milner opened a store of general merchandise. T. H. Powell soon followed with a grog-shop, the liquor business proving quite as profitable as any other for some time.

Uncle Henry Smith came to Georgiana immediately after the Rev. Milner, Miles and Peter Simpson, John W. Wheeler, Richard Gardner, Jerry Farlo, Dr. Clemons, the town's first physician, Joseph Roberson, and Thomas Cargle, were among the earlier citizens. Before the coming of the railroad the mails were run to and from Greenville on horse-back two or three times a week.

The first school was taught in this place in 1856 by Miss Eunice Eskew[2] in a log school house erected by Pitt Milner. E. C. Milner and John A. Milner, sons of the minister, had a steam saw and grist mill in operation in the city as early as 1858.

Here is an account of the coming of the first train into Georgiana, written by some pioneer citizen at that time who signed her article "Ancient Dame", taken from The Butler County News of June 12, 1912, when the paper was being edited by R. W. Pride: "The first train rolled into our town on July 4, 1859. The track had been laid this far and the train was expected that day. There was a big barbecue and political speaking (The Civil War was then brewing) which was held under a large brush arbor located where uncle K. L. Davis' house now stands. The excitement was intense. You can imagine how excited the people were if you can recall the day the airship came. There were old people who had never seen a train, and when the whistle blew there was a regular stampede--one poor old lady began to hallo, "Stand back, stand back for God's sake, they tell me that thing runs a mile a minute." On the train were speakers and candidates for some office, I don't remember what. However, I remember that they halloed, "Hurrah for Bell and Everett". All day the railroad gave free rides to Bolling and back and it was a day never to be forgotten in life, though there are few of us living to tell the tale."

After the establishment of the railroad through Georgiana, the town began to grow steadily. Rev. Milner started the construction of the Baptist church in 1865, and began preaching in it in 1866. The Metho-

---

1. The Greenville Advocate. 1931.
2. Niece of Pitt S. Milner and daughter of Miriam Milner & Rev. Isaac Eskew.

dists started their church the following year. The Baptist Church was organized with 20 members by Rev. Milner in 1856 and the Methodists a few years later. The present fine structures of both of the churches were erected in 1903 and 1907, respectively. Jerry Farlo, one of the earliest residents, gave the lot for the first Methodist Church.

Georgiana was incorporated as a town in 1869 and received a new charter in 1872. Rev. Milner was very probably the first mayor of the city. Major A. N. Glenn was mayor for several years around the 1885 period.

In 1868 the citizens of the town erected a large school building, called the Georgiana Academy. From this has been gradually evolved the present efficient public school. The present building was constructed about 12 years ago.

In 1885 Georgiana had a population of 600. Today it has over 1500 people."

In 1898 Georgiana had an excellent weekly paper, the Georgiana Guardian, edited by Messrs. Oscar C. Sims and George Bryan. It had a good subscription list and enjoyed a splendid advertising patronage.

It had an educational advantage over other towns of like size in the area with its Pensacola District High School. Under the leadership of Prof. J. B. Adams, it had established prestige among the educational institutions of this section, furnishing thorough instruction in all of the intermediate and high school branches.

Mr. John D. Bryan was one of Georgiana's most popular and enterprising merchants. He served the people well as Mayor and later as a member of the city council. He was a great advocate of improvement and took a leading part in all movements which had for its object the improvement of the town or the bettering of its religious, social or commercial conditions.

The health of the city was well looked after by several excellent physicians, among them Dr. W. W. Mangum, whose professional skill was appreciated by the people and whose professional services were in constant demand.

Georgiana was also known in the literary world as the home of Thad L. Rose, whose work "The Devil's Balance Sheet" met with a most favorable reception and his reputation as an entertaining and instructive lecturer extended over the entire country. He was one of the most public spirited men in Alabama and devoted much of his time and money to the improvement and development of the town.

Mr. George H. Brayan, associate editor of the Guardian, was a leading druggist in town. He was one of the most popular young men in town and a newspaper man of great talent.

Mr. Oscar C. Sims, also with the Guardian, was a young man of versatile talents. In addition to his editorial work Mr. Sims devoted much of his time and attention to the mercantile business and to the buying and shipping of cotton. As a writer he possessed superior ability, and was a poet of no mean order. His poems possessed real merit and are read and appreciated by hundreds who knew the author only by his pseudonym "J. Ralph Reny". Each week he filled half a column with charming verses which were often copied in the state papers. He was the son of the Rev. Alexander T. Sims, pastor of the Baptist Church, and was born in Forest Home on March 5, 1872. He moved with his parents to Georgiana in 1887 and after leaving school he engaged in the fancy grocery and confectionary business. He later went into business with an uncle, Arthur, Forest Sims, opening a general merchandise firm.

Mr. J. E. Cheatham was one of Georgiana's most popular and enterprising merchants, was born nine miles East of Greenville in 1859. His father, James Cheatham, was a son of one of the wealthy land owners of Butler County. He died in 1862 in Tupelo, Miss. while in the army. Upon the death of young Cheatham's father, the late Dr. Thomas Stallings was made his guardian. The tragic death of Dr. Stallings at a time when J. E. Cheatham was being prepared for school interfered very seriously with his early education. He received a common school education, provided by his mother and later spent three years at a school at Highland Home, Ala. Early in life he took an active part in the management of the farm. For some years he worked on the farm of his uncle, Rev. W. H. Cheatham, earning for himself a reputation for industry, honesty and sobriety which did much to shape his later career of usefulness. He married in October 1888 Miss Lila Dewberry. He had attended Lebanon College where he trained in the educational field, and for two years he taught and was in charge of the Georgiana Academy, being ably assisted in the work by Mrs. M. J. Motes as primary teacher and Miss Hallie Cochran as music and art teacher.

HISTORY OF CHAPMAN
GIVEN BY RESIDENT OF BREWTON

"Lumbering Along" January 16, 1953.   by Thomas A. Ludham

In a letter to the editor of The Brewton Standard a short sketch of the history of Chapman was written which was re-printed in "Lumbering Along".

"The first sawmill was built (in Chapman) by K. L. Davis and sons. It was known as the Old Chapman Hill Mill. This mill cut about 12 or 15 thousand feet of lumber per day. After a while the mill changed hands to a Mr. Sutton. Mr. Sutton operated the mill a short while and then it was operated by a Mr. Thuston and then by Mr. Chapman and Mr. Kirkland.

While they were operating the mill, they purchased the first log engine. It ran on a pole road. The name of this old engine was the Florence Baldwin. While this was in operation, it went by the name of Rocky Creek Lumber Company. While Mr. Chapman and Mr. Kirkland were in charge, they built a large sawmill down by the old hill. The mail was carried to and from Georgiana by an old schoolmate of mine, Bert Graves.

About 1890, Mr. Chapman purchased the second log engine, which ran on a narrow gauge iron track. The name of this little locomotive was Old Prince. After Mr. Chapman left here, he went over in Georgia. The mill was then operated by Mr. Kirkland and Mr. Mallette.

About 1890, Mr. W. T. Smith came from north of Montgomery and purchased the entire mills at Chapman and changed the name from Rocky Creek Lumber Company to W. T. Smith Lumber Company. Mr. Smith operated this mill for about 10 or 12 years and sold out to Mr. Pad Foshee, of Brewton, Alabama. About 50 years ago, Mr. Foshee and the McGowins operated this business under the same name, W. T. Smith Lumber Company. They made a pretty good town out of Chapman, Alabama. They built two other sawmills, which are still in operation.

The first commissary on the Old Mill Hill was built of round pine poles and later they built a new commissary out of lumber. Mr. Zema Shepherd of Georgiana, was the clerk in the new commissary. Mr. Shepherd was a fine young man. The writer of this letter was a water boy on the tram road under Mr. S. E. Graves in the Summer of 1890, at 35¢ a day.

Mr. Ludham was asked if he remembers what year the mill was moved from Old Mill Hill down into Chapman. He replied that he was quite sure it was 1887. When the little mill was built on the hill in 1883, Mr. Ludham was about nine years of age. Now he is 78.

One of the fond recollections, Mr. Ludham said, was: "Back in the 1890s, Mr. W. T. Smith would send his little log engine, "Old Prince" with about four flat cars with seats on them of pine boards, out eight or ten miles east of Chapman to bring the people into church on Sunday mornings. Billy Williams was the engineer and would go out and get these people and bring them in on his train and that Old Prince engine ran so fast until the people had to hold their hats on to keep them from blowing off. They would attend church and they had plenty of drinking water. After church, Billy Williams would carry them back across Persimmon Creek. Billy was a fine fellow and liked by everybody. Billy has been dead 50 years and I do not know where the Old Prince engine is today."

W. T. SMITH LUMBER COMPANY

14

At Chapman, twelve miles south of Greenville, are situated the mills and offices of the W. T. Smith Lumber Company, the largest single enterprise in Butler County and the largest lumber mill in the state. Although Chapman looks like a hustling little city, and is one, yet is is really the lumber company, for hardly a dozen people live in this little town of nearly a thousand inhabitants who do not work at the mills or in the woods. Here are situated the office, the stupendous mills, the commissary and the machine shops, and here also are the homes of the men and the officers of the company. These homes would do credit to any city and are delightful residences. The mills themselves, with their dry kilns and other adjuncts, cover many acres and here in a day train loads of logs are converted into lumber, totaling up to about four million feet of the long leaf yellow pine every month. Of this product, about half is exported and the other finds ready market here in the United States, though principally north of the Ohio River.

The history of the W. T. Smith Lumber Company is indeed an interesting one. About nine years ago the present stockholders purchased the company and immediately set about the rehabilitation of the whole plant. At Chapman they started as if there had never been a mill there and in a little while a most modern mill rose where the old had stood. Presently another mill was built, the two having a monthly capacity of three and a half million feet of lumber. In the seven or eight years since that time other improvements have been added, new machinery installed and the whole has kept even pace with every stride of progress.

At first only the long leaf yellow pine on their sixty thousand acres of timber land was used, but later a stave factory was erected so as to make use of the large amount of splendid hardwood growing along the creek banks of their land. A veneer mill was put up and here poplar and other woods are turned into patent shipping crates.

Growing out of the lumber industry and an important part of it is what really amounts to a little private railroad system some seventy five miles or more in all, over which the logs are brought to the mill. Some of the trains run over the Louisville and Nashville line from Chapman to a point below McKenzie, where they branch off to other land belonging to the W. T. Smith Lumber Company. At Chapman are the railroad machine shops, and here the engines and cars are kept in repair.

In the United States we have learned to look for the man behind every great business and to feel that the growth of the enterprise is just an expression of that man's power and thought. In this instance, however, we could not look for the man, but for the men who have taken this plant and in a short ten years made it a great power in the lumber world. Working together toward a common goal in perfect harmony and accord, the officers of this lumber company have written their names indelibly in the history of both the lumber industry and the History of Butler County. They are: Mr. J. F. McGowan, president; Mr. W. E. Foshee, vice-president; Mr. J. G. McGowan, secretary and treasurer, and Messrs. J. C. and W. M. McGowan, woods superintendents. These are all comparatively young men who have done much and will do more in their chosen field. They are respected citizens of the county as a whole and have the trust and respect of their employees and associates as well as that of the citizens of the entire county."[1]

MCKENZIE HISTORY[2]

"McKenzie was named for Captain McKenzie, who was the engineer of the first train to run through the community, the railroad between Montgomery and Mobile being constructed through this point in 1899. Bob Lee owned the first store in the immediate vicinity, which was located just south of the present site of the town.

---

1. Greenville Advocate, 8 Apr. 1914.
2. Greenville Advocate. 1931.

Previous to this time there were few homes within miles of the location. When the railroad began to clear its right of way, the present site of the town began to take on the semblance of a settlement. J. C. Huggins, who still resides in McKenzie, worked on the railroad right of way. He came to the place and built the first home in March, 1899, at the present north end of town on the west side of the railroad tracks. At that time McKenzie was merely the intersection of the public roads now known as U. S. Highway No. 31. Mr. Huggins built his present home in the summer of the same year.

The following year, after the railroad had been completed through the place, the building of homes was begun. G. W. Lee, former Representative of Butler County in the Alabama Legislature, constructed a home and a store. S. D. Majors followed the same procedure and D. B. Sellers built a home and a hardware establishment.

Mr. Huggins moved the postoffice from Lumber Mills to Persimmon Creek in 1899, by which name it was called until the town was named McKenzie in 1900. Mr. Huggins was postmaster for many years after that time.

In 1901, the first school house for the community was built, a small wooden structure. The Methodist Church was organized in 1903, and built its house of worship the same year, the first pastor being Rev. J. L. Mathewson. Rev. A. T. Sims, of Georgiana, organized the Baptist Church here a few years later. B. J. Griffin was one of the first elders. Among those who might be counted as pioneer citizens of McKenzie are: J. C. Huggins, J. D. Sellers, R. A. Lee, H. J. Huggins, J. L. Sellers, J. W. Huggins, R. W. Johnson, J. W. Hall and John W. Baldwin.

McKenzie was incorporated in 1913, and since that time its civic affairs have been directed by the mayor-council form of government, made up of able and energetic citizens. H. E. Mancil was first mayor of the city, and the following, with one other who could not be determined, composed the first council: J. C. Huggins, E. A. Barrow, J. L. Sellers, and W. I. Lee.

Since its very beginning McKenzie has been gradually growing, seeing an increase in population and prosperity with each decade. It is located in the southern part of Butler County and is a fine country town with a population of about 500 at present. It is ideally located as the heart of an excellent agricultural section, is on the A&F branch of the L&N railroad, on the U. S. Highway No. 31, running from Montgomery to Mobile and also on the Montgomery to Andalusia highway, which leaves the Mobile road at McKenzie. It is 21 miles from Evergreen, the county site of Conecuh, 25 miles from Andalusia, the county site of Covington, 25 miles from Greenville, the county site of Butler, and is on the south end of a stretch of paved highway coming from Fort Deposit, in Lowndes county.

B. F. Beesley is postmaster at present and is assisted by J. D. Hubbard and L. G. Sellers as carriers. W. I. Hall serves as superintendent of education and W. L. Walsh as director of vocational agriculture. T. J. Spear, as mayor, is the present head of McKenzie's competent city government. E. B. Odom, Gip B. Lee, W. J. Hall, J. L. Sellers, and Wilson Lee, councilmen: H. E. Mancil, treasurer, K. L. Huggins, clerk; J. C. Avant, chief of police.

GREENVILLE

Although Greenville is the County seat it was a relatively small town until the advent of the railroad in 1855, and the Eradication Act which passed in Congress about this same date. The southern half of the county had land open to entry at $1.25 per acre and had lain idle for many years at the same price, in no demand except for an occassional new comer. The Eradication Act reduced the price to actual new settlers, or in limited amounts for increasing established properties, for fifty cents an acre. These lands contained much valuable timber and soil for cultivation. The railroad made accessable markets which had been only partially available due to the sea of prairie which was impassable in wet seasons in various parts of the county.

The lower price of land brought in the Milners, Broughtons, Flowers and Thames along with many other families. Greenville increased rapidly in size and as it grew there became an increasing need for lawyers. The first lawyer to settle in the County was Anderson Crenshaw for whom Crenshaw County was named. He was circuit judge from 1821 to 1839, a member of the Supreme Court of Alabama from 1821 to 1832 and the Chancellor of the Southeastern Division of Alabama from 1838 to 1847. He held the first circuit court in Butler County under the spreading branches of an oak tree at Fort Dale.

Other lawyers were Jack Herbert, Nathan Cook, Thomas Hill Watts, John K. Henry, David B. Parmer, Mr. Abney, John W. Womack, T. H. Hampton, I. S. McMean, Samuel Adams, Benjamin F. Porter, M. C. Lane, Hilary A. Herbert, J. J. McLemore, Mr. Thomasson, J. L. Powell, John Gamble, E. Y. Hill, Bryan Whitfield, Tom J. Judge, Sam Seawell, J. M. Whitehead, L. M. Lane, R. F. Cook, Mr. Evans, L. D. Brooks, J. A. Minnis, W. A. Dukes, H. B. Pilley, John Padgett, Edward Crenshaw, Jesse F. Stallings, Smyth & Bozeman, Zell Gaston, J. W. Posey, Philemon O. Harper, H. D. Lampley, Julius Ceasar Richardson, Claude E. Hamilton, Dempey M. Powell, Lee Andrews, John Gamble, Jr., Arthur Emmett Gamble, Earnest Bryan, Gen. Robert E. Steiner, Calvin Poole, Claude E. Hamilton, Jr.

Among the Judges who have served in Butler County were Anderson Crenshaw, Herndon L. Henderson, William Lee, James Lane, Daniel Gafford, Samuel J. Bolling, J. F. Johnson, H. W. Watson, Jonathan L. Powell, John R. Tyson, J. C. Richardson, Arthur E. Gamble, T. Werth Thaggard, Arthur E. Gamble, Jr.

Four Court Houses have served the county. The first one, a frame building, was erected in 1822 and was destroyed by fire April 12, 1853. A second frame building was soon erected on the previous site and was used until 1871. This was then torn down and replaced by a brick building with a pair of steps in front which curved to meet at the second floor entrance. This building was replaced in 1903 when the present building was constructed. A shortage of space in recent years resulted in the additional rooms being added to the front of the building which altered its appearance considerably.[1]

The Hon. W. H. Crenshaw left at the office of the Advocate a manuscript copy of "A Bill to be entitled an Act to incorporate the City of Greenville" in February, 1867. This Act of incorporation was to be submitted to the citizens of Greenvile at any early day, for their acceptance or rejection. It conferred the usual powers and privileges which are given by Charter to cities and nothing more.[2]

---

[1]. Greenville Advocate
[2]. Greenville Advocate, 28 February, 1867.

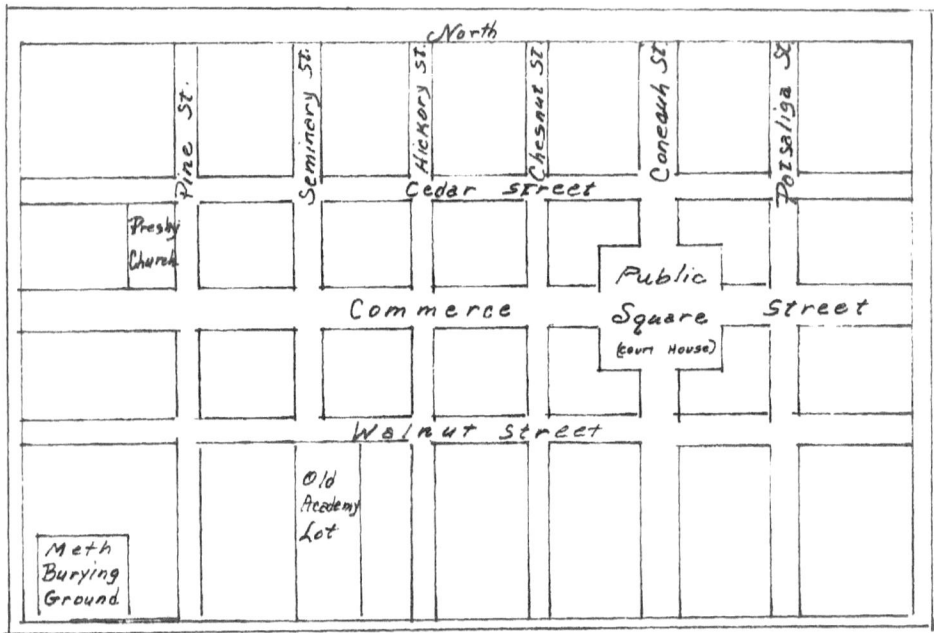

Greenville 1854

This plat of Greenville was made on 22 August 1854 by William Graydon, the county surveyor. It is reproduced from the Greenville Advocate of November 29, 1947. The plat was furnished to the Advocate by Wallace R. Hill, a descendant of Mr. Graydon, who was a banker in Selma. This was probably the first, or one of the first plats, drawn of Greenville following the Court House fire. At that time Greenville was huddled around the Court House. Some years later after the completion of the railroad the city built up around the railroad station. Gradually the city expanded and the two business sections closed in on each other.

The present city hall was just outside the city limits of Greenville in 1854. The Presbyterian Church occupies the same site as it did then, while the "Methodist Burying Ground" has been doubled in size, and is now known as Pioneer Cemetery. The Methodist Protestant Church was just outside the city limits on the site of the present First Methodist Church, which is located across the street from Pioneer Cemetery, or to the left of the cemetery as shown on the plat. The square between the church on Walnut Street and Commerce Street has been made into a beautifully maintained park in which is found the statue of the Confederate Soldier which was erected by the Father Ryan U.D.C. Chapter.

The first church in the city was a community church and was located at the site of that "burying ground" and the early funerals were held on the church grounds. The streets as shown on the plat have remained the same with the exception of Seminary Street which has been changed to Mallett Street.

LAYING OF THE CORNER STONES
OF THE COLLEGIATE INSTITUTE AND THE CITY HALL[1]

The laying of the corner stones of the Greenville Collegiate Institute and the City Hall took place on August 19, 1880, and despite the intense heat there was a large number of spectators to witness the impressive ceremony which was conducted by the Masonic fraternity.

THE PROCESSION

was led by the Greenville Light Guards, under command of Lieut. Porter, then came the Fire Companies, Knights of Pythias, Odd Fellows and Masons.

The corner stone of the Collegiate Institute was first laid, and owing to a reversal of the programme as published, not more than half of the crowd witnessed the interesting ceremony. The ladies had gathered at the City Hall, where seats had been provided in the shade, and on account of the misunderstanding, did not go to the college, expecting the corner stone of the City Hall to be laid first as per published programme. This was the only thing that occured to mar the pleasure of the day. Quite a number of articles were deposited in the stone. Catalogues of the two colleges, constitutions, and by-laws of the various secret orders of the city, gold, silver and copper coins, greenbacks, Light Guards brass button, corn, cotton, barley, Greenville Advocate, etc.

Rev. Mr. Boling delivered a prayer, after which, Prof. Holcombe was introduced, and made an eloquent address of about fifteen minutes length. He paid a handsome tribute to each of the secret societies present, the fire and military companies, and heartily thanked them for participating. The procession then reformed, and marched to the City Hall, where an immense concourse of people were waiting to witness the ceremony.

A prayer was given by the Rev. Mr. Holcombe after which the corner stone was adjusted and deposits called for. The various societies deposited by-laws and constitutions, the city code, oats, barley, corn, gold and silver coins, a copy of each of the city papers, and numerous other articles, after which came an address by Rev. J. D. Porter.

GREENVILLE'S SCHOOLS OF THE PAST[2]

"In presenting and connecting Greenville of the past and present in the matter of schools, information for the first fourth of a century depends wholly on the memory of one person--a lady. She remembers Mrs. Harriet Herbert (mother of Phil Herbert, who in the 1850s was a representative in Congress from California and was killed in Louisiana in one of the battles of the late war) teaching a mixed school for boys and girls between 1825 and 1830 and again in the thirties. Also that a Presbyterian clergyman from Connecticut, a friend or relative of the Demings, came down and taught and preached several years in the thirties.

Greenville, although the county seat, was a mere village, and most of the patrons residing outside, the teaching was more often in the country than in the town. There seems to have been no separate school or building for females until 1847. Mr. and Mrs. Thomas E. Herbert had the year before purchased a body of splendid land on Muscle Creek, nearly all timbered and put a strong force to prepare it for

1. Greenville Advocate 25 August 1880. 2. Greenville Advocate 5 Jan. 1898.

cultivation and had settled themselves in Greenville. They had taught with success in another locality and were pressed into service. An Academy was built in which they taught successfully as long as it suited them to do so, about four years.

The next teacher equal to all requirements was the Rev. Dr. Capers in 1859 (Greenville's boom year) took the building and with assistants ran the school with success until subsided by the war.

The male branch by accident or otherwise seems to have kept in better shape, as in the thirties the male academy was built, and connected with it were more men who later attained distinction then, perhaps, any similar building in the State. About 1840 a gentlemen named Murrah[1] held the rod over Dan Dunklin, Jeff Burnett and others, and afterward became Governor of Texas. In 1847 a gentleman named Eaton, from Connecticut, taught--an accomplished man. Some suppose that he is the same man who since represented that State in the Unites States Senate, but the Congressional Directory does not confirm the supposition. Samuel Adams, a graduate of the South Carolina College, taught in 1852. He afterwards represented Butler County in the legislature, and while a rapidly growing lawyer he went down as Colonel of the Thirty third Alabama Regiment in the late war, idolized by his command, and wringing a tribute of tears from his commander, Pat Cleburne. Edward A. Perry, who taught in 1855 and 1856 became an eminent lawyer, Brigadier-General in the late war and Governor of Florida. Robert Garlington, a first-honor student of the South Carolina College, taught in 1858, and returned to take charge, as president of a female college.

Since the war, Thomas C. Pinckard, since mayor of Opelika, taught boys one or two years, and one year a select group of twenty females. Rev. Mark Barnes had charge of the Male Academy in the days of Reconstruction, and has since built up, in another locality, one of the finest institutions in the State. Col. William Seawell, a graduate of Chapel Hill, North Carolian, and afterward of the University of Virginia, one of the most finished scholars, born with a silver spoon in his mouth and having lost it and also an iron spoon, as a result of the war, endeavored to recoup the bread question by imparting part of what he knew, and was given possession of the building and opened the school, to appearance for success, but before reaching the middle of the first term he threw up the sponge and went into politics, declaring that a horse that had run to pasture thirty years could not stand pressure to back and shoulder.

P. Carolan, a highly educated Irishman, also taught during the reconstruction, but a victim to a too common weakness, he lost his mind and was taken charge of by a Priest of St. Louis, Mo. and cared for.

Thomas E. Royall, of Virginia, taught the female school first after the war. Messrs. Mack and George Thigpen, followed soon after and arranged for permanence. The Methodist people, about the same time, secured a lot of their own and erected thereon a commodious building.[2] The

---

1. Pendleton Murrah was born in S.C. He came first to Alabama and then moved to Texas in the late 1840s or early 1850s. In 1857 he was elected representative of Harrison County, Texas, in the State legislature and in 1863 was made governor. When the Confederacy surrendered he fled to Mexico where he died in Monterey in 1865.
2. The Greenville Collegiate Institute. Among the men who served this school were the Revs. John W. Rush, Henry Urquhart and R. S. Holcomb. This school was operated by the Methodist Conference.

former school, under the Thigpens, was called the Baptist school, on account of their prominence as members; the other was called the Methodist school, because the head officers were under their denominational control. Assistants were chosen for character and qualification without reference to creeds."

GREENVILLE PUBLIC SCHOOL

GREENVILLE'S CENTENNIAL, 4 JULY 1922[1]

8:10 A.M.--Arrival of distinguished guests, including General R. E. Steiner, who will proceed up Commerce Street from the station, escorted by Butler Horse Guards and Masonic Home Band.

9:30 A.M.--Band Concert at City Hall.

10:00--Welcome to Former Citizens at City Hall: Mayor W. S. Blackwell, Chairman.
Invocation---------------------------------Dr. J. O. Grogan
Song, "Home, Sweet Home."
Address of Welcome on Behalf of Greenville--Col. C.E. Hamilton
Response on Behalf of Former Citizens-------Brig. Gen. Robt. E. Steiner
Song, "America."
Benediction--------------------------------Dr. H. Ross Arnold

11:00--Pagent-Parade: Starts at Court House, goes down Commerce Street to station, turns to left and goes to Herbert Street; then up Herbert Street to Episcopal Church, thence to Commerce Street at First National Bank; back up Commerce Street to Court House.

[1]. Greenville Advocate, 28 June 1922.

ORDER OF PARADE

Marshal of the Day, Duke Guice.
1. Masonic Home Band.
2. Butler Horse Guards.
3. City Officials.
4. Boy Scouts.
5. Historical Floats.
6. Decorated Automobiles.

1:00 P.M.--Barbecue, Basket dinner and Brunswick Stew on School Campus, and on Cedar Street immediately behind City School building.

2:00 P.M.--Community Sing on School campus.

3:30 P.M.--Baseball Game at the Ball Park--Butler County vs. Crenshaw County.

All Day--Stunt Flights by aviators from the Intermediate Air Depot of Montgomery.

Band concerts during the day.

All Day--Dancing on Platform on Beeland's Square.

Merry-Go-Rounds, Ferris Wheels.

On this float are descendants of the Dunklin family, one of the pioneer families of the county.

FOREST HOME, INC.

Forest Home has been incorporated and is now a town. On Monday of last week an election for city officers was held and resulted as follows: Intendent--J. G. Reynolds; Councilmen: E. M. Lazenby, W. H. Shanks, J. P. Benson and B. T. Bryson.   (Advocate, 1 Apr. 1891)

CHAPTER 8.

ELECTION OF FIRST MONDAY IN MAY 1859[1]

Two men from each precinct were running for Justice of the Peace and one for Constable. Following the names of these men are the three inspectors and the returning officer for each precinct.

Pct. 1. Starlington
Jas. W. Page, Benj. Norris
Alford Gandy, J. M. Page, L. A. Callier

J. W. Prim
Elihu Sims, R.O.

Pct.2, South Butler
Newton M. Rhodes, Wm. Palmore
Eli Hudson, N. W. Rhodes, W. C. Saitor

William Riley
W. Riley, R.O.

Pct. 3. Oakey Streak
Henry C. Smith, Richard S. Hughes
John T. Dees, H. C. Smith, J. Crittenden

J. H. Wells
D. L. Thomas, R.O.

Pct. 4, Shut-Eye
Geo. J. Staggers, P. P. Davenport
W. F. Mahone, D. Clancy, J. Kettler

David Staggers
J. Y. Smyth, R.O.

Pct. 5. Solomon's
C. Campbell, Jeff Cote
A. G. Morrison, G. W. Thagard, G. Miller

James Churchwell
W. Churchwell, R.O.

Pct. 6. McCormick's
Z. Daniel, John Henderson
J. Henderson, Z. Daniel, T. H. Briggs

J. N. Baxter
J. N. Baxter, R.O.

Pct. 7. Graydon's
William Graydon, Jas. G. Colvin
J. G. Colvin, T. Graydon, S. S. Seawright

Jas. A. Stubb
T. R. Morgan, R.O.

Pct. 8. Dead Fall
Albert Gafford
P. J. Brock, J. Barganier, A. G. Gafford

James Butler
J. M. Butler, R.O.

Pct. 9. Manningham
J. B. Simpson, Artimus Peagler
E. H. Furgerson, B. Butts, G. Thigpen

Jas. P. Boggan
J. P. Boggan, Sr., R.O.

Pct. 10. Monterey
Thos. Trawick, Warren Thompson
W. R. Trawick, R. Yeldell, L. J. Knight

Vinson Watts
V. Watts, R.O.

Pct. 11. Butler Springs
S. B. Brookins, Augustus Green
S. B. Brookins, J. Eady, John Murphy

J. Sims
J. Mullins, R.O.

[1]. The Southern Messenger, 28 April 1859.

Pct. 12. Greenville
Alexander McKellar, Benjamin Newton   J. P. Routon
W. P. Routon, D. G. Payne, A. Newton   W. D. Perryman, Shff.

Pct. 13. Rhode's
Geo. H. McClure, S. B. Otts   Benj. J. Parker
H. S. Presley, J. S. Brooks, J. Chancelor   W. Allen, R.O.

Pct. 14. Shepherd's
W. C. Shepherd, Coleman O'Gwin   R. L. Black
J. Shepherd, H. Smith, J. M. Black   Jacob Turner, R.O.

Pct. 15. Owen's
T. C. Owen, James S. Watson   T. F. Cleghorn
A. Burnett, J. M. Jordan, L. B. Jackson   T. F. Cleghorn, R.O.

W. D. Perryman, Sheriff, March 30, 1859.

LETTERS IN THE POST OFFICE FOR THE QUARTER ENDING JUNE 30, 1860. PUBLISHED IN THE GREENVILLE ADVOCATE.

H. H. Armstrong	Miss M. Davis	B. F. Hamet
Redden Alford	A. W. Dinna	Samuel Ingram
E. Ashley	M. A. Deavenport	D. D. H. James
S. J. Atkins	John Denson	Mrs. C. Johnson
Charles Amos	John Dickens	F. M. Jones
W. J. Anderson	W. L. C. Evans	J. Jones
E. C. Adams	John Evans	A. F. Jones
William Adams	R. H. Evans	Kargler & Walker
E. B. Arms	L. Estella	John Kuykendall
W. J. Adkins	D. Ellis	Mrs. M. Keeler
John Baynes	J. A. Eubanks	J. C. Kendall
W. R. Brown	Ellis & Simontin	William Knight
J. W. Beel	Benj. Franklin	Dr. James Lester
Mrs. E. Blackshear	Brunetta Fostor (Col.)	J. Limsey
Jonathan Bliss	Jerusha Freeman	Mrs. M. Lasaste
Mrs. Becey Butler	Mrs. M. Felps	Mrs. Julia Loins
P. J. Bennett	A. J. Feagen	J. F. Long
Jorge Boyce	A. P. Feagen	W. Lee
J. N. Bunkley	W. Grace	J. W. Lenoir
M. B. Breedlove	S. Godwin	G. W. Lance
W. M. Benis	Mrs. M. J. Gibson	E. Love
Jessy A. Berry	Mrs. J. Garard	M. McCarty
W. W. Barrington	H. Gragg	Rev. E. Wadsworth
A. P. Blake	T. Gray	J. C. McEachern
Miss L. Brantly	Robt. Garlington	Miss Anne McLerey
Mrs. M. P. Calhoun	Miss M. Garner	Mrs. S. McCaskill
Miss A. Carrecter	Mrs. M. L. Gafney	Mr. McNulty
Hart Collins	W. R. Grogan	Mrs. M. E. Moyl
H. T. Crumpton	Gowan, Cox & Marley	Miss Missoura Morris
C. Calloway	B. M. Garner	Mrs. Mary E. May
Miss Sallie Carter	C. F. Gerkey	Miss S. E. May
C. A. Cox	W. B. Gaines	J. B. Mullins
George W. Carr	T. J. Ganey	John Meads
John Cato	L. Husdt	Miss Mary Moore
D. B. Cokman	J. Hobbs	J. B. Manly
J. Collins	Miss M. Harrington	S. J. Nalls
E. Carnathan	H. Henderson	H. J. Nissis
John Dykes	G. W. Hays	Mrs. M. Narcus

Mrs. F. Norris	Miss M. Rape	Mrs. M. Williams
P. O'Dwyer	Z. L. Rudulph	Mrs. Annie Wilson
G. H. Oliver	J. S. Robins	Henry Whirt
Madam St. Owen	T. H. B. Rinerse	E. C. Warren
Miss Laura Owen	Mrs. Talitha Smith	Miss B. C. Wallace
Mrs. Sarah Oliver	W. Scott	M. J. Williams
Joel Porter	A. Swaner	Miss M. A. White
T. B. Pollard	Prof. R. Schmit	Nelson H. Wheaton
Mr. Pritchett	Britton Stamps	Mrs. Dusey Williams
M. L. Pane	Mrs. S. Troutman	Mrs. Nancy Williams
Mrs. L. C. Phillips	James C. Travis	Marlin D. White
N. B. Peacock, M.D.	Walter Tobin	Dr. G. R. Y. White
Allen Prince	J. L. Tyle	S. J. Ward
Miss Sallie Phipps	Sim Tyner	E. Winslow
Mrs. M. A. Prater	G. F. Todd	Miss E. White
N. Perritt	James R. Taylor	Rev. E. Wadsworth
Miss M. M. Phipps	J. T. Trentlin	J. B. Williams
Miss A. M. Parker	Miss E. Tollent	G. Zelk
Henry Pane	Obediah Vernon	
Miss G. Remington	Mrs. E. E. Varner	

Persons calling for any of the above letters will please say they are advertised.

W. C. Caldwell, P. M.

LETTERS IN THE GREENVILLE POST OFFICE 7 JUNE 1875

H. M. Arnold	M. O. Dawson	Josiah Lewis
Thomas Anderson	Miss Lizzie Day	James Murpha
Miss Georgiana Ashwood	George Earl	Miss M. McGinnis
S. O. Aplin	N. W. Hapy	Hester McNicola
Enoch Blair	M. R. Henly	T. J. Mullens
Cindia Brown (Col.)	William Harrison	L. B. Martin
Rebecker Babbet	T. E. Harrison	A. W. Martin
E. B. Barnes	W. H. Haper	Sarah McCarty
James Campbell	M. B. Johnson	L. E. Murry
Henry Chesnut	Mrs. Mary M. Johnson	M. A. McCall
Miss Alice Cook	Mrs. Maria Jackson	Miss W. J. Majors
Richard F. Cook	J. Jordan	J. G. Miller
Mrs. Nancy Davis	N. Jerry	O. G. Pitts
	Armstead King (Col.)	

SEVENTH ANNUAL DISTRIBUTION OF THE GREENVILLE ADVOCATE

The Greenville Advocate   April 2, 1884.

"The Distribution passed off pleasantly at noon at the City Hall, on the 28th to the perfect satisfaction of all parties. So far as we have learned there has not been a single word of disapproval uttered concerning it. We believe that all of our readers are satisfied that is is conducted fairly. A sufficient proof of this exists in the fact that the committee was composed of the following gentlemen: Capt. L. Harrell, Messrs. L. M. Lane, John Bush, E. Pollard and Harris Lampley. They were assisted by Secretaries King and Pilley. To them and to the several little boys taken from the audience without premeditation, we return thanks for assistance.

The following is the list of names and presents awarded them. Wherever the postoffice is in this State the name of the State is omitted-other States being given.

Andress, Dan'l, Ft. Deposit, shirt studs.
Allen Z. T., Georgiana, shirt studs.
Andress, W. T., Ft. Deposit, $1.00.
Ashcraft, Mrs. M. E., Manningham, shirt studs.
Andress, E. M., Bellville, $1.00.
Andress, R., Greensboro, pocket knife.
Anderson, C. P., Simpkinsville, $1.00.
Adams, J. H., Greenville, butter knife.
Allen, W. T., Pine Apple, shirt studs.
Adams, J. P., William Station, $1.00.
Armstrong, W. H., Greenville, sewing machine.
Allman, J. A., Citra, Fla., $2.00.
Bragg, Mrs. M., Camden, butter knife.
Barker, J. L., Montgomery, $1.00.
Bryant, H. E., Best, $1.00.
Blow, Dr., J. W., Georgiana, silver castor.
Benson, Tom, Andalusia, $2.00.
Buchanan, A. H., Ft. Deposit, silver syrup pitcher.
Bankister, E. A., Bay Minette, $2.00.
Brooks, R. A., Whiting, $1.00.
Butts, J. D., Manningham, $1.00.
Ballard, J. R., Ft. Deposit, silver castor.
Brown, W. A., Olustee Creek, $2.00.
Brook, T. H., Oaky Streak, butter knife.
Burch, Mrs. M. J., Milton, Fla., silver goblet.
Balderee, G. H. N., Greenville, $1.00.
Bozeman, J. E., Dawson, Texas, $1.00.
Bankester, Henry, Bromley, china tea set.
Barganier, Mrs. M. C., Searcy, $2.00.
Barrett, E. R., Greenville, plow.
Barrow, J. G., Cohasseet, $2.00.
Bates, T. J. & J. P., Ft. Deposit, $1.00.
Black, R. L., Georgiana, sewing machine.
Bruner, Dr. P. M., Braggs, silver butter dish.
Burnett, W. A., Castleberry, $1.00.
Barganier, M. H., Greenville, $2.00.
Brown, D. A., Gravilla, $2.00.
Body, J. C., Ft. Deposit, $1.00.
Bozeman, D. T., Greenville, $2.00.
Brooks, Lee, Bolling, $1.00.
Beel, V. H., Calhoun, $1.00.
Black, A. J., Ft. Deposit, $1.00.
Benson, W. L., Shirley, $2.00.
Barge, T. H., Monterey, $1.00.
Balderee, J. W., Greenville, $1.00.
Burke, William, Castleberry, sewing machine.
Bush, J. J., Greenville, $1.00.
Baldwin, Miss O. B., Georgiana, $1.00.
Black, W. S., Bolling, $1.00.
Burke, W. P., Castleberry, $1.00.
Bryant, R. C., Leon, $1.00.
Beasley, E. S., Repton, breach loading gun.
Bowman, E. R., Canoe Station, $1.00.
Boutwell, J. C., Ft. Deposit, $2.00.
Beasley, H. B., Georgiana, $1.00.
Biggs, B. F., McKinney, Texas, $2.00.
Boggan, Mrs. S. E., Bay Minette, $1.00.
Bradley, A. B. Shell, $2.00.
Bailey, M. J., Greenville, $1.00.
Christian, L. W., Weatherford, Texas, $2.00.
Crenshaw, J. W., Phoenix, Arizona Territory, $1.00.

Creech, W. J. Coalburg, $1.00.
Coker, W. B., Honoraville, $2.00.
Coleman, W. R., Pine Apple, shirt studs.
Chapman, Dr. R. B., Leon, $2.00.
Castleberry, Miss Lucy, Vera Cruz, shirt studs
Coleman, Mrs. Hellen, Manningham, $1.00.
Crews, W. D., Childersburg, $2.00.
Corley, Mrs. R. A. Pine Apple, wagon.
Coleman, J. O., Ft. Deposit, $1.00.
Corry, Mrs. R. E., Greenville, $1.00.
Calloway, M. P., Bashi, $1.00.
Carter, Ike, Monterey, $1.00.
Cohran, Rev. J. A., Monterey, $1.00.
Campbell, S. J., Forest Home, $1.00.
Chapman, Mrs. J. B., Evergreen, $1.00.
Cheatham, W. F., Greenville, $1.00.
Carey, John P., Molino, Florida, $1.00.
Cheatham, Mrs. Ida, Georgiana, $1.00.
Creig, Wade, Bolling, shirt studs.
Curtis, G. W., Milton, Florida, $1.00.
Campbell, T. D., Bolling, $1.00.
Cheatham, Mrs. L. E., Greenville, $2.00.
Campbell, G. E., Ft. Deposit, $1.00.
Calloway, C. W., Sandy Ridge, shirt studs.
Clipper, J. R., Georgiana, silver butter dish.
Craddock, Jack, Atlanta, Georgia, organ.
Crenshaw, Mrs. C. E., Ft. Deposit, $2.00.
Clarke, S. D., Leon, silver butter dish.
Crenshaw, Anderson, Sumpterville, Florida, $2.00.
Cook, N. B., Pensacola, Florida, $1.00.
Cowart & Bro., E. T., Mobile, $2.00.
Crenshaw, W. H., Sumpterville, Florida, $1.00.
Dantzler, A., Manningham, silver castor.
Davidson, J. C., Georgiana, $1.00.
Donald, Mrs. J. M., Monterey, $2.00.
Dumont, A., Molino, Florida, shirt studs.
Daniel, Mrs. E., Honoraville, $2.00.
Dunklin, W. T., Greenville, $1.00.
Davis, S. P., Georgiana, butter knife
Donaldson, W. J., William Station, $2.00.
Dampier, Mrs. J., Greenville, butter knife
Duke, Sam'l D., Atlanta, Georgia, $2.00.
Dickinson, Mrs. J. T. Letohatchie, $2.00.
DeLoney, W. C., Brewton, $1.00.
Davis, S. W., Hurricane Bayou, butter knife.
Davis, J. H., Georgiana, $2.00.
Deming, S., Evergreen, $2.00.
Davis, Mrs. E., Hot Springs, Arkansas, silver castor.
Ellis & Bates, Ft. Deposit, butter knife.
Earnest, Miss R. C., Ft. Deposit, butter knife.
Edge, J. W., Mt. Carmel, $1.00.
Emmons, Jesse, Whiting, shirt studs.
Ewing, S. F., Aiken, cooking stove.
Emmons, J. A., Whiting, $2.00.
Ellis, J. E., Burnt Corn, butter knife.
Ealum, S., Oaky Streak, silk dress pattern.
Fountain, H. T., Burnt Corn, $2.00.
Furguson, S. F., Montgomery, $2.00.
Fail, J. J., Greenville, butter knife.
Fife, J. H., Greenville, $1.00.
Files, Miss Fannie, Mobile, silver goblet.

Fields, J. W., Greenville, $1.00.
Frazier, R. S., Best, $1.00.
Flowers, W. M., Greenville, $1.00.
Farrior, R., Greenville, $1.00.
Fonville, W. D., Tuskegee, $150.00.
Forshee, F. J., Lewis Station, $2.00.
Fagin, A. B., Fairfield, $1.00.
Fendlay, Mrs. M. A., Stellar, Texas, $1.00.
Green, Mrs. Sarah, Marion, $2.00.
Gafford, A. G., Greenville, $2.00.
Garvin, W. R., Hamptonville, $1.00.
Green, J. E., Ella, shirt studs.
Godwin, David, Farmersville, $1.00.
Golson, Jno., Ft. Deposit, $1.00.
Gantt, Mrs. M., East Tallassee, $2.00.
Giddens, Abram, Pine Apple, $1.00.
Grant, J. W., Greenville, $2.00.
Gainey, N. J., Rutledge, $1.00.
Garrett, R., Waverly, Tennessee, $2.00.
Graham, W. P., Ella, $2.00.
Gist, Mrs. Rose, Six Mile, $1.00.
Glenn, T. J., Forest Home, $2.00.
Gardner, Mrs. Adaline, Washington, D. C., $10.00.
Griffin, Mrs. J. M., Forest Home, gents gold watch.
Giddens, J. C. Olustee Creek, $1.00.
Gilmore, J. W., Bluff Springs, Florida, $1.00.
Hawkins, J. M., Rutledge, shirt studs.
Hutchenson, D. A., Red Level, $1.00.
Horn, O. W., New Providence, $2.00.
Hairston, W. L., Ft. Deposit, $2.00.
Harrison, C. B., Bolling, $1.00.
Hartley, Mrs. M. F., Ft. Deposit, $1.00.
Hartley, A. C., Greenville, $1.00.
Howell, J. P., Bryant, Texas, $1.00.
Holcombe, J. G., Greenville, $10.00.
Howard, J. P., Brooklyn, $2.00.
Hughes, Mrs. Mary, Nashville, Tenn., Chamber's Encyclopedia.. 10 Vols.
Hancock, Miss M. F., Greenville, shirt studs.
Herbert, L. D., Greenville, $1.00.
Hatton, H. B., Pensacola, Florida, $1.00.
Hamels, M. C., Georgiana, $1.00.
Hightower, H. C., Brewton, $1.00.
Hamil, A. F., Bolling, $1.00.
Hambrick, Mrs. S. E., Greenville, $1.00.
Hardy, Jesse, Whiting, shirt studs.
Hill, Miss Lelia, Evergreen, $2.00.
Herbert, Lee, Bolling, $2.00.
Holzer, Ben, Greenville, $1.00.
Harrison, Mrs. F. O., Searcy, shirt studs.
Harwell, J. T., Georgiana, $1.00.
Higdon, W. R., Commerce, $1.00.
Harrold, Mrs. Andrew, Brewton, $1.00.
Harris, J. W., Calhoun, $2.00.
Hoyett, J. L., Ferry Pass, Florida, silver castor.
Harrell, Mrs. F. E., Greenville, shirt studs.
Harold, Mrs. George C., Brewton, $1.00.
Hamner, W., Elba, $1.00.
Hinson, A. T. & Brother, Greenville, $1.00.
Harrison, Mrs. H. L., Searcy, $1.00.
Henderson, J. B., Evergreen, $1.00.
Hood, James, Georgiana, $2.00.

Harris, Mrs. F. L., Montgomery, $1.00.
Hawkins, W. H., Evergreen, silver goblet.
Irvine, Miss Mary, Tuscaloosa, $1.00.
Johnson, Rev. J. C., Lower Peachtree, $1.00.
Jay, Dr. A., Evergreen, $2.00.
Johnson, T. B., Shell, $2.00.
Johnson, Tom, Greenville, $1.00.
Jones, W. H., Georgiana, $1.00.
Joiner, W. H., Shell, butter knife.
Judge & Carr, Morganville, $1.00.
Jernigan, T. J., Pollard, fine saddle.
Jones, S. F., Simpkinsville, $1.00.
Johnson, A. M., Pollard, $2.00.
Kirkpatrick, E. M., Greenville, $1.00.
Kirkpatrick, M. W., Ft. Deposit, $10.00.
Kendrick, Davis, Sepulga, shirt studs.
King, J. O., Garland, $2.00.
Knight, William, Greenville, $1.00.
Kelley, J. W., Pollard, $1.00.
Kyser, J. K., Belville, butter knife.
Knight, T. D., Strata, $1.00.
Knight, J. T., Greenville, $2.00.
Kellough, A. H., Ft. Deposit, $1.00.
Liddell, Forbes, Montgomery, $1.00.
Long, Dr. N. W., Greenville, plow.
Lloyd, Mrs. M. E., Butler Springs, $1.00.
Lewis, J. B., Jr., Greenville, set chairs.
Lambert, Capt. James, Perdue Hill, silver goblet.
Lee, Mrs. A. M., Farmersville, $1.00.
Lasseter, B. F., Greenville, $1.00.
Lenard, Mrs. S. W., Winn, $1.00.
Lowrey, R. B., Greenville, $2.00.
Lucky, A. C., Pine Apple, $1.00.
Little, D. J., Ft. Deposit, $2.00.
Lambeth, J. M., Whiting, $1.00.
Lee, M., Aiken, cotton-planter.
Larkins, W. R., Georgiana, butter knife.
Lowry, S. A., Burnt Corn, $10.00.
Ludlam, S. P., Georgiana, $1.00.
Lehman, Durr & Co., Montgomery, butter knife.
Lehman, L., Greenville, $10.00.
Maxwell, W. R., Kempville, $1.00.
Melton, Mrs. Mary, Ft. Deposit, rocking chair.
Morgan, E. H., Sepulga, $1.00.
McCoy, W. J., Greenville, $1.00.
Mock, Mrs. M. E., Pensacola, Fla. $1.00.
McGowan, T. J., Brewton, 1 bbl. flour.
Mayo, M., Whiting, $1.00.
McCall, T. M., Holland, $2.00.
Milton, T. J., Pine Apple, $2.00.
Merriwether, Mrs. A. H., Hayneville, $2.00.
Milner, E. C., Georgiana, shirt studs.
Moore, J. C., Troy, $2.00.
McCoy, C., Searcey, $1.00.
Maddox, J. F., Greenville, $1.00.
McKinzie, B. B., Dunham, $2.00.
McCrory, Jno., Forest Home, $1.00.
McCreary C., Evergreen, $1.00.
Moore, L. E., Greenville, $2.00.
McQueen, J. S., Greenville, $1.00.
McCane, T. U. T., Eclectic, $2.00.

Morris, J. M., Mt. Vernon, Texas, $1.00.
McIntyre, Z. T., Evergreen, $2.00.
Moseley, Mrs. M. A. Searcey, $1.00.
Mixon, N., Commerce, $2.00.
Moorer, Gilbert, Braggs, $1.00.
Mendilshon, Ben, Greenville, silver butter dish.
McCreary & Co., Turn Bull, $1.00.
Melton, H. & J., Pine Apple, silver watch.
Morris, Lewis, Whiting, $2.00.
Massengill, W. W., Jayvilla, $1.00.
McQueen, Mrs. M. E., Belton, Texas, $1.00.
May, A. C., Bolling, $1.00.
Moseley, William, Searcey, $1.00.
Monroe, Miss A. E., Evergreen, cotton-planter.
McPherson, J. D., Garland, $1.00.
Neumann, Chas., Greenville, $10.00.
Newman, W. D., Greenville, China tea-set.
Noles, William, Whiting, cotton-planter.
Norris, G. B., Ft. Deposit, family Bible.
Norsworth, W. J., Greenville, $1.00.
Norris, J. J., Bolling, pocket-knife.
Norwood, James, Ft. Deposit, $2.00.
Norred, William, Bellville, $1.00.
Newton, Mrs. C., Bolling, silver syrup pitcher.
Nelson, J. W., Whiting, $1.00.
Owen, J. G., Repton, $1.00.
Oland, Henry, Montgomery, shirt studs.
Owen, J. D., Greenville, 1 bbl. flour.
Pouncey, W. T., Best, $2.00.
Parker, Mrs. F. B. E., Three Runs, $1.00.
Perry, Robert, Glasgow, $1.00.
Parks, Prof. M., Greenville, $2.00.
Perry, J. T., Greenville, butter knife.
Parmer, W. K., Greenville, $1.00.
Peavy, Miss S. E., Shell, China tea-set.
Purifoy, Jno., Camden, $2.00.
Parker, D. T., Mobile, $2.00.
Powell, J. B., Greenville, $1.00.
Pryor, G. W., Greenville, $1.00.
Pierce, Miss Alice, Pigeon Creek, $1.00.
Pitts, C. J., Oaky Streak, butter knife.
Purnall, Mrs. L. A., Georgiana, $2.00.
Pou, J. C., Pensacola, Florida, $1.00.
Parker, S. A., Ft. Deposit, $1.00.
Parker, Noah, Red Level, $1.00.
Perdue, S. F., Live Oak, $2.00.
Parkman, J. B., Honoraville, $1.00.
Porterfield, Mrs. J. B., Cross Plains, $2.00.
Parker, G. J., Oaky Streak, $1.00.
Pilley, R. S., Shell, $2.00.
Perryman, Katie, Greenville, $1.00.
Peavy, L. B., Shell, $1.00.
Pritchett, J. J., Bolling, $1.00.
Palmer, Miss Cora E., Birmingham, $2.00.
Purifoy, Mrs. Maggie, Snow Hill, $1.00.
Perdue, Peyton, Three Runs, shirt studs.
Peacock, N. B., Garland, $1.00.
Palmer, A. L., Georgiana, $1.00.
Russell, J. S. Pigeon Creek, $1.00.
Roach, H. T., Greenville, $1.00.
Reddoch, W. L., Rutledge, $1.00.

Rabb, Mrs. M. E. Reagon, Texas, $1.00.
Rigsby, P. D., Shell, $2.00.
Raley, Sam, Andalusia, $2.00.
Riley, Autry, Hamptonville, shirt studs.
Rhames, F. C., Cook's Stand, $1.00.
Russell, Dr. J. H., Sandy Ridge, $2.00.
Roberts, J. S., Pensacola, Florida, $1.00.
Rice, Mrs. M. P., Prescott, Arizona, $1.00.
Reid, H. H., Greenville, $10.00.
Rogers, W. D., Greenville, buggy harness.
Robinson, J. C., Greenville, $1.00.
Ross, R. E., Whiting, butter knife.
Roberts, J. M., Corryell, Texas, $2.00.
Robertson, B. H., Cook's Stand, $1.00.
Roberson, C. E., River Ridge, $2.00.
Rhodes, Mrs. Sue E., Brundidge, $1.00.
Robinson, J. D., Simpkinsville, $1.00.
Roper, E. M., Greenville, butter knife.
Routon, J. C., Honoraville, $1.00.
Skinner, Rev. J. P., Wildersville, Texas, $2.00.
Smith, A. A., Tarkingston's Prairie, Texas, $1.00.
Sellars, Miss Martha, Greenville, $2.00.
Savage, L. E., Evergreen, $1.00.
Stubbs, J. C., Jayvilla, $1.00.
Smyth, J. E., Greenville, $1.00.
Stallings, T. N., Honoraville, lady's gold watch.
Smith, R. H., Monterey, $2.00.
Stott, J. R., Georgiana, $1.00.
Salter, T. E., Snow Hill, $1.00.
Shanks, F. M., Kerens, Texas, $1.00.
Savage, L. J., Bagdad, Florida, butter knife.
Seale, W. H., Greenville, silver syrup pitcher.
Smith, Mrs. E. E., Butler Springs, $2.00
Swanson, Mrs. C. A. Palestine, Texas, $1.00.
Steiner, Dr., S. J., Greenville $1.00.
Staggers, O. J., Greenville, $1.00.
Slater, S., Bolling, $1.00.
Starks, J. R., Blackwater, Florida, $2.00.
Sawyer, S. D., Anniston, $1.00.
Stringfellow, J. W., Butler Springs, butter knife.
Stewart, Alex, Ft. Deposit, sewing machine.
Steinhart, J. D., Greensboro, $2.00.
Sneed, Mrs. S. E., Centreville, $2.00.
Smith, H. C., Oaky Streak, butter knife.
Steiner, J. M., Greenville, pocket knife.
Stuart, S. M., Greenville, $1.00.
Smith, W. R., Oaky Streak, $1.00.
Stinson, Josiah, Simpkinsville, $2.00.
Scarborough, Miss Lula, Greenville, $10.00.
Salter, Miss Amanda, Evergreen, $2.00.
Smith, G. L., Oaky Streak, shirt studs.
Simpler, William, Georgiana, $1.00.
Shanks, Elizabeth, Ft. Deposit, cotton planter.
Shine, E. L., Greenville, $1.00.
Smith, J. Q., Greenville, $1.00.
Stamps, Mrs. Sallie, Evergreen, butter knife.
Scott, J. A., Jemison, $1.00.
Smith, A. G., Hurricane Bayou, silver goblet.
Touart, Joseph, Georgiana, $1.00.
Toler, Jno., Whiting, butter knife.
Thigpen, J. M., Pleasant Hill, $1.00.

Thigpen, William, Manningham, $1.00.
Talley, Mrs. M., Ft. Deposit, $2.00.
Turner, J. W., Honoraville, $1.00.
Thigpen, D. M., Pigeon Creek, $2.00.
Tomlin, W. R., Rutledge, $1.00.
Thames, T. J., Greenville, $1.00.
Thompson, Mrs. L. L., Sandy Ridge, $1.00.
Taylor, William, Manningham, $1.00.
Thigpen, G. W. Greenville, French china tea set.
Teal, J. H., Ella, $2.00.
Thames, N. B., Greenville, $1.00.
Till, J. N., Braggs, $1.00.
Teague, Miss Lizzie, Atlanta, Georgia, $1.00.
Thigpen, Mrs. E. T., Pine Apple, $1.00.
Thigpen, Grey, Greenville, silver syrup pitcher.
Thagard, T. S., Greenville, $10.00.
Thagard, A. J., Greenville, $1.00.
Thomas, T. P., Greenville, $1.00.
Vann, A. H., Greenville, $2.00.
Williams, E. E., Commerce, $1.00.
Williams, S. J., Georgiana, butter knife.
Williams, C. L., Ella, silver butter knife.
Wimberly, M., Greenville, $1.00.
Williams, Mrs. L. E., Louisville, Ky., $2.00.
Walker, Judge F. M., Columbia, $1.00.
Wyatt, T. H., Bullock, shirt studs.
Webb, James B., Wallace, $1.00.
Wright, W. L., Bolling, $1.00.
Wall, J. E., Forest Home, $1.00.
Wilkinson, Mrs. H. Z., Greenville, $2.00.
Womack, Mrs. E. S., Cade, Texas, $2.00.
Webster, G. B., Argus, $2.00.
Waters, Miss M., Manningham, $2.00.
Whittle, W. H., Mt. Willing, $10.00.
Williams, George, Bolling, $1.00.
Waters, R. H., Cameron, Texas, $1.00.
Wiggins, C. L., Pollard, $1.00.
White, J. C., Shirley, $1.00.
Wright, Mrs. J. W., Greenville, silver syrup pitcher.
Watson, T. E., Snow Hill, $1.00.
Williams, Clara, Buffalo, N. Y., $2.00.
Watts, R. P., Greenville, $2.00.
Walker, Mrs. J. F., Rutledge, $1.00.
Young, George, Molino, Florida, $1.00.

HOTELS IN BUTLER COUNTY

Bedell House: operated in Greenville by W. H. Bedell. This was a large two story frame building erected prior to 1865.
Bell House: a large two story hotel on the present site of Haynes Store in Greenville. Judge Benjamin F. Porter died in this hotel.
Binion Hotel: in Georgiana. Mrs. E. C. Binion, Prop. In operation in 1889.
Bolling Hotel: John Bolling, Prop. A very popular hotel South of the Court House in Greenville.
Butler Springs Hotel: in the village of Butler Springs. On the site of the famous mineral springs. Several hotels existed under this name from the mid 1800s to the early 1900s.
Martha Calloway: a negress, ran a large two story boarding and lodging house and served fish you could smell cooking for three blocks away. Was on the site of the Belk-Hudson store.

City Hotel: In Greenville near the Court House.
Ehlbert House: In Greenville run by Mr. & Mrs. Ehlbert. Formerly called the Perry House. Was located acress the street from the depot and was THE HOTEL of Greenville. Rooms were neatly and comfortably furnished and Mrs. Ehlbert was experienced in making a stranger comfortable.
Hotel Fleming: located three blocks from the depot in Greenville and two blocks from the Post Office. Advertised rooms for $1.00 and $1.50 per day.
Foster House: in the depot end of Greenville. It was finished in Feb. or March, 1890. Had two spacious brick store rooms on the first floor and a number of rooms on the second and third floors which were either rented as a hotel or occupied as a private dwelling.
Gafford House: A. F. Gafford, Prop. Was built on Commerce St. in 1858 in Greenville.
Grenala Hotel: also known as the Stark House and Waller Hotel. First brick building erected in the downtown area of Greenville and was located by the train overpass on Commerce.
Holzer House: operated by Ben and Mylth Holzer and was located in the center of Greenville.
Johnson Hotel: was located in Georgiana, John Johnson, Prop. Building was destroyed in the big fire in Georgiana.
Mallett House: J. W. Mallett, Prop. Was in operation by 1865 in Greenville. This was an immense building later to become known as the Holzer House. Later a three story building was erected on this lot to attrack Northern tourists, but the building was never completed.
Morrow Hotel operated by Mrs. Morrow in Greenville by 1881.
Oaks Hotel: operated by Charles McRae. Originally built as a home for Jeff Burnett around 1860-1865. Previously called the Wilkinson House.
New Boarding House: run by Ganus and Harry and located on the corner of Commerce and Walnut Streets in Greenville in 1858.
The Palings or Fort Dale Stage Coach Stop: One of the earliest structures in the county. Among the earliest owners were Matthew Wood and Joseph Hartley.
Perry House: F. M. Harrison, Prop. Erected near the depot in Greenville.
Reddoch Springs Hotel at the site of the springs.
Rocky Creek Inn: located in Chapman, ranked with the best in the nation. Located in the heart of the mill property and was operated by the firm on a practically non-profit basis. The pine-panelled hotel included a dining room serving the most economical, sumptuous meals found anywhere. Run by Mrs. Lewis.
Travelers Home Boarding House: Mrs. M. E. McLain, Prop. in operation by 1886.
Vinson Hotel: T. J. Vinson, Prop., located in Georgiana.
Virginia Hotel: in Georgiana in the early 1900s. Run by Virginia and Lit Johnson. Was located on the site of the hospital. It was a popular place for entertaining. Destroyed by fire.
Wilkinson House: by by Mr. & Mrs. H. Z. Wilkinson. It was a homelike hotel which was popular with traveling people as well as local people. Many families resided permanently in this hotel. It served the same lavish and wonderfully prepared meals which made the Purifoy Hotel in Talladega nationally famous. This tradition carried over when the hotel was operated by Mr. McRae. Seven meats were offered twice a day with only four or five offered at breakfast. Located in Greenville.
Williams Hotel: located in Georgiana.

THE VIRGINIA HOTEL, GEORGIANA

OAKS HOTEL, GREENVILLE

STOP AT THE
EHLBERT HOUSE,
FORMERLY PERRY HOUSE.

NEAR DEPOT.

STRICTLY FIRST CLASS.

GOOD SAMPLE ROOMS FOR COMMERCIAL TRAVELERS.

MRS. M. EHLBERT, Proprietor.
GREENVILLE, ALA.

HOLZER HOTEL,
GREENVILLE, ALA.

MRS. M. HOLZER, Proprietress.

The only Hotel in the Business Portion of the City. Has the advantage of all the markets, which no other house has. The table and attendance will be equal to any in the State. The patronage of the public generally, and of Commercial Travelers, especially, solicited.
A free hack for the benefit of Customers.

DRAYAGE & SAMPLE ROOM FREE.

A TRIAL IS EARNESTLY REQUESTED.

GRENALA HOTEL, GREENVILLE

BUTLER COUNTY NEWSPAPERS

1. ALABAMIAN. Established in 1845 by Curtis and assisted by Moody. John S. Davies, foreman, later bought the paper and was both editor and business manager according to Little's "History of Butler County".
2. BANNER AND MESSENGER. A negro publication. Dunklin, editor, according to The Living Truth, Jan. 11, 1900.
3. BUTLER COUNTY CITIZEN. Established 1883 by Col. William C. Howell. Suspended before the end of the year.
4. BUTLER COUNTY NEWS. Established 1911 by Moses Pride. Has been run continuously by members of the Pride family since its beginning.
5. THE ECHO. Established in 1880 to support John L. Powell for Judge of Probate; edited by J. T. Thomas, Mrs. I. M. P. Henry, Rev. B. H. Crumpton. Ceased publication in 1882. There were two publications, THE WEEKLY ECHO and THE DAILY ECHO.
6. THE FREE LANCE. Suspended publication following the death of the publisher and editor during World War 1.
7. GEORGIANA GUARDIAN. Editors Oscar S. Sims and George Bryan in 1898. Mr. Lilliard became publisher in Dec. 1899 and in Feb. 1900 Eugene Colley bought the paper.
8. GEORGIANA INDEPENDENT. Editor and Proprietor, J. R. McKean. First issue run in July or August, 1873.
9. GEORGIANA WEEKLY MONITOR. Mentioned in the Echo of 13 Oct. 1880.
10. THE GREENVILLE ADVOCATE. Founded by James Berney Stanley, Prospectus for this paper was in the MONTGOMERY ADVERTISER in the latter part of 1865, soon after Mr. Stanley returned from the Civil War. Other early editors and associate editors were Leatherwood, Lucien J. Walker, Charles R. McCall, Mrs. Ina Marie Porter Henry and Rev. E. F. Baber. It is the longest running paper in the county.
11. THE GREENVILLE LEDGER. Editor and Proprietor, Vernon Thagard, in 1915.
12. GREENVILLE WEEKLY OBSERVER. Jno. S. Davies, Prop. Only one issue has been located, an extra, published by the Federal troops 21 Apr. 1865. Prospectus for the paper was run in this edition. Rates for three months were $1.00.

13. GREENVILLE WHIG. Established in 1834 and edited by John W. Womack. Published by Thomas J. Judge.
14. INDEPENDENT THINKER. J. W. Whitehead, Editor. Was a late editor of the GREENVILLE ADVOCATE. Was short-lived.
15. THE LIVING TRUTH. Abe Lehman, editor. An Anti-Populist paper. Published from 1894 to 1914.
16. LUMBERING ALONG. Published in Chapman from 1951 to 1956. Editor: Olive Swann.
17. MIRROR. Edited by Watson. In publication soon after 1834. Was a paper of little influence and soon suspended.
18. SOUTH ALABAMIAN. John S. Davies, Editor and Prop. Established in 1846. James D. Porter, editor in 1869. Mrs. I. M. P. Henry also associated with this paper. Purchased by Porter, Drake and Harbin in 1874 with J. D. Porter, editor until August 1876 when T. J. Parmer appears as editor until the paper suspended in October of that year.
19. SOUTHERN MESSENGER. Steele and Osboune, Publishers from December 1857 to November 1858. L. D. Steele and L. A. Livingston, Editors and Publishers 1859-1861. Supported the American party and Whigs.
20. SOUTHERN NEWS. Irregularly published in 1864 by Captain George I. Henry, and in 1865-66 by W. W. Beasley, assisted by Hon. Benjamin F. Porter.
21. SPIRIT OF THE TIMES. George D. Reid, Publisher, November 1879 to May 8, 1880.
22. VOICE. Established in 1880 to support J. C. Richardson for Probate Judge in opposition to John L. Powell.[1]

ABE LEHMAN, Editor
THE LIVING TRUTH

1. Much of this information came from "ALABAMA NEWSPAPERS TO 1900" by Dr. Rhoda Ellison.

GEORGE H. BRYAN, standing, and OSCAR C. SIMS, seated, Editors of THE GEORGIANA GUARDIAN.

JAMES B. STANLEY

General Stanley was the first editor and proprietor of the Greenville Advocate, the longest running newspaper in Butler County and the oldest establishment in the county. This newspaper has been invaluable as a source of material for this book.

HIPP AND KELLEY

In 1891 and 1892 two men named John Hipp and Charley Kelley went on a rampage in Georgiana and the surrounding territory which shocked the citizens of the county.

The first crime charged to these men was the illegal sale of liquor, followed by a series of robberies and murders. Their first victim apparently was a negro woman who was killed in Georgiana where the Methodist Church is now situated. The next victim was a man named Dunn. Following this was the ruthless murder of Joseph Touart.

Mr. Touart was one of the leading merchants in Georgiana. He was foully murdered in his store at an early hour on Wednesday, September 9, 1891. He had gone to his store for the purpose of fixing up some papers he intended sending to Greenville on the train that morning. About 4 o'clock a farmer heard two pistol shots. Half an hour later another man passed the store and seeing the door open looked in and saw Mr. Touart slumped on the floor against the counter dead. A bullet from a 38 caliber pistol had entered his left side over his heart, passed through his body and shattered his right arm. Over turned boxes and chairs gave evidence that Mr. Touart had fought valiantly for his life. As two or three stores in Georgiana were robbed late Tuesday night there was no doubt but that robbery had been the motive.

Next on the list was the double murder of Eliza L. and Thomas Shepherd. They were brutally slain with an axe November 1, 1891 at their home. It was evident from the state of their house that robbery was the motive for this deed also. Every drawer and trunk was ransacked. Mr. Shepherd had sold some cotton a few days before and this must have been known to the culprits. The two old people were alone in the house when Hipp and Kelley got there and killing them was easily done. From the bloodstains it could be seen that one was killed in the hall and the other in the dining room and then both bodies were dragged to the bedroom. They were murdered in the early part of the evening as they had not retired. This brought to five the number of murders in Georgiana in a short span of four months. There were no clues leading to the identification of the killers. The citizens of the city were terrified and took what measure they could to protect themselves. Shortly after the murders of the Shepherds a negro man named Edmond Moore and his wife were arrested when blood stained clothing was found in their wood pile. The Moores testified that the blood was from a steer that they had butchered. The clothing was sent to Auburn so that tests could be made and the couple was soon released. Suspicion then fell on Tom Rhodes who had signed a contract to rent and cultivate part of the land belonging to the Shepherds and then had mysteriously disappeared.

The last murder charged to these two men, and which took place over a year later was that of Charles Jacob Armstrong, better known as Jake, who was the tax collector for Butler County. He had left Greenville on December 11, 1892, for Monterey where he collected the taxes on Monday; Tuesday he went to Forest Home; Wednesday to Butler Springs; Thursday was spent at Purnall's' and Friday at J. M. Y. Sellers' store. He spent the night with Mr. Sellers and left early Saturday morning to fill his appointment in the Rocky Creek precinct. He had traveled only about three miles to Panther Creek, and while crossing the bridge was shot by the culprits who had lain in wait for him under the bridge. One shot hit Mr. Armstrong above his right eye entering his brain and rendering him unconscious. He died a short time later. Mr. Armstrong was a veteran of the Civil War where he lost one of his legs. He had been the County surveyor before being elected tax assessor and was thoroughly competent and well liked by everyone. He was survived by his wife and six children.

Later when Judge L. M. Lane examined the stubbs in Mr. Armstrong's receipt book, it was discovered that only $12.00 was missing from the more than one thousand dollars which had been collected. Most of the taxes had been paid by check, but the robbers had overlooked several hundred dollars which had been placed in an inside coat pocket.

Upon hearing about the murder, Sheriff J. T. Barganier immediately formed a posse and set out in pursuit of the killers. Hipp was caught several days later as he attempted to board a train belonging to the Dunham Lumber Company. In the posse of thirty men were Oliver Bryant, Chink Williams, Tom Owens and Dave Kern along with Sheriff Barganier, Capt. Porterfield and the other men. When captured Hipp had on his possession a 44 calibre pistol, a Winchester rifle and extra ammunition. He appeared to be about 30 or 32 years old, well built and muscular. Hipp was wounded in the arrest when he refused to surrender; instead opening fire on the posse. There appeared to be no doubt as to his guilt as he was suffering from an earlier bullet wound believed to have been inflicted by Jake Armstrong.

Charley Kelley was soon arrested in Monroe County where he was found hiding in a cotton house about five miles south of Pine Apple on Christmas Eve. He was discovered by H. L. Soloman who owned the building in which he was hiding. Mr. Solomon with the assistance of several friends captured him without any show of resistance. Messrs. T. P. Buffington, J. H. Remley, H. L. Solomon, James Anders, C. M. Myrick, R. L. Evers and J. R. Bailey are given credit for his capture.

Kelley was placed in the Greenville jail on Christmas Day. Thursday, December 29, 1892, two men went to the home of Deputy Sheriff Hill Barganier and said they had a prisoner they wished to have arrested. Barganier and Deputy Robert Harrison then went to the jail with the men, and on arriving there around 100 men appeared from all directions and demanded to be let into the jail. The sheriff asked if his life depended on it and was told "Yes". Six of the men rushed into Hipp's cell and carried him out of the building. Hipp may have already been dead by this time as the wound he had received in his capture had been a fatal one. Kelley was then awakened and led out of the building with a rope around his neck. Then the law officers were told to leave the premises.

The next morning the bodies were found hanging from the columns in front of the Court House. Upon examination by Acting Coroner H. R. Goolsby it was discovered that the bodies had been raised from the ground instead of being dropped from above as the necks of neither man had been broken. Death came by strangulation.

Mr. Goolsby empannelled a jury on the morning the bodies were discovered and an inquest was held in the Tax Collector's office in the Court House. The following verdict was returned:

"We, the jury empannelled by Acting Coroner H. R. Goolsby, find after making an examination, that John Hipp and Charles Kelley came to their death by unlawful hanging at the hands of parties unknown. A. Lehman, Foreman, G. W. Hinson, A. T. Hinson, R. H. Stanley, J. O. Lee, and H. Howard."

The feelings in the county had been very bitter since the arrest of the desperadoes, but it had been thought that the excitement had subsided. To my knowledge the men responsible for the hangings were never apprehended.[1]

HIPP AND KELLEY

BUTLER COUNTY COURT HOUSE BUILT IN 1871
The site of the hangings

1. This information was taken from several editions of the Greenville Advocate in 1891 and 1892.

CHAPTER 9.

ALEXANDER MCKELLAR

Alexander McKellar was not born in Butler County, but went there shortly after the establishment of Greenville and had a great deal to do with the building of the city. He was not a man of many words, but one who earned and kept the respect of those who knew him. This was exemplified by the many offices he filled with distinction and also by the way he acted under pressure.

When the Union soldiers finally reached Greenville at the close of the War Between the States, Mr. McKellar was the Tax Assessor. Knowing from their actions elsewhere that one of the first things those occupying troops would do would be to seize the books of the county, Mr. McKellar took the tax records to his home and hid them safely and securely in a place that proved to be the last one that searchers would think of--in his well.

This well was, as was the custom then, located close to the back porch. The well house was roofed over and the well itself was covered with planks, with a hole in the center for the bucket to get through. Trap doors in the well house floor gave access to a series of shelves where milk and butter were stored for coolness. It was on the shelves that the county records were placed, and there they stayed until it was safe to remove them.

His office was searched, of course, and when the books were not found, the three men in the party repaired to Mr. McKellar's home and conducted a most thorough search there, turning the beds upside down; going through every receptable in the house.

Mr. McKellar's life before the war must have been an interesting one. He was first the Intendent of the city (an office similar to that of mayor) and later Mayor. He was also Justice of the Peace, and he served for some years as Postmaster. This was after the war. His daughter, Miss Margaret, was his assistant, and after his death was appointed in his place serving until the next change of administrations.

Squire McKellar's home stood on the lot behind the present post office, his lot being bounded on three sides by Commerce, Fort Dale and Cedar Streets. His home faced Cedar. The whole was enclosed by a fence at first, but later the fence on Commerce was moved back and a building erected there which served for many years as the Greenville post office. The home itself had three rooms across the front with a hall between. Back of these were three more rooms. Later another room was added at the back. Across the front ran a wide verandah with a small shed at the end. This was one of the first homes built in Greenville.

Mr. McKellar was married to Miss Mary Caldwell who was closely related to the Henrys, Milners, Caldwells, Otts and other pioneer families, prominent in Butler County beginnings. Of their seven sons and five daughters, Nat was killed in one of the battles of the War Between the States in Virginia and another son, Jim, died of measles while in camp at Mobile. Other sons were Pomp, Felix, Pickens, William and James. Their daughters were Isabella, who married Ed Newton, a member of Company C, 17th Alabama Regiment, Sarah, Margaret, Antoinette and Emma. Isabella was the only one of the children who married. Her daughters, Mary (Mrs. R. E. Smith) and Rose (Mrs. Lee Kettler) recalled the erection of the old city hall. The lower floor was modeled on the system that was so popular in those days, as a city market. It was devoted almost entirely to meats and seafoods, with each merchant having a stall for his wares with a refrigerator in the rear and a counter at the front. This building was finished in 1880 and was the pride of the citizens. They also recalled going to Greenville's first ten-cent store (or "Racket") and spending the whole sum of a dime on one item.

RULINCY HILSON SEALE

Rulincy Hilson Seale was born in Milledgeville, Georgia in 1807, the daughter of Aaron and Sarah Hilson and granddaughter of John and Dianna Hilson of Warren County, Georgia. John was a veteran of the Revolutionary War, serving with the State Militia in South Carolina's Cheraw District. She came to Butler County in 1817. From her obituary we learn that she was in the fort near Butler Springs when Captain Butler was killed by the Indians and could point to the very spot where the hero of the hour held the savages at bay before the last unerring blow; could show the path by which the others escaped and could tell of those trying days that are tracked with blood in our country's history, as if they were but yesterday. Rulincy was married to William Seale and was the mother of a large family of children, among them Ranson Seale who was Clerk of the County Court for many years. From his obituary it was said that the greatest sorrow in his life was the loss of his beloved mother.

JOHN TURNER MILNER

One man who played an important part in the history of Butler County and the State of Alabama was John Turner Milner. His whole life was devoted to industry and to the spread of civilization. He rose to prominence as a railroad builder, then as a developer of our state's mineral and timbered wealth, and finally as a legislator.

He was born in Hannel, Pike County, Georgia in 1826, the son of Willis J. Milner and Elizabeth Turner, and grandson of John Milner and Eunice Calloway of Pike Co., Georgia (now Lamar Co.). He learned the mining business in the gold mines of Lumpkin County, Ga. In 1858 he was commissioned by Gov. Moore to locate a line connecting the navigable waters of the Alabama River with those of the Tennessee. The line upon which the present South and North Alabama division of the L&N was surveyed. He was elected chief and placed under control of the L&N in 1872. Retiring from the railroad, Col. Milner began the development of mining and timber properties. He founded the big saw mills at Bolling. He projected the city of Birmingham some years before it was founded. He developed the Coalburg coal property on the Georgia Pacific Railroad at Newcastle where he had built up an immense business. In 1888 he was elected State Senator from Jefferson County and was re-elected in 1892. The achievements accomplished by Mr. Milner in his lifetime list him among the greatest men in Alabama. His record will rank him with that of any man in the South. It was while he was living in Butler County that he founded the Milner, Caldwell & Flowers Lumber Co. at Bolling.

SIMS

A large family of Sims settled in the Pine Flat and Forest Home section of Butler County in the 1830s, arriving here from Lancaster Co., S.C. Much research was done on the ancestry of the Sims family by Henry Upson Sims of Birmingham in 1940. The first of this family to come to America from England was George Symes who settled in the Isle of Wight Co., Virginia as early as 1688. Many of his descendants served in the Revolutionary War, one of these being Sherrod Sims. Following the war Sherrod and his wife, Sally Ashburne, with their children moved to Lancaster Co., S. C. where Sherrod died in 1825 at age 95. Sherrod's son, Stephen, with his wife, Rhoda, moved to Butler Co. where he is first recorded as entering land in 1836.

The children named in the settlement of Stephen's Estate in 1856 were Stephen, Jr. (deceased), Sherrod, Arthur C., Jane Franklin (Mrs. Morris), Wiley (of Lowndes Co., Tex.), James (deceased), Elihu, Isaac, Sarah Ann Riley (Mrs. Travis M.) and Jackson. Some of these children moved into Wilcox County and other neighboring counties in later years but many remained here for the rest of their lives. Two of the sons of Arthur and his wife, Sarah Caroline Austin, entered the ministry, Alexander Theodore Sims and Americus Arastus Sims, who were ordained in the Forest Home Baptist Church and served many churches in the county in the late 1800s.

THOMAS STEVENSON

Thomas DeLoach Stevenson was born around 1818 in Orangeburgh, S.C. At age 17 years on or about 16 Feb. 1836 he enlisted in the Seminole War as a Private in the company commanded by George Whitmore, Regiment of Volunteers of Cavalry, under the command of Col. Goodwin. He served for a term of three months and was honorably discharged in Charleston, S. C.

In 1838 he moved to Butler County where in July of that year he married Margarette E. Wyrosdick. He lived in Butler County for 30 years, before moving to Hempstead Co., Arkansas where he died 27 Feb. 1897. His wife was the daughter of Andrew P. Wyrosdick and Linda Delilah Sojourner. Two of their daughters married in Butler Co.; Dellia Ann to William H. Knotts and Sarah Mildred to Manning Russell.

SUE GLASGOW

An interesting story is told in the obituary of Mrs. Sue Holmes Glasgow. "In the Light Guards Armory hangs a faded, tattered and torn, blue banner, bordered with silver lace. On this is painted an oak tree, and the familiar design on an unrolled map which represents the coat of arms of the State of Alabama. Over this is the motto: "QUID NON PRO PATRIA". On the other side is the "Bonnie Blue Flag that bore a single star!". In letters of green and gold are the words, THE YANCEY GUARDS.

Its officers and men were mostly from Pigeon Creek, nine miles east of Greenville. It was commanded by Capt. Glasgow. The ladies of that neighborhood made this banner for the company, at the residence of Mr. James Black, and the young lady who presented the same in the name of "The Women of Pigeon Creek" was Miss Sue Holmes. The presentation ceremonies were very interesting and took place in the presence of numbers of visitors from Greenville and other places, on the broad lawn in front of the residence of Capt. Glasgow. It was accepted in behalf of the Company by Hon. H. A. Herbert, then the young Captain of The Greenville Guards. That banner which now idly hangs in the Armony, which then glittered in the sunshine of that bright May morning, fluttered its silken folds over as brace a set of men as ever answered the pibroch's call to arms for one's native heath--brave, young, handsome and hopeful--and now alas, where are they! Out of 106 volunteers, only 6 returned out of that company! And the Greenville Guards, who stood in rank and file with them that day? 10 men cannot answer the master roll!

Miss Sue Holmes became the bride of Capt. Glasgow, and was afterward present in deep mourning as his widow, when the same banner was presented to the Light Guards several years ago, by the late Rev. J. D. Porter, in behalf of the donor, Mr. W. J. Warrington of New Orleans.

The silken folds have waved over her once as maiden, once as widow; and now in the mute presence of the dead, let us lift the dear old bullet-torn banner of blue to her memory."

DR. HENRY MARTIN CALDWELL[1]

Henry Martin Caldwell was born in Greenville, Alabama 5 September 1836, the son of John and Elizabeth Black Caldwell, early emigrants from Georgia. After completing his studies in medical school at the University of Pennsylvania he entered practice in Greenville. At the onset of the Civil War he was appointed an assistant surgeon in the Confederate Army and was assigned to duty with the 33rd Alabama Regiment then in Corinth, Mississippi. In August 1862 he was assigned to duty with Surgeon E. H. Moren, then in charge of the Confederate General Hospital in Greenville. From there he served at Spring Hill Hospital near Mobile and in the fall of 1864 this hospital was removed to Greenville where Dr. Caldwell remained on duty until the hospital was captured by Smith's Corps early in April, 1865, a few days after the surrender of Lee's army. Two years after the war Dr. Caldwell abandoned the practice of medicine and engaged in the drug business and lumber business in Greenville. In the days of Birmingham's infancy he moved to that city where in 1875 he was elected president of the Elyton Land Company. No man played a more important role in the development of early Birmingham than did Dr. Caldwell. He was also president of the Caldwell Hotel, director of the First National Bank, of the Williamson Iron Co. and the Birmingham Iron Works. He was marmied to Elizabeth Milner, daughter of Willis J. Milner of Greenville.

W. H. FLOWERS

Mr. W. H. Flowers emigrated to Butler County in 1856 and located on a tract of land between Greenville and Bolling. A few years after this Messrs. John T. Milner and Henry M. Caldwell formed with him and erected a saw mill at Forest under the name of the Milner, Caldwell & Flowers Lumber Co. He was elected the first president and general manager and held these positions continuously until his death. Subsequently the mill was moved to Bolling. Under his management the company grew until it became the largest and most lucrative business in the county, if not in South Alabama. He was born in South Carolina on January 7, 1813, and died August 24, 1895, rich in good deeds and public esteem. His wife was the former Sarah Thames. They were consistent members of the Methodist Church.

1. Birmingham Evening Chronicle, Sept. 19, 1885.

KINCY LEWIS DAVIS

Kincy Lewis Davis was born in 1828 in the Durham/Raleigh section of North Carolina, the son of James Thomas Davis. He moved to Columbus, Ga. where he married on 17 Feb. 1853 Harriet Pattillo Piggott, daughter of William A. Piggott and Nancy C. Kirkland; grandaughter of Abner Piggott and Susannah Camp and of Snowden Kirkland and Elizabeth Buchanan. For about ten years he lived in Columbus and near Pensacola, Florida before moving to Georgiana during the Civil War.

For a while he was active in the lumber business in Chapman with his sons under the name of the Old Chapman Hill Mill, and then later operated a grist mill a block from the heart of Georgiana. He was one of the founders of the First Methodist Church serving as Trustee throughout the remainder of his life. His home was headquarters for the circuit riders where was always found a warm Christian welcome. He was a Charter member of the Masonic Lodge and served as Secretary for 32 years. On the day he died the Methodist Church that had played such a great part in his life caught fire and was totally destroyed. When the present church was erected a stained glass window was placed to the right of the altar in memory of K. L. and H. P. Davis.

The children of this couple include the following: Arthur Lewis who married Martha Sue McLeod of Grove Hill, Ala.; Harriet Eugenia, who married Nat G. Foster; Joseph Kemp who married Floy Seegar; Katie Louella who married Daniel McLeod; William Bruner who married Dump Hubert; Kincy Levozia who was married to Olivia Moore, daughter of Rev. Seborn Moore; Lillie Ruby who was married to a Mr. Sheats and 3 children who died young. No descendants are known to live in the county now.

AUSTIN

The Austin family settled in Butler County in 1835 migrating there from Albany, Georgia. Prior to that they are believed to have lived in Sunsbury, Georgia, where a Davis Austin served our nation in the Third Georgia Batallion in the Revolutionary War. His wife was Mary Ann Forsyth. Davis Austin who settled in Butler County is thought to be the son of this Patriot. His wife was Elener Hill, the niece of Thomas Hill, one of the pioneer settlers of the county, and possibly the daughter of Benjamin Hill.

Among their children were Sarah Caroline, who married Arthur C. Sims; Davis Washington Austin, who married Amanda Seals; George H. and John Austin. Davis Washington Austin lived for some years in Pensacola where he was a ship builder. At the onset of the War Between the States he volunteered his services, but was detailed to the Navy Yard due to his knowledge of ship building. At the end of the War he returned to Butler County where he stayed until moving to Birmingham in 1871 where he became a contractor and builder, coroner, deputy sheriff and city jailer. His son, Conrad Wall Austin, was also prominent in the law enforcement bodies of Birmingham, where he served for eight years as Chief of Police.

George H. Austin died around 1855 and in 1857 his widow married William J. Heap and moved to Lowndes County. One of their daughters, Mary Ann Austin married James M. Morgan.

JAMES KEY BENSON

James Key Benson was the son of William Benson, who was born about 1745 in Fairfax County, Virginia; married Eleanor Key; moved to Spartanburg District, S. C. where he joined the S. C. Forces in the Revolutionary War.

James Key Benson married Lucy Drake of South Carolina and served as a quarter master in the War of 1812. Shortly after his war services he came to Butler County as a government surveyor. In 1818 he was listed as Justice of Peace in Monroe Co. (This portion of Monroe Co. later became part of Butler Co.) In 1820 he was Justice of the Peace in Butler Co. For his skill and integrity while surveying he was presented with a citation by President James Monroe. Before joining Pine Flat Church he was prominent in the Methodist Protestant Church and was listed in the "Methodist Roll of Honor" by Dr. M. E. Lazenby's "History of Methodism in Alabama and West Florida". He is credited with building the first house in Butler County, erected of logs, in the area of Pine Flat, not far from the Wilcox County line. Many of his descendents have engaged in the teaching profession in Alabama.

REYNOLDS

The Reynolds family, descended from Christopher Reynolds, born in 1530 in Kent Co., England, came to America ca 1637. Reynolds was born in Greene Co., Georgia, where his grandfather, James Reynolds, had come from Richmond Co., Virginia. His mother was Mary Leftwich, daughter of John Leftwich who fought with the Virginia troops in the Revolutionary War. The Leftwich family is traced to Lord Richard de Vernon, who accompanied William the Conqueror to England in 1066, and was awarded the English estate of Leftwich.

James H. Reynolds and his wife, Martha Barge Reynolds, gave the deed to the land for the Pine Flat Methodist Church. He was Postmaster from 1848 to 1899, mail delivered from Greenville three times a week to Post Office "Reynolds" later to be called "Butler Springs".

The nephew of James H. Reynolds, Joseph G. Reynolds, married Lucy Frances Lazenby, daughter of Elias Marion Lazenby. He was associated with his father-in-law in the mercantile business at Forest Home, later moving to Greenville where he engaged in the same business. He was one of the County Commissioners when the Court House was built, was deacon in the First Baptist Church.

LAZENBY

The Lazenbys of Butler and Monroe Counties trace their English ancestry to Robert Lazenby, 1, of Md. whose six sons fought in the Revolution. After the War, Robert's son, Elias Lazenby, 1, emigrated to Columbus Co., Ga. Elias Marion Lazenby, son of Elias, came to Forest Home in 1853. He engaged in farming and was prominently identified with the milling and mercantile business here. He also operated a saw and grist mill and personally looked after a large plantation. He served as County Commissioner for seven years. When the Forest Home Methodist Church was organized in 1879 he was elected a steward and served until his death in 1896.

Dr. Marion Elias Lazenby, son of James Elias Lazenby, and grandson of Elias Marion Lazenby, was born at Forest Home. He was a member of the Alabama-West Florida Methodist Conference, was pastor at Forest Home 1908-9, was editor of the Alabama Christian Advocate 1950-53, and was author of "History of Methodism in Alabama and West Florida."

Elias Marion Lazenby's son, George Samuel, married Carolyn Greene, daughter of Capt. A. C. Greene, in 1875. He became owner of his father's mercantile business, served as one of the first directors of First National Bank of Greenville, was elected to the Legislature, House of Representatives during Gov. Kilby's administration.

Harry Drake Lazenby, youngest son of Elias Marion Lazenby, was born in 1858, was educated at the Greenville Collegiate Institute, married Ella Lloyd, daughter of William H. Lloyd of Pine Apple, granddaughter of Benjamin Lloyd. Harry D. Lazenby engaged in agricultural and commercial businesses at Forest Home. He was Supt. of the Methodist Sunday School for many years, was President of Butler Co. Farm Bureau and Chairman of the County Board of Education.

A grandson, Dr. O. C. Weaver, Jr., member of the Alabama-West Florida Methodist Conference, is Professor of Religion and Philosophy at Birmingham-Southern College.

POOLE

Several generations of the Poole family lived in Spartanburg District, S. C. before Calvin Poole came to Alabama prior to 1848. He was the son of Elisha Poole and his wife, Harriet Wells. Calvin Poole married Laura Frances Davidson, whose parents were also from S. C. Their two sons were Joseph Davidson Poole and Elisha Calvin Poole. Elisha Calvin Poole's son, Calvin Poole, 11, associated with his son, Elisha Poole, 11, established a successful law practice in Greenville.

Joseph Davidson Poole served four terms in the Alabama legislature, representing Lowndes Co. before moving to Pine Flat in 1900. His extensive agricultural operations were on what is known as the Carter Place and the John Smith Place. In 1889 he married Jessie Bloxom from the cultured community of Monterey. Their son, Joseph Neil Poole, Sr., though born at "Palmyra", Lowndes Co., Dec. 29, 1892, spent his life from early childhood in Butler Co. He married Helen Lazenby of Forest Home, 21 Feb. 1922 & they resided at Pine Flat where their sons, Joe Neil Poole, Jr. and Harry Davidson Poole, now continue the farming operation successfully engaged in by their father and grandfather.

In 1923 Joe N. Poole, Sr. was elected to the lower House of the Legislature, served four terms, was chairman of Public Roads and Highways Committee, chairman of Joint Recess Committee in 1927, was author of Alabama Highway Code. He was elected to the Senate from the 17th Ala. District, was President Pro Tem during the administration of Gov. Frank Dixon. The press corps noted him "the most influential senator" in 1938. He served as Commissioner of Agriculture and Industries from 1943-1947, and ran for Governor in 1946. During his twenty-eight years of service to his County and State he was engaged in promoting agricultural interests, was active in the committee codifying the agricultural laws of the State. He introduced and actively supported the laws making possible the establishment of the Rural Electrification Administration in Alabama. He introduced the Constitutional Amendment which set up the present Pardon and Parole Board.

LLOYD

The Benjamin Lloyd Family Cemetery is located on Highway 185 N adjoining the home of Mrs. Cecil Cross and Mr. Zell Taylor.

The authentic Lloyd Family history begins with John Lloyd who was born in London, England, 1705, emigrated to Maryland in 1726, resided in Frederick Co., Va. His great-grandson, Benjamin Lloyd was born in 1804 in Hancock Co., Georgia; married Naomi Ann Cox of Putnam Co., Ga.; died 1860 in Greenville, Ala. Benjamin Lloyd came from Coosa Co., Ala. to Butler Co. after 1850. He served as Elder of the Mt. Zion Primitive Baptist Church until his death. He compiled a Hymn Book still used by this denomination.

Nine of his sons engaged in the War Between the States, joining the Confederate forces. A son, Cary Chappelle Lloyd, was a physician and minister of the Missionary Baptist Church. He completed his medical studies at the Jefferson Medical Colleges Philadelphia and Atlanta, graduated with honors in 1856. He began the practice of his profession at Greenville, but in 1861 enlisted in the Confederate Army, was made a Captain of Cavalry. He was Clerk of the Alabama Baptist Assoc. for 25 years. His son, Francis B. Lloyd, writer, was elected to the State Legislature from Montgomery and Butler Counties. Frank B. Lloyd, Jr. was Probate Judge of Crenshaw Co. for many years.

Benjamin's son, James B. Lloyd was Representative to the Legislature from Wilcox Co. in 1911.

Mrs. Ruby Lloyd Apsey, daughter of David Lloyd and granddaughter of Benjamin is an author, playwright and active in Birmingham Little Theatre.

Benjamin's son, Emory Eugene Lloyd was elected Superintendent of Education, Butler Co. He died in 1860.

One of Benjamin's sons, William Holt Lloyd was a druggist for many years at Pine Apple and was married to Mary Frances Reynolds. His Civil War Services were with Co. L, 6th Ala. Inf. and was Hospital Stewart at General Hospital, Richmond, Va. Many of his descendants have inherited marked musical talents, serving as organists for church and civic organizations, and as choir directors. One of his great-grandsons is a minister with the Alabama-West Florida Methodist Conference, and a great-great-grandson a member of the North Carolina Methodist Conference.

JESSE FRANCIS STALLINGS

Jesse Francis Stallings, lawyer and representative in Congress was born 4 April 1856 near Manningham, the son of Reuben and Lucinda Ferguson Stallings. His ancestors were early pioneers coming into Butler Co. in 1818. He studied law under J. C. Richardson and was admitted to the bar in 1879. He practiced first with L. E. Brooks and later with C. L. Wilkerson. He served in the State Congress from Butler for several terms, later on moving to Birmingham. He was married to Miss Ella McCallister of Eufaula.

EDWARD NIX

Edward Nix was born 5 November 1817 and married Miss Jane Perry in Russell County, Ala. 14 December 1839. He lived for a while in Macon Co. Alabama and by 1857 was living in the Oaky Streak community of Butler Co. He volunteered in the War Between the States and was fatally injured in a railroad accident in Cleveland, Tenn in 1862.

His son, Dow Perry Nix, was born in Oaky Streak in 15 Mch. 1857. He married twice, the first wife being Zula Eleanor Owen whom he married 3 Mch. 1880 and the second being Rowan Almaine Owen on 11 August 1886. Oscar H. Nix, the son of Dow and Rowan Nix, was born 23 Dec. 1887 in Oaky Streak and married Eula Mae Russell on 12 Sept. 1915 in Butler County.

JOHN H. CRITTENDEN

John H. Crittenden was born 18 May 1810, the son of Senator Robert Greene Crittenden (1783-1868) and Nancy Crowder (1788-1860) who are buried near Ozark in the Pleasent Hill Methodist Cemetery. He was married to Caroline Stoneham on 24 May 1837. Both are buried in the Oaky Streak Cemetery.

Caroline Elizabeth Greenway Crittenden, sister of John H., was married to Robert E. Owen, and the mother of Zula Eleanor Owen and Rowan Almain Owen who were both married to Dow Perry Nix.

BROOK, SHINES, SMITH, STALLINGS

Preston Brook was born in Virginia and migrated first to Georgia, living in Wilkes County and later in Oglethorpe. He and his wife, Mary, entered land in Butler Co. in 1836. Of their children, their son, E. Hardeman Brook married Mary Smith and had three children, Mary, who married a Merrill, James I. and Thomas H. Brook who married Shines sisters.

Elias Stallings, Jr. lived in Bertie County, N. C. He had several children one of these who was named Jessie. He moved to St. Johns Parrish, Ga. and later to Wilkes Co., Ga. and was a Colonel in the Revolutionary War. One grandson, William Sheets, was State Superintendent of Education in Florida for several years. Malachi Stallings, son of Jessie, lived in Greene County, Ga. and left a will in 1803 naming his children, three of whom moved to Butler Co. These were Jessie, who settled in the northern part of the county and was named to the Committee who built the first Court House in Butler County. Another son was Daniel Stallings, who settled in the Oaky Streak area. The third was Susannah Stallings who was married first to a Reid. Among her children was Archie M. Reid who was married to Elizabeth Herbert, a sister of Hillary A. Herbert who was Secretary of the Navy during the administration of President Cleveland. Mr. Reid acquired the land where the Methodist Church is located at Oaky Streak, deeding ten acres of this land to the Trustees of the Church naming himself, Daniel B. Shines, James W. Shines, Jr. and two others.

In 1818 Susannah married James T. Lane in Putnam Co., Ga. and they came to Butler Co. soon after. Mr. Lane took the first Census in Butler County in 1830 listing himself and Daniel Stallings as living next to each other. This Census was taken and witnessed only by members of the family.

SARAH FRANCES REANDER WIMBREY BROWN

Sarah Frances Wimbrey married Francis Marion Brown in Pike Co., Ga in 1845 and was the daughter of William B. and Gilley Moody Wimbrey. Sarah Frances and Francis M. Brown moved to Butler Co. in the 1850s where they remained until the Reconstruction Period living in the area near Forest Home where several of their children were born. During the War Betwen the States when Francis was in Virginia with the 61st Infantry Regiment Sarah Frances was left to keep things going on the farm. One day the Yanks came by and took all the meat in her smokehouse except for one ham that had fallen behind a box. Then they ordered her to cook a meal for them. In the meantime, Sarah Frances had hidden the children in the attic and had warned them to be quiet. In later years, Lena (Brown) Lloyd of Vernon, Texas, said she crawled under a trundle bed up there and almost smothered. After serving dinner to the Yankees, Sarah Frances was told they were going to take her horses. She pointed to one of her horses and said: "See that one out yonder with her head down? All she wants to do is eat. She is a lazy, no-count mare, and you will be doing me a favor if you take her!" The Yanks by-passed that horse, much to her delight, as it was her best farm horse! Another story is told of this delightful lady that her husband became ill in the Army. She wrote several letters to his Captain requesting his discharge due to illness. The letters were ignored. Sarah Frances got hoppin' mad and made the trip to Virginia, speaking her mind to the Captain in person. When she returned home her beloved Frances Marion Brown went with her. The family eventually moved to Texas.

Among their children were Texana Victoria Brown Beason-Nelson, John Buchanan Brown, Salena Havana Brown Lloyd (married to Albert Adam Lloyd, son of Benjamin Lloyd of Butler Co.), Mattie Elizabeth Brown Byrd and William Moss Brown.

Frances Marion Brown had three brothers, Andrew J., John W. and William R. O. Brown. He was married first to Martha Horn in Pike Co., Ga. by whom he had a daughter Mary Ann who married Henry C. Thomason in Butler County. Frances Marion was the son of William T. Brown.

BENJAMIN FANEUIL PORTER

Benjamin Faneuil Porter was born in 1808 in Charleston, South Carolina and died 4 June 1868 in Greenville. He was the son of Benjamin Richardson Porter and Eliza Seabrook Ficklin Porter. While he was serving as court reporter he brought out 15 volumes of reports. Among the outstanding acts on his record were the abolishment of imprisonment for debt and the establishment of a penitentiary for criminals.

He was married to Elizabeth Taylor Kidd by whom he had ten children. One son, John Richardson Porter, was a physician and planter and was killed in the Battle of Franklin, Tenn. He was married to Lucy Meriwether Howard. Another son, the Rev. James D. Porter was rector of St. Thomas Church in Greenville, a lawyer like his father and an editor. His wife was the former Ellen Ferguson. Benjamin F. Porter, Jr. was a railroad official in California, and was married to Mary Thomas. Laura E. M. Porter was married to Major Joseph R. Abrams, a civil engineer. Julia R. Porter was married to John Pratt, the inventor of the first typewriter in the world. Emma Porter was married to Capt. Harry Bedell of Texas. Annice Porter was married to Capt. John Anderson of Tennessee. R. Yeadon Porter, fire adjustor, was married to Etta Wilson. Ina Marie Porter was married twice, first to Capt. George L. Henry and second to Albian Ockenden. She was well known in the literary world.

Elizabeth T. Porter was the daughter of Judge John Kidd and Adelaide Adair of Chester County, S.C.

WILLIS JULIAN MILNER[1]

Willis J. Milner was born in Barnesville, Ga. 3 May 1842. He served in the Confederate Army where he rose from a private to the rank of Major in the 33rd Alabama Regiment. After the War he moved to Greenville to live with his mother, his father having died 15 March 1864.

From his autobiography in the Department of Archives and History in the Birmingham Public Library he tells of beginning life as a citizen, having attained his majority while a soldier. It was difficult to describe conditions confronting Confederate soldiers upon their return to their homes, many of them devasted and in ruins. He was much more fortunate than many others and had much to be thankful for. He had had no opportunity for a professional or business training by which he could earn a living. He had given special attention to civil engineering while in school and there was no prospect of employment along that line following the War. He went into the drug business with his brother-in-law, Dr. H. M. Caldwell, who furnished most of the money while he did most of the work. He also learned to keep books in which he became expert. His knowledge of Latin helped him in translating the doctor's prescriptions.

In July, 1869 he was engaged to survey certain lands situated in Jefferson and Shelby counties which had been entered as homesteads by persons living in Butler and Montgomery counties and for that purpose obtained leave of absence from his work. From Greenville to Elyton at that time the only public conveyance was by rail to Montgomery, then by boat to Selma, and then again by rail to Montevallo from which point a hack ran every other day, carrying the mail and such occasional passengers as wished to go.

From this point in his life Mr. Milner concentrated all of his efforts in Jefferson County becoming Secretary of the Elyton Land Company, Superintendant of the Highland Ave. & Belt R.R. and Superintendent of the Water Works Company.

Willis Milner was the son of Willis J. Milner and Elizabeth Turner Milner and a brother of John Turner Milner.

HENRY URQUHART

Dr. Henry Urquhart was born 18 June 1833 in Ramer, Alabama and died 6 July 1902 in Tate Springs, Tennessee. He was married on 15 June 1855 to Miss Missouri Ann Phillips of Mobile.

Dr. Urquhart joined the Methodist Church in 1846 and on 11 Nov. 1851 was licensed to preach at age 18. His work as a Christian leader was outstanding. He was one of the early presidents of Auburn Female College, the forerunner of Auburn University which was run by the Methodist Conference at that time. He was one of the presidents of Greenville Collegiate Institute, and pastor of the Greenville Methodist Church and other churches in the county. His final years were spent as Editor of the Christian Advocate. He was buried in Eufaula by the side of his wife who preceded him in death on 7 Nov. 1884.

1. Journal of Birmingham Historical Society. Vol. V. No. 1. January, 1977.

ALEXANDER THEODORE SIMS

Alexander Theodore Sims was born in Starlington, the son of Arthur C. Sims and Sarah Caroline Austin. His father was a veteran of the Creek Indian Wars and was in the group that assisted the Indians in boarding boats on the coast of Florida for their trip West. His grandparents were Stephen and Rhoda Sims who emigrated to Butler County in the early 1830s.

Alexander T. Sims was licensed to preach in July 1870 and was ordained in July 1872 in the Forest Home Baptist Church. He served as minister for this church, Georgiana Church and many others in the county. During his ministry he organized and built 25 churches and organized over 300 Sunday Schools. For 11 years he worked in the mission field of South Alabama and West Florida. According to Rev. B. H. Crumpton in his book called "A Book of Memories" some of the quotations from Sims' diary sound like the incidents in the New Testament. He baptised over 3,000 converts during his ministry. For many years he served as Chaplain of the Sepulga Lodge #233 of the Masons & was Relate of Lodge of Pythians in Mobile. He wanted to preach as long as he lived and wanted to die just as he had lived--serving his Master the best way that he could up to the last. At the end of his life he was taken sick during a revival and passed away two weeks later after truly serving his Master well for 57 years.

He was married twice. First to Sarah Nancy Adelia Hilson, daughter of Pinkney Hilson and Anna Odom, and grandaughter of Aaron and Sarah Hilson. His second wife was Annie Laurie Harper, daughter of James B. Harper, Esq. and Margaret Watts of Wilcox Co. The children born of these marriages were Oscar Capus who married Hally M. Cochran; Comer Sherrod and Graves; Maude Carline (Mrs. Charles Sims); Enda (Mrs. Philip K. Urquhart); Lillian; Nina (Mrs. James W. Coor); Gladys Scott (Mrs. Fred Lewis Davis); and by his second marriage: Margaret (Mrs. Byron Hendrix): Alexander T., Jr.; and Grace (Mrs. Wyatt Thomas).

INA MARIE PORTER OCKENDEN

Ina Marie Porter was born in Tuscaloosa in 1837, the daughter of Benjamin F. Porter and Eliza S. Ficklin. She moved to Greenville with her parents around 1860. Interesting insight into the development of the Greenville Confederate Hospital was told by Ina Marie by her own pen: "My father was appointed a Colonel by President Davis and commanded at the camp of instruction located on an old playground in East Greenville. My father soon saw the necessity for a place for the sick. He and Mother were the founders of the (Greenville Confederate) Hospital. At first it was only another room in our home. My mother had a room back of the parlor prepared tastefully and most comfortably, where the draperies were red and white. There were pictures on the walls, books on the tables, easy chairs and a bed that was a dream of luxury to those boys afar from home.

Of course, the room that was called the "Soldier's Rest" would not hold more than four. My father went to Judge Henry, Judge Bolling and perhaps others to confer and decide upon where and how to take care of the increasing number of wounded and sick soldiers. It was decided that beds would be made in the Presbyterian Church and in the Boy's Schoolhouse on the hill. The ladies came to my mother's assistance and I suppose every lady in that historic little town took her turn at sending meals to the church and school rooms, which had been converted into a hospital.

My father reported the necessity for establishing a government Hospital, but until that was done, the physicians took turns and the ladies were devoted nurses, all serving under my mother, who acted as volunteer matron. I cannot tell you the details of buying the spot on which the Government Building was erected. It may have been given. Work went on rapidly and noble work was done by the men and women of Butler County."

Today the site of this hospital can be located on West Commerce Street by a marker which is inscribed, "Site of Confederate Hospital 1861-65. Placed in 1914 by Father Ryan Chapter."

Ina Marie Porter was married twice. Her first husband was George L. Henry whom she married in 1867. He was a lawyer and editor of the Greenville Southern News. After his death in 1877 she married Albion Ockenden, an English engineer with whom she traveled extensively in Europe and America. After being widowed for the second time she returned to Greenville where she remained until her death. She had an outstanding reputation in the field of journalism, writing for several papers during her career. She was the first woman in Alabama admitted to the Alabama press association.

DR. JOHN R. BARGE

John R. Barge was the son of Lewis and Christiana Barge. He settled in Pine Flat around 1825 and married Elizabeth Webb Hill, the daughter of Thomas Hill who with his sons, Reuben and Josiah, his brother, Benjamin, and his son, Isaac, and with his son-in-law, John Hughes Watts, husband of Prudence Hill, came to Butler County from Clark County, Ga. in 1816.

Dr. Barge and his wife lived in the house previously owned by her parents. In 1836 as an inducement to persuade his brother, Abel, to come to Butler County he offered him this house, later known as the "Reynolds Place". Abel Barge accepted and Dr. Barge built on land known as the Barge Plantation. Here they reared six sons and two daughters. In 1845 he was buried in the Barge family burial plot. His wife died in 1862.

Their children all settled in Butler County and married as follows: Sarah Christiansen to Rev. Duncan Fowler; Lewis to Elefare Barge (daughter of Abel); Josiah to Sally Powers; Edward Webb to Minerva Traweek; John R., Jr. to Adeline Bowen; Elinore first to Dr. Adden Harris and second to Henry Paul Watts; Thomas Hill to Talitha Traweek and Essex was killed in 1864 in the War Between the States.

John R. and Elizabeth Barge were charter members of the first small chapel to be erected on the site of the Pine Flat Methodist Church. The Rev. Abiezer Clark Ramsey in 1834 and his co-worker the Rev. Isaac Mullins were assigned as Circuit Riders on the Cedar Creek Circuit. In his Journal the Rev. Ramsey writes of their coming on a week day to preach at "Dr. Barge's Church" and mentions that "Dr. Barge and his wife; Squire Benson and his wife were in the congregation." The cross that is now being used in the Pine Flat Church was dedicated in memory of this fine couple in recognition of their labors in the service of the church, and the rich heritage they bequeathed to their descendants.

STEPHEN FATHERLY PILLEY

Stephen F. Pilley, the son of Robert Pilley, was a Methodist minister in the Georgiana Church. His grandfather came to American as a British soldier during the Revolutionary War, and at that time his name was Paley. He was captured by the Americans with whom he sympathized. He then joined the American side and to escape detection changed his name to Pilley when he was later captured by the British. Years later in 1830 Stephen's mother, Mrs. Robert Pilley, sailed with relatives from New York in 1830 and the ship was captured by pirates and all of the crew was killed, the passengers being released unharmed. Stephen moved to Butler County from N. C. in 1822.

His children include three Methodist ministers, W. B. Pilley, Stephen A. Pilley and Charles B. Pilley. Others were G. A. Pilley and H. B. Pilley, a lawyer; Mary who married Benjamin Lafayette Selman, who was a minister and another daughter who was married to a Rev. Mathis.

COL. JESSE STALLINGS

Jesse Stallings, born 24 Nov. 1794; married Mary Mallory 11 Mch. 1813. His wife was born 9 Sept. 1796. They were early settlers in the Manningham area of Butler County. He served three terms as Congressman from the Second District of Alabama and refused to run for the fourth term.

The following were his children: Lucinda, born 22 Mch. 1814, married to James Gafford 7 Nov. 1853; Martha Mosely, born 14 Nov. 1816, married David Davenport; Celia Ann, born 14 Nov. 1819, married Francis Swanson 1 Nov. 1845; Reuben Reid, b. 14 June 1821; married Lucinda Ferguson 10 Sept. 1850; Jesse Chambers, born 8 Jan. 1825; Robert Reid, married Lidia, daughter of Ransom Seale and Ellen Murphy; Mary Mallory, born 20 Sept. 1828; Archibald Reid, born 12 Jan. 1831, married Nannie Cheatham; Elizabeth Sara, born 8 May 1833, married Allen B. Seale, son of Ransom Seale; Thomas Daniel, born 12 Jan. 1836, Gracie Allen, born 20 Sept. 1838, married John Wilson Seale, son of Ransom. All of these children lived in or around Manningham.

DUNNAM - ANTHONY

Theodore Woodberry Dunnam was born in 1833 in Butler Co., Alabama the son of Andrew Johnson Dunnam and a descendent of Robert Dunnam of Marion Dist., South Carolina, who was a Patriot in the Revolutionary War, furnishing supplies for the Continental Army. He was married to Nancy Terrell Anthony in 1855 and resided in the Starlington and Garland section of Butler County. Nancy was the daughter of Dr. Thomas Anthony and Sara King Wright of Garland. T. W. Dunnam served in the Confederate Army in the Fourteenth Alabama Artillery.

Andrew Johnson Dunnam or Dunham was an official with the L&N Railroad and it was more than likely for this man that the Dunham Community was named. He and his wife, the former Martha Watson eventually moved from Butler Co. and settled in Monroe Co., Alabama.

Dr. Thomas B. Anthony was a long time resident of Butler County where he died in 1886 and is buried in the Garland Cemetery. He was a member of the Garland Masonic Lodge. Lemuel B. Anthony, who was Tax Collector for Butler Co. was probably a member of his family.

MARTIN

The Martin family was instrumental in the development of industry in Greenville. In 1873 the firm of Martin & Hunt became the Greenville Mills manufacturing cedar buckets and hickory handles for hoes and axes and was owned by W. R. Martin, G. J. and T. W. Peagler. In 1893 the firm expanded into the Greenville Mills & Ice Co. and was the only ice plant between Mobile and Montgomery. The electricity generated by this company was used by the city to light the Opera House, the telephone exchange, Peagler's Drug Store and several residences. Warm water from the condenser of the plant supplied the city with its first public bath. A shed behind the building contained a wooden tub 2 to 3 feet deep and 6 to 8 feet in size which was available to bathers who were required to bring their own towels and soap. The Mills also operated a grist mill, a gin and a cotton seed oil mill. Mr. Martin was joined in the business by his son, Henry Porter Martin.

WHITMILL BUTLER

Whitmill Butler was born 2 Aug. 1791 in Edgefield District, S. C., the son of John Butler from Virginia and his wife, Sarah Ward. His mother died in 1818 in Edgefield District. Whitmill moved to Alabama around 1820 living first in Autauga County, then Macon and Montgomery Counties, before moving to Butler County in 1867.

He was married twice. His first wife, Penelope, died while he was living in Montgomery County leaving three children, Albert, James and Sarah. In August 1865 he married Rebecca Wade in that county and of this marriage Eugenia, Josephine and Anna R. were born. Albert and James both predeceased their father. Albert and Irena, his wife, moved to Ashley County, Arkansas and their children included Penelope Russell, who was widowed early in her marriage, William, Narcissa Finley (Mrs. James), Lafayette, John and Louisa. James stayed in Montgomery County and his children included Mary Ann Wilson (Mrs. Thomas), John W., William A. and James B. Butler. Whitmill's daughter, Eugenia, married William E. Tobias 27 Sept. 1849 in Montgomery County. Even though Whitmill had first entered land in Butler County in 1836 he apparently didn't live there until 1867. It was in this county that he died 2 February 1874.

MIRIAM MILNER ESKEW

Miriam Milner was the youngest child of Rev. John Milner. She was born 1 Mch. 1822 in Georgia and died in Butler County 21 June 1881. It was not until after the death of her husband, Dr. Isaac Richardson Eskew, on 13 June 1854 in Georgia that she migrated to Alabama. She was the sister of the Rev. Pitt Sanders Milner, founder of Georgiana to which place she moved. Other brothers included Willis J. and John T. Milner.

Her children included: Eunice, the first teacher in the school started by her uncle in Georgiana, and who later married a Mr. Haralson; Sarah Elizabeth, who married Judson Mercer Archer; Miriam L. who married a Mr. Shephard; Martha B.; Lillie Ora, wife of William Turner Dunklin; Isaac R., who moved to Selma; Mary Margaret, who married Thomas J. Thames and Miranda Isabel. Some of the descendants of the Archers moved to Texas, one of these being Sellers G. Archer, who has written a book "Descendants of Thomas & Alice Archer 1734-1975 & Related Families". Most of the information for this sketch came from his book.

GANDY

The first of the Gandy family to settle in Butler County was Brinkley Gandy, a veteran of the Revolutionary War. He was born around 1742 in Edgecombe County, North Carolina, later moving to Darlington County, South Carolina. He married for the second time in Darlington to Patty Chambliss, daughter of John Chambliss. Among their children were Elias, Abijah, Meshack, Patsy and Molly. The Gandys moved to Butler County before 1830, settling in the Pigeon Creek community. It was here that Brinkley applied for his Pension on 13 August 1832. Shown on the Pension application as witnesses were Noah Whidden also from South Carolina and a Revolutionary War veteran, and Robert Reid, Clerk of the County Court. At that time Brinkley was between 90 and 100 years of age. He died prior to 1840 and is buried in Butler County.

Abijah Gandy and his wife, Susannah Moore were married in South Carolina where their first three children, John L., Martha (Patsy) and Nichols W. were born. After moving to Butler County around 1828 five additional children were born; Brinkley, Mashack, Arthur Moore, Susannah and Abijah C. Gandy. They remained in the county until at least 1841 when their last child was born, moving on to Wayne County, Miss. between that date and 1850.

Another Gandy living in Darlington as shown on the 1810 Census was John Gandy who migrated to Cotaco County (later Morgan Co.). He is thought to be a son of Brinkley by his first marriage. Two of John's sons later on migrated to South Alabama with Oxford settling in Conecuh County and Alford in Butler County only one or two miles apart. Alford was married to Anne E. Kinnebrew and for many years operated a successful mercantile business in Greenville. Oxford's home in Conecuh burned and for a while he and his family lived with his brother in Butler County in his home shown on page 177. Many years later one of Oxford's sons, John Oxford Gandy, before moving to Escambia Co., Fla., visited the area and found the house still standing. It was owned by a Davis family at that time and they had a grist mill in operation right behind the house. Oxford's wife, Phebe, is buried in Old Bethel Cemetery, and he is probably buried in an unmarked grave by her side. He was a veteran of the Civil War.

John Oxford Gandy lived to the ripe old age of 108 years and was a real celebrity in the Panhandle of Florida. He was the oldest citizen of that section of the state and was one of the most beloved and respected men in the area. The community he started when he settled in Escambia County grew and because of the large number of Gandys living there the State Legislature named it Gandyville, Fla. in 1973. John never lost his love for Butler County and could talk for hours about the people and communities that he remembered so well. His wife, the former Victoria Black of Georgiana, died many years before he did. He was survived by 61 descendants when he passed away in 1977.

REV. DAVID BUTLER

David Butler was born 28 Aug. 1816 in New York, N. Y., the son of one of the owners of Butler Bros., Inc., retail and wholesale dealers in general merchandise. David was well educated having studied law to please his father; religion to please his mother and medicine to please himself. Soon after graduating from medical school he left home after a quarrel with his brother and mother over putting out the cat, never to return.

He married Narcissa Sarah Douglas Raymond Tibbett, daughter of Thomas, in Elbert County, Georgia on Dec. 17, 1842. By 1844 they had moved into Butler County settling in the Monterey Community where he was a planter and a Methodist minister. He lived between the Methodist Meeting House and Dr. Atkins. In 1851 after 8 years in the Methodist Ch., he was baptized into the Baptist Church in the Ridgeville community. On Aug. 21, 1851 he was authorized to perform marriages and was pastor of the Ridgeville Baptist Ch. This authority was approved by the Presbytery of Baptist Ministers one of whom was Rev. K. Hawthorne. From this church he went forth as a missionary. In his report in 1853 he stated that in 163 days he had preached 117 sermons, delivered 23 exhortations, made 95 visits and traveled 1418 miles.

On leaving Alabama he moved to Paducah, Kentucky, and then to Jonesboro, Illinois where he remained during the War Between the States. After the war they moved to Jonesboro, Arkansas. He worked too hard there as a physician and in March, 1877 after riding his horse at night through a flooded creek trying to save the life of a sick man in a remote area he died from exposure.

The children born to this couple were: Andrew Strother Harris, James Laurence, Sarah Anna Leonard, Josephine Alice, Mary Ann Eugenia, Brownell, Rosalie Naomi, David Brooks, Helen Ada, Almeta Ann and David Oliver Butler.

PITTS

A family of Pitts settled in Butler County in the mid-1800s. Named in the settlement of the Estate of Sarah Pitts in 1861 were her children John and Mathew of Polk County, Texas; Creed F., William F., Elizabeth Barrett, and Nancy Nichols of Butler County; Henry of Virginia; and the children of David, deceased.

William F. Pitts was married to Louisa Pruett 29 Dec. 1857 by Henry Smith, J.P. Creed F. Pitts married Elizabeth Lee, daughter of Jackson Lee 29 Dec. 1856, John T. Deen, J. P. officiating. David W. Pitts was married to Anna Barrett on 26 July 1855 with B. S. Barrett as Surety. Nancy H. C. Pitts and Jasper N. Nichols were married 30 Dec. 1856 by Harry Smith; Surety by Matthew C. Pitts. Matthew C. Pitts and Willia Barrett were married by John Deen on 28 Jan. 1858. William R. Barrett, Surety. All of these marriages took place in Butler County. Elizabeth's husband was Benjamin Barrett who died before 1861. David also predeceased his mother, leaving minor heirs, Ghatsey, Francis, Mellia, Isaiah, Mary and Martha.

BENJAMIN JOHN COOPER

Rev. B. J. Cooper settled in Butler County in 1858 from his home state of Georgia. He was pastor of Sardis, Spring Hill, Oak Grove and Friendship Baptist Churches. He died in 1899 and was buried in Pleasant Home Baptist Church Cemetery.

He was married three times; first to Edna Rosanna Craig; second to Louvenia Crawford; third to Mary Pitts. To these marriages 21 children were born. Among these children were Bulah (Mrs. Fletcher Herrington), Callie (Mrs. Tom A. Knight), Ella Henrietta (Mrs. Elijah Mack Pitts), Ida (Mrs. Frank Armstrong), Ada (Mrs. Elisha Pitts), Robert Benjamin (mar. M.F. Wesley), Edna Rosana (Mrs. Willie Hinson), Rosie (Mrs. Clyde Foster) and Emma Lou (Mrs. Jake Mercer) There were three sets of twins in this family by the first marriage.

CHAPTER 10.

REAL ESTATE TAXES FOR 1856

The earliest Real Estate Tax book remaining in the Butler County Court House is for the year 1856. The following is a listing of the people ennumerated in this book.

PRECINCT #1.

Burkill, William, Sr.
Burkill, Manuel
Bilberry, Henrietta
Barran, Jacob
Bryant, John A.
Burkill, Thomas
Burkill, Henry
Burkett, John
Burkett, Joseph
Burkett, Jno.
Bilberry, John
Coalman, Phillip
Coalman, John
Coalman, Jesse
Coalman, Rachael
Coalman, Joab
Deen, William
Davis, Sinia A.
Dean, L. D.
Dean, Thomas M.
Ealum, John
Finkley, Hugh
Fuller, William R.
Failes, Osburn
Franklin, Mark
Franklin, Edmund
Garner, Levi, Jr.
Gibson, Springer S.
Garner, Levi, Sr.
Garner, Nathan
Gardney, Richard S.
Grayson, Lavia
Grayson, Sarah
Gandy, Alfred
Harrison, Henry
Hood, John
Howell, James
Lee, Thomas
Lee, Yong (Young ?)
Lee, Jackson
McBride, Lavia
Moon, James
Myrich, Moses
Norris, Benjamin

Page, J. W.
Phepps, Samuel
Page, A.
Rials, Jesse
Sims, Elihu
Sims, Stephen
Sirmon, Levi
Sims, Susan
Smith, Elizabeth
Sims, Arthur
Stinson, Leander
Thomas, James T.
Tupton, Joseph

PRECINCT #2.

Arant, Jacob
Berry, Rhoda
Bowden, W. E.
Brooks, Rachael
Brooks, Samuel
Bush, William P.
Casleberry, John
Cravey, Amos
Dean, Jephton, Jr.
Duglas, James A.
Dean, John
Dozier, Thomas R.
Friddle, John
Hudson, Eli
Henderson, John T.
Hudson, Mornen
Hinson, Nancy
Hinson, Tillman G.
Hudson, Nelson
Hodges, James
Hinson, Andrew
Hinson, Eliza
Hinson, Asa E.
Hair, John
Jones, Elbert
Jones, William H.
Jones, James R.
Kervin, Morris
Little, Thomas

Mancus, William L.
McCormick, James
Michell, R. M. J.
Mosley, Mark
Moore, Lewis
Northcutt, Wm. A.
Northcutt, Henrietta F.
Northcutt, Ann W.
Northcutt, John G.
Overstreet, Lavia
Parker, John
Peavey, Daniel
Peavey, William J.
Peavey, Asa (2)
Preslar, William J.
Preslar, R. A.
Perritt, Needham
Preslar, Allen
Pierce, Levi
Preslar, William A.
Rogers, Francis
Rhodes, Newton M.
Riley, H. C., agt. for James A. Rabb
Stewart, Nimrod
Stewart, Robert W.
Stewart, William H.
Stewart, Charles
Sarter, Richard F.
Sarter, William
Williams, Winney
Whiddon, Bennett
Wilkerson, John

PRECINCT #3

Allen, L. R.
Arnold, A. P.
Armstrong, James W.
Barrett, Timothy
Brogdon, James C.
Brogdon, William
Barrett, B. J.
Curry, Ebeneaser
Campbell, Philip J.
Dees, John T.

166

Edward, William J.
Fowler, Eli
Feagan, A. P.
Feagan, S. J.
Huggans, Dianna P.
Hughes, T. M.
Halso, Stephen
Halso, John W.
Hart, Jordan
Hammonds, William
Hughs, R. S.
Hughs, Willson
Jordan, Charles B.
Josey, James W.
  & James S.
Jones, Samuel J.
Jordan, James M.
Jordan, John, Est. of
Lewis, Charles
Lee, Jackson
Lee, Hillary
Minyard, Thomas
Maxey, John
McLean, J. C.
Monroe, A. C.
Maxey, Allen
Martin, David
Morgan, John A.
Nichols, Joel
Pruitt, Winnaferd
Pitts, Sarah
Pitts, J. S. C.
Rogers, William
Rose, Mary
Reide, A. M.
Stalling, Daniel
Shines, William P.
Shine, Daniel B.
Jernagan, William
Stallings, James
Shine, Elizabeth
Smith, Henry C.
Smith, J. R.
Shines, James W.
Stallings, R. R.
Smith, Clarrisa W.
Stallings, W. M. D.
Skipper, Silas
Skipper, B. B.
Skipper, Needham
Tillman, George
Tinis, John H.
Turk, Laban
Thomas, Daniel L.
Williams, Calvin D.
Williams, George
Wall, Wright, agt for
  Jonathan Harrison
Wall, Wright
Willson, L. H.
Willson, L. B.

Williams, Mary L.
Wall, William R.
Wade, William F.
Williams, J. S.

PRECINCT #4

Armstrong, Mac
Boane, Jacob M.
Boane, John L.
Brown, Daniel A.
Blackmon, E. H.
Brown, Mary
Boggs, James
Browder, Thomas
Burk, Nancy
Boyster, L. T.
Bedgood, Richard
Bentley, Mary
Barter, James M.
Boane, Fedrick
Bedgood, John
Burk, J. M.
Benson, S. C.
Boswell, William J.
Burke, D. J.
Campbell, David
Callaway, D.J., agt.
  Francis Calloway
  Seaborn Moore
  Thomas Cooper
Capps, Alexander
Claghorn, John
Childers, P. W.
Coe, William
Cartlidge, B. M.
Cook, James B.
Caldwell, Elizabeth
Capps, William H.
Coe, Ransom
Cowart, James A.
Carr, William
Clansey, Daniel
Capps, Daniel
Capps, James
Drake, Patrick
Dyer, Cornelius O.
Davis, William M.
Davis, Helton
Davis, John J.
Davis, John, est.
Davis, A. C. L.
Davis, Robert B.
Davenport, P. P.
Davenport, P. O.,
  Guardian
Davis, James
Franklin, Henry C.
Gainey, Elizabeth
Gilchrist, Henry
Goodson, Josiah

Gibson, Lewis E.
Harrison, John H.
Herrenton, Jos. W.
Hasting, Benjamin
Holland, James
Holland, John N.
Harbin, Wm. P.
Harrill, Lewis
Holland, James Sr.
Jordan, Wiley
James, Mahala
James, Arnollus
Jackson, L. B.
Johnson, Robert
Johnson, Joseph B.
Ketter, Thomas S.
Kingsley, James
Kennington, Arnold
Long, Ann
Long, Mary
Long, Robert B.
Long, Sarah
Mahone, Thomas, agt
  James L. Pollard
  L. Cook
  Wm. B. Marshall
Mahone, Thomas & Co.
Mormon, D. J.
Mahone, Thomas agt.
  C. H. Word
Morris, James B.
McCall, Ruel E.
Moore, L. J.
Moye, George A.
Nix, Edward, agt.
  Thomas Slaton
  Edward B. (?)
Nix, Edward
Pickett, John
Pittman, Elizabeth
Rhodes, Josiah
Roach, P. B.
Rayner, James L.
Rhodes, Charlotta
Reeves, William W.
Rees, George
Ridgeway, William
Swanner, Amariah
Swanner, William
Skipper, Samuel
Stephens, James
Staggars, George J.
Swanner, John
Skaines, Thomas
Sanford, H. H.
Skains, Sam'l S.
Thomasson, Thomas R.
Thomasson, J. F.
Thaggard, James L.
Thaggard, J. L., agt.
  A. M. Sellers

Thomasson, L. M.
Upshaw, Leroy
Upshaw, Rebecca
Vann, Calvin
Wood, Lavia
Williamson, Wiley
Wilkerson, Benj. F.
Wren, William
Wilkerson, Joshua

PRECINCT # 5

Adkinson, Alexander
Bishop, Stephen
Bryant, George
Bishop, Stephen, agt
   Mark E. Moore
Boanhan, N. S.
Ball, John
Bridges, D. B.
Burk, William P.
Bonner, Robert A.
Clemment, David
Courtney, Wm. R.
Conner, Michael,
   1855 & 1856
Churchwell, James
Cooper, Wm. D.
David, Archibald
Davis, Abram E.
Duke, Ransom
Dukes, Stephen
Davis, Isaac
Ellington, David
Ellington, Joseph
Ellington, W. D.
Fuller, Joseph
Fowler, John W.
Fowler, Warran
Fuller, Henry C.
Green, George
Goare, James
Gibbs, John W.
Guy, James
Gardney, T. J.
Harrison, S. C.
Haynes, R. D. (?)
Holland, D. F.
Holland, Joseph
Hamrick, Jason H.
Hutton, Levi
Hall, Clemmon
Jones, John
Jones, William, Sr.
Jackson, Henry F.
Jones, Jeremiah
Johnson, William, Sr.
James, John
Jones, Littleton
Knotts, Nancy
Kent, James L.

Kent, Arnold
Loftin, A. J.,
   Trustee for
   Eliz. Davenport
Liles, William J.
Liles, Hampton
Lowery, James
Lowery, J., agt
   Albert Butts
Mapes, Maletta
Mosley, William E.
Moody, C. W.
Miller, Ezra
Martin, Bird
Mills, Isaac L.
Mitchael, Peter
Lowery, Thomas est.
Newman, William
Norris, A. B.
Parrish, John
Pipens, Lewis
Perritt, Rebecca
Rogers, John
Rogers, Henry
Rogers, Elizabeth
Rogers, Nathaniel
Rabb, Ezekial
Rabb, William
Rogers, Harvy
Rhodes, G. W.
Smith, C. W.
Summerlin, Wm. R.
Sikes, William
Stephenson, S. T.
Summerlin, Smith
Soloman, Henry
Skipper, Samuel
Sturgis, A. M.
Sanders, Josiah
Thaggard, George
Tobias, B. R.
Trainum, George
Thaggard, T. S.
Thaggard, G. W.
Thaggard, W. R.
Typett, William H.
Thomas, James F.
Typett, Susan
Vinson, M. E.
Willis, John G.
Welch, William
Wyche, George E.
Wyches, Anna
Welch, James
Walker, H. P.
Wyrodick, Thomas Z.
Wright, Ezekiel W.
Winsley, Nancy
Wright, George W.
Welch, Seaborn
Wyrodick, Andrew

Wyche, Peter
Welch, J. Littleton
Williamson, Arasmus

PRECINCT # 6

Anthony, L. B.
Anthony, M. W.
Allen, Washington W.
Ambrose, Ashley
Armstrong, Jessee M.
Andress, William J.
Burough, James
Barrett, Andrew J.
Beasley, William A.
Beasley, W. A., agt.
   Nathan Mash
----Hancock
Boyett, Gibson
Bell, Thomas W.
Briggs, Thomas H.
Boyler, Thomas
Bell, William J.
Bell, Washington
Black, Thomas J.
Black, F. M.
Black, A. M.
Boggus, Jasper
Boyett, Thomas
Barnes, Lanchlin
Barrenton, Wm. W.
Barnes, Archibald
Barnes, Sam'l
Barrett, Joshua
Black, Robert W.
Bishop, Mathew
Camp, L. G.
Cook, A. H.
Callens, R. H.
Camp, E. H.
Daniel, W. J.
Daniel, T. J.
Daniel, E. F.
Daniel, A. J.
Davis, Levi
Daniel, Thomas
Daniel, Abel
Davidson, James T.
Day, Sarah
Daniel, Z.
Dean, Thomas
Daniel, T. F.
Daniel, Leonard
Dorman, James T.
Daniel, Theophilus
Edward, David
Frost, Y. H.
Fails, S. W.
Gandy, Augustus
Griggs, Lewis
Gillian, Isaac

Graham, Joseph J.
Henderson, John
Hartin, Hugh
Harrison, Augustus
Harton, John
Hays, Jessee
Jay, John, Sr.
Knowles, Robert
King, Thomas M.
Keily, Elisha
Kirkpatrick, Wm.
Kent, John
Kent, Levi, Est.
McBride, J. J.
McGinney, J. A.
McGough, J. R.
Marlow, John
McCharthee, Alex
McCullough, Rachael
Mosley, John
McKingey, Charles
McCormick, Isabella
McCormick, Patrick
McCormick, Thomas
Morgan, William
Mercer, William
McMullin, J. S.
Norman, J. J.
Nichols, William
Pollard, R. M. C.
Pollard, Elizabeth
Powell, Coalman
Petty, Mathew
Perdiew, William E.
Perdiew, Joshua A.
Phelps, Terrill
Peterson, Thomas D.
Perdiew, J. E. W.
Peterson, William B.
Pollard, Nathaniel
Pharough, Thomas
Reeves, James M.
Reeves, Joseph M.
Reeves, James E.
Reeves, Jessee W.
Reeves, Chislin M.
Rhame, Ranson
Raburn, David
Reeves, Joseph J.
Reeves, U. G.
Reeves, William
Rogers, Wesley
Reeves, Miles
Roach, David C.
Riley, F. D. N.
Raburn, Richard
Smith, A. A.
Staggars, John H.
Stringer, William J.
Skipper, Mary
Searcy, Sarah

Spraggins, Thomas
Sims, Waller
Stringer, William R.
Scarborough, Addison
Staggars, Henry S.
Stiner, Joseph
Sheales, Willson E.
Stringer, John A.
Thornton, Eli
Taylor, Margaret A.
Turner, John T.
Taylor, Joseph
Turner, Mary
Turner, Jacob, agt.
  S. Word
Thomason, James R.
Taylor, J. R.
Thomas, William
Thompson, John P.
Terry, Henry
Thornton, Jacob A.
Vernell, C. C.
Veasey, Jessee H.
Williamson, William J.
Whiddon, William
Whiddon, Elias
Williams, Drucilla
Roper, John M.

PRECINCT # 7

Adams, J. L.
Andress, Nancy
Andress, S. F.
Andress, Jeremiah
Alexander, Lavney
Brownlee, A. C.
Ballard, J. T.
Ballard, Theophilus
Bolling & Ewing
Bundrick, A. M.
Bates, W. T.
Bell, J. E. and
  Jones, Wash
Burnes, Henry
Bell, Edward
Colley, Allen
Cheatham, Gutridge, Jr.
Cheatham, Gutridge, Sr.
Cheatham, Andrew
Cheatham, Archer
Callaway, Claiborn
Callens, Ross
Daley, Michael
Day, Zack
Day, Fed
Day, Joseph
Day, William
Ewing, William W.
Easterlin, Bennett
Fuller, Thomas

Frost, Thomas
Frost, Henry
Fost, Derrill
Flinn, L. W.
Fuller, Archibald
Failes, Elsberry
Failes, Elsberry, agt.
  Mary A. Senter
Finley, William
Failes, D. N.
Failes, William
Failes, William, agt.
  Joseph Bell
Ewing, Jonathan & Nancy
Gafford, A. P.
Gafford. A.P., guardian
  Wm. F. Gafford
Gafford, Thomas P.
Gafford, David W.
Gafford, D. W. for
  M. L. Gafford
Gafford, Pheraba
Gholson, William T.
Gafford, Grant
Gafford, Jeremiah P.
Getlin, Moses
Glass, Francis
Graydon, William
Gafney, D. F.
Herlong, William F.
Hamilton, Elvira
Harriman, L. R.
Huckaby, A. J.
Hammond, M. G.
Herrendon, William
Harrison, William agt.
  Stan Hillard
  John Stewart
Jordan, Samuel
Jones, Washington
Kellough, Samuel
Kelley, William
Kite, C. A.
Kirkpatrick, R. H.
Kirkpatrick, James S.
Kirkpatrick, James
McKinzie, Elias G.
Mercer, Seth
McQueen, Daniel
McKinzie, John
Martin, Bartlet
Murrey, Willson
McCoy, Mary
Mosley, Robert
Manning, Richard
McLean, John
Martin, George W., Jr.
McKinzie, William T.
Morgan, M. S.
Mosley, Gutridge
Mosley, William

Morgan, Thomas R.
McCoy, John R.
McCoy, John R., Adm.
   Est. John McCoy
McCoy, Patience
McPherson, John
Norman, James
Norman, James, agt
   Wm. E. Thompson
Ott, James P.
Pickens, Hanna
Petillo, George H.
Payne, D. G.
Payne, T. J.
Phelps, Edward
Phelps, Lorenzo
Riley, Daniel
Roper, John B.
Reynolds, Abner
Reynolds, Robert R.
Reynolds, Overton
Rains, Mary
Sheppard, Francis, agt
   William Collins
   Dennis Hodges
Salter, Mary Ann
Shaw, J. J.
Sims, William
Sheppard, Francis
Tally, James C., agt
   A. B. Collier
Tillery, John
Tally, John
Tillery, John R.
Tillery, Washington
Tillery, Thomas
Tillery, James W.
Tillery, Richard
Talley, James C.
Wight, James W.
Wrincher, William
Wood, G. W.
Wicker, Thomas

PRECINCT # 8.

Brown, Joseph
Butts, Benjamin
Butts, Rebecca
Barganier, James F.
Butler, Edmund
Butler, Reubin
Chesnut, James
Cates, Josiah
Cheatham, Peter, guard.
   Jesse Mosely
Cheatham, Peter
Daniel, James
Gafford, A. G.
Grant, John

Hartley, Hiram
Hartley, William
Hinson, Asa
Hartley, Joseph G.
Hartley, Anderson C.
Hampton, Thomas H.
Hatcher, Rutledge
Heaton, John, Sr.
Heaton, John, Jr.
Harrison, G. W.
Hawkins, John
Harrison, John
Hersting, W. J.
Harrison, Henry
Harrison, Levi
Harrison, William
Harrison, Jonathon
Harrison, King S.
Leonard, C. W., Sr.
Matthews, Samuel M.
Miles, J. C.
Martin, G. W.
Mealin, Jonathan
Orum, James
Oliver, H. P.
Peagler, Nancy
Parker, Sherrod
Perry, Robert
Parmer, William H.
Pierce, John Estate
Rogers, Joseph
Roper, E. M.
Ramage, J. C.
Rogers, P. H.
Ray, W. H.
Smith, W. T.
Smith, W. B.
Smith, George W.
Whittle, William
Wilson, Cyrus
Waller, William
Wallace, Linia
Waller, James
Waller, William A.
Waller, Clark

PRECINCT # 9

Adams, James
Adams, Martin
Ashcraft, John
Armstrong, J. W.
Brown, J. E.
Boggan, J. P., Jr.
Bragg, Rachael B.
Boggan, Rebecca
Boggan, D. G.
Bowin, Edward
Cooper, Augustin
Crenshaw, Edward T.

Coalman, W. C.
Chesnut, Nehemiah
Cross, Franklin
Caldwell, John C.
Crenshaw, F. W.
Crenshaw, Mary
Crenshaw, W. H.
Crenshaw, T. C.
Davison, Joseph
Davis, James L.
Dickerson, Archibald
Davison, William R.
Donald, A.
Duberry, Wiley
Ernest, Boliver
Ernest, Asa
Ferguson, Elizabeth
Ferguson, D. J.
Ferguson, Elias H.
Ferguson, D. J. & Co.
Gafford, James M.
Giddens, W. R.
Harrilson, W. B.
Herbert, C. B.
Hagler, James
Hutchison, Abraham
Jackson, Matthews
Jones, John
Koulb, Thomas
Kinsey, Martin
Kinsey, Mary H.
Martin, Kin
Martin, A. W.
Matthiss, J. D. & Bro.
Mathess, J. D.
Mathess, J. S.
Phillips, William H.
Powell, Martha
Patton, Eliza
Patterson, John P.
Patton, Matthew, Sr.
Peagler, Martin
Peagler, George S.
Powell, George
Peagler, A.
Pool, Calvin
Pierce, Moses
Rayney, William
Stallings, R. R.
Shanks, R. S.
Smith, W. G.
Sartin, A. B.
Seals, William
Stallings, Jesse
Smith, J. C., Guard.
   Mrs. Judith Coalman
Simpson, J. B.
Stallings, Reuben
Seale, R. H.
Seal, Anderson

Smith, A. J.
Till, Hampton
Thigpen, Gray
Waller, John
Waller, Briget
Waller, Levin
Walker, William
Wade, W. H.
Womack, J. L.
Womack, T. A.
Walker, James
Jones, Joseph
Pruitt, Hardin

PRECINCT # 10.

Atkins, J. W.
Atkins, R. Y.
Atkins, J. O.
Barge, J. T.
Barge, John R.
Barge, E. W.
Benson, James H.
Boggan, Patrick
Boggan, Holan W.
Beverly, A.
Beverly, Alexander
Boggan, Ann
Boggan, Elizabeth
Benson, J. W.
Boggan, J. P.
Caldwell, A. J.
Chancellor, Gilbert
Crain, C. H.
Donald, G. J.
Dailey, John S.
Foller, D. C.
Gasting, David
Gray, J. M.
Greene, Thomas
Green, Joshua
Glenn, N. R.
Gregory, Opian
Hutchinson, F. W.
Herbert, G. B.
Hutcheson, J. D.
Hays, Thomas
Hixon, Ezra
Homes, Zabuel
Horton, Daniel
Hays, J. N.
Hawkins, Wiley
Knight, L. J.
Lazenby, E. M.
Lewis, E. E.
Little, Amos
Lewis, J. C.
Lackey, E. J.
Lewis, J. B.
McKay, Hugh
McWhorter, John

Moorer, N. J.
Moorer, Elizabeth
McLoud, Rodrick
Palmore, Marshal
Palmore, John
Powers, J. D.
Parks, F. F.
Powell, William
Perkins, J. L.
Perkins, E.
Powell, John
Smith, William
Smith, Thomas
Smith, Henry
Smith, Martha P.
Smith & Benson
Salter, Wadkins
Steen, Curtis
Thigpen, John
Thompson, Warren A.
Traweek, William H.
Traweek, T. M. G.
Traweek, L. W.
Watts, Vincent
Ward, H. R.
Yeldell, James R.
Yeldell, Robert
Yeldell, J. M.
Yeldell, James A.

PRECINCT # 11.

Amos, William
Augburn, Allen
Ainsworth, J. C.
Blackmon, William
Blackmon, J. C.
Burket, Calib, Jr.
Baldree, Robert
Carter, Alfred
Carter, Alfred for
   Rufus K. George
Carter, John, Est.
Cole, Robert
Cole, James Est.
Creamer, Michael
Dailey, E. H.
Green, Elijah
Green, Joshua
Harrison, Jonathan A.
Hunter, H. M.
Hill, Isaac
Hawkins, Thomas W.
Henderson, Jas.
Hilson, Anna
Jones, Allen
Liles, Francis A.
Mullins, Josiah
McCrory, Thomas
Martin, P. F.
Green, John

Murphy, Wilson
McCord, R. P.
McGinney, A. J.
McNeil, Daniel
Nixon, A. W.
McCrory, John
Murphy, John
McCrory, John E.
McCrory, Mary
Nevills, John
Odom, J. H.
Phillips, Wiley
Phillips, Isham
Park, Henry B.
Park, Tempy D.
Park, James D.
Pinkerton, James
Reynolds, James
Saucer, Mary
Seale, Hardaway & Co.
Seale, Ransom
Serman, Ransom
Sims, Isaac
Sims, Sherwood
Stringfellow, Reubin
Stringfellow, John W.
Stokes, M.
Stinston, Reubin
Stinston, J. W.
Stinston, George
Stinston, Joseph H.
Thompson, J. C.
Thompson, James
Thompson, Andrews
Thompson, Mary
Vickrey, Franklin
Vickrey, Rhoda
Vickrey, Francis
Vickrey, John J.
Vickrey, G. W.
Womack, J. M.
Willson, Calvin
Watts, John H. Estate

PRECINCT # 12

Allen, Gideon
Banister, John
Broughton, John T.
Barrett, Ghatsey
Braden, Harvy C.
Bennett, Ryan
Bailey, Sarah
Bailey, Isaac
Baldwin, J. G.
Brightwell, William
Briant, Elisha
Buckellew, John
Bullock, Alfred
Bush, Richard
Bolling, John

Brenton, John H.
Burnett, T. J.
Burnett, William
Bolling, S. J.
Bolling & Gonder
Bolling, S. J. for
   Hyman Gratz
   J. D. Craig
   C. J. Edward
   Richard Catlin
   Stideman & Barry
   J. J. Crocheran
   Muller Grieve
   Sarah Rorie
Bolling & Burnett
Bragg, Thomas M.
Branton, Thomas A.
Bryers, William H.
Colvin, James G.
Cooper, Benjamin
Carlow, Andrew
Craig, James
Cheatham, Daniel H.
Creach, William
Chambliss, D. E.
Corlee, M. C.
Camp, John T.
Clute, John H.
Craig, Wm. G. Est.
Craig, Jincy E.
Corlee, Jessee
Davidson, William
Dunklin, James L.
Davies, John S.
Davis, Jane M.
Davis, Martha
Davis, Henrietta
Dunklin, William A. T.
Dunklin & Haralson
Dickens, Thomas
Dickens, Clinton
Duke, Joel
Deming, Ezra
Deming, Simeon & Co.
Deming, Simeon, Sr.
Deming, Simeon, Jr.
Deming, Ezra
Deming, John
Dunklin, Daniel G.
Erwin, Henry
Evans, Uriah
Erwin, Matthew
Ernest, John R.
Fife, John
Fail, William
Flowers, William H.
Fails, M. F.
Glassgow, John
Gideon, Thomas
Glass, B. A.
Gray, Joseph P.

Gilbert, Eliza
Gandy, Mavina
Gilbert, Webster
Gafford, James L.
Gedian, Alfred
Gafford, S. F., Guard.
   Mary Jane and
   Josiah M. Gafford
   Agt.C.M. Allister
Gafford, S. F.
Gill, R. W.
Goodall, William C.
Henry, John K.
Herbert, Hillary Est.
Herbert, Thomas E.
Hodges, Alfred
Harper, Henry S.
Hortman, Abraham
Holliday, William
Holliday, Martha
Herrington, Harvy
Hopper, Joseph D.
Hartley, Wm. F.
Hugla, George
Jay, John
Jackson, William
Jay, Joseph
Jones, Joseph
Lee, Joseph
Lee, Seaborn
Locklear, W. W.
Lovett, Alley
Long, John T.
Martin, Green
Mattel, John W.
Moran, W. B.
McLemore, J. J.
McKellar, Alex.
Moye, John
McCann, James Est.
McQueen, Nancy
McQueen, Louisa
McQueen, John C.
May, Seth S.
Newton, Caswall
Newton, Thomas
Newton, Benjamin
Newton, B. for
   F. Armstrong
   M. Fife
Newton, Amos
Ormand, G. M.
Oliver, Sam'l, Sr.
Perry, John, Sr.
Peevy, Thomas
Peevy, Benjamin
Pickens, E. H.
Parmer, M. H.
Parmer, John M.
Parmer, Fleming
Parker, Henry E.

Payne, William W.
Payne, John
Posey, A. F.
Pollard, Albert
Porter, William J.
Porter, Wm. for
   Guilford
Perry, John, Jr.
Perry, Simon
Parmer, J. M.
Perry, James
Peters, R. & Co.
Parmer, D. B.
Payne, Sam'l
Payne, C. J.
Parker, Hoab, Sr.
Rhodes, Sanford
Rhodes, Mancil
Rhodes, Kinchen (2)
Rhodes, John
Robert, William A.
Rhodes, James W.
Reddoch, W. W. Est.
Reddoch, Wm. C. for
   B. B. Saunders
Reddoch, William C.
Rhodes, Reddin
Rhodes, William
Riley, John
Richards, Lucinda
Roberson, N. J.
Rhodes, Benj., Sr.
Rendolph, John
Rendolph, John & Son
Routon, Wm. R.
Rhodes, Berry
Rhodes, Robt.
Rhodes, Benj., Jr.
Ruffin, Alex
Rhodes, Martha
Rhodes, Jonathan
Smyth, John P. E.
Stewart, A. D.
Shealy, George
Smith, Ambrose
Smith, Daniel L.
Skinner, Asa
Skinner, Asa for
   Wiley Skinner
Smyth, Jacob A.
Smyth, Daniel C.
Smyth, Robert B.
Smyth, D. J.
Sirmon, R. P.
Staley, William and
   Alfred Hodges
Staton, Thomas
Smyth, John
Thomas, John T.
Thames, J. G.
Taylor, H. B. Est.

Thomas, Harnett
Thomas, William R.
Turner, William D.
Turner, Thomas
Thornton, Jacob
Thornton, Jacob agt.
   E. Harrison
Thomas, Daniel
Thomas, Robt.
Thomas, Richard D.
Taylor, Alex
Uhink, John
Vann, Sanders R.
Vines, Jos.
Wright, William
Wright, Robt. R.
Winn, R. P.
Waters, P. B.
Wheeler, John Est.
Waters, P. B., Adm.
   F. C. Davis
Wallace, John
Wilkerson, Joseph
Williams, Martha
Watts, T. H.
West, Elizabeth
Waid, William E.
William, Joshua F.
Whited, William
Williams, Williamson
Whitted, William
Wiggins, Joshua
Amerson, Benjamin
Brooks, D. W.
Brooks, E. P.
Brooks, John S.
Briers
Burkett, James, Sr.
Chancelor, Jackson
Cook, S. E.
Creach, William
Coker, Daniel
Dunham, A. J.
Driver, Leroy
Fail, John O.
Hood
Johnson, Elliott
Morgan, Thomas R., Sr.
   additional
Moore, Isham
Power, James, Agt.
   Widow Cook
Parker, Benj.
Peacock, H. B.
Pollard, William P.
Rhodes, Eli
Riley, L. G.
Riley, Travis M.
Sanders, E. H.
Smyth, Robert

PRECINCT # 13.

Allen, Warran
Beasley, Lelia
Bell, William
Burkett, William, Jr.
Beesley, John
Black, Elijah
Burkett, Caleb
Burkett, Enoch
Burkett, Wiley
Burkett, Alfred
Bransford, Nathan
Bransford, J. H.
Bennett, Thomas
Cone, Lewis for
   Jessee Cone
Driver, Chas.
Ethridge, Lewis
Evans, A. B.
Ellis, Nathan G.
Gallaway, Nathan
Gillmore, Wm.
Gillmore, John
Huston, Dorson
Huston, Isaiah
Hobbs, Jacob
Harper, Berry
Howell, Benj. J.
Ingram, Isaac
Ingram, Irid (?)
Jones, James
Kelsoe, Eliz.
Kelsoe, Angus
Kebler, Peter
Kebler, John
Kebler, Samuel
Lee, Alex
Lee, John by
   D. B. May
Lee, Bryant
Lee, Benj. N.
May, Drury
McClure, Wm. D.
Morrow, Abraham
McClure, Geo. H.
McPherson, John F.
May, Jos. J.
Myers, John P.
Norris, Abud
Odom, Jethro J.
Obed, Ham
Parker, Noah, Jr.
Preslar, Elias
Price, David S.
Price, Geo. W.
Preslar, Elias B.
Preslar, James
Preslar, H. S.
Rustin, E. C.

Shell, John
Skipper, Wesley
Stinson, Elias D.
Simpson, N. L., agt.
   Winston Billings
Sellers, Elizabeth A.
Sellers, J. D.

PRECINCT # 14.

Blair, William
Burkett, James, Jr.
Black, James M.
Brown, F. M., agt.
   A. J. Brown
Brown, F. M.
Brown, F. M., Agt.
   John W. Winley
Blackburn, Stephen
Bradley, George W.
Blair, William, Jr.
Black, Hugh L.
Bradley, Aston
Black, Robert L.
Blair, James M.
Bradley, G., Agt.
   John Bradley
Corley, John
Campbell, H. E.
Duck, Timothy
Davis, William
Faile, William
Faile, John
Faile, Leonard
Guinn, Colman O.
Heap, William J.
Hammond, Nancy
Harrison, James E.
Hood, Isaac
Ingram, Marshall
Jones, Levi
Johnson, Robt.
Kuykendall, Isaac J.
Lee, John H.
Lee, Edward, Jr.
Lee, Edward, Sr.
Lee, Irvin
Lee, Alex
Lee, Isaac
Lee, Joel W.
Myers, David B.
Moore, M. J.
Moore, A. W.
McBride, Rich'd
Martin, R. H.
Milner, Pitt S.
Milner, Pitt S., agt.
   M. M. Eskew
Methany, T. B.
Norris, Ingram

Overstreet, Sam'l
Oatley, George
Parker, Arthur
Pugh, Albert
Pugh, Ivey
Pugh, Maston B.
Stott, David
Shepperd, John A.
Stott, Abdial
Shepperd, W. B.
Shepperd, Jas.
Shepperd, Jas. C.
Shepperd, Thomas
Smith, Henry
Shepperd, John
Stott, Marshall
Singleton, Jos. T.
Wadkins, Jessee
Whittington, Jonathan
Waters, Bryan

SUPPLEMENT

Albritton, Arnold
Acre, John E.
Antony, Thos.
Andrews, Daniel
Buckloo, Geo. D.
Bell, Robt.
Black, T. M.
Butler, Daniel
Bennett, T. B.
Burk, John M.
Bogan, Wingate
Clopton, N. V.
Deen, Drury
Dillard, Nathaniel
Davis, Sophia
Duck, Timothy
Dubury, Wiley

Ficklin, Thos.
Fail, Jeremiah
Gray, Joshua
Gibson, Henry T.
Gibson, Robert C.
Gill, R. W.
Gilbert, James
Hightower, William
Hollenhead, John
Howard, Benjamin
Harris, J. F.
Hassey, W. B.
Hughla, John A.
Hobbs, Marada
Jones, Rich'd
Jordan, Turner
Jordan, William
Jordan, Felix
Johnson, James E.
Jones, Sebron
Kelley, Elarsah, Jr.
Kite, C. H.
Kill, Sam'l
Lane, James B.
Mercer, Noah
Massey, Joseph
Morrow, Geo. H.
Myers, L. H.
Morgan, J. W.
Maniece, John B.
McMullen, John
McWhorter, John
Miller, Mary
Milner, John T.
Milner, Willis J.
Milner, Benj. C.
Norris, David J.
Owens, Richard
Oswalt, L. H.
Perkett, Ervin

Parker, L. B.
Parker, Sam'l
Perry, S. G.
Porterfield, Henry
Powell, H. C.
Pulaski, John C.
Rabon, Delpha
Shell, John
Skipper, John
Smith, D. E.
Smith, Robt.
Smith, Wm. M.
Scarborough, A. B.
Shanks, R. T.
Stringer, Sarah
Stinson, J. B.
Seal, Wilson M.
Turner, Sam'l
Tankersley, T. P.
Tankersley, Mary
Tines, Wiley
Varner, John H.
Williamson, Augustus
Williams, Theophilus
Williams, James E.
Williams, Franklin
Wilson, A. J.
Waters, Levi M.
Waters, W. C.
Worrell, J. D.
Watson, Gilbert
Whitted, William
Womack, Mary

Lemuel B. Anthony, Tax
  Coll., Butler County
Amos Newton, Tax Assessor
  Butler County

GRAND JURORS, FEBRUARY 9, 1877

W. C. Bennett
G. W. Brown
J. T. Carter
Geo. R. Crittenden
W. M. Flowers
Daniel Harrison

Joseph Hartley
S. A. Hickman
J. H. Johnson
J. E. Josey
W. R. Luckie
William McBride

J. A. Norman
A. L. Palmer
J. A. Reid
C. M. Sellars
B. W. Stewart

PETIT JURORS

W. H. Armstrong
S. J. Balderee
Jno. Burt
Jno. Bush
A. H. Cook
K. L. Davis
A. F. Day
J. M. Donald

W. A. Graydon
W. E. Hinson
J. G. Lazenby
F. C. Mize
F. J. McCormack
T. J. Newton
J. R. Peacock

J. W. Powell
G. W. Searcy
G. H. Smith
A. J. Thagard
J. F. Thames
A. C. VanPelt
B. F. Webb

HONOR LODGE # 21, K of P

The officers of this Lodge as listed in the Advocate on 23 Jan. 1884.

P. C.; W. M. Wimberly
V. C.; B. Wimberly
P. R.; H. Lichton
M of F; W. B. Barrow
I. G.; W. F. Jones

C. C.; J. T. Steiner
K of R. S.; A. W. Metcalf
M of E; J. M. Steiner
M of A; Samuel Ewing
O. G.; A. Sanders

Trustees; J. M. Steiner, A. Steinhart, J. C. Richardson.
Representatives to Grand Lodge; J. M. Steiner, J. C. Richardson.

SECTION 15 FOR THE ENDOWMENT OF K. OF P.

Pres.; J. Lang
Sec. & Treas.; A. W. Metcalf
Chaplain; A. Steinhart
Sentinel; A. Sanders

Vice Pres.; W. M. Wimberly
Guide; J. M. Steiner
Guard; A. Lichten
Medical Examiner; S. J. Steiner

ASHE LODGE, #302, I.O.B.B.

Pres.; A. Drum
Sec.; J. Lang
O. G.; Joseph Neumann

Vice Pres.; H. Lichten
Treas. & I.G.; A. Steinhart
M.; F. Flexner

Representative to Grand Lodge; A. Steinhart

DEMOCRATIC AND CONSERVATIVE PARTY

The Greenville Advocate   March 17, 1884

The Executive Committee of the Democratic and Conservative party of Butler County will meet in Greenville on Saturday the 22nd at 12. Members of the Committee are:

Beat 1. Jesse Owen
Beat 2. N. M. Rhodes
Beat 3. Henry C. Smith
Beat 4. J. M. Hickmon, Box 2
Beat 4. D. L. Milton, Box 1
Beat 5. J. B. Taylor
Beat 6. J. J. McBride
Beat 7. W. F. Cheatham
Beat 8. Daniel Harrison

Beat 9. J. F. Brown
Beat 10. John G. Little
Beat 11. John D. Vickory, Box 1
Beat 11. W. H. Shanks, Box 2
Beat 12. L. M. Lane
Beat 13. Willis Darby
Beat 14. J. W. Blow, Esq.
Beat 15. Robert Perry
Beat 16, B. F. Saucer

GEORGIANA LODGE OF GOOD TEMPLARS

Officers as listed in the Greenville Advocate on 16 Jan. 1884.

Rev. T. E. Atkinson, W.C.T.
C. S. Adams, W.A.S.
Miss Mattie Palmer, W.T.
Miss Mollie Bracken, W.D.M.
Zema Shepherd, W. Sentinel
Miss Minnie Palmer, W.R.S.
William Porter, P.W.C.T.

Miss Mollie Bell, W.V.T.
W. J. Bell, W.F.S.
R. H. Davis, W.M.
Rev. J. E. Bell, W. Chaplain
Miss Mittie Atkinson, W.I.G.
Miss Fannie Clark, W.L.S.
J. R. Stott, Lodge Deputy & W.S.

This Lodge was organized by Maj. Demaree December 4, 1883 with 31 members. Considerable interest is manifested.

GRAND JURORS, OCTOBER 19, 1898

John Branum	Beat 15	Will Hutchins	Beat 10
John Brown	9	W. A. Jackson	7
B. F. Burns	6	J. R. Kendrick	13
J. H. Dunklin	12	J. T. Porter	14
W. A. Flowers (Not found)	18	D. M. Presley	2
F. J. Harrison	8	W. C. Shines (Not found)	3
J. T. Harwill	1	J. H. Sirmon, Jr.	11
W. H. Hays	16	F. C. Smith	12
C. B. Hester	17	J. H. Williams	17

PETIT JURORS FIRST WEEK

S. B. Barganier	8	S. P. May	5
J. P. Benson	11	J. R. Merritt	2
R. L. Bogan	18	J. E. Middleton	13
E. L. Brooks	18	J. C. Morrow	14
W. B. Browder	17	A. D. Murphy	1
W. C. Brown	9	J. T. McPherson	16
C. N. Dickens	8	W. E. Phelps	6
J. C. Dunklin	7	J. F. Phillips	3
C. H. Ellington	7	J. T. Rhodes	2
Robert Gandy	15	R. J. Smyth	12
H. S. Gradon	5	W. J. Thigpen	9
J. H. Hartley	12	J. P. Vickory	11
Tom Kendrick	10	J. H. Vinson	14
Henry Ketler	4	J. C. Weaver	19
W. A. Leysath	1	J. R. White	12

PETIT JURORS SECOND WEEK

W. J. Andress	7	G. L. McClure	13
F. S. Boan	8	J. B. Perry	15
H. W. Browder	17	James A. Phelps	6
H. W. Burt	12	W. W. Pouncy	15
W. F. Colly	12	J. F. Rhodes	13
Edward Cox	12	E. P. Rigsby	2
P. W. Cunningham	9	F. M. Rodgers	8
J. L. Dean	1	D. B. Sellers	19
Hugh Gamble, Jr.	1	J. F. Thompson	5
J. E. Harrison	8	C. N. Till	10
J. L. Henderson	11	W. H. Watson	14
W. W. Johnson	14	J. W. Williams	17
W. T. Jornigan, Fla.	3	W. L. Wright	18
John Kendrick	10	T. J. Wyrosdick	2
J. H. Murphy	16	J. P. Zeigler (No beat shown)	

GEORGIANA DIXIE LODGE NO. 2844, KNIGHTS OF HONOR
Officers as listed in the Greenville Advocate on 9 Jan. 1884.

A. L. Palmer, D.	W. C. Vinson, V.D.
William Simpler, A.D.	D. T. Sellers, Guide
Ralph Larkins, Financial Reporter	J. R. Stott, Reporter
N. M. Bayzer, Treasurer	T. E. Atkinson, Chaplain
John T. Palmer, Guardian	Dr. J. W. Blow, Post Dictator
_____, Sentinel	

THE ALFORD GANDY HOME
STARLINGTON, ALABAMA
This house was started before the onset of the War Between the States and completed afterwards.

OLD ABRAMS HOME
Built in 1859. Nice example of a raised cottage style house. Was the home of Gov. Gordon Person's mother. This house is listed on the Alabama Register of Landmarks & Heritage. Located in Greenville, Ala.

LANE-KENDRICK-SHERLING HOME
GREENVILLE, ALA., ca. 1840

THAGGARD-POOLE HOME
ON HIGHWAY 10 NEAR GREENVILLE ca 1850

CRENSHAW HOME

The home and carriage of the Hon. Anderson Crenshaw, first Chancellor of Alabama. Located on the Ridge. Mrs. Lewis Crenshaw is depicted in pilgramage costume. Ca 1835.

T. W. PEAGLER HOME
GREENVILLE, ALABAMA

A. G. STEWART HOME
GREENVILLE, ALABAMA

DR. W. E. MORRIS HOME
GEORGIANA, ALABAMA

MILNER-VINSON-BOONE HOME
GEORGIANA, ALABAMA
Built by Rev. Pitt S. Milner, founder of Georgiana.

J. G. MCGOWIN HOME
CHAPMAN, ALABAMA

MILNER - SPEIR HOME
GREENVILLE, ALABAMA
Listed in the Alabama Register of Landmarks & Heritage. Built by John T. Milner who was influential in the founding of Birmingham.

THE SPEIR HOSPITAL
Was located in Greenville on the lot adjoining the Milner-Speir Home above.

BLYTHEWOOD-TRAWEEK-KNIGHT-
ATKINS HOME
Monterey
Built in 1845 and added to
by later owners.

YELDELL-OLIVER-TILL-
CARMICHAEL HOME
The Ridge
Built in 1858 by Robert
and Frances Powers Yeldell

GEORGE S. LAZENBY HOME
Forest Home
Remodeled in 1875.

E. M. LAZENBY & SON
Forest Home

DUNKLIN-BEELAND-KENDRICK HOME
Greenville

CARTER-SMITH-POOLE HOME
Pine Flat
Built about 1825 by William
Carter. Residence of Mrs.
Joe N. Poole

TWO-STORY SMOKE HOUSE
POOLE PLANTATION

WESLEY CHAPEL METHODIST CHURCH

SARDIS BAPTIST CHURCH
Established 1856

MONTEREY METHODIST CHURCH
Established 1858

MT. MORIAH BAPTIST CHURCH
Established 1828

Liberty United Methodist Church

Listed on the Alabama Register of Landmarks & Heritage

GREENVILLE FIRST BAPTIST CHURCH
The lot for the church was donated by Milton Parmer in 1858. The original building was replaced by the above structure in the 1890s.

THE FIRST BAPTIST CHURCH
GEORGIANA, ALABAMA
Organized 1865 by
Rev. Pitt S. Milner

1903

FIRST METHODIST CHURCH
GREENVILLE, ALABAMA
Organized ca 1823

After remodeling in the early 1900s.

PRESBYTERIAN CHURCH
Greenville
Organized in 1820. Present building erected 1885/6. Was used as a "dead-house" by the Union troops during the occupation of Greenville. Listed on the Alabama Register of Landmarks & Heritage.

ST. THOMAS
EPISCOPAL CHURCH
Greenville
1896

PINE FLAT METHODIST CHURCH
Organized ca 1834. Church erected 1857. Listed on the Alabama Register of Landmarks & Heritage.

FOREST HOME BAPTIST CHURCH
Organized 1856.

MCKENZIE METHODIST CHURCH
Organized 1903

SHILOH BAPTIST CHURCH
Located on the Old Federal Road.

A.M.E. ZION THEOLOGICAL INSTITUTION
LOMAX-LANNON JR. COLLEGE
Founded 1893
Listed on the Alabama Register of
Landmarks & Heritage.

BARTRAM TRAIL
Follows the approximate route taken
by William Bartram in 1775/6. Listed
on the Alabama Register of Landmarks
& Heritage.

FIRST METHODIST CHURCH
Georgiana, Alabama
Organized 1866

BUTLER SPRINGS BAPTIST CHURCH
The land was deeded to the church
in 1890 by the Rev. A. T. Sims. Picture taken from Rev. J. W. Joyner's
"History of the Baptists of Butler
County".

HALSO GRIST MILL
Built on Pigeon Creek in the late 1800s.
In operation until 1970.

OAKY STREAK METHODIST CHURCH
Listed on the Alabama Register of
Landmarks & Heritage

Forest Home Methodist Church

A TRIBUTE
TO THE PIONEERS

God gave to every man a role in life to play;
   How well that he performs it is up to him to say.
Looking through the pages of Butler's history;
   You'll find men of valor and high integrity.

They came into a new land and settled down to live;
   Each giving to society the best that he could give.
They built their homes in hardship and then prepared their fields;
   They planted crops, prayed to God and gathered in the yields.

One thing that I have noticed 'bout those men of long ago;
   Who had so many problems that we will never know;
Is the courage that was dwelling deep within each heart;
   To face the many dangers that beset them from the start.

They had a deep awareness of God in all they did.
   When He spoke they listened and did as they were bid.
We can take a lesson from Butler's men of yesteryear;
   Faith in God will help _us_ to face the things we fear.

And so, my hat is off today in tribute to them all,
   To the men who lost their lives when they heard our nation's call.
To the pioneer women who toiled and taught and prayed.
   To the pioneer children who did chores and seldom played.

They performed the roles God gave them the best way that they could;
   They lived throughout the county--in every neighborhood.
Here's hoping that this book keeps the memories in store,
   Of the nineteenth century settlers of Butler's land of yore.

                                          Madge Hahn

INDEX

ABNEY, 116, 125
ABRAMS/ABRAM, 39, 83, 84, 85, 86, 90, 103, 158, 176
ACRE, 174
ACREMAN, 39
ADAIR, 158
ADAMS, 17, 30, 36, 39, 54, 101, 110, 125, 128, 132, 134, 169, 170, 175
ADKINS, 132
ADKINSON, 168
AINSWORTH, 16, 171
ALEXANDER, 39, 112, 169
ALFORD, 29, 132
ALLBRITTON/ALBRITTON, 39, 174
ALLDAY, 27
ALLEN, 39, 97, 113, 132, 134, 166, 168, 171, 173
ALLISON, 114
ALLISTER, 172
ALLMON/ALLMAN, 39, 134
AMBROSE, 168
AMERINE, 39
AMERSON, 173
AMOS, 39, 96, 132, 171
ANDERS, 147
ANDERSON, 39, 132, 133, 134, 158
ANDRESS, 39, 61, 100, 134, 168, 169, 176
ANDREWS, 28, 90, 96, 125, 174
ANSLEY, 96
ANTHONY/ANTONY, 39, 96, 162, 168, 174
APLIN, 133
APSEY, 156
ARANT, 39, 68, 100, 166
ARCHER, 34, 40, 90, 163
ARDIS, 86, 90, 110
ARDLE & MOORE, 97
ARMS, 86, 132
ARMSTRONG, 29, 40, 105, 108, 132, 134, 146, 147, 165, 166, 167, 168, 170, 172, 174
ARNOLD, 1, 40, 129, 133, 166
ARRAUK, 25
ARRINGTON, 17
ASBERRY, 164
ASHBURNE, 151
ASHCRAFT, 71, 86, 134, 170
ASHFORD, 37, 40, 116
ASHLEY, 59, 132
ASHWOOD, 133
ATKINS, 33, 40, 105, 132, 165, 171
ATKINSON, 28, 175, 176
AUGBURN, 171
AUSTIN, 71, 108, 151, 153, 160
AUTREY/AWTREY, 27, 40
AVANT, 124

BABBET, 133
BABER, 143
BAGGETT, 34
BAILES/BAIL, 9, 86
BAILEY, 28, 29, 40, 77, 97, 134, 147, 171
BAISDEN, 40
BAKER, 25, 102
BALDEREE/BALDREE, 134, 171, 174
BALDWIN, 40, 96, 124, 171
BALL, 168
BALLARD, 134, 169
BANISTER, 171
BANKISTER/BANKESTER, 134
BANKS, 22, 31
BARDEN, 34
BARFIELD, 97
BARGANIER, 33, 40, 100, 101, 131, 134, 147, 170, 176
BARGE, 17, 18, 33, 40, 86, 90, 95, 110, 134, 154, 161, 171
BARGE & POWERS, 100
BARGE & SHANKS, 102
BARKER, 34, 40, 134
BARKSDALE, 8
BARLOW, 25, 27
BARNES, 34, 40, 96, 128, 133, 168
BARNETT, 17
BARRAN, 166
BARRETT, 30, 40, 90, 100, 134, 165, 166, 168, 171
BARRINEAU, 25
BARRINGTON/BARRENTON, 132, 168
BARROW, 35, 40, 124, 134, 175
BARROW & SON, 97
BARTER, 167
BASS, 40, 101
BATCHELLER, 86
BATES, 40, 134, 169
BATTENHAUSSEN, 34
BAUGH, 90
BAXTER, 131
BAYLOL, 40
BAYLS, 12
BAYNES, 132
BAYZER/BAZER, 34, 176
BAYZER & ADAMS, 97
BEAR, 86, 90, 97
BEASLEY/BEESLEY, 16, 40, 41, 53, 124, 134, 144, 168, 173
BEASTON/BEASON, 41, 158
BECK, 97, 98
BECKWORTH, 41
BEDELL, 86, 140, 158
BEDGOOD, 17, 90, 167
BEEL, 132, 133

BEELAND/BEALAND, 33, 37, 41, 104, 184
BELL, 29, 41, 86, 168, 169, 173, 174, 175
BELTON, 29
BEMENT & BURBANK, 86
BENBOW, 69, 86
BENIS, 132
BENNETT/BENNET, 34, 41, 47, 90, 96, 132, 171, 173, 174
BENSON, 6, 15, 16, 17, 18, 33, 41, 96, 101, 108, 109, 110, 114, 117, 130, 134, 154, 161, 167, 171, 176
BENTLEY, 167
BERDEAUX, 41
BERNEY, 34
BERRY, 25, 110, 132, 166
BETHENA, 41
BETTERTON, 41
BEVERLY/BEVOLEY/BEAVELY, 16, 27, 171
BIBB, 6, 11, 12
BIGGS, 134
BILBERRY/BILBRAY, 41, 166
BILLINGS, 173
BINION, 90, 140
BINION & BRO, 96
BISHOP, 18, 90, 168
BLACK, 15, 16, 22, 41, 105, 132, 134, 151, 152, 164, 168, 173, 174
BLACKBURN, 173
BLACKMAN/BLACKMOND/BLACKMON, 41, 90, 102, 167, 171
BLACKSHEAR/BLACKSHIRE, 4, 132
BLACKWELL, 129
BLAIR, 133, 173
BLAKE, 132
BLALOCK, 34, 41
BLAUM, 41, 98
BLISS, 132
BLOW, 133, 175, 176
BLOXOM, 108, 109, 111, 155
BLYTHEWOOD, 41, 183
BOAN/BOANE, 33, 41, 167, 176
BOANHAN, 168
BODIFORD, 118, 121
BODY, 134
BOGGAN/BOGAN, 24, 41, 105, 106, 110, 111, 131, 134, 170, 171, 174, 176
BOGGS/BOGGUS, 28, 29, 167, 168
BOLAND, 41
BOLLING/BOLING/BOLDING, 1, 16, 22, 28, 30, 41, 42, 90, 98, 100, 103, 107, 108, 113, 115, 125, 127, 160, 171, 172, 191
BOLLING & BURNETT, 172
BOLLING & EWING, 169
BOLLING & GONDER, 172
BOND, 27, 49
BONNER, 108, 115, 116
BOOKER, 42

BOONE, 181
BOSWELL, 42, 167
BOUTWELL, 42, 96, 134
BOWDEN/BOWDON, 42, 90, 166
BOWEN/BOWAN/BOWIN, 16, 42, 90, 106, 107, 115, 116, 161, 170
BOWMAN, 42, 134
BOYCE, 132
BOYD, 42
BOYETT, 168
BOYLE/BOYLER, 42. 168
BOYSTER, 167
BOZEMAN, 16, 42, 134
BRACKEN, 175
BRADEN, 29, 42, 171
BRADLEY, 42, 118, 134, 173
BRAGG, 42, 86, 98, 114, 115, 134, 170, 172
BRANCEFORD, 15
BRANNON, 5, 9, 12, 13
BRANSFORD, 27, 173
BRANTLY, 132
BRANTON/BRENTON, 27, 108, 172
BRANUM, 176
BRASWELL/BRASSELL, 27, 42
BRAUNNER, 86
BREEDLOVE, 132
BRENT, 90
BREWER, 16, 17
BRIDGES, 168
BRIERS, 173
BRIGGS, 16, 17, 23, 27, 131, 168
BRIGHTWELL, 171
BRINKMAN, 86
BROCK, 131
BROGDON, 110, 166
BRONNER, 90
BROOKINGS/BROOKINS, 39, 131
BROOKS/BROOK, 27, 29, 42, 90, 95, 111, 125, 132, 134, 156, 157, 166, 173, 176
BROOKS & STALLING, 98
BROUGHTON, 36, 42, 86, 90, 98, 117, 125, 171
BROWDER, 167, 176
BROWN, 16, 33, 36, 42, 58, 59, 86, 98, 101, 111, 132, 133, 157, 158, 167, 170, 173, 174, 175, 176
BROWNLEE, 169
BRUNER, 43, 134
BRUNSON, 43
BRYON/BRYANT/BRIANT, 43, 96, 120, 125, 134, 143, 145, 147, 166, 168, 171
BRYAN & CARROL, 98
BRYERS, 172
BRYSON, 130
BUCHANAN, 134, 153
BUCK, 43

BUCKELLEW/BUCKLOO, 171, 174
BUCKHAULTS, 42, 43, 100
BUELL/BUILL, 27, 43
BUELL & LANE, 98
BUFFINGTON, 147
BULLOCK, 171
BUNDRICK, 169
BUNKLEY, 132
BURCH, 43, 134
BURK/BURKE, 16, 90, 97, 134, 167, 174
BURKETT/BURKET, 43, 111, 166, 171, 173
BURNETT, 35, 43, 47, 86, 90, 98, 100, 108, 115, 128, 132, 134, 172
BURNETT & SMITH, 86
BURKILL, 166
BURNS/BURNES, 100, 169, 176
BURNSIDES, 16
BUROUGH, 168
BURT, 174, 176
BURTON, 28
BUSBY/BUSBEY, 43, 96
BUSBY & PORTER, 86
BUSH, 33, 43, 95, 100, 101, 108, 111, 133, 166, 171, 174
BUTLER, 4, 5, 6, 7, 8, 9, 10, 12, 18, 23, 24, 43, 90, 100, 131, 132, 150, 163, 164, 165, 170, 174
BUTTS, 4, 90, 105, 109, 131, 134, 168, 170
BYRD/BIRD, 16, 74, 158
CAINE, 44
CALDWELL, 3, 15, 16, 17, 18, 25, 44, 59, 61, 87, 91, 109, 115, 133, 149, 152, 159, 167, 171
CALES, 100
CALHOUN, 44, 132
CALLENS, 168, 169
CALLIER/COLLIER, 131, 170
CALLAWAY/CALLOWAY, 132, 135, 140, 150, 167, 169
CALVIN, 44
CAMP, 44, 73, 108, 153, 168, 172
CAMPBELL, 44, 86, 96, 100, 131, 133, 135, 166, 167, 173
CANNON, 86
CAPERS, 128
CAPPS, 167
CAREY, 135
CARGLE, 119
CARLOW, 44, 172
CARNATHAN, 132
CAROLAN, 128
CARPENTER, 44
CARR, 23, 31, 70, 132, 167
CARRECTER, 132
CARTER, 2, 6, 15, 25, 33, 44, 77, 91, 95, 101, 102, 106, 117, 132, 135, 155, 171, 174, 184

CARTLIDGE, 167
CASTLEBERRY/CASLEBERRY, 135, 166
CATER, 28
CATES, 44, 170
CATLIN, 172
CATO, 132
CAULFIELD & BELL, 3
CHAMBERS, 29
CHAMBLISS, 87, 164, 172
CHANCELLOR/CHANCELOR, 44, 75, 96, 111, 132, 171, 173
CHANDLER, 44, 86
CHAPMAN, 108, 121, 135
CHAPPELL, 44
CHEATHAM/CHEATAM, 25, 29, 33, 44, 58, 72, 73, 91, 100, 101, 121, 135, 162, 169, 170, 172, 175
CHEPPEN, 96
CHESNUT, 25, 133, 170
CHILDERS, 44, 167
CHILES, 100
CHITTY, 107
CHRISTIAN, 134
CHULE, 96
CHUMBY, 44
CHURCHWELL, 131, 168
CLAGHORN/CLEGHORN, 44, 167
CLANCY/CLANSEY, 81, 131, 167
CLARK/CLARKE, 34, 41, 44, 98, 107, 135, 175
CLAY, 23
CLEBURNE, 128
CLEGHORN. 132
CLEMMENT, 168
CLEMONS, 119
CLINTON, 2
CLIPPER, 135
CLOPTON, 100, 174
CLUTE, 172
COBURN, 51
COCHRAN, 121
COCKE, 104
COE, 167
COFFINBERRY, 30
COGBURN, 6
COGHLAND, 30
COHRAN, 135
COKER, 16, 135, 173
COKMAN, 132
COLE, 44, 102, 171
COLEMAN/COALMAN, 17, 18, 27, 41, 42, 44, 64, 135, 166
COLLEY/COLEY/COLLY, 44, 102, 143, 169, 176
COLLINS/COLLEN, 1, 22, 91, 132, 170
COLQUHOAN, 17
COLVIN, 45, 87, 101, 131, 172
CONDON, 45
CONE, 25, 45, 173
CONNER, 28, 45. 168

CONWAY, 45
COOK/COOKE, 1, 4, 8, 13, 15, 18, 22, 33, 35, 45, 75, 86, 87, 91, 100, 108, 109, 111, 125, 133, 135, 167, 173, 174
COOK & EVANS, 108
COOLEY, 29
COOPER, 30, 45, 164, 165, 167, 168, 170, 172
CORLEY/CORLEE, 135, 172, 173
CORRY, 33, 37, 45, 135
CORY & FLOWERS, 98
COTE, 131
COURTNEY, 9, 168
COWART, 45, 135, 167
COWART & BRO., 133
COWELL, 31
COX, 29, 45, 112, 132, 156, 176
COXWELL, 45
COYNE, 45
CRADDOCK, 135
CRAIG/CREIG, 13, 22, 25, 45, 100, 107, 111, 135, 165, 172
CRANE/CRAIN, 33, 45, 101, 102, 171
CRAVY/CRAVEY, 25, 166
CRAWFORD, 70, 98, 165
CREAMER, 171
CREATH, 45
CREECH/CREACH, 28, 29, 33, 45, 100, 135, 172, 173
CRENSHAW, 2, 4, 33, 34, 37, 44, 45, 86, 90, 91, 98, 108, 125, 134, 135, 170, 179
CRENTH & BREWSTER, 98
CREWS/CREW, 45, 46, 64, 91, 101, 135
CRISWELL, 27
CRITTENDEN, 33, 46, 91, 101, 131, 157, 174
CROCHERAN, 172
CROSS, 46, 100, 155
CROWDER, 157
CRUM, 46
CRUMPTON, 132, 143, 160
CURINGTON, 46
CUMBIE, 46
CUNNINGHAM, 25, 176
CURRY, 166
CURTIS, 13, 46, 135, 143
CUSHING, 87
DAILEY/DAILY/DALEY, 111, 169, 171
DALE, 6, 11, 12, 13
DAMPIER, 46, 135
DANIEL, 18, 25, 46, 131, 135, 168, 170
DANIEL & SMITH, 98
DANNELLY, 68
DANTZLER, 135
DANVIS, 110
DARBY, 46, 96, 175

DARLEY, 3, 46, 118
DASH, 46
DAVENPORT/DEVANPORT, 1, 15, 16, 22, 25, 108, 131, 132, 162, 167, 168
DAVES, 27
DAVID, 168
DAVIDSON, 108, 109, 111, 135, 168, 172
DAVIES, 30, 32, 143, 144, 172
DAVIS, 22, 28, 46, 97, 100, 105, 110, 113, 119, 121, 132, 133, 135, 153, 160, 164, 166, 167, 168, 170, 172, 173, 174, 175
DAVISON, 22, 46, 98, 101, 170
DAWSON, 46, 133
DAY, 46, 87, 92, 101, 133, 168, 169, 174
DEAN, 46, 55, 92, 113, 165, 166, 168, 174, 176
DEES, 46, 131, 166
DELONEY, 135
DEMAREE, 175
DEMING, 27, 46, 92, 108, 111, 114, 115, 127, 135, 172
DENDY, 28, 29, 30
DENNIS, 18
DENSON, 132
DERBIN, 7, 10
DESHIELDS, 47
DE VERNON, 154
DEWBERRY, 47, 121
DEY, 36
DICKENS, 132, 172, 176
DICKSON/DICKERSON/DICKIRSON/DICKINSON, 2, 3, 5, 13, 16, 22, 47, 135, 170
DILLARD 174
DINNA, 132
DISMUKE, 47
DIXON, 15, 98, 155
DODSON, 29
DOHRMEIER/DOHMIEIR, 47, 98
DONALD, 33, 47, 87, 100, 101, 102, 135, 170, 171, 174
DONALD & DONALD, 100
DONALDSON, 135
DORMAN, 168
DOTMAN, 87
DOTZHEIMER, 87
DOUGHERTY, 115
DOUGLASS/DUGLASS/DOUGLAS, 8, 9, 27, 47, 166
DOWD, 47, 118
DOWLING, 27, 47
DOWNING, 16
DOZIER, 166
DRAKE, 34, 41, 47, 144, 154, 167
DRIVER, 28, 29, 100, 173
DRUM, 175
DRYESS, 100
DUBERRY/DUBURY, 96, 113, 170, 174

DUCK, 173, 174
DUGAN, 28
DUKE/DUKES, 28, 47, 71, 91, 125, 135, 168, 172
DULANY/DULANEY, 1, 2, 22, 109
DULIN, 47, 87
DUMONT, 135
DUNCAN/DUNCAND, 27, 75, 87
DUNKLIN, 1, 18, 22, 27, 30, 34, 35, 36, 47, 74, 87, 91, 100, 102, 108, 109, 115, 116, 128, 130, 135, 143, 163, 172, 176, 184
DUNKLIN & HARALSON, 172
DUNKLIN & SON, 98
DUNKLIN & STEINER, 87
DUNLAP, 25
DUNN, 45, 98, 146
DUNNAM/DUNHAM, 162, 173
DURR, 47
DYER, 167
DYKES, 132
EADY, 131
EAGERTON, 25
EALUM, 47, 135, 166
EARL, 133
EARNEST/ERNEST, 2, 15, 16, 17, 28, 48, 135, 170, 172
EASLEY, 97
EASON, 25
EAST, 10
EASTERLIN, 169
EASTERWOOD, 2, 22
EATON, 128
ECHOLS, 47
EDDY, 117
EDGE, 135
EDMONSON, 18
EDWARD/EDWARDS, 167, 168
EHLBERT/ELHBERT, 37, 47, 98, 141
ELLINGTON/ELINGTON, 100, 101, 111, 168, 176
ELLIOTT/ELLIOTTE, 15, 16
ELLIS, 27, 54, 132, 135, 173
ELLIS & BATES, 135
ELLIS & SIMONTIN, 132
ELLISON, 144
ELLSWORTH, 91
ELY, 77
EMMETT, 109
EMMONS, 135
ERWIN, 172
ESKEW, 47, 48, 74, 119, 163
ESSELMAN, 105
ESTELLA, 132
ETHERIDGE, H & CO., 98
ETHRIDGE, 173
EUBANKS, 132
EVANS, 48, 60, 92, 106, 111, 113, 125, 132, 172, 173
EVANS, TEAT & CO., 87
EVERS, 147

EWING, 42, 48, 64, 108, 109, 135, 169, 175
FAIL/FAILS/FAILES, 48, 60, 92, 100, 102, 135, 166, 168, 169, 172, 173, 174
FALLOW, 48
FARLO, 119, 120
FARMERS ACADEMY, 107
FARRAR/FARRIOR/FARRER, 2, 15, 48, 75, 91, 98, 114, 136
FARRIS, KAMP & CO., 87
FEAGIN/FEAGEN/FAGIN/FEAGAN, 16, 48, 97, 132, 136, 167
FEDERICK, 27
FELTON, 96
FERGUSON/FURGERSON/FOGERSON, 18, 27, 48, 87, 105, 108, 110, 131, 135, 156, 158, 162, 170
FERRELL, 91
FICKLING/FICKLIN, 91, 158, 160, 174
FIELDS, 58, 136
FIFE, 48, 100, 106, 135, 172
FILES, 135
FINCH & MELTON, 87
FINDLEY/FENDLAY, 48, 136
FINKLEY, 166
FINLEY, 163, 169
FITZPATRICK, 4, 103, 104
FLEMING, 27
FLEXNER & LICHTEN, 98, 175
FLINN, 169
FLOOD, 87, 91
FLORENCE, 48, 91, 96, 102
FLOWERS, 9, 29, 34, 48, 91, 98, 100, 125, 136, 152, 172, 174, 176
FLOYD, 5, 6, 9
FOLLER, 171
FONVILLE, 136
FORD, 8, 87
FOREST HOME ACADEMY, 96
FORT BIBB, 5, 6
FORT CLAIBORNE, 6
FORT DALE, 1, 2, 5, 6, 11, 13
FORT DECATUR, 5
FORT JACKSON, 5, 7
FORT MITCHELL, 5, 7
FORT TOULOUSE, 7
FOSHEE/FORSHEE, 121, 123, 136
FOST, 169
FOSTER/FOSTOR, 35, 48, 97, 98, 132, 153, 165
FOSTER BROS., 98
FOUNTAIN, 96, 135
FOWLER, 48, 161, 167, 168
FRANCIS, 7
FRANK, 34
FRANKLIN, 48, 87, 132, 151, 166, 167
FRAZIER, 136

FREAR, J.B. & CO., 87
FREEMAN, 48, 91, 100, 112, 113, 132
FRIDDLE, 166
FROST, 28, 29, 48, 101, 106, 168, 169
FROW, 107
FULLER, 17, 25, 27, 166, 168, 169
FUNDERBURKE, 48
FUSSELL, 33, 48
FUTCH, 25
GAFFE, 17
GAFFORD, 1, 15, 16, 28, 48, 92, 100, 101, 105, 106, 109, 111, 115, 118, 125, 131, 136, 141, 162, 169, 170, 172
GAFNEY/GAFFNEY, 87, 92, 132, 169
GAILLIARD, 92
GAINES, 12, 132
GAINEY, 136, 167
GALLAGHER, 49
GALLAWAY, 173
GAMBLE, 35, 37, 49, 87, 92, 125, 176
GAMBLING & BOLING, 98
GANDRUD, 9
GANDY, 27, 49, 92, 112, 131, 164, 166, 168, 172, 176, 177
GANEY, 132
GANTT, H. & SON, 98, 136
GANUS, 29, 49, 141
GARARD, 132
GARDNER/GARDNEY/GARNER, 4, 5, 6, 12, 27, 49, 119, 132, 136, 166, 168
GARLINGTON, 128, 132
GARRETT/GARETT, 5, 7, 8, 9, 22, 33, 49, 98, 101, 136, 27
GARRISON, 75, 92
GARTHY, 92
GARVIN, 136
GARY/GAY, 1, 5, 7, 11, 12, 14, 16, 27, 49
GASGON, 92
GASS, 87
GASTING, 171
GASTON, 37, 49, 101, 125
GAYLE & BOWER, 107
GEDIAN, 172
GENTRY, 111
GEORGE, 98, 171
GERKEY, 132
GETLIN, 169
GIBBS, 16, 168
GIBSON, 25, 49, 61, 87, 92, 132, 166, 167, 174
GIDDENS, 49, 65, 136, 170
GIDEON/GEDIAN, 111, 172
GILBERT, 1, 8, 9, 22, 49, 172
GILCHRIST/GILDCRIST, 49, 92, 167
GILES, 87
GILL, 172, 174
GILLESPIE, 49, 96

GILLION/GILLIAN, 49, 168
GILMORE/GILLMORE, 136, 173
GINGLES, 25
GIPSON, 49
GIST, 136
GLANTON, 111
GLASGOW/GLASSGOW, 49, 92, 151, 152, 172
GLASS, 169, 172
GLENN, 43, 49, 96, 98, 101, 120, 136, 171
GOARE, 168
GODWIN, 50, 132, 136
GOHLSON/GHOLSON/GOLSON, 50, 60, 65, 91, 92, 111, 136, 169
GOINS, 71
GOLAY, 92
GOLDSMITH, 50, 92
GOLDTHWAITE, 4
GOMILLIAN, 50
GOODALL, 115, 172
GOODSON, 28, 167
GOODWIN/GOODWYN, 25, 27, 50, 151
GOOLSBY/GOLDSBY, 35, 50, 98, 147
GORDON, 2
GOWAN, COX & MARKLEY, 132
GRACE, 50, 132
GRAGG, 132
GRAHAM, 24, 34, 50, 60, 92, 136, 169
GRAMLING/GRAMLIN, 36, 50, 117, 118
GRANT, 31, 50, 101, 136, 170
GRATZ, 172
GRAVES, 50, 55, 121, 122
GRAY, 25, 50, 87, 101, 132, 171, 172, 174
GRAYDON/GRAYSON, 15, 16, 22, 29, 33, 50, 91, 100, 126, 131, 166, 169, 174, 176
GREEN/GREENE, 27, 34, 50, 101, 106, 111, 131, 136, 155, 171
GREENING, 4
GREENVILLE ADVOCATE, 98, 145
GREENVILLE COLLEGIATE INSTITUTE, 98
GREENVILLE OIL & GRIST CO., 98
GREGORY, 50, 87, 92, 171
GRIEVE, 172
GRIFFIN/GRIFFINS, 33, 50, 96, 136
GRIGGS, 109, 168
GROGAN, 129, 132
GUGENHEIM, A. & CO., 114
GUICE, 130
GUILFORD, 172
GUINN, 173
GUY, 168
HAGERMAN, 50
HAGLER, 170
HAGOOD, 50
HAINESWORTH, 102

HAIR, 166
HAIRSTON, 136
HALE/HAILE, 12, 27, 101
HALL, 26, 29, 50, 101, 124, 168
HALSO, 33, 51, 167, 192
HAM, 51
HAMET, 132
HAMIL/HAMILL/HAMELS/HAMMELL, 9, 51, 87, 136
HAMILTON, 35, 37, 51, 98, 101, 125, 129, 169
HAMMOND/HAMMONDS/HAMOND, 27, 51, 110, 167, 169, 173
HAMNER, 51, 53, 136
HAMPTON, 125, 170
HAMRICK/HAMBRICK, 51, 136, 168
HANCOCK, 51, 136, 168
HAPY, 133
HARALSON, 163
HARBIN, 43, 51, 144, 167
HARDY, 107, 111, 136
HARPER/HAPER, 28, 33, 98, 125, 133, 172, 173
HARRELL/HARRILL, 133, 136, 167
HARRILSON, 170
HARRIMAN, 169
HARRINGTON/HERRINGTON, 115, 132, 165, 172
HARRIS, 51, 87, 101, 136, 137, 161, 174
HARRISON, 1, 22, 28, 29, 30, 33, 51, 72, 92, 98, 100, 101, 112, 133, 136, 141, 147, 166, 167, 168, 169, 170, 171, 173, 174, 175, 176
HARRISON & PAYNE, 87
HARROLD/HAROLD, 51, 92, 136
HARRY, 141
HART, 167
HARTON, 169
HARTLEY, 14, 33, 51, 87, 92, 100, 105, 112, 136, 141, 170, 172, 174, 176
HARTSFIELD, 52
HARVILL/HARVELL/HARWILL/HARWELL, 9, 33, 52, 136, 176
HASKEW, 26
HASSEY, 174
HASTING, 167
HATCHER, 25, 27, 104, 170
HATLEY, 27
HATTON, 136
HAWKINS, 27, 33, 52, 87, 93, 96, 100, 101, 136, 137, 170, 171
HAWTHORN/HAWTHORNE, 52, 87, 165
HAYLEY, 92
HAYNES, 140, 168
HAYS/HAYES/HAYSE, 27, 52, 57, 110, 132, 165, 169, 171, 176
HEAP, 153, 173
HEARD, 34, 97

HEARTSILL, 52
HEATON, 22, 33, 52, 100, 101, 170
HEMPHILL, 17
HENDERSON, 15, 17, 18, 23, 27, 28, 33, 52, 70, 106, 107, 112, 125, 131, 132, 136, 166, 169, 171, 176
HENDRIX, 28, 52, 87
HENLEY, 133
HERRENTON, 167
HENRY, 52, 87, 92, 93, 98, 104, 109, 115, 116, 125, 143, 144, 149, 160, 161, 172
HERBERT, 1, 3, 4, 15, 22, 29, 43, 44, 45, 52, 59, 61, 65, 70, 74, 87, 92, 98, 105, 107, 109, 110, 112, 115, 125, 127, 136, 152, 157, 170, 171, 172
HERLONG, 53, 169
HERNDON, 28, 68
HERRENDON, 169
HERRON, 33
HERSTING, 170
HERVEY & WEIRICK, 97
HESTER, 17, 27, 28, 53, 176
HICKMAN/HICKMON, 53, 174, 175
HICKS, 53, 98
HIGDON, 53, 136
HIGHTOWER, 18, 53, 87, 136, 174
HILDRETH, 53
HILL, 1, 6, 7, 9, 15, 53, 125, 136, 153, 161, 171
HILLARD, 169
HILSON, 70, 71, 106, 109, 110, 113, 150, 171
HINSON, 6, 33, 53, 74, 98, 100, 101, 136, 147, 165, 167, 170, 174
HIPP, 146, 147
HITSON, 53
HIX, 111
HOBBS, 26, 34, 110, 132, 173, 174
HODGES/HODGE, 17, 109, 112, 170, 172
HODGSON, 13
HODNETT, 34
HOLCOMB/HOLCOMBE, 53, 127, 128, 136
HOLLAND, 29, 92, 111, 167, 168
HOLLENHEAD, 174
HOLLIDAY/HOLADAY/HOLLODAY, 27, 101, 111, 172
HOLLOWAY, 9, 53
HOLLY, 24
HOLMAN, 25
HOLMES/HOMES, 27, 53, 108, 151, 152
HOLT, 97
HOLZER, 98, 136, 141
HOOD, 136, 166, 173
HOOK, 53
HOOP, 31

HOPPER, 172
HORN, 136
HORNDAY, 53
HORTMAN, 172
HOUSON, 112
HOWARD, 28, 33, 53, 92, 136, 147, 158, 174
HOWELL/HOWEL, 23, 57, 96, 98, 136, 143, 166, 173
HOUGH, 27
HOYETT, 136
HUBBARD, 124
HUBERT, 40, 153
HUCKABY, 169
HUDSON, 35, 53, 92, 131, 166
HUGGINS/HUGGANS, 34, 53, 124, 167
HUGHES, 30, 33, 53, 101, 131, 136, 167
HUGHSTON, 54
HUGULEY/HUGHLY/HUGLA, 33, 54, 172, 174
HULONG, 92
HUNT, 54, 98, 163
HUNTER, 4, 171
HUSDT, 132
HUSON, 96
HUSTON, 173
HUTCHINS, 93, 176
HUTCHINSON/HUTCHISON/HUTCHENSON/HUTCHESON, 1, 16, 22, 54, 56, 101, 105, 136, 170, 171
HUTSON, 27
HUTTO, 54
HUTTON, 54, 87, 168
HYDE, 87
IBELL, 97
INGRAM, 54, 132, 173
IRVINE, 137
IVEZ, 54
JACKSON, 7, 27, 28, 54, 98, 102, 132, 133, 167, 168, 170, 172, 176
JAMES, 11, 12, 112, 132, 167
JAY, 28, 137, 169, 172
JEFCOAT, 87
JENNINGS, 54
JERNIGAN/JORNIGAN, 34, 54, 101, 137, 167, 176
JERRY, 133
JOHNSON, 15, 28, 29, 33, 34, 54, 60, 68, 98, 112, 118, 124, 125, 132, 133, 137, 141, 167, 168, 173, 174, 176
JOHNSTON, 54, 115, 116
JOLLY, 1, 16, 22
JONES, 7, 9, 10, 12, 16, 17, 18, 22, 23, 25, 27, 33, 35, 36, 49, 54, 55, 87, 93, 96, 98, 100, 101, 112, 117, 132, 137, 166, 167, 168, 169, 170, 171, 172, 173, 174, 175
JONES & TRAWICK, 88

JORDAN, 34, 55, 112, 132, 133, 167, 169, 174
JORDAN & KNIGHT, 88
JORDAN & MCPHERSON, 88
JOSEY, 55, 93, 167, 174
JOYNER/JOINER, 55, 88, 137
JUDGE, 23, 27, 35, 37, 47, 55, 125, 144
JUDGE & CARR, 137
JUDSON, 59
JUSTICE, 30
KARGLER & WALKER, 132
KATES, 102
KEATING, 88
KEEBLER/KEEBLE/KEBLER/KEELER, 55, 96, 132, 173
KEEFER, 88
KEILY, 169
KEITH, 55
KELLAM, 55
KELLEY/KELLY, 28, 55, 137, 146, 147, 169, 174
KELLEY & COLE, 88
KELLOUGH, 137, 169
KELSOE, 173
KEMON, 84, 85
KENDALL, 132
KENDRICK, 29, 33, 35, 37, 55, 96, 99, 101, 137, 176, 178, 184
KENNEDY, 55
KENNINGTON, 167
KENT, 27, 55, 112, 168, 169
KERN, 55, 147
KERSEY, 55
KERVIN, 95, 166
KETTLER/KETLER, 33, 54, 55, 58, 93, 131, 150, 167, 176
KEYS/KEY, 55, 153
KIDD, 158
KILBY, 155
KILGORE, 55
KILL, 174
KIMMONS, 56
KINBALL, 56, 89
KING, 33, 42, 56, 93, 96, 99, 102, 133, 137, 169
KINGSBURY, 56, 93, 99
KINGSLEY, 167
KINNEBREW, 164
KINNEY, 30
KINSEY, 170
KIRKLAND, 62, 121, 153
KIRKPATRICK/KIRPATRICK, 18, 26, 35, 37, 56, 88, 93, 100, 137, 169
KIRKSEY, 56, 100
KITE, 29, 169, 174
KNIGHT, 34, 35, 36, 56, 88, 93, 99, 101, 117, 131, 132, 137, 165, 171, 183

KNIGHT & RANTYN, 100
KNOTTS, 151, 168
KNOWLES, 56, 169
KNOX, 56
KONKLIN, 56
KORNEGAY, 50
KOULB, 170
KRAM/KRAHM, 34, 56
KUYKENDALL, 132, 173
KYSER, 137
LACKEY, 171
LAMBETH/LAMBERT, 137
LAMPLEY, 56, 125, 133
LANCE, 132
LANE, 3, 15, 56, 88, 93, 125, 133, 147, 157, 174, 175, 178
LANG, 175
LANGDON, 107
LANGLEY, 78
LANIER, 88, 89
LANSDON, 56
LANY, 28
LARD, 28
LARKIN/LARKINS, 56, 176
LASASTE, 132
LASETER/LASSETER, 56, 137
LAWSON, 56
LAYNE, 56, 68
LAZENBY, 33, 37, 56, 102, 109, 130, 154, 155, 171, 174, 183
LAZENBY, E.M. & SON, 96, 102
LEATHERWOOD, 56, 143
LEATHERWOOD & STANLEY, 88
LEDLOW, 57
LEE/LEA, 1, 2, 3, 15, 18, 22, 27, 28, 30, 31, 33, 34, 35, 36, 37, 39, 57, 99, 109, 115, 124, 125, 132, 137, 147, 152, 165, 166, 167, 172, 173
LEFTWICH, 154
LEGRIFF, 57
LEHMAN, 37, 99, 137, 144, 147
LENOIR, 132
LEONARD/LENARD, 1, 22, 57, 99, 137, 170
LESTER, 33, 57, 132
LEVEN, 29
LEVY, 95, 99, 102
LEWIS, 2, 18, 23, 33, 57, 88, 101, 106, 112, 133, 137, 141, 167, 171
LEWIS & WADE, 88
LEY, 17, 93
LEYSATH/LAYSATH, 33, 57, 93, 176
LICHTEN/LICHTON, 34, 35, 174
LICHTEN & CO., 99
LIDDELL, 137
LILES, 168, 171
LILLIARD, 143
LIMSEY, 132
LINAN, 57

LINTON, 27
LITTLE, 26, 49, 57, 65, 101, 115, 143, 166, 171, 175
LIVINGSTON/LEVINGSTON, 1, 15, 22, 57, 144
LLOYD, 28, 33, 57, 88, 137, 155, 156, 158
LOCHE, 57
LOCKHART, 93
LOCKLEAR, 57, 88, 172
LOE, 57
LOFTIN, 168
LOINS, 132
LONG, 34, 36, 57, 70, 95, 99, 132, 137, 167, 172
LOVETT, 172
LOWE, 57, 132
LOWHORN, 55
LOWRY/LOWERY, 16, 27, 29, 57, 93, 113, 137, 168
LUCAS, 7, 8
LUCKIE, 33, 58, 75, 88, 93, 101, 109, 174
LUDHAM/LUDLAM, 58, 121, 122, 137
LUNDY, 26
LUT, 58
LYMAN, 33, 93
LYMAN & GOLDSMITH, 88
LYNN, 107
MCALLISTER/MCALISTER, 58
MCARTHUR, 31
MCBRIDE, 33, 58, 100, 166, 169, 173, 174, 175
MCCALL, 34, 35, 36, 58, 133, 137, 143, 167
MCCALLISTER, 156
MCCANE/MCCAN/MCCANN/MCKAIN, 17, 58, 88, 93, 108, 137, 172
MCCARTER, 58
MCCARTY/MCCHARTHEE, 133, 169
MCCASKILL, 58, 132
M'CEANNE, 26
MCCLURE, 58, 96, 132, 173, 176
MCCOMBS, 58
MCCORD, 171
MCCORKLE, 96
M'CORLEY, 26
MCCORMICK/MCCORMICH/MCCORMACK, 27, 28, 33, 58, 100, 166, 169, 174
MCCOY, 17, 27, 58, 102, 112, 137, 169, 170
MCCREARY, 137, 138
MCCRORY/MCCRARY, 28, 58, 74, 96, 102, 105, 137, 171
MCCULLOUGH, 59, 169
MCCUNE, 27
MCCURRY, 17
MCDANIEL/M'DANIEL, 1, 16, 22, 26, 59, 93

MCDONALD, 105
MCDOWELL, 59, 89
MCDUFFIE, 59
MCEACHERN, 132
MCELROY & HUNTER, 107
MCFARLAND, 93
MCFERRIN, 59
MCGEHEE/MCGHEE, 18, 54, 59
MCGINNEY, 169, 171
MCGINNIS, 133
MCGLAUN, 59
MCGOUGH, 169
MCGOWIN/MCGOWAN, 123, 137, 181
MCGREW, 6
MCINTOSH, 5
MCINTYRE/MCINTIRE, 17, 138
MCKAY, 171
MCKEAN, 143
MCKEE, 30, 59, 93, 108
MCKELLAR/MCKELLAN, 18, 26, 59, 99, 100, 109, 115, 116, 132, 149, 172
MCKENZIE/MCKINZIE/MCKENSIE, 34, 39, 59, 88, 96, 99, 123, 137, 169
MCKINGEY, 169
MCKINNEY, 59
MCLAIN/MCLEAN, 59, 141, 167, 169
MCLEMORE, 125, 172
MCLEOD/MCLOUD, 153, 171
MCLEREY, 132
MCMEAN, 24, 125
MCMILLIAN/MCMILLEN/MCMILLAN, 59, 93, 97, 99
MCMULLAN/MCMULLEN/MCMULLIN, 35, 59, 88, 99, 103, 114, 169, 174
MCMURTRY, 30
MCNEIL, 171
MCNICOLA, 133
MCNULTY, 132
MCPHERSON, 17, 34, 59, 96, 100, 138, 170, 173, 176
MCPURIFOY, 59
MCQUEEN, 33, 59, 93, 106, 137, 138, 169, 172
MCRAE, 141
MCTIER, 93
MCWHORTER, 59, 171, 174
MCWILLIAMS, 59
MADDOX, 137
MADISON, 60
MAGERTS, 12
MAHONE, 60, 131, 167
MAJORS, 34, 60, 133
MALLETT, 34, 88, 93, 115, 116, 121, 141
MALLETT, DEWING & CO., 88
MALLETT, DEMMING & CO., 88
MANAC, 11, 12
MANCIL, 60, 124
MANCUS, 166
MANGUM, 120

MANNIS/MANICE/MINNIS, 22, 125, 174
MANLY, 132
MANNING/MANING, 2, 16, 17, 27, 60, 169
MAPES, 29, 168
MARAMAN, 60
MARLOW, 169
MARSH, 60
MARSHALL, 167
MARTIN, 1, 15, 24, 27, 30, 48, 53, 60, 93, 99, 100, 102, 133, 163, 166,168, 169, 170, 171, 172, 173
MASH, 29, 60, 93, 168
MASON, 30, 60, 99
MASSENGILL, 138
MASSEY, 36, 174
MASTON, 60
MATHEWSON, 124
MATHEWS/MATTHEWS, 16, 17, 34, 60
MATHIS/MATHYS/MATTHISS/MATHESS, 85, 162, 170
MATLEY, 12
MATTEL, 172
MAURICE, 30
MAXEY, 167
MAXWELL, 30, 137
MAY, 60, 88, 114, 132, 138, 172, 176
MAYNARD, 60
MAYO, 137
MEADS, 132
MEEKS, 26
MELTON, 60, 137, 138
MEMBO, 37
MENDILSHON, 138
MENIFEE, 55
MERCER, 29, 33, 50, 60, 61, 100, 118, 165, 169, 174
MERRILL, 157
MERRITT, 26, 176
MERRIWEATHER/MERIWETHER, 50, 60, 137
MERTIEF, 99
METCALF, 61, 99, 175
METHANY, 173
MIDDLETON, 61, 176
MILLER, 26, 27, 28, 29, 61, 88, 93, 106, 133, 168, 174, 131
MILLS, 61, 88, 96, 168
MILNER, 48, 61, 88, 93, 97, 99, 119, 120, 125, 137, 149, 150, 152, 159, 163, 173, 174, 182, 187
MILNER, B. C. & CO., 88
MILNER, CALDWELL & FLOWERS LUMBER CO., 95, 150
MILTON, 28, 29, 61, 137, 175
MIMS, 112

MINIARD/MINYARD, 61, 167
MINSE, 61
MIROT, 28
MITCHELL/MICHELL/MITCHAEL, 61, 166, 168
MIXON, 138
MIZE, 61, 96, 174
MOCK, 137
MOTES/MOATS, 61, 121
MONCRIEF, 33
MONROE, 138, 154, 167
MOODY/MOODEY/MOODIE, 61, 115, 143, 168
MOON, 166
MOORE, 27, 61, 96, 101, 132, 137, 146, 150, 153, 164, 166, 167, 168, 173
MOORER, 43, 55, 61, 138, 171
MOREN/MORAN, 152, 172
MORGAN, 29, 33, 61, 88, 112, 131, 137, 153, 167, 169, 170, 173, 174
MORMON, 167
MORRILL, 61
MORRIS, 61, 99, 101, 132, 138, 167, 181
MORRIS & JONES, 101
MORRIS & WRIGHT, 88
MORRISON, 74, 131
MORROW, 34, 62, 99, 109, 141, 174, 176
MOSLEY/MOSELEY/MOSELY, 51, 62, 99, 100, 102, 138, 166, 168, 169, 170
MOYE/MOYL, 132, 167, 172
MULLES, 26
MULLINS/MULLENS, 131, 132, 133, 161, 171
MURPHY/MURPHA, 7, 33, 51, 62, 75, 88, 93, 99, 100, 101, 102, 105, 106, 110, 114, 131, 133, 162, 171, 176
MURRAH, 128
MURRY/MURREY, 133, 169
MURTAUGH, 62
MYERS, 62, 173, 174
MYRICK, 62, 101, 147, 166
NALL/NALLS, 62, 132
NARCUS, 132
NEAL, 27
NELSON, 138, 158
NELSON & BATES, 107
NEVILLS, 171
NEWCOMER, 62
NEWMAN/NEUMANN, 62, 99, 138, 168, 175
NEWTON, 16, 33, 62, 93, 100, 106, 132, 138, 150, 172, 174
NICHOLS/NICKLES, 29, 62, 165, 167, 169
NICHOLSON, 34, 63, 96
NISSIS, 132

NIX, 63, 156, 157, 167
NIXON, 2, 18
NOLES, 138
NORMAN, 30, 63, 99, 105, 169, 170, 174
NORRELL/NORRED, 88, 138
NORRIS, 33, 63, 102, 131, 133, 138, 166, 168, 173, 174
NORSWORTHY, 33, 63, 138
NORTHCUTT, 96, 166
NORVELL, 99
NORWOOD, 16, 138
OATIS, 63
OATLEY, 174
OBED, 173
O'BRIEN, 63, 88
OCKENDEN, 63, 158, 160, 161
O'CONNELL, 63
O'CONNOR, 88
ODEN, 96
ODOM, 63, 71, 109, 112, 124, 171, 173
O'DWYER, 133
OGLE/OGLEY/OGLESBY, 5, 6, 10, 93
O'GWYNN/O'GWIN, 63, 132
OLAND, 138
OLD CHAPMAN HILL MILL, 121
OLIVER, 4, 63, 64, 93, 115, 116, 133, 170, 172
OPY, 16, 17
O'NEAL, 63
ORMAND, 63, 114, 172
ORUM, 170
OSBOUNE, 144
OSWALT, 174
OTTS/OTT, 27, 63, 132, 149, 170
OVERSTREET, 166, 174
OWENS/OWEN, 33, 54, 63, 88, 100, 112, 132, 133, 138, 147, 156, 157, 174, 175
PACE, 29, 30, 100, 102
PADGETT, 34, 63, 88, 125
PAGE, 27, 63, 112, 131, 166
PALMER, 22, 34, 63, 74, 99, 138, 174, 175, 176
PALMORE, 52, 57, 64, 94, 131, 171
PARKS/PARK, 35, 64, 112, 138, 171
PARKER, 16, 18, 29, 61, 64, 107, 111, 132, 133, 138, 166, 170, 172, 173, 174
PARKMAN, 64, 138
PARMER, 1, 3, 17, 35, 64, 88, 89, 94, 99, 109, 115, 125, 138, 144, 170, 172, 186
PARMER & WEBB, 89
PARRISH, 168
PARSONS/PARSON, 4, 23, 64
PASCIE, 64
PATE, 16, 17
PATILLO/PETILLO, 64, 99, 170

PATRICK, 64
PATTERSON, 26, 28, 170
PATTON/PATON, 16, 26, 41, 64, 69, 105, 113, 170
PAYNE/PAINE/PANE, 1, 17, 22, 26, 28, 30, 34, 35, 64, 88, 94, 99, 101, 108, 109, 132, 133, 170, 172
PEACOCK, 65, 96, 133, 138, 173, 174
PEAGLER, 33, 35, 38, 65, 88, 94, 99, 118, 131, 163, 170, 180
PEARCE, 65
PEASON, 96
PEASTER, 65
PEAVY/PEEVY, 26, 65, 138, 166, 172
PENN, 33, 65
PENTECOST/PENTTICOST, 65, 89
PERDUE/PERDIEW, 29, 34, 65, 94, 138, 169
PERINE & CROCHERON, 107
PERKINS, 65, 88, 94, 171
PERRITT/PARRITT, 27, 64, 94, 133, 166, 168
PERRY, 1, 4, 10, 17, 22, 27, 28, 29, 33, 34, 65, 88, 89, 94, 99, 100, 128, 138, 156, 170, 172, 175, 176
PERRYMAN, 28, 30, 94, 114, 132, 138
PERSONS, 99
PETERS, 102, 172
PETERSON, 28, 29, 66, 169
PETRY, 69
PETTIT, 84
PETTY, 27, 29, 66, 113, 169
PHAROUGH, 169
PHELPS/FELPS/PHIPPS, 66, 100, 105, 132, 133, 166, 169, 170, 176
PHILLIPS, 17, 26, 102, 133, 159, 171, 176
PHYLYAW, 28
PICKENS, 18, 27, 66, 100, 102, 105, 106, 108, 115, 170, 172
PICKETT, 7, 13, 167
PIERCE, 22, 25, 29, 33, 35, 66, 99, 138, 166, 170
PIERSON, 66
PIGGOTT, 153
PILLEY/PALEY, 34, 37, 66, 70, 125, 133, 138. 162
PINCKARD, 128
PINKERTON, 66, 171
PINNEY, 35
PINSON, 16
PIPENS, 168
PITTMAN, 167
PITTS, 9, 66, 101, 113, 133, 138, 165, 167
PIVY, 22
PLANT, 66
POLLARD, 29, 33, 66, 100, 133, 167, 169, 172, 173

POOLE/POOL, 5, 26, 109, 125, 155, 170, 178, 184
POPE, 66
PORTER, 33, 34, 37, 66, 88, 94, 125, 127, 133, 140, 144, 152, 158, 160, 161, 172, 175, 176
PORTERFIELD, 35, 100, 102, 138
POSEY, 28, 29, 67, 88, 94, 101, 103, 109, 114, 116, 125, 172
POTTER, 67, 88, 89, 99
POTTS, 89
POU, 30, 99, 138
POUNCEY/POUNCY, 138, 176
POWELL, 15, 28, 29, 30, 33, 34, 35, 37, 67, 89, 100, 101, 105, 108, 109, 119, 125, 138, 143, 144, 169, 170, 171, 174
POWERS/POWER, 40, 67, 79, 101, 110, 161, 171, 173
POWERS & ETHERIDGE, 89
PRATER, 133
PRATT, 158
PRESLAR, 166, 173
PRESLEY/PRESSLEY, 94, 96, 110, 132, 176
PRICE, 67, 110, 173
PRIDE, 67, 119, 143
PRIM, 131
PRINCE, 133
PRITCHETT, 133, 138
PROCTOR, 77
PRUETT/PRUITT/PRUIT, 16, 27, 67, 114, 165, 167, 171
PRYOR/PRIOR, 67, 88, 94, 99, 101, 138
PUGH, 67, 174
PULASKI, 67, 174
PURDON, 63
PURIFOY, 67, 138
PURNALL, 138
QUINLEY, 27
RABORN, 27, 67
RABUN/RABURN/RAIBURN/RAYBURN, 27, 29, 41, 100, 169
RABB, 139, 166, 168
RAGSDALE, 101
RAINER, 67
RAINS, 67, 170
RALEY, 139
RAMAGE/RAMMAGE, 36, 67, 170
RAMSEY, 29, 161
RAPE, 67, 133
RAWLS/RAWLES, 67, 101
RAY, 18, 27, 170
RAYNER/RAYNEY, 167, 170
REDDOCH/REDDOCK/REDDECK, 6, 67, 106, 110, 113, 138, 172
REESE/REES, 67, 74, 100, 102, 167
REEVES/REAVES, 27, 64, 67, 102, 167, 169
REID/READ/REED, 16, 22, 25, 47,

67, 89, 94, 99, 110, 118, 139,
144, 157, 164, 167, 174
REMINGTON, 133
REMLEY, 147
RENDOLPH, 172
REYNOLDS, 18, 35, 68, 95, 110, 130,
154, 156, 170, 171
RHAMES/RHAME, 139, 169
RHODES, 14, 16, 17, 27, 29, 32, 33, 68,
89, 94, 100, 108, 113, 118, 131,
139, 146, 166, 167, 168, 172,
173, 175, 176
RHODES & GRAHAM, 97, 102
RIALS, 166
RICE, 24, 139
RICHARDS, 33, 68, 172
RICHARDSON, 99, 125, 144, 156, 175
RIDDLE, 11, 13
RIDGEWAY, 167
RIGSBY, 33, 68, 139, 176
RILEY, 12, 34, 68, 131, 139, 151,
166, 169, 170, 172, 173
RILEY & COOLEY, 89
RINERSE, 133
RINGGOLD/RENGOLD, 22, 68
RIVES, 29
RIVIERE, 55, 68
ROACH, 16, 68, 105, 138, 167, 169
ROBERTS/ROBERT, 68, 94, 99, 139,
172
ROBERTSON/ROBERSON, 89, 119, 139,
172
ROBINS, 133
ROBINSON, 68, 96, 139
ROBINSON & POWELL, 89
ROBISON, 68
ROCKY CREEK LUMBER, 121
RODGERS, 68, 94, 176
RODGERS & FLORENCE, 89, 96
ROGERS, 16, 17, 23, 26, 29, 68, 101,
111, 139, 166, 167, 168, 169, 170
ROLLINS, 69
ROPER, 33, 69, 100, 139, 169, 170
RORIE, 172
ROSE, 120, 167
ROSS, 7, 139
ROTTON, 22
ROUGH, 31
ROUGHTON, 101
ROUNDTREE, 69
ROUSE, 29, 33, 35, 69, 89, 100
ROUSE & THAGGARD, 99
ROUTEN/ROUTON, 35, 56, 69, 107, 132
139, 172
ROWDON, 1
ROYALL, 69, 128
RUDULPH, 56, 69, 94, 133
RUFFIN, 69, 172
RUNYAN, 30
RUSH, 128

RUSSELL, 12, 29, 34, 69, 138,
139, 151, 157, 163
RUSTIN, 173
RUTLEDGE, 69
RYAN, 36, 37
RYE, 69
SAFFOLD, 5, 6, 22
SAITOR, 131
SALCHER, 69
SALTER, 69, 106, 139, 170, 171
SAMPLER, 69
SANDERS, 29, 69, 168, 173, 175
SANDERSON, 26
SANFORD, 167
SAPP, 69
SARTER, 166
SARTIN, 170
SAUCER, 69, 171, 175
SAUNDERS, 79, 87, 94
SAVAGE, 139
SAVANNAH JACK, 6, 7, 12
SAWYER, 69, 96, 139
SCARBOROUGH, 69, 110, 111, 139,
169, 174
SCHMIT, 133
SCHOOLCRAFT, 69
SCHULER, 48
SCOGGINS, 69
SCOTT, 55, 67, 68, 75, 101, 133,
139
SCRUGGS, 17, 107
SEABORN, 111
SEALES/SEALE, 28, 29, 70, 99, 101,
102, 105, 108, 110, 113, 139,
150, 153, 162, 170, 171, 174
SEARCY, 70, 100, 101, 102, 169,
174
SEARCY & PERRY, 99
SEAWELL, 122, 125
SEAWELL & CO., 89, 128
SEAWRIGHT, 36, 70, 100, 131
SEEGER, 153
SELLERS, 70, 78, 97, 102, 110,
124, 139, 146, 173, 174, 176
SELMAN, 70, 162
SERMON, 100, 171
SHALLY, 89
SHANKS, 70, 100, 130, 139, 170,
174, 175
SHARP, 70
SHAW, 5, 6, 12, 26, 170
SHEALES, 169
SHEALY, 172
SHEATS/SHEETS, 153, 157
SHELL, 33, 70, 173, 174
SHEPPARD/SHEPHEARD/SHEPERD, 16,
17, 27, 28, 63, 70, 75, 89,
94, 105, 119, 122, 132, 146,
163, 170, 174, 175
SHERLING, 178

SHERWOOD, 89
SHINES/SHINE, 16, 33, 70, 99, 101, 110, 139, 157, 167, 176
SHIP/SHIPP, 26, 107
SHORTER, 103, 104
SHULTZ, 71
SHUSTER, 89
SIMMONS/SIMONS, 33, 42, 60, 71, 89, 96, 102, 106
SIMPLER, 139, 176
SIMPSON, 71, 76, 89, 94, 119, 131, 170, 173
SIMS, 17, 28, 29, 33, 34, 71, 94, 96, 97, 102, 110, 113, 117, 118, 120, 121, 124, 131, 143, 144, 151, 153, 160, 166, 169, 170, 171, 191
SIMS & BAYZER, 97
SINGLETON, 174
SIRMON, 34, 71, 166, 172, 176
SKAINES/SKAIN/SKEIN/SKAINS, 16, 26, 27, 113, 167
SKINNER, 71, 100, 139, 172
SKIPPER, 28, 29, 71, 99, 113, 167, 168, 169, 173, 174
SLATER, 139
SLOCOMB, 18
SMITH, 15, 16, 17, 26, 28, 29, 31, 32, 33, 34, 41, 51, 58, 71, 89, 94, 96, 99, 100, 101, 110, 111, 114, 119, 121, 122, 131, 132, 133, 139, 150, 152, 155, 157, 165, 166, 167, 168, 169, 170, 171, 172, 174, 175, 176, 184
SMITH & SIMMONS, 102
SMITH, W.T. LUMBER CO., 121, 122, 123
SMOOT, 9
SMYTH/SMYTHE, 26, 29, 34, 72, 114, 131, 139, 172, 173, 176
SMYTH & BOZEMAN, 125
SNEED, 139
SNELL, 67
SNYDER & ROUGHTON, 101
SOJOURNER, 151
SOLEER, 72
SOLOMON, 17, 147, 168
SO. ALA. FEMALE INSTITUTE, 99
SPANN, 72
SPEAR/SPEIR, 16, 17, 72, 182
SPIVEY, 72
SPRADLEY, 29
SPRAGGINS, 169
SPRATLING, EDWARDS & AVERY, 96
SPRIG, 16
SPURLING, 30, 32
SPURLOCK, 29
STABLER, 72
STAGGERS/STAGGARS, 17, 18, 72, 131, 139, 167, 169
STALEY, 172
STALLINGS/STALLING, 33, 36, 60, 72, 89, 94, 106, 108, 109, 110, 121, 125, 139, 156, 157, 162, 167, 170
STAMPS, 73, 94, 133, 139
STANFORD, 73, 95
STANLEY, 29, 37, 73, 89, 94, 100, 104, 143, 145, 147
STARKS, 139
STATON, 172
STEELE, 73, 144
STEEN, 47, 54, 72, 73, 101, 171
STEINER/STINER, 18, 35, 73, 94, 100, 112, 125, 129, 139, 169, 175
STEINHART, 35, 139, 175
STEPHENS, 59, 100, 167
STEVENS, 28, 42
STEVENSON, 73, 110, 151
STEWART/STEWARD, 29, 36, 37, 73, 74, 88, 139, 166, 169, 172, 174, 180
STEWART & PEAGLER, 100
STINSON/STINSTON, 73, 139, 166, 171, 173, 174
STOCKTON, 73
STOKES, 73, 171
STONE, 73
STONEHAM, 46, 157
STOTT, 73, 139, 174, 175, 176
STOUSE & STEINHARDT, 100
STOW, 50
STREETY, 15, 16, 26, 108, 115
STRICKLAND, 30
STRINGER, 29, 73, 169, 171, 174
STRINGFELLOW, 74, 105, 139, 171
STROUD, 6, 10
STUART, 13, 26, 74, 139
STUBBS/STUBB, 66, 100, 131, 138
STUCKEY/STUCKIE, 29, 74
STURDIVANT, 114
STURGES/STURGIS, 34, 168
STYLES, 60
SUMMERFORD, 33
SUMMERLIN, 168
SUTHERLIN, 34
SUTTON, 121
SWANER/SWANNER, 133, 167
SWANN, 144
SWANSON, 110, 139, 162
SWEATT, 74
SWINDLE, 101
TALBOT, 70, 110
TALLANT, 74
TALLEY/TALLY, 1, 17, 22, 23, 29, 74, 100, 140, 170
TANKERSLEY, 174
TARVER, 16, 54
TATE, 95
TAYLOR, 1, 2, 13, 14, 16, 17, 22, 25, 28, 33, 34, 42, 74, 115, 116, 133, 140, 155, 169, 172, 175

TEAGUE, 140
TEAGUE, A.A. & CO., 89
TEAGUE & NEWMAN, 100
TEAT, 74, 94
TENSLEY, 22
TERRELL, 74
TERRY, 26, 74, 169
THAGARD/THAGGARD, 18, 29, 33, 34, 36, 57, 74, 100, 105, 106, 125, 131, 140, 143, 167, 168, 169, 174, 178
THAMES, 34, 35, 54, 74, 89, 100, 125, 140, 163, 172, 174
THIGPEN, 22, 35, 74, 89, 95, 100, 101, 114, 128, 129, 131, 139, 140, 171, 176
THOMAS, 27, 28, 75, 95, 96, 106, 131, 140, 143, 158, 166, 167, 172, 173
THOMASON/THOMASSON, 102, 125, 167, 168, 169
THOMPSON, 7, 10, 14, 29, 33, 57, 72, 75, 94, 96, 101, 110, 114, 131, 140, 169, 170, 171, 176
THORNTON/THORTON, 29, 75, 94, 106, 115, 169, 173
THROWER, 75
THUSTON, 121
TIBBETT, 164
TIGNER/TIGNOR, 4, 15, 23, 28
TILL/TEAL/TEEL, 33, 74, 75, 140, 171, 176, 183
TILLERY, 75, 114, 170
TILLMAN, 22, 167
TINIS/TINES, 167, 174
TINSLEY, 1
TOBIAS, 168
TOBIN, 133
TODD, 133
TOLER, 139
TOLLENT, 133
TOMBLINSON, 51
TOMLIN, 140
TOMPKINS, 65
TOMPSON, 89
TONAF, G. & CO., 89
TOUART, 97, 139, 146
TRANUM/TRAINUM, 29, 168
TRAVIS, 133
TRAWEEK, 29, 30, 40, 41, 76, 161, 171
TRAWICK, 28, 89, 95, 101, 131
TRENTLIN, 133
TROUTMAN, 29, 114, 133
TULIN, A.B. & CO., 89
TUPTON, 166
TURK, 76, 167
TURNER, 45, 61, 68, 76, 132, 139, 150, 159, 169, 173, 174

TYLE, 133
TYNER, 133
TYPETT, 168
TYSON, 125
UBANKS, 117, 118
UHINK, 76, 173
UPSHAW, 168
URQUHART, 128, 159
VAN BUREN, 23
VAN PELT, 34, 76, 95, 174
VANN, 76, 140, 168, 173
VARNER, 133, 174
VERNON/VURNON, 76, 133
VICE, 29
VICKORY/VICKERY/VICKREY, 17, 33, 76, 96, 102, 105, 106, 113, 171, 175, 176
VINCENT, 1, 4
VINES, 1, 173
VINSON, 34, 76, 78, 97, 141, 168, 176, 181
VEAL, 26
VEASEY, 169
VERNELL, 112, 169
WADE/WAID, 1, 3, 15, 17, 22, 95, 163, 167, 171, 173
WADSWORTH, 132, 133
WAGSTER, 27
WALKER, 4, 26, 76, 96, 100, 102, 103, 140, 143, 168, 171
WALL, 33, 76, 89, 95, 96, 140, 167
WALLACE, 15, 16, 22, 28, 29, 34, 76, 107, 108, 133, 170, 173
WALLER, 76, 112, 170, 171
WALLIS, 28
WALTON, 29, 76, 89, 100, 105, 106
WARD, 16, 22, 26, 30, 76, 95, 133, 163, 171
WARDEN, 95
WARDLAW, 76
WARE, 17, 18, 25
WARLEY, 76
WARREN, 23, 33, 67, 76, 133
WARRICK, 76
WARRINGTON, 151
WATERS/WATTERS, 17, 18, 76, 102, 108, 115, 140, 173, 174
WATFORD, 76
WATKINS/WADKINS, 6, 33, 76, 184
WATSON, 14, 34, 35, 76, 107, 125, 132, 140, 144, 162, 174, 176
WATTS/WATT, 7, 15, 16, 17, 33, 62, 75, 77, 95, 96, 101, 102, 107, 114, 115, 125, 131, 140, 161, 171, 173
WEALCH, 28
WEATHERFORD, 7
WEATHERLY, 26

WEATHERLY & BARRON, 100
WEATHERS, 77
WEAVER, 18, 29, 155, 176
WEBB, 35, 77, 89, 97, 100, 101, 140, 174
WEBSTER, 140
WELCH, 26, 168
WELLBORN, 100
WELLS/WELL, 77, 95, 131
WESLEY, 77, 165
WEST, 77, 107, 108, 173
WETHERS, 26
WHEATON, 133
WHEDDON, 27
WHEELER, 17, 26, 119, 173
WHIDDON, 77, 114, 164, 166, 169
WHIRT, 133
WHITE, 23, 77, 89, 95, 96, 102, 133, 140, 176
WHITEHEAD, 33, 77, 100, 118, 125, 144
WHITFIELD, 125
WHITMORE, 151
WHITTED/WHITED, 107, 173, 174
WHITTINGTON, 38, 77, 174
WHITTLE, 33, 77, 96, 170
WICKER, 170
WICKS, 114
WIGGINS/WIGGINGS, 71, 77, 96, 110, 140, 173
WILCOX, 108
WILKERSON, 78, 100, 156, 166, 168, 173
WILKINSON, 36, 37, 78, 89, 117, 140 141
WILLIAMS, 1, 16, 22, 56, 61, 78, 95, 100, 102, 113, 114, 115, 116, 122, 133, 140, 147, 166, 167, 169, 173, 174, 176
WILLIAMSON, 28, 29, 33, 78, 168, 169, 174
WILLIS, 29, 78, 168
WILSON/WILLSON, 16, 17, 33, 35, 78, 101, 105, 111, 117, 118, 133, 158, 163, 167, 170, 171, 174
WIMBERLY, 35, 36, 55, 78, 97, 100, 140, 175
WIMBREY, 157
WINDERWOOD, 28
WINDHAM, 17, 26, 28, 78, 107
WINKLER/WINLER, 78, 100
WINN, 78, 173
WINSLEY, 28, 168
WINSLOW, 78, 133
WINZER, 43
WIRTHEN, 78
WOMACK/WOMMACK, 2, 3, 9, 15, 16, 17, 22, 23, 24, 26, 28, 34, 45, 78, 95, 105, 106, 108, 109, 114, 125, 140, 144, 171, 174

WOOD, 1, 13, 28, 48, 78, 89, 95, 141, 168, 170
WOODHAM, 8
WOODRUFF, 78
WOOLDRIDGE, 102
WORD, 167, 169
WORRELL, 174
WRASH, 79
WREN, 17, 168
WRINCHER, 170
WRIGHT/WIGHT, 17, 18, 26, 28, 36, 79, 89, 95, 96, 106, 109, 111, 140, 162, 168, 170, 173, 176
WRIGHT & ROUSE, 89
WYATT, 140
WYCHE/WYCHES, 29, 168
WYRICK, 114
WYROSDICK/WYRODICK, 10, 151, 168, 176
YANCEY, 3
YARBROUGH, 181
YELDELL, 18, 33, 73, 76, 79, 89, 108, 109, 111, 114, 131, 165, 183
YOUNG, 67, 79, 96, 109, 140
ZEIGLER, 79, 176
ZELK, 133

BUTLER COUNTY COURT HOUSE

www.ingramcontent.com/pod-product-compliance
Lightning Source LLC
Chambersburg PA
CBHW030549080526
44585CB00012B/316